The Art of Maya™

3rd EDITION

AN INTRODUCTION TO 3D COMPUTER GRAPHICS

Alias | Learning Tools

The Art Of Maya™

Copyright © 2000-2005, Alias Systems, CORP.

Trademarks:

Disclaimer

International Standard Book Number 1-894893-82-4

First printing: October 2000
Second printing: September 2002
Third printing: May 2004
Fourth printing: January 2005

2005   2003   2002   2001   2000   7   6   5   4

The Art of Maya™

3rd EDITION

AN INTRODUCTION TO 3D COMPUTER GRAPHICS

Introduction

By Danielle Lamothe I Project Manager, Learning Tools and Training

My colleague's eight-year old son thinks 2D animation looks weird. He'll vehemently argue that 2D is for kids. If it isn't 3D, he's just not interested and his friends will nod vigorously in agreement to these bold statements. But 3D? That's another story. And it's a story that surrounds us. In the past 20 years, 3D animation and effects have become virtually ubiquitous. From station identifications on television, to video games and full feature-length animations, 3D permeates the world of entertainment. But the possibilities are not limited to diversion. Maya, the world's most powerful 3D software is also used as a visualization tool for the medical and scientific communities. Need to perform a tricky operation but want to minimize the risk for your patient? Visualize it with 3D. Want to create awareness and understanding for your space exploration projects? Show them how it will work with 3D. Need to solve a crime? Prove how it happened through 3D visualization.

Introducing 3D software into your artistic toolkit will open a myriad of possibilities to you. Maya is an integrated package that mixes modeling, animation, texturing, dynamics, lighting and rendering into one consistent user interface. This book is your guide to how those tools work and to how you can work with them. *The Art of Maya 3rd Edition* seeks to provide you with an understanding of what Maya can do. With practice, we leave it up to you to discover what you can do with Maya.

Included with this book is Maya Personal Learning Edition so that you can start working in Maya right away.

Foreword

By Duncan Brinsmead | Alias Principal Scientist

The computer is a fantastic tool for the creative mind. In some ways it is the ultimate medium: a canvas of the mind that can represent anything we dream through its internal, esoteric strings of 1s and 0s. Like a telescope, the computer is a power extension to our visual sense, to our brain's visual cortex. Through these extensions, we can see much more than we could otherwise.

Creating 3D graphics on a computer is more than just generating images. Working in 3D is about modeling our world and finding its essence. When creating animations or when developing software, our goal is to convey our creative vision through the simplest possible representation. Doing so might involve using a bump map instead of modeling features on an object, or using a keyframed walk cycle instead of an elaborate dynamic simulation.

Yet, frequently, these simpler solutions may prove unconvincing to the eye. At this point, and as artists, we must try to observe the world at a deeper level in order to come up with a model that will resonate with our audience. An example of these different levels of representation can be found in considering shading models. A surface can simply have a color. At a deeper level we modulate brightness using the surface light angle (Lambert shading). Deeper still we model specular highlights (Phong shading), add reflections (raytracing), then bounced light (global illumination) and finally light scattered within the surface (subsurface scattering). Each level brings us closer to conveying the way we see the world to our audience.

Oftentimes I walk outdoors and am amazed by the richness of the world compared with my latest attempts on the computer. Recently I showed a new toy to Jos Stam, who invented the Maya fluids solver. The toy shoots huge smoke rings into the air and we took turns firing it and marveling at the gossamer shapes it generated. We saw a humbling level of complexity beyond what we could do with our current Fluids solver...it was back to the whiteboard!

Now that you've decided to enter the world of 3D, you've made the right first step in buying this book. *The Art of Maya* is a uniquely visual introduction to the concepts and practices of creating images with 3D computer graphics. Though told from the perspective of Maya, the principles you'll learn here apply to all 3D applications.

This 3rd edition has been expanded to cover Maya Unlimited topics: fluid dynamics, hair, fur and cloth. The mental ray renderer is also introduced. Rounding things out are a new set of industry profiles illustrating the use of Maya for creating movies, games and visualizations.

There is a tremendous amount to learn in this field, but the future looks good. As models get more complex we will at the same time be making programs smarter and providing simpler means of manipulation. Eventually an animator may become a director of sorts, where using the software is like playing a video game. For example, instead of modeling soldiers in battlefield garb one might instead simply specify the range of body types and clothing styles. Instead of keyframing thousands of limbs and expressions one would tell the program to stage a battle, how bloody the battle should be, and who wins. In anticipation of that future, I encourage you to dive in and start creating. The world is out there. How do you see it?

About This Book

Layout

This book is made up of several chapters that each contain a series of two-page spreads focusing on specific Maya concepts. This breakdown makes it easy to read the book in a non-linear fashion as each concept can be explored on its own. Information in the top left corner of each spread contains more fundamental concepts, while information in the bottom right corner explores more advanced ideas.

How to Use This Book

If you are new to computer graphics, you may want to read the book from cover-to-cover. This will enable you to take advantage of the build-up of ideas throughout the book and to get a more complete picture of how Maya works. If you are already a Maya user, you may want to take a more non-linear approach and focus on concepts that interest you. Many spreads deal with ideas that are not specifically linked to a single tool in Maya and these spreads will offer you more workflow-based information.

Maya Packaging

This book can be used with either Maya Complete, Maya Unlimited, or Maya Personal Learning Edition. The focus is on Maya Complete concepts which apply to both packages. Maya Unlimited software features such as Maya Cloth are highlighted to help you compare these tools to Maya Complete workflows. Not all tools in Maya are covered in the book.

The Art of Maya CD-ROM

At the back of this book, you will find *The Art of Maya* CD-ROM. This CD includes Maya Personal Learning Edition software, Maya Mentor, as well as scene files and movies that support the visual concepts highlighted in this book.

Feedback

We welcome comments and suggestions for improvements and for future editions of *The Art of Maya*. Please contact us at learningtools@alias.com.

Acknowledgments

The intricate task of putting together a book of this magnitude has been handled with great passion, enthusiasm, care, and dedication. Creating *The Art of Maya* has truly been a collaborative effort and we wish to acknowledge and thank all those involved.

Authors:
Tim H. Brown, Steve Christov, Shawn Dunn, Lee Graft, Deion Green, Marc-André Guindon, Bob Gundu, Danielle Lamothe, Robert Magee, John Patton, Lorna Saunders, Carla Sharkey. and Heather Kernahan.

Technical Reviews:
Barb Balents, Bob Bennett, George Daves, Bill Dwelly, Chris Ford, Erica Fyvie, John Gross, Jill Jacob, Sang Kim, Tom Kluyskens, Rick Kogucki, Doug Law, Julio Lopez, Cory Mogk, Andrew Pearce, Farhez Rayani, Damon Riesberg, Kevin Tureski, Martin Watt, Andrew Woo, and Jeffrey Zoern.

Additional Artwork and Illustration:
Frank Belardo, Yiqun Chen, Matt Dougan, Pierre Dueny, Marcel de Jong, Jason Ungerman, Mitch Frazao, Lee Irvine, Rick Kogucki, Gary Mundell, Terry Stoeger, and Ian McFadyen.

Editorial Services:
Claudia Forgas and Erica Fyvie.

Printing:
Von Hoffmann

Additional thanks:
Govind Balakrishnan, Don Chong, Greg Curgenven, Jackie Farrell, David Haapalehto, Yuko Isoda, Rachael Jackson, Alan Kennedy, Bernard Kwok, Lenni Rodrigues, Daniel Rotman, Paul Saitowitz, Rob MacGregor, Sylvana Chan, Michael Stamler, Leilei Sun, Ken Taki, Leon Vymenets, and Fianna Wong for their contributions.

Education Team:
Carla Sharkey: Product Development Manager
Danielle Lamothe: Project Manager, Learning Tools and Training
Lenni Rodrigues: Production Coordinator
Ian McFadyen: Graphic Designer
Julio Lopez: Sr. Media Specialist
Roark Andrade: Audio Video Producer

Alias Systems Corp. Education
Toronto, January 2005

Table Of Contents

Table Of Contents

3D Computer Graphics

Animation is an art form created and cultivated over the last century. While drawing, painting, sculpting and photography allow artists to represent shape and form at a single point in time, animation lets artists explore a world in motion. Through animation, new worlds can be imagined. This modern art form evokes emotion through the movement of a sequence of drawings, paintings, photographs or rendered images.

The introduction of 3D computer graphics over the last couple of decades has had a big impact on the world of animation. Digital characters and sets can now be built and animated, then presented in different media formats such as film, video and interactive games. Characters and visual effects can even be seamlessly integrated into live-action footage.

Maya is a 3D animation system that lets artists play the roles of director, actor, set designer and cinematographer.

3D Computer Animation

The world of 3D computer graphics has grown from experimental short films to full integration into the creative process for many types of media. From flying logos to digital actors, the field of 3D computer graphics has evolved rapidly over the last two decades. The use of 3D graphic tools is now an important part of many television, film, and multimedia projects.

What makes 3D such a useful tool is the way it simulates real objects. The way objects appear in perspective, the way a surface bends and twists, or the way a light illuminates a space – all of these complex 3D effects can now be recreated on the computer. The resulting digital images can then be integrated into other media types using familiar compositing and editing techniques.

Maya is a 3D animation system that addresses the needs of a wide variety of digital content creators. The Maya Software tools and techniques have been developed with the artist in mind, while command-based scripting offers ways to build customized tools that suit more integrated production workflows.

Bingo © 2000 Alias Systems CORP

Animated Short Films

For many years 3D computer graphics were used primarily in animated short films. The experimental nature of these films was a good match for this new computer graphics technology. Smaller teams of artists, or even individual artists, could explore the use of computers to generate animation without the pressures of a larger feature production schedule.

In fact, an animated short film, Chris Landreth's *Bingo*, was created at Alias while Maya was still in development. Using Maya, Chris and his team were able to tell a compelling story about the influences of our society on the average person.

Short films provide a fertile ground for experimentation that help drive innvation in the computer graphics industry. It is also a great way for young animators and students to begin using their animation skills as a vehicle for storytelling.

CNN Headline News. © 2000 CNN. Image courtesy of David Price

Broadcast

There is a good chance that anyone involved in the early years of 3D computer graphics has had to animate a flying logo. This use of 3D offered a new and dynamic way of getting the message across – always important in the world of advertising. Since then, the use of 3D in broadcast has evolved and more sophisticated artwork is being produced.

Flying logos are now integrated into more complete 3D environments where a product is advertised or a corporate message introduced. Character animation is also used more to bring objects to life and help sell the message.

Maya has helped open the door to a more complex use of 3D in the broadcast world. With integrated modeling, animation, characters, visual effects and rendering, a smaller video production house can now easily add 3D into their existing 2D workflow.

© Blockbuster Entertainment 2002

Feature Films

The last few years have seen a sharp rise in the use of 3D in feature films. While many films have integrated 3D into existing live action scenes, Pixar's Toy Story® became the first feature-length animation that used 3D exclusively for characters and sets. Recently Sony Pictures Imageworks' Stuart Little® took this one step further and made a digital mouse the star of a live-action movie. Digital creatures, characters and sets continue to show up in the movies and even traditional filmmakers are starting to consider 3D a standard part of the production process.

Feature films tend to use many computer programs to complete a project, including in-house software and off-the-shelf software such as Maya. Maya is most often used for modeling, animation, character animation and dynamics simulations such as cloth. The Maya Software open architecture makes it easy for computer graphics (CG) supervisors to build custom tools to help streamline production.

Visual Effects

While CG actors star in movies of their own, 3D computer graphics is changing how visual effects are used for both film and television. Smaller productions can now afford to integrate 3D graphics into their work while large film productions can now achieve effects only dreamed of in the past.

Film sets can be partially built and then extended with detailed 3D digital sets. Also, animated stunt people can be thrown off buildings in ways not recommended for real people. And smoke, fire, and exploding objects can now be simulated within the safety of a computer screen.

The Maya Software tools, especially Maya dynamics, are ideal for generating visual effects that can be fully integrated into live-action shots. The best effects make it impossible to find the line between reality and where computer graphics are used.

Interactive Video Games

Over the years, video games have developed from black and white pixels to real-time virtual environments built with 3D characters and sets. The graphics used in these games have always conformed to the capabilities of the game console on which they are delivered. Tomorrow's next-generation game systems use the same kind of computing power as the workstations that you use today to run Maya. This is breaking down limitations of the past.

Game artwork is becoming more sophisticated with complex 3D models, texture maps, lighting and even dynamics. Maya is an ideal tool for generating this kind of 3D artwork and includes tools to address the special needs required to build content for real time.

Visualization and Web

Digital content creation tools are used in a number of fields including fine arts, architecture, design, education, and scientific research.

Some of these fields require 3D computer graphics to produce highly realistic images for the evaluation of projects or prototypes. With advances in the web's ability to present graphic and 3D information, visualization on the internet is emerging as an important tool for many companies.

Technical Creativity

As an artist working in a new medium, you must first understand the technical aspects of your new tools before you can reach your full creative potential. Just as a painter must learn how a particular paint mixes and dries on canvas, and a photographer must learn what film speed works best with a particular lens, a 3D artist must learn the basics of setting keyframes, working with 3D geometry, and setting up materials and lights for photorealistic rendering.

To fully master computer animation, you must have a balance of artistic and technical skills. Not only must you learn how to work with shape, form, motion, color, and texture, but also you must learn how the computer interprets all of these elements. While Maya will allow you to go far without understanding all the technical details, you will have greater creative freedom with more knowledge.

Getting to Know Your Computer

If you are sitting down at the computer for the first time, you may be intimidated by the many computer-based tasks you must learn such as opening applications, moving and saving files, and even how to work over a network. If you work in a larger production house, you probably have technical assistance on-site to help you get through this part of the learning process. In a smaller production house, you likely have less assistance and must learn more on your own. Luckily, these skills come quickly with experience. The best way to learn is to dive in and start working.

Getting Started with Maya

There are several steps to getting started with Maya. This book is designed to give you a conceptual understanding of how Maya works, while the *Learning Maya | Foundation* book gives you project-based experience. You can also use the reference manuals and web tutorials offered at the Alias web site.

While these academic tools are important, they can't replace true production hands-on experience. One good way to begin using the software is to model, render, and animate a real object - an object you can study, document and accurately turn into a digital scene. Try to build and animate your favorite old toy, a household appliance or even your own face.

By using a real object, you will be able to evaluate your success against the real object. By focusing on creating something you will be able to apply the knowledge you have gained from this process.

Transferring Traditional Skills

Artists with skills in traditional media will find the transition to 3D computer graphics easier once they get used to working on a computer. In fact, new 3D artists should take the time to learn one or more of the following traditional art forms because they can help enhance 3D skills:

Drawing and Sketching

Drawing is a technique of representing the real world by means of lines and shapes. This skill requires the ability to observe and record the three-dimensional world. This skill can also be used to create storyboards and character sketches, great tools for developing an idea before proceeding to computer graphics.

Cel Animation

Cel animators create 2D art through motion. Cel animation includes traditional techniques such as squash and stretch, anticipation, overlapping action and follow through. Many of these 2D techniques translate very well into 3D environments.

Painting

Painters learn to work with color, light, shape, form, and composition. On the computer, these skills help create texture maps, position lights and compose scenes.

Cinematography

Knowledge of traditional cinematography will help artists use real-world techniques when setting up CG lights and cameras. This skill is very important when working with 3D graphics that are integrated into live-action plates.

Photography

Still photography requires an understanding of lighting and camera effects such as key lights, focal length, and depth of field. Photography also teaches good composition techniques that are useful for framing scenes.

Sculpture

Sculpturing with clay, stone and metal requires an intimate understanding of shape and form. Hands-on experience in shaping complex surfaces is a great asset when working with digital surfaces in Maya.

Architecture

Architects often make good 3D artists because they are trained to think in plane, section, elevation, and perspective. Building models by hand is another skill they develop that makes it much easier to work in a digital environment.

Right and Left Brain Thinking with Maya

Maya has a creative and a technical side. The creative side of Maya offers you tools that make it easy to work in a 3D world with shape and form. These tools free you up to make creative decisions on your project. The technical side of Maya offers you access to the inside workings of both your scenes and Maya itself. This access makes it possible to build your own custom tools and to speed up production where repetitive tasks appear. By having this dual nature, Maya is able to contribute to different stages of a production and to different ways of working.

Switching Sides

While working as a 3D artist, you will be required to be both technical and creative at the same time. One strengths of Maya is that you can start off with a technical approach as you rig up your characters and models with controls. Once this work is complete, you can focus on the creative process using a few higher level controls that let you put aside the technical issues for a while.

Left Brain Thinking

The Technical Edge

Maya has many editors that give you access to all parts of a scene. For example, the Attribute Editor can access the mathematical values assigned to all objects, shaders, and animated sequences in your scene.

The Maya Software MEL-based scripting language can be used to execute commands or build custom user interface elements. This is the ideal tool for technical leads who need to create tools that support production workflows used by their teams.

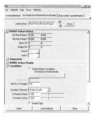

Maya lets you group objects together to build complex hierarchies. These groups help you organize your models while offering methods of animating complex objects.

Maya is built on a complex interconnection of objects known as the Dependency Graph. This establishes the connections between objects and can be viewed and manipulated for incredible control. Understand the Dependency Graph and you understand the technical side of Maya.

Right Brain Thinking

The Creative Edge

Many tools in Maya use Manipulator Handles to offer visual clues as you edit an object. By using the manipulator, you are able to make your decisions visually without relying on the actual numbers stored in Maya.

Maya includes fully shaded and textured views so that what you see in your interactive scene resembles what your final rendering will look like.

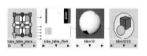

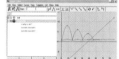

Materials and textures are presented visually using icons and swatches that help you make decisions. This is one step in the creation of rendered scenes. Material changes can also be explored using Maya IPR (Interactive Photorealistic Rendering).

Animation information is presented in visual graphs that help you visualize motion. This makes all the numbers easier to understand. You can then easily edit this graph in the same way you would edit a curve in 3D.

Mathematics, Scripting and Programming

Mathematics is used by Maya in a number of ways. Objects in Maya exist in a 3D coordinate system, colors are stored as RGB values, and animation is created as values that are mapped against time. A Maya scene is basically a database of numbers that is interpreted by the software into geometry, color, and texture. In some cases, you may need to do some math outside of Maya to make sure the right numbers are plugged in. Also you may want to set up a mathematical equation or expression to create more complex motion in your scene.

Maya is built on MEL™ (Maya Embedded Language), a scripting language that you can use to build custom tools and workflows. This language is fairly easy to learn and more technically minded artists might want to explore its use in their work. If you want the tool integrated into Maya, you can also program plugins using Maya API. To develop these skills, a foundation in C++ programming is an asset. However, you can get quite far by using existing scripts and source code as inspiration.

Creative Awareness

One of the goals of creating artwork in a 3D graphics application such as Maya is to mimic the real world. This means that the more you are aware of the world around you, the easier it will be to recreate it on the computer.

As you come into contact with people, places and objects, take a closer look and imagine that you have to model, animate and render all of the details that you see. Details such as how a person swings his or her arms while walking, or how light enters a room, offer great reference for the 3D artist to incorporate into their work. Any seasoned animator will tell you the importance of observing the world around you.

You should continue this kind of awareness when you go to the movies. In many ways, your animations will have roots more in movies than in real life. While watching movies, observe camera angles, set lighting, the staging and framing of actors, and performances. An understanding of how people, places, color, shape, and form are captured on film can help you become a better animator.

The Animation Pipeline

A number of different stages lead up to a final animated 3D sequence. When computers were first used for 3D graphics, these stages were broken down into modeling, animating, and rendering. These stages have since been expanded with the introduction of character animation, effects, and more sophisticated camera and lighting tools.

Each stage of 3D animation is a full area of study on its own. It is useful to be familiar with all the stages, even if you find yourself focusing on only one later on. Knowing how the stages in the animation pipeline work together will help you make decisions that benefit everyone down the line.

Modeling, Animating and Rendering

The animation pipeline can be summarized in seven stages: modeling; characters; animation; materials and textures; lights and cameras; effects; and rendering and compositing. These general stages describe the main tasks required to create an animation.

On a project, you will often work on different parts of the pipeline at the same time. It is a good idea to have teams work closely using storyboards and sketches to tie elements together. If you work in a larger office, you may focus on one of these areas although having an understanding of several areas is beneficial.

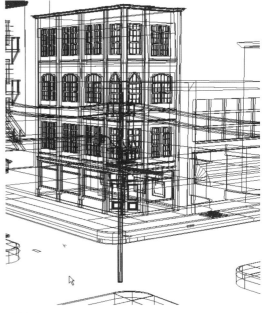

1. Modeling
This is the stage where you build geometry to represent objects and characters. This geometry describes the position and shape of your models and can be manipulated in the 3D workspace of Maya.

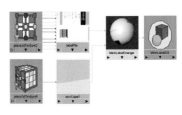

2. Characters
Characters are models that use special controls such as skeleton joints and inverse kinematics for animation. These controls make it possible to create the complex mechanics required by characters.

3. Animation
Once a model has been setup for animation, you can begin to animate it. By changing its position or shape over time, you bring it to life. The timing can then be tweaked to create very specific motion.

4. Materials and Textures
In order for geometry to be rendered, it must be given material attributes that define how it will be shaded by light. Texture can also be added to bring detail and visual richness to the surfaces.

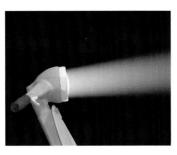

5. Lights and Cameras
As you would on a movie set, you must set up lights and cameras to illuminate and frame objects. You can then animate both the lights and the camera to further mimic Hollywood effects.

6. Effects
There are many effects such as fire, fields of grass, and glowing lights that can't be easily represented using models and textures. Tools such as particles and Maya Paint Effects™ can be used to add effects.

7. Rendering and Compositing
Once all the scene's parts are ready, you can render a single image or a sequence of images. You can also render objects separately, then bring them back together in 2D using a compositing system.

Animating in Maya

Looking at the animation pipeline from the perspective of a Maya user, several stages - such as modeling, characters, and effects - use animation as their foundation. Since almost any attribute in Maya can be animated, you can begin preparing for the animation process at any time.

After setting up and animating a scene, you can render and composite the 3D objects and bring them into a 2D bitmap world. The rendering and compositing stages seem to stand on their own at the end of the pipeline. However, you can apply test renderings throughout the animation process and undertake compositing earlier on.

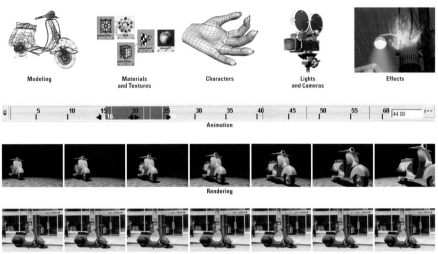

Modeling   Materials and Textures   Characters   Lights and Cameras   Effects

Animation

Rendering

Compositing

Production Pipelines

The way in which you approach the animation pipeline will depend on the environment you create in. From a single artist on his or her own to an artist in a large corporation, the approach to using 3D graphics may differ. Here are some general descriptions of the production pipelines you can expect to encounter.

Single Artist

As a lone artist, you will be in charge of all aspects of the production process. You will, therefore, work in a more linear fashion. As technical lead for yourself, you may want to set up a consistent control strategy for your characters and scenes so that when you are animating you can think more creatively.

Small Production House

In a smaller production house, the focus is on cutting production time and making the most of limited resources. You will be called upon to play a few roles, although some specialization will occur. Custom tools may be put into place to streamline production.

Large Production House

In a large production house, specialization is more likely. You will focus on either modeling, texturing, lighting, animating, effects, or rendering. Technical leads will take care of custom tools and character rigging. Maya will also be part of a larger production tool kit and MEL scripts and plugins will be required for data transfer to proprietary tools.

Gaming Company

A game company can work like either a small or large production house. Here the focus is on modeling with polygons, setting up texture UVs, painting textures, and animating. The exact workflow for your models and scenes will depend on the game engine and which custom tools are available for exporting.

School/Student

If you are at school and working on a production, you can either work alone, which may limit the complexity of your animation, or you can work with your fellow students to create a production-house scenario. Here you would choose an area of expertise and specialize in that area with your classmates' support. The first approach offers a more general view of the pipeline while the second approach gives you production-level experience in a particular area.

Technical Leads

In production houses, technical directors (TDs) and CG supervisors offer their teams support with scripts, expressions, plugins, and character rigging. Technical leads set up controls that allow animators to focus on creating motion.

In building up a character, the technical lead might also build high-level controls that create a particular kind of motion for use by the animators. For example, if many different animators are working on a bird character, the technical lead might want to make sure the wing beat is always animated the same way. Therefore, a single control can be created that drives all the components of the wing beat. The high-level control makes sure all of the wings beat the same way. Management of the production workflow may also involve creating custom tools. Since many production houses use in-house software, MEL scripts might also be used to pipe Maya scenes out to a custom file format.

High-level Controls
For example, custom attributes make it easier for an animator to control a character's hand.

Animators

While the setup of scenes and characters is an important part of the process, the animation of these elements is where the art is created. Animators must tell a story using motion as the main tool.

A well set up scene gives an animator space to focus on setting keys on the various high-level controls built by the technical lead. With non-linear animation, a whole library of motion can be saved and used in different parts of a project. Such a library provides an animator with a sort of animation palette.

Well-built controls and skilled animators are the ideal combination for creating art through animation.

Trax Editor and Visor
The non-linear workflow of Maya is an ideal tool for animating a scene. High-level clips and poses can be mixed and blended in the Trax Editor. Motion can be quickly laid out, then edited with simple click+drag actions.

Computer System

While most digital artists have a good understanding of the technology they work with, some traditional artists may find themselves facing the computer screen for the first time with very little computer knowledge. Graphics applications, like Maya, make it possible to quickly begin creating, while technical aspects can be addressed by others, simultaneously or at a later time.

Acquiring some technical knowledge yourself will strengthen your skills as a 3D artist. Therefore, you should become familiar with the various hardware and software components available to you. This will help make the computer in front of you less intimidating.

Anatomy of a Computer Workstation

Buying a computer system involves finding a balance between power and affordability. With a more powerful system, you can create more complex scenes and render them faster. If you are focused on afford-ability, then you will need to build more efficient models and spend more time keeping your rendering times down. Luckily, the results will not be any less impressive, as long as your animations tell their story effectively.

Maya is qualified to run on a specific list of workstations. Visit the Alias Web site (www.alias.com) for the latest list of qualified systems. It is possible to build a more cost-effective system that matches the capa-bilities of a qualified system, but problems arising from a non-standard configuration may not be something that can be fixed. For this reason, only qualified systems are recommended.

Computer Terms

CG (Computer Graphics)
The use of computers to create and present 2D and 3D visual imagery.

GUI (Graphical User Interface)
A computer interface that uses buttons and menus to access tools.

Command-line Interface
A computer interface where you enter text-based commands. Requires more in-depth knowledge of the system.

Input Device
A tool such as a mouse, keyboard, or tablet helps you enter information into the computer.

workstation

CD-ROM (DVD) drive
The CD-ROM drive is used to install Maya and to work with files stored on CD-ROMs. Computers now ship with DVD-ROM drives which also run CD-ROMs.

CPU
The central processing unit is the heart of the computer. Typical workstations can run one or more processors at the same time. Maya can get a speed boost from all of these processors when creating rendered images.

Memory (RAM)
A system's memory, or RAM, is where the system stores instructions that are being used by the processor(s). A basic system would have around 128 MB of RAM, although at least 256 MB is recommended for Maya. The more RAM the better.

Hard Drive
All the files that make up your computer system are stored on one or more hard drives. This storage space contains application files such as Maya, and scene files and image files that you create with Maya. External storage solutions are also available to support your main drives.

display

Monitor
To work effectively in 3D, you need a monitor with sufficient resolution to view a large workspace. You need at least a 17" monitor, although 19" or 20" monitors are preferable.

Graphics Card
A graphics accelerator card drives the display of 3D graphics on your monitor. A good card provides interactive performance when working with 3D textured models. The card also determines your desktop area – 1280 x 1024 pixels is a recommended size.

Graphics Tablet
A graphics tablet is an input device that uses a pen to draw with pressure sensitivity. A tablet is not required, but is highly recommended since it greatly enhances the Maya software brush-based tools such as Maya Artisan™ and Maya Paint Effects™. Tablets are available in sizes as small as 4" x 5" at very affordable prices.

Keyboard and Mouse
The two input devices that are standard on most workstations are the keyboard and the mouse. Be sure to get a three button mouse since Maya makes extensive use of all three buttons.

input devices

Operating System

The software that controls how your computer works is the operating system. Maya runs on Microsoft® Windows 2000®, Windows XP, SG®IRIX®, Apple® Mac OS® X and on the Linux® operating system. Maya Batch renderer also runs on Linux which offers UNIX® operating system-style administration and reliability on a typical PC.

Maya works virtually the same way on all these systems. The main differences lie in system-specific file management tools and the hardware and graphics that are supported by each system.

Windows 2000/XP

These operating systems work on PC workstations developed by a number of hardware vendors. Maya does not run on Windows ® 95 or Windows® 98.

IRIX

IRIX is an Operating System for SGI's UNIX-based workstations. It's usage is limited to a number of workstations produced by SGI.

Expanding Your System

To expand your basic workstation, there are a number of tools ranging from storage solutions to Internet connectivity. Each of these tools offers you functionality that is not required to run Maya successfully but will enhance your production. The list below is a small sampling of the options available to you. Keep your eyes on industry magazines and Web sites to learn about advances in these support tools.

Removable Media

As you create scene files and rendered images, you will quickly fill up your hard drive space. Removable storage devices, such as the Iomega® JAZ®, offer file access similar to a hard drive. These files can be used to back up your work or to transfer it to another computer.

Writable/Re-writable CD/DVD

Storing your data on a writable CD or DVD is ideal for sharing data with others since most people have a CD-ROM or DVD-ROM drive. Writable disks only let you store data once, while re-writable disks let you overwrite files with new data.

Video Capture Board

If you want to upload your animations to video, you need a video board. These boards take the animated frames and upload them to tape. There are many video boards available and you should research which one suits your needs. Alternatively, you may rely on an outside service bureau for this work.

Scanner

A scanner lets you turn sketches and photographs into bitmap images as references for modeling or texture maps. A scanner is a great tool for transferring images from traditional media to digital media. Scanners that capture slides are also available.

Modem-Internet Access

A lot of 3D reference material is available on the internet, while email is a great tool for sending data to colleagues and clients. With a fast modem, you can download or upload a lot of useful material.

Related CG Applications

While many digital artists focus on a 3D software package like Maya, other software packages offer complementary tools that support Maya 3D projects. Learning about these tools will help empower you when it comes to taking a project from concept to reality. Listed below is a small sampling of related software that complements Maya.

2D Paint Applications

Paint applications let you create and manipulate single frame bitmap images. You can work with images that were either painted by hand, derived from scanned data, or even rendered in Maya. Bitmap images can also be used as texture maps in Maya. Some popular 2D paint applications include:

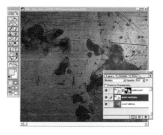

• Adobe® Photoshop®
• GIMP (Freeware)
• Alias StudioPaint™

3D Paint Applications

3D paint applications let you paint directly on 3D surfaces to create bitmap textures. While Maya has built-in 3D paint capabilities, you may find a wider set of brush options and layering capabilities in a stand-alone paint package. Some popular 3D paint applications include:

• Deep Paint 3D
• Alias StudioPaint
• Amazon 3D Paint

Compositing and Video Editing

Compositing packages let you layer, color correct, and add special effects to animations. Video editing software lets you assemble different clips together with sound. In Maya, you can generate multiple render passes to support a compositing workflow. Some popular compositing and video editing packages include:

• Digital Fusion™
• Adobe® After Effects®
• Adobe® Premiere®

Illustration and Graphic Design

Illustration programs can be useful for creating textured graphics, while graphic design applications can be used to create presentations of storyboards and work-in-progress images. Some popular design applications include:

• Adobe® Illustrator®
• Macromedia® FreeHand®
• QuarkXpress®
• Adobe® In Design®

Time and Space

With 3D computer animation, artists work in a digital world where space, color, texture, time, shape, and form are tools for creating images and sequences of images.

All of these physical realities must be translated into a computer language based on numbers. In fact, Maya scenes and images are really just databases of numbers that are interpreted by Maya and presented on the computer screen in a more visual and artist-friendly manner.

While artists do not have to know how the numbers are interpreted by the computer, they do need to understand some of the ways in which space, color, and time are quantified and recorded. Learning how the computer interprets digital information such as 3D coordinates, frames per second, or the RGB information stored in a bitmap image can help artists understand how this information relates to their own perception of time and space.

3D Space

Every day, you come into contact with three dimensional objects and spaces. You have learned how to recognize and work with three dimensions in your daily routine and have an intuitive feel for how it works. If you have ever drawn a sketch, built a model or sculpted a model, you also have a creative feel for how shape and form can be described in 3D.

Three-dimensional objects can be measured and quantified. If you have ever measured the length, width, and height of an object, you have analyzed its three dimensions. You can also determine an object's position by measuring it in relation to another object or to a point in space. In Maya, you can explore three-dimensional objects and recreate them on screen as rendered images complete with lights and shadows.

XYZ Coordinate Space

In Maya, 3D space is measured using three axes that are defined as the X-axis, the Y-axis, and the Z-axis. If you imagine looking into a movie screen, the width would be the X-axis, the height would be the Y-axis, and the depth would be the Z-axis. In Maya, these axes are presented with X and Z on the ground and Y as the height.

You can find any point in this 3D world by defining a coordinate for each of the axes. To help you visualize these coordinates, a grid with axis indicators shows you their orientation.

Two Dimensions
When you measure the width and height of an object, you are analyzing two of its dimensions. The X and Y axes can be used to find points on an object, such as the center of the wheel or the position of the headlight in this two-dimensional space.

Three Dimensions
When you measure the length, width, and height of an object, you must consider a third dimension as defined by the Z-axis when defining points in space.

Origin
Points in a 3D coordinate system are measured against an origin point. This point is assigned a value of 0, 0, 0.

Axis indicator
To help you visualize the three axes, each is given a corresponding RGB color.
    X – red
    Y – green
    Z – blue

Transformations
When an object is moved, rotated, or scaled, the xy and z axes are used for reference. An object is moved along, rotated around, or scaled along the chosen axis line. Values for these transformations are stored for each of the three axes.

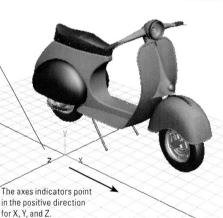

The axes indicators point in the positive direction for X, Y, and Z.

The Ground Grid
To create a ground surface to reference your work in XYZ, Maya includes a grid that maps out an area 24 x 24 units. The X and Z axes are on the ground and form the lines of the grid. The Y-axis is the height.

Y-up and Z-up Worlds
By default, Maya is Y-up where the Y-axis represents the height. Some 3D packages, especially CAD applications, might use Z as the height. If you import a model from one of these packages, you have to either re-orient the model or set up Maya as a Z-up world.

3D Space

time and space

Perspective Space

When you visualize objects in the real world, you do not usually think about axis lines and 3D coordinates. Instead, you see the world in perspective where lines vanish to the horizon and objects get smaller as they get further away. A perspective view allows you to visualize a 3D space in a way similar to how you view the world through either your eyes or the lens of a camera.

Most artists have learned to sketch a 3D scene in perspective or use drafting techniques to create more accurate perspective drawings. With Maya, the 3D perspective view is automatically calculated for you based on a camera position and a view angle that you set.

Orthographic Projections

While a Perspective view can help you compose a shot, it is not always the ideal method for modeling and animating objects. Therefore, an Orthographic view lets you analyze your scene using parallel projections of only two axes at a time. Using these views, you can more accurately determine how an object is positioned.

Most 3D animators find themselves using perspective views to compose a shot while Orthographic views offer a place to view the scene in a more analytical manner. Both views are crucial to working properly in 3D.

World Space and Local Space

When you build objects in 3D, it is possible to parent one object to another. This creates a hierarchy where the parent object determines the position of the group in world space. The child objects inherit this positioning and combine this with their own local space position. This parent-child relationship is used during the animation of an object where keyframes can be set on both the child and the parent.

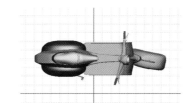
Top view

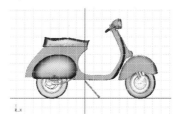
Perspective view

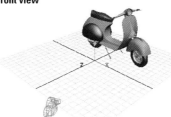
Front view

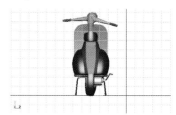
Side view

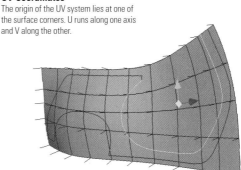
Perspective Camera

The Complete Picture
The different points of view afforded by Orthographic and Perspective views let you build and evaluate your models.

The Camera
Perspective views are generated by cameras that simulate real-world camera attributes. It is possible to set up a number of cameras and then choose your preferred shot later.

UV Coordinate Space

One of the object types you will build in Maya is surfaces. While surfaces are positioned in 3D space using X,Y,Z coordinates, they also have their own coordinate system that is specific to the topology of the surface. Instead of using X,Y,Z axes, this system uses U, V, and N, where U and V represent the two axes that lie on the surface and N is the "surface normal" axis that points out from the front of the surface.

When you create a curve, it has a U direction that lets you measure points along the curve. When a surface is created, it has a U and a V direction that define the surface parameterization. You can draw and manipulate curves in this 2D surface space. The placement of textures can also take place in UV space.

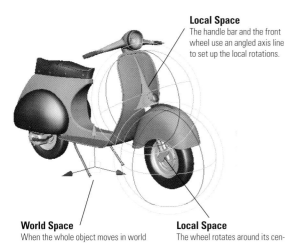

Local Space
The handle bar and the front wheel use an angled axis line to set up the local rotations.

UV Coordinates
The origin of the UV system lies at one of the surface corners. U runs along one axis and V along the other.

Curve-on-Surface
Curves can be drawn in UV space. Later edits will be in 2D along U and V axes.

World Space
When the whole object moves in world space, child objects such as the handle bar and the wheels move with it.

Local Space
The wheel rotates around its center using a local rotation axis.

Normal
The surface Normal always points out from the front of the surface. You can see the Normal lines pointing out from each intersection on the UV grid.

Moving Curves
When you select and move a curve in UV space, you can only move along the two axes of the surface grid. Curve control points can also be edited in UV space.

Time

In the world of 3D animation, time is the fourth dimension. An object will appear animated if it either moves, rotates, or changes shape from one point in time to another. Therefore, learning how time works is crucial to the animation process.

Both live action and animation use either film or video to capture motion. Both media formats use a series of still images that appear animated when played back as a sequence.

Film and video images are often referred to as frames and most animation is measured using **frames** as the main unit of time. The **relationship** between these frames and real time differs depending on whether you are working with video, film or other digital media.

Frames per Second

Frames can be played back at different speeds that are measured in frames per second (fps). This is known as the **frame rate** and it is used to set the timing of an animation. The frame rate is required to output animation to film or video, and to synchronize that animation with sound and live-action footage.

In Maya, you can set your **frame rate** in the **Preferences** window. By default, The Maya Software frame rate is 24 fps. If you have a background in animation, confirm your time units to ensure you set keys properly.

Game (15 fps)
Film (24 fps)
PAL (25 fps)
NTSC (30 fps)
Show (48 fps)
PAL Field (50 fps)
NTSC Field (60 fps)
milliseconds
seconds
minutes
hours

Because seconds are the base unit of time, it is possible to set keys at 24 fps, then change your frame rate to 30 fps. This will scale the timing of your animation to match the timing as measured in seconds.

Playback

When you preview your animations, you will often use interactive playback. You can set the playback speed in the **preferences** window. The default is **free** where Maya plays frames as fast as possible. Simple scenes play back faster and complex scenes play back slower. You can also choose **normal** playback where Maya attempts to maintain the chosen frame rate even if some frames have to be dropped out. If you are synchronizing to sound, then **playback speed** should be set to **normal**, while for Dynamic simulations **playback** Speed should always be set to **free**. It is important to note that **free** playback does not give you an accurate preview of the timing. Instead, you can focus on the motion itself.

Time Code

Time code is a frame numbering system that assigns a number to each frame of video that indicates hours, minutes, seconds, and frames. This is what gets burned onto video tape. This gives you an accurate representation of time for synchronization. You can set up time code display in Maya from the Preferences window.

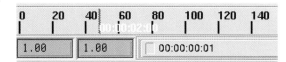

Fields

The concept of Fields is important if you output your animation to video. To make video play back smoothly, Fields are used in place of frames. Each Field uses alternating rows of pixels – called scanlines – that are interlaced during playback. Fields are timed at 60 fps for NTSC, with each Field containing only half the number of scanlines as a typical frame.

In Maya, you can render directly to Fields that have the 60 fps (50 fps PAL) timing or you can output a 30 fps (25 fps PAL) sequence and use a compositing system to convert it to Fields. For fast-moving objects, rendering directly to Fields offers smoother playback since each Field displays half-frame intervals.

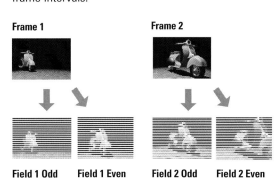

Frame 1   Frame 2

Field 1 Odd   Field 1 Even   Field 2 Odd   Field 2 Even

Double Time

At a frame rate of 24 fps, a 6-minute animation would require 8640 frames (24 fps x 360 sec.). Animators working with either cel animation or stop motion sometimes use double time, where only every second frame is created, then repeated twice. Double animations don't play back as smoothly as the full frame rate, but they save you in rendering time. Students, especially, might consider this option when confronted with a tight deadline. You can set up double time by setting By **Frame** to **2** in Maya **Render Globals** window.

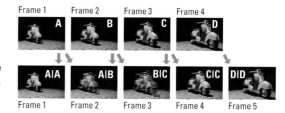

3:2 Pulldown

When an animation created for film at 24 fps is transferred to NTSC video, a 3:2 pulldown can be used in place of re-rendering at 30 fps. This technique spreads every four frames into five frames by remixing the fields of the first, second, and third frames to match film's frame rate. A 3:2 pullup takes NTSC back to film. Both these techniques can be accomplished in a compositing package such as Maya Fusion™ or Maya Composer™. PAL video does not generally require a pulldown because PAL's frame rate (25 fps) matches film more closely.

How Objects Are Animated Using Keyframes

Keyframe animation is created by capturing values for attributes such as translation or rotation at key points in time. An animation curve is then drawn between the keys that defines or interpolates where the object attribute would be at all the in-between frames.

Animation curves can be viewed as a graph where time is mapped to one axis and the animated attribute is mapped to the other. In Maya, virtually every attribute can be animated in this manner. The way in which you set keys and control the in-between motion determines the quality of an animation. As scenes become more complex, you will learn to create control attributes that can drive the motion of different parts of your scene to help simplify the process of setting keys.

One Frame at a Time
When you render an animation, images are created for every frame. The accurate playback of these frames will be based on the **Time Units** you choose in the **Preferences**.

Setting Keys
When you know that your object or character needs to be at a certain place at a certain time, you set a key. With characters, you can create poses out of a number of keys set for different parts of the character.

In-between
The position of objects in-between the two key-frames is determined by the shape of the animation curve.

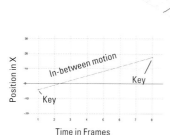

Mapping Against Time
Two keyframes are mapped against time, then an animation curve interpolates the motion between the keys. The shape of the curve determines the quality of the motion.

Pivot Points
You animate objects in Maya based on a single point called the pivot point. The pivot for the whole scooter would lie on the ground, while the pivot for a wheel would be at its center. The position of the pivot sets the center of the axes for rotating or scaling objects in your scene.

In-between motion

Key

Key

Position in X

Time in Frames

Bitmap Space

A bitmap is a representation of an image, consisting of rows and columns of pixels, that is stored color information. Each pixel (picture element) contains a color value for a number of channels – red, green and blue. When you view these channels together, at a high enough resolution, all of the different colors form a complete image. These images can then be output to video, film, or printed on paper.

Bitmap images play a number of roles in an animation system such as Maya. When Maya renders a scene, the geometry, lights, and materials are calculated from the camera's point of view and a bitmap image or a series of images results. Further manipulation of the image in two dimensions is then possible using compositing or paint packages. Bitmap images are also used as texture maps to help add color and detail to the surfaces in scenes.

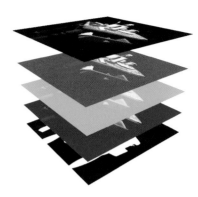

Pixels
Up close, you can clearly see the grid of pixels that make up the bitmap image.

Bitmap Sources
Bitmap images are common in computer graphics and can be created and manipulated in paint, compositing and 3D rendering packages.

Full Resolution
As pixels are presented at a higher resolution, the grid is no longer visible and you get a clearer view of the final image.

Bitmap Channels
Each pixel is made up of at least three color values – red, green and blue. These channels combine to create the visible color.

Image and Display Resolution

Maya uses the term **Image resolution** to refer to the total pixel size of the bitmap image. **Display resolution** refers to how many pixels you will find in 1 inch on the screen. This resolution is measured in pixels per inch (ppi) or dots per inch (dpi). Monitors have a display resolution of about 72 dpi, although your graphics card may offer several settings which will alter this value.

As an animator, you will focus on producing images with a particular **Image resolution** such as 640 x 480 pixels for video or one of a variety of resolutions for film. The default **Display resolution** for these images is 72 dpi. If you are taking an image to print, you will need to consider a Display resolution of around 300 dpi. This value may be higher or lower depending on your printing needs. Below, you can see how different resolutions look when printed. You can see how the 300 dpi image provides a higher quality image on the printed page.

2" x 2" @ 72 dpi (144 x 144 pixels)   2" x 2" @ 150 dpi (300 x 300 pixels)   2" x 2" @ 300 dpi (600 x 600 pixels)

Aliasing and Anti-aliasing

The bitmap image grid can create a staircase-like or jagged effect within an image where lines run diagonally against the pixel grid. To create realistic bitmap images, you must soften these jagged edges using an effect called **anti-aliasing**.

Anti-aliasing modifies the color of pixels at the edges between objects to blur the line between the object and its background. This results in a softer look. Anti-aliasing is most important when you are working with lower display resolutions (72 dpi). Higher display resolutions (300 dpi), used for printing, hide jagged edges better.

Anti-aliasing is important when you render your scenes. You can set an anti-aliasing value in the **Render Globals** window. An accurate calculation of anti-aliasing increases rendering time, but yields better results. Later, when you learn more about rendering, the issue of anti-aliasing will be explored in more detail, including the issue of anti-aliasing an animated sequence.

No Anti-aliasing
Without anti-aliasing, a bitmap image will display jagged edges where one object meets another and on the interior of a surface where a texture map can appear jagged without proper anti-aliasing settings.

With Anti-aliasing
An anti-aliased image removes the staircase-like effect by creating in-between pixels that soften the edge. This gives results that more closely resemble a real photograph that has been scanned into the computer as a bitmap.

Other Channels

In a typical bitmap, the first three channels contain color information. You can also create other channels that offer useful information about the image. Maya is able to render images with mask and depth channels for use in compositing packages. These channels can be used when you want to layer several images together seamlessly, including live-action plates created outside Maya.

Mask Channel
A mask (or alpha) channel, defines where an image needs to be solid or transparent. This channel can be used to layer images for compositing or to texture map attributes such as transparency or bump. White is opaque and black is empty.

Depth Channel
A depth channel can provide actual 3D information about an image. Images are very useful in a compositing package where you can combine layers or add effects such as fog or depth of field. White is close to camera and black is far.

Image Formats

Over the years, many different image formats have been created. You can choose one of these in Maya **Render Globals** window. The Maya Software default format is called IFF and it handles RGB, mask, and depth channels. Maya also has several movie formats that contain sequences of bitmap frames.

In the Rendering chapter of this book, image formats are discussed in more detail.

Alias PIX (als)
AVI (avi)
Cineon (cin)
DDS (dds)
EPS (eps)
GIF (gif)
JPEG (jpeg)
Maya IFF (iff)
Maya16 IFF (iff)
PNG (png)
Quantel (yuv)
RLA (rla)
SGI (sgi)
SGI16 (sgi)
SoftImage (pic)
Targa (tga)
Tiff (tif)
Tiff16 (tif)
Windows Bitmap (bmp)

Maya Image (mi)
Sony Playstation® (tim)

Non-square Pixels

While most bitmap images use square pixels, digital video uses pixels that are slightly taller than they are wide. Therefore, an image that uses non-square pixels will appear squashed on a computer monitor that uses square pixels.

On a video monitor, the image would appear with its pixels stretched to their proper aspect ratio. If you are rendering to digital video, you must take the pixel aspect ratio into account.

Computer Monitor Display   Video Monitor Display

Bitmap File Textures

Bitmaps can be used to texture objects in Maya. They can be used to add color, bump, transparency, and other effects on a surface. The RGB and the alpha (mask) channels can all be used to texture the object.

Bitmaps used as textures can add detail to geometry without requiring any extra modeling. These bitmaps are ideally saved as Maya IFF files and work best with image resolutions that use base-2 such as 256 x 256, 512 x 512, or 1024 x 1024. This is because these sizes fit best with Maya bip-mapping algorithm used to filter textures.

When objects are rendered, textures are affected by the lighting and shading on the object, then output as another composed bitmap image. In an animation, each frame would be rendered as a different bitmap that creates motion when played back at the right frame rate. These images can also be output to video or to film.

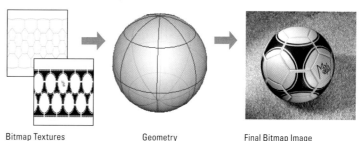

Bitmap Textures   Geometry   Final Bitmap Image

Color Space

Color adds richness to our visual world and helps define how we perceive it. On the computer, color is stored as numbers that are then interpreted for viewing on the monitor. Most operations performed in computer graphics involve some form of manipulation of these numbers.

In Maya, color is a key component of the rendering process. As you choose colors for your objects, you need to consider how they will be altered by shading, lighting, reflections, and other rendering effects. Later, you can color correct your rendered images in a compositing or paint package to enhance their look.

RGB Color Space

Red, green and blue (RGB) are the primary colors in the RGB color space. RGB images are based on the way light mixes color. As such, RGB images on computer screens and video monitors add red, green and blue light to define the final color.

The secondary colors of the RGB palette are cyan, yellow and magenta and are found where the primary colors overlap. RGB is considered to be an additive model because colors must be added to achieve white. In the illustration below, you can see that when all the colors overlap, you have white.

Primary Colors
Most traditional artists learn that red, yellow and blue are the primary colors. In fact, these are the primary colors when mixing paint pigment. On a computer monitor, the primary colors are red, green and blue since this is how light mixes color.

In Maya, RGB color information is defined by three channels that contain values ranging between 0 and 1. If all the RGB channels are set to 0, you have black, and if they are set to 1, you have white.

Other programs such as Adobe® Photoshop might measure each channel as a value between 0 and 255. The color palette of Maya, you can choose to use either a **0** to **1** or **0** to **255** range of color values.

Color Channels
Color is stored in the channels of a bitmap image. The RGB color channels each contain values ranging from 0 to 1. When combined, these form a final color image.

HSV Color Space

HSV stands for hue, saturation and value. The HSV model offers artists an easier way to build up color based on actual color properties instead of color values.

The HSV color wheel is easy to understand visually. **Hue** is the color that appears on the wheel while **saturation** defines the color's intensity, and **value** defines its brightness.

When you set HSV values in the color palette of Maya, they are stored as RGB values. Therefore, you can't set keys on HSV values. However, you can set up a special utility node to extract HSV values for other purposes.

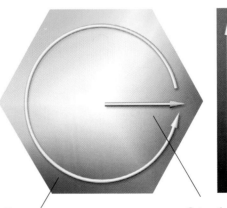

Value
Value controls the brightness of the color. A value of 0 is the darkest while a value of 1 is the brightest. The value setting darkens or lightens the whole color wheel.

Hue
Hue is defined by the color around the edge of the wheel. The value range is 0 to 360 degrees and is measured around the wheel. The hue starts and stops at the color red.

Saturation
Saturation controls the intensity of the color. A saturation value of 1 offers the most saturated and a value of 0 offers the least intense color. On the wheel saturation runs from the center to the outside.

Shading

One of the main benefits of working in a 3D animation system such as Maya is the ability to create complex 3D surfaces that render with shading that respects a particular lighting setup. A final shaded scene is a combination of the color qualities of surface color and shading qualities.

In Maya, you can add color and define how the surface will react to lights. A photorealistic image is the result of combining geometry, surface properties and lighting.

The first object shows color without any shading. The second object shows the shading properties of the surfaces and the third image shows the combination of both color and shading.

Color Synchronization and Gamma

Depending on whether you are outputting to print, video, or the web, you must set your monitor's gamma to match your chosen output to help you better preview your work. You may need to take some time comparing images on your monitor and in their output format so you can synchronize your monitor correctly.

Super White

While an RGB value of 1, 1, 1 produces white, there are cases when these values can be exceeded to create super white. As you build textures in Maya, you may want to use superwhite values to help you achieve certain effects. When these images go to a compositing or paint package, super-white values will return to 1, 1, 1.

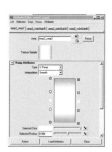

The light's incandescence is mapped with a ramp that is more intense at the center. By using RGB values of 1.66, 1.66, 1.66, the rendered lamp appears extra intense in this area.

Color Palettes and Pixel Depth

Color can be stored on the computer using different palettes and pixel depths. A color palette makes only certain pixel values available to an image. Most images are stored with a large common palette, but multimedia and games artists may have to work with smaller palettes to meet the limited memory requirements of their delivery formats. Images on the web also require different pixel depths and color palettes. The need to keep file sizes small necessitates a lower color quality.

Pixel (or bit) depth is used to define the number of colors in an RGBA (Alpha) image. The more colors used, the smoother the image. one-bit is two colors - black and white; 2-bit is four colors; 4-bit is 16 colors, and 8-bit is 256 colors, etc. The number of colors at any bit depth = 2bitdepth. For example, 8-bit = 28 = 2x2x2x2x2x2x2x2 = 256 colors.

While converting pixel depths is not typically necessary when using Maya, you may need to convert your Maya images later in the production process. If you don't need a reduced color palette for your images, then be sure to avoid certain file formats such as GIF that are designed for Web delivery. You may want to choose another format like Maya IFF or TIFF so that your final renderings have top color quality. If you need to reduce your file sizes later, you can use an image manipulation package such as Adobe Photoshop. Movie formats such as Apple QuickTime and AVI can also reduce the color quality to keep file sizes down.

24 bit Millions of Colors   **8 bit** 256 Colors   **4 bit** 16 Colors

CMYK Color Space

Cyan, magenta, yellow and black are the primary colors used by the printing industry. This color model is based on the use of ink on paper where the ink values absorb light. While most animators will not have to work in CMYK, you may need to take an image to print for promotional purposes and some knowledge of this topic can be useful.

To achieve white in CMYK, all color is removed from the image. That is why CMYK is considered to be a subtractive color model. Where colors overlap you have red, green, and blue and where all the colors are at full strength you have black.

Maya does not create CMYK images. To work with this color model, you need an image manipulation program with graphic design features. If you import a CMYK file texture into Maya, the CMY values will be interpreted as RGB and the image will not look correct.

Exploring Maya

Before exploring modeling and animation concepts, it is a good idea to become familiar with the Maya user interface. The user interface is where 3D artists display and organize scenes, save and open files, and transform and animate objects. While developing these skills 3D artists learn just how they can make Maya do what they want it to.

Maya has a very clean user interface where many of the elements share generic editor windows. At first, this may make it difficult to distinguish different parts of a scene, but with experience 3D artists learn the power of this paradigm. The generic way in which Maya presents information makes it very easy to transfer skills from one area of Maya to another. This lets 3D artists focus on learning the underlying concepts of Maya instead of always re-learning how the user interface works.

The Maya Software Dependency Graph concept links virtually all objects in a scene to each other. As 3D artists learn more, they discover this underlying structure plays a key role in how they work and animate in Maya.

The Workspace

Creating an animation in Maya involves the manipulation of many graphic elements such as curves, surfaces, colors and textures. Information about these elements is stored in Maya as numeric values that can be viewed in a number of different ways. In the workspace of Maya, you can choose how you want to view a scene and access different tools to alter its 3D information. Maya offers several ways of accessing and altering your scene, giving you the flexibility to build workflows that best suit the way you work.

User Interface Elements

When you first launch Maya, the workspace is presented to you with a number of user interface (UI) elements. Each is designed to help you work with your models, access tools and edit object attributes. Initially, you should learn the locations of the UI elements so you can easily find them while you work.

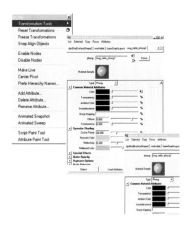

Many UI panels can be set up as floating windows in case you need them just temporarily. Menus can also be broken off from menu bars in case you need to focus on the menu's contents.

Menu Sets
The first six menus are always available in Maya, the remaining menus change depending on which menu set you choose. This helps focus your work on related tools.

Menus
Menus contain tools and actions for creating and editing objects and setting up scenes. There is a main menu at the top of the Maya window and individual menus for the panels and option windows.

Status Bar
The Status Bar contains shortcuts for a number of menu items as well as tools for setting up object selection and snapping. A Quick Selection field is also available that can be set up for numeric input.

Shelf
The Shelf is available for you to set up customized tool sets that can be quickly accessed with a single click. You can set up shelves to support different workflows. Press Shift+Ctrl+Alt when selecting a menu item to add it to the Shelf.

Layers
Maya has two types of layers. Display Layers are used to manage a scene, while Render Layers are used to set up render passes for compositing. In each case, there is a default layer where objects are initially placed upon creation.

QWERTY Tools
The "qwerty" hotkeys can be used to select (q), Move (w), Rotate (e), Scale (r), and Show Manipulators (t) as well as access the last tool used (y) in the scene.

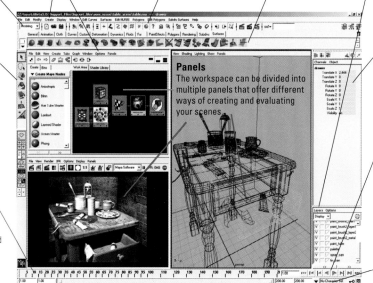

Panels
The workspace can be divided into multiple panels that offer different ways of creating and evaluating your scenes.

Channel Box
The Channel Box lets you edit and key values for selected objects.

Playback
The Playback controls let you move around time and preview your animations as defined by the Time Slider range.

Time Slider
The Time Slider shows you the time range as defined by the range slider, the current time, and the keys on selected objects or characters. You can also use it to "scrub" through an animation.

Characters
The Character Menu lets you define one or more characters, then prepare them for being animated.

Range Slider
This bar lets you set up the start and end time of the scene's animation and a playback range if you want to focus on a smaller portion of the T ime Line.

Help Line
The Help Line gives a short description of tools and menu items as you scroll over them in the UI. This bar also prompts you with the steps required to complete a certain tool workflow.

Command Line
This bar has an area to the left for inputting simple MEL commands and an area to the right for feedback. You will use these areas if you choose to become familiar with the MEL scripting language.

Simplifying the User Interface

All of the UI tools that are available when Maya is first launched can be turned off or on as needed. In fact, you can turn them all off and focus on one single view panel if this is how you like to work. In this case, you would use interface techniques such as the hotbox, hotkeys, or the right mouse button to access tools and options.

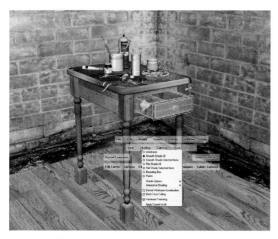

This is a single shaded view panel with the hotbox being used to access tools. Most likely, you will configure the workspace somewhere between this minimal setup and the default setup.

Hotkeys

Hotkeys will give you quick access to many of the tools found in Maya. To set up hotkeys, select **Windows > Settings/Preferences > Hotkeys**. The Hotkey Editor lets you set up either a single key or a key and a modifier key such as Ctrl, Shift, or Alt,

to access any tool in Maya that is listed in the Editor.

It is also possible to build custom commands using a MEL (Maya Embedded Language) script. This feature allows you to set up the UI to completely reflect your own workflow.

The Hotkey Editor gives you access to all of the tools in Maya.

Mouse Buttons

Each of the three buttons on your mouse plays a slightly different role when manipulating objects in the workspace. Listed here are some of the generic uses of the mouse buttons. When used with modifiers such as the Alt key, they also aid in viewing your scene.

The Hotbox

The hotbox gives you access to all of the menu items and tools right at your cursor position. When you press and hold down the space bar on your keyboard, after a short delay the hotbox appears. The hotbox is fully customizable and lets you focus on the tools you feel are most important to your workflow. The hotbox Controls let you turn off the main menus and the panel menus in the workspace. When the menus and panels are off, you can focus entirely on using the hotbox.

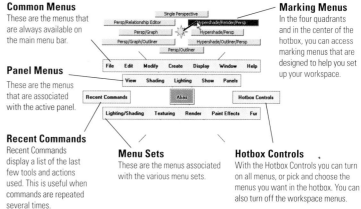

Common Menus
These are the menus that are always available on the main menu bar.

Panel Menus
These are the menus that are associated with the active panel.

Recent Commands
Recent Commands display a list of the last few tools and actions used. This is useful when commands are repeated several times.

Menu Sets
These are the menus associated with the various menu sets.

Marking Menus
In the four quadrants and in the center of the hotbox, you can access marking menus that are designed to help you set up your workspace.

Hotbox Controls
With the Hotbox Controls you can turn on all menus, or pick and choose the menus you want in the hotbox. You can also turn off the workspace menus.

Marking Menus

Marking menus are accessed by selecting a hotkey and clicking with your left mouse button. The menu appears in a radial form so that all your options are simply a stroke away. Once you learn the location of the menu options, you can quickly stroke in the direction of an option without having to see the menu itself. Because the menu is radial, it is very easy to remember the location of each menu option. It will only take a short time for you to master this way of accessing tools.

You can set up your own marking menus by building them in **Windows > Settings/Preferences > Marking Menus,** then assigning the new marking menu to a hotkey.

First Use
When you first use a marking menu, press the hotkey, click and hold it with the mouse while you view the options, then drag to the desired location in the menu.

Expert Use
As you become an expert, you can quickly press the hotkey and click+drag to the desired location in the menu. The menu doesn't appear and your selection quickly flashes by.

Left Mouse Button
This button is used to select tools and objects and access visible manipulators.

Middle Mouse Button
This button is used to edit objects without the manipulator. This button is also used to click+dragging. If your mouse has a wheel, it can be used to scroll into windows.

Right Mouse Button
This button is used to invoke context-sensitive menus and marking menus such as the one shown here.

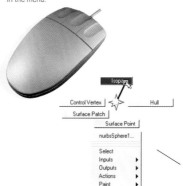

File Management

Working on a computer involves saving and retrieving files from your hard disk. Directory structures are used to organize these files in a hierarchical relationship.

A typical Maya project is made up of many files that need to be easily accessible. To organize these files, Maya uses a special directory structure for different file types such as 3D scenes, texture files, and final rendered images. You may also want to make specific directories for importing and exporting files. It is, therefore, important to learn about the file types you will be working with and how they apply to your Maya project.

As your production workflow becomes more sophisticated, you may want to begin sharing files with other users or create libraries for your own long-term use. With a few modifications, these alternative workflows can easily make use of Maya file management capabilities.

The Maya Directory

A new Maya directory is created for each user. This makes it possible for multiple users on the same machine to have personalized UI setups, scripts, and project files. Some of the directories found in the Maya directory are: projects, source images, and scripts.

Scripts
The Scripts directory is where you can store scripts available for any versions of Maya, quickly accessed from the Maya Software Command Line.

6.0 Directory
The 6.0 directory is where your version 6 preferences are kept. This directory also contains a scripts folder for scripts specific to version 6.

Projects
The projects directory is where all project files are saved. Each project has a dedicated hierarchy that keeps a project organized.

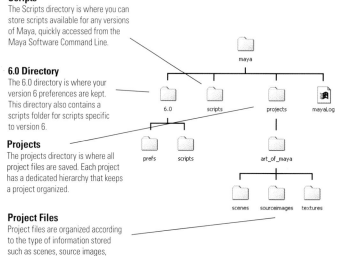

Project Files
Project files are organized according to the type of information stored such as scenes, source images, and textures.

Creating Projects

The projects directory stores and organizes all the information related to a scene. It contains sub-directories in which different scene elements, such as textures and scene files, are located.

When you start a new production, you will want to create a new project, with directories specific to that production's needs. To create a new project, select **File > Project > New...**

A window will open where you can name the project and set up the various sub-directories that you will refer to as you work.

Maya File Types

Maya has several dedicated file types for saving scenes, images, and scripts. These formats store files created in Maya.

Maya Binary (.mb)
This scene file description uses binary code to efficiently store information about objects, shaders, and animation. This format is only accessible from within Maya.

Maya ASCII (.ma)
This scene file description is written with ASCII text and can be opened and edited using any Text Editor. Its file size is larger than a Maya binary file, but allows those familiar with Maya a chance to tweak parts of a scene without opening the file within Maya.

Maya IFF (.iff)
The Maya bitmap file format is called IFF. It can save RGB channels as well as mask and depth channels. It can also be used to save rendered images and file textures used when rendering. While other industry standard image file formats can be used, Maya IFF is more efficient when used within Maya, because it is a file created for Maya.

BOT Files (.bot)
A BOT file is used for texture caching during the rendering process. It is a rapidly accessible tiled version of a texture file that is stored on disk rather than in memory during rendering. This process uses more disk space but less memory.

MEL Scripts (.mel)
MEL scripts are ASCII text files saved using a .mel extension. If written using MEL syntax, the script can be used to extend the Maya Software capabilities.

The Projects Directory

The projects directory is where all your Maya files are stored. The new project options window is divided into three separate sections: Scene File Locations, Project Data Locations, and Data Transfer Locations. You can use The Maya Software default settings or enter your own in the text field. If you leave a field blank, a folder will not be created for that section and the default location directory will be used.

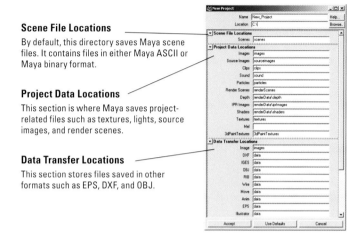

Scene File Locations
By default, this directory saves Maya scene files. It contains files in either Maya ASCII or Maya binary format.

Project Data Locations
This section is where Maya saves project-related files such as textures, lights, source images, and render scenes.

Data Transfer Locations
This section stores files saved in other formats such as EPS, DXF, and OBJ.

Scenes
The scenes folder is where Maya binary or Maya ASCII scene files are stored.

Clips
Exported Animation clips created in the Trax Editor are stored in the clips folder.

Sound
Sound files to be imported into Maya are stored in the sound folder.

Particles
Particle cache files are saved in the particles folder.

Render Scenes
Maya scene files to be rendered are saved in the render scenes folder.

Render Data
IPR images, shaders, and depth maps are saved in the render data folder.

Source Images
Images used to create surface materials are stored in the source images folder.

Textures
Exported texture nodes used to add detail to surface materials are stored in the textures folder.

Data Transfer

Transferring data from one scene to another can be done in one of two ways. Scenes can be imported to merge with your current scene or they can be referenced into your scene.

Importing data into your present scene merges the material, making the file size larger. When you import data, you can make any changes needed to that file. Files that have not been created in Maya, such as Adobe Illustrator, and EPS files can also be imported into a scene . This feature can be useful when creating 3D text and flying logos, where the artwork is created in a 2D package and imported as a NURBS curve. To import a scene into Maya, select **File > Import**.

Referencing a scene file allows you to share that same file with other scenes. The scene content is not copied into your scene, but a visible reference of the scene to which changes cannot be made appears. The benefit of referencing a scene file is the ability to work with multiple scenes that use the same reference file. If that file requires changes, all you need to do is change the original file and all scenes containing reference to that file will automatically be updated. To reference a scene file, select **File > Create Reference**.

Setting Projects

Setting a project in Maya allows you to specify the location of your current project. This is useful when working with multiple projects, allowing you to save and open files from the appropriate directories. To set a project, select **File > Project > Set**.

Editing Projects

Editing the current project allows you to change the path to where Maya looks for certain elements of a scene. By editing a project, you re-assign the path to which Maya is going to search for information. To edit a project, select **File > Project > Edit Current...**

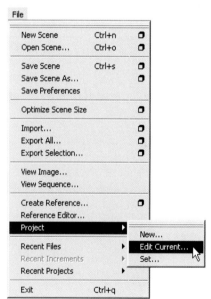

Shared Directories

When sharing a project with other people, you may want to set up a common folder where information can be shared.

Under the Project Data Locations menu, you can specify more than one directory from which to retrieve information. Shared directories can be useful when working on different scene files that share common source images.

Viewing 3D Scenes

When building a scene in Maya, you work in three-dimensional space. Orthographic and Perspective view cameras offer several ways of looking at the objects in your scene as you work. There are also different display options that change the way objects in your scene are shaded.

Default Views

In Maya, the default views are set as Perspective, top, front, and side.

The Perspective view is a representation of your object in 3D space allowing you to move along the X, Y and Z-axis. The top, front, and side views are referred to as Orthographic views and allow you to move in two dimensions at a time.

Extra Views

In addition to the default views, you can also create your own camera angles. To add a new **2D view**, select **Panels > Orthographic > New**. Also, to add a new 3D view, select **Panels > Perspective > New**.

Orthographic views

To create new orthographic views, select Panels > Orthographic > New. Make a back view panel by creating a new front view and change Translate Z to -100 and Rotate Y to 180 in the Channel Box.

Camera views

To create a new camera, select Panels > Perspective > New. You can also select Create > Camera from the menu which offers some unique camera options.

Default Top View

Default Perspective View

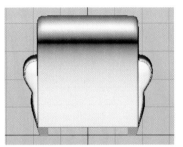
New Back View

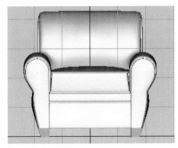
Default Front View

Default Side View

New Perspective View

View Tools

By pressing the Alt key along with different mouse button combinations, you can navigate the objects around in your scene.

While the Tumble Tool is only used to rotate a 3D Perspective view, you can track and dolly in many other views including the Orthographic, Hypergraph, Hypershade, Visor, and Render View.

Tumble
Press the Alt key plus the left mouse button to rotate the camera around a 3D Perspective view.

Track
Press the Alt key plus the middle mouse button to pan from left to right, and up, and down.

Dolly
Press the Alt key plus the right mouse button to dolly in and out of your scene. Using the mouse wheel also has the same effect.

Shading

The Shading menu in Maya offers several options for displaying objects in a scene. Shading can be different for each view panel, allowing geometry to be shown at different levels of complexity.

The more detailed a scene becomes, the greater the need to simplify the objects in it. Although Maya is very good at processing complex levels of geometry, it is a good idea to view your objects in a less complex shading mode until you are ready to render or make adjustments to those objects.

There are several shading display options to choose from. The default shading in Maya is Wireframe. Other display options include: Bounding Box, Points, Flat Shade, Smooth Shade, Hardware Lighting, Wireframe on Shaded, and X-Ray.

Show Menu

The Show Menu allows you to show and hide different elements of a scene. You can show all or none or specific items such as NURBS curves, lights, or cameras.

The Show Menu is accessible from all views and can hide items in one view while displaying them in another.

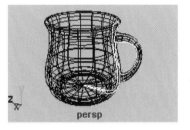
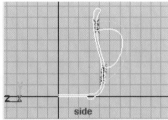

The Show Menu allows you to edit a NURBS curve in the Side view with NURBS surfaces turned off while viewing the Perspective view panel with NURBS surfaces visible.

Isolate Select

The Isolate Select option allows you to hide surfaces at both the object and component level, on a per-panel basis. To hide the Control Vertices (CVs) of an object, choose the CVs you want to modify and select **Show > Isolate Select > View Selected**. This will hide all unselected CVs.

Another advantage of using Isolate Select is that it affects hardware rendering only, allowing hidden objects to be viewed during software rendering.

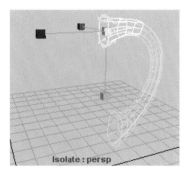

Using Isolate Select allows you to hide CVs on a NURBS surface.

Bounding Box
Bounding Box displays objects as boxes. This is useful when working with complex scenes.

Points
Points shading displays objects as a group of points that represent the shape of the object.

Wireframe
Wireframe shading is the default shading quality in Maya.

Flat Shade
Flat Shade displays all or only the selected objects with lower resolution faceted display.

Smooth Shade
Smooth Shade displays all or only the selected objects as smooth surfaces with surface color and shading properties.

Hardware Texturing
Hardware Texturing displays smooth-shaded surfaces with textures.

Hardware Lighting
Hardware Lighting displays smooth-shaded surfaces with textures and lighting.

Hardware Fog
Hardware Fog displays surfaces with a user defined fog. This is useful to simulate a scene fog.

High Quality Rendering
High Quality Rendering displays surfaces with more accurate texturing, bump mapping, transparency and lighting.

Shade Options

In addition to the default shading mode, there are two shading options for viewing your models: Wireframe on Shaded and X-Ray modes. Both of these options can be used at the same time.

Viewing your model in Wireframe on Shaded mode will allow you to easily view surface isoparms for all objects in your view panel without viewing through the object.

Viewing your model in X-Ray mode will allow you to view through your model using a semi-transparent shading. This is useful when you want to see a surface that is behind other surfaces or inside objects such as skeletons within a character.

X-Ray
X-Ray shading displays objects with a semi-transparent surface.

Wireframe on Shaded
Wireframe on Shaded displays a wireframe on a shaded surface.

Objects and Components

Y ou can transform objects in Maya by selecting objects and their components. Selection masks allow you the flexibility to select only the items you want in a scene. These masks are grouped into three categories: Hierarchy, Object type, and Component type selections.

Object Types

Scene objects are items such as cameras, curves, surfaces, dynamics, joints, handles, and deformers. Objects created in Maya are made up of two parts: a Transform node and a Shape node. The Transform node contains basic information about an object's position, orientation, and scale in space. The Shape node defines what the object looks like.

Rendering
Scene objects such as lights, cameras, and textures placement are rendering object types.

Curves
Turning off the curve selection means you can not select the curves in the scene.

Surfaces
Selecting by surfaces allows you to select the surface geometry of an object.

Dynamics
Dynamic objects such as particles can be separately selected by toggling the Dynamics button on.

The Outliner can be used to select and view hierarchical relationships between the objects in your scene.

Skeleton Joints
Skeleton joints are used to help control characters.

Handles
IK handles are applied to joint chains for animation control.

Deformations
Deformers such as cluster flexors and lattices modify the shape of an object.

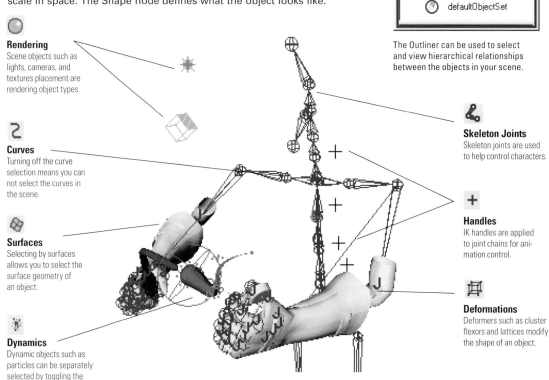

Component Types

In order to change the shape of an object in Maya, you need to modify component-type information.

There are a variety of component types such as points, isoparms, faces, hulls, pivot points, and handles. These components can be used to interactively modify and reshape the appearance of an object.

Points
Points such as CVs and polygonal vertices are used to modify the shape of an object.

Param Points
Param points are points that lie directly on a curve or surface.

Lines
Lines such as isoparms and trim edges define the shape of an object.

Faces
Faces are patches created by intersecting lines.

Hulls
Hulls are guides that connect CVs. They can be used to select and transform rows of CVs at once.

Pivot Points
Pivot points determine the location around which transformations occur.

Hierarchy   Object   Component

Selection Masks

Selection masks allow you to select the specific items you want to work on. There are three main groups of selection masks: Hierarchy, Object, and Component.

Hierarchy mode allows you to select nodes at different levels. In this mode you can select the Root, Leaf, and Template nodes.

Object mode allows you to select scene elements at the Transform node level. These include objects such as surfaces, curves, and joints.

Component-type selections are selections made to objects at the Shape node level, such as isoparms and CVs.

Selection Priority

Objects and Components are selected in order of priority based on an assumed production work-flow. For example, if you want to select both joints and surfaces, Maya anticipates that you want to select joints first. To select more than one object with different priorities, select the first object and Shift+click on the object of different priority.

Hierarchies

When working with a group of objects that are arranged in a hier-archy, you may want to specifically work at the Root node or Leaf node level.

If you choose to work at the Root node level of a group, also known as the top node in a hier-archy, you can toggle on the Select by Hierarchy: Root mask. In this selection mode, you can click on any object in the hierarchy and only the top node of the object picked will be selected.

If you want to work at the Leaf node level, toggle on the Select by Hierarchy: Leaf button. In this mode, only the leaf nodes or children of a hierarchy will be selected.

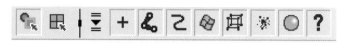

Hierarchy

Selecting by hierarchy allows you to select objects at either the Root, Leaf or Template node level. Unlike Object and Component selection masks, you are not able to turn on more than one mask at a time.

Object

Object selection masks allow you to make selections based on the object types you specify. Left-clicking on the arrow to the left of the pick masks displays a menu allowing you to turn all objects on or off.

Component

Component selection masks offer a variety of pick masks to choose from. Right-clicking on a mask displays more selection options.

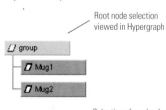

Preferences

The selection priority list can be found under Windows > Settings/Preferences > Preferences. In this window, you can change the order in which Objects and Components are selected.

Root node selection viewed in Hypergraph

Selection of any Leaf node will select the root node

Toggling on the Select by Hierarchy: Root mask allows you to select any Leaf node in a hierarchy and the Root node will become selected.

Right Mouse Button Selections

Clicking the right mouse button over an object will bring up a marking menu that allows you to choose from both Object and Component selection types, while remaining in Component mode. The menu choices are specific to the object selected or the object beneath the marking menu.

Quick Select

Using Quick Select, you can type in the name of an object in the text field and it will become selected in your scene.

This is particularly useful when there are several objects in a scene with a common name. You can type in the name followed by an asterisk (*) and all objects containing that same name will be selected.

Dependency Graph

Everything in Maya is represented by a node with attributes that can be connected to other node attributes. This node-based architecture allows connections to be made between virtually everything in Maya. Node attributes determine such things as the shape, position, construction history and shading of an object. With this architecture, you can create inter-object dependencies, shading group dependencies, and make your own node connections.

Nodes with Attributes that are Connected

The Dependency Graph is a collection of nodes which are connected together. These connections allow information to move from one node to another and can be viewed in a diagrammatic fashion through the Hypergraph and Hypershade windows.

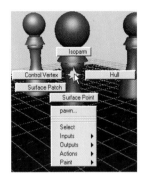

Right Mouse Button
Clicking the right mouse button over a selected object will give you access to an object's input and output connections.

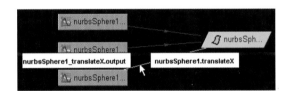

Animation Curve
When an animation is produced in Maya, node dependencies are created between the animation curves and the object being animated.

Node Dependencies

In the diagram below you can see the nodes that are dependent on each other to make up a chess piece. Each node plays a part in creating the final rendered object. Here you see that the Shader node is dependent on the Shape node to render the material, the Shape node is dependent on the revolve node for the chess piece surface, and the Revolve node is dependent on the Curve node to make the revolve.

Shading Group Dependencies

When a material is created in Maya, a network of node dependencies is built. This network is referred to as a Shading Network.

The Hypershade window allows you to make and break connections between shading group nodes. The Hypershade displays thumbnail images representing each node. The diagrams below both show the same shading group dependency in the Hypershade and Hypergraph windows.

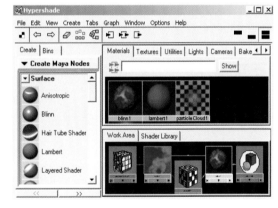

Hypershade
Using the Hypershade, you can make materials and textures and view the node dependencies used to create them.

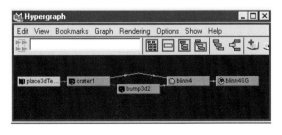

Hypergraph
The Hypergraph window can also be used to view and create shading group dependencies. However, it does not have swatches as the Hypershade does.

Viewing Dependencies

Dependencies are relationships created between nodes that are connected. There are many ways to view and edit dependencies in Maya including the Hypergraph, Attribute Editor, and Channel Box.

By selecting a node and clicking the Up and Downstream Connections button in the Hypergraph window, you can view node dependencies on a selected node. This window visually displays the connection between nodes with arrows showing the direction of their dependency to one another.

The Attribute Editor is made up of several tabs allowing you to view related nodes of a dependency group. In the Attribute Editor, you can edit the attributes that affect these nodes.

In the Channel Box, the selected node is shown with a listing of any keyable attributes that belong to it. Depending on the node selected, it will also show input, output, or shape nodes. If you select more than one node with the same keyable attributes, you can modify them at the same time using the Channel Box.

Channel Box
In the Channel Box, you can edit any keyable attributes on the selected node.

Attribute Editor
In the Attribute Editor, you can adjust the attributes on the input and output connections of a selected node.

Hypergraph
In the Hypergraph window, you can see the input and output connections of a selected node.

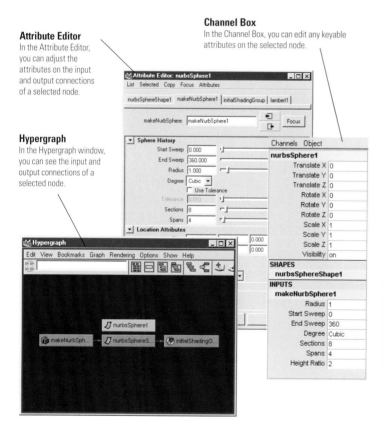

Construction History

When an object is built in Maya, Input nodes can be viewed in the Dependency Graph containing information on how the object was created. These Input nodes allow you to edit an object based on the geometry used to build it. For example, if you were to create a curve and use the Revolve Tool to make a surface from it, the curve used to create the surface would hold information as to how the surface was created. Using construction history, you can go back to the original curve and alter the shape of the object.

Making Connections

Connections made in Maya represent the flow of information from one node to another. You can make your own connections between nodes as well as break connections using the Connection Editor.

The Connection Editor offers a list of node attributes that can be connected to other node attributes. For example, you can map the scale of one object to influence the rotation of another. This creates a connection between the two nodes where every time you scale one, the other automatically rotates.

The Connection Editor can extend the possibilities of your production by automating tasks done through the connection of nodes.

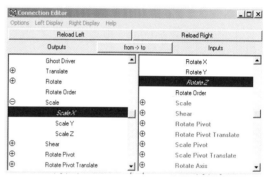

Connection Editor
The Connection Editor allows you to make connections between nodes attributes.

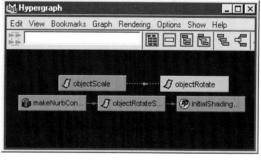

Hypergraph
In the Hypergraph, you can view the result of connections made in the Connection Editor.

Construction History On

Construction History Deleted

Transformations

Transformations are changes made to an object's position, orientation, and scale in space. The Transform node holds all of this information and the Transform manipulators such as the Move, Scale and Rotate Tools are used to transform an object along the X, Y and Z axes.

Manipulators

Manipulators are used to move, scale, and rotate objects in orthographic and 3D space. Each of the manipulators uses red, green, and blue color handles matching the colors of the X, Y, Z locator at the bottom left corner of the view, making it easier to distinguish the direction of the transformation. These handles are designed to constrain the transformation to one, two, or three axes at a time, allowing for complete control.

Move Tool

The Move Tool has a handle for each X, Y, and Z axes and a center handle to move relative to the view.

Rotate Tool

The Rotate Tool has a ring for the X, Y, and Z axes. One ring moves relative to the view, and a virtual sphere rotates in all directions.

Scale Tool

With the Scale Tool, you can scale non-proportionally in X, Y, or Z. You can also scale proportionally by selecting the center handle.

Setting Pivot Points for Transformations

Objects are transformed around their pivot point location. This is important to be aware of because the position of your pivot point affects the outcome of your transformation. To change the location of your pivot point, select a Transform manipulator and press the Insert key on the keyboard. Move your pivot point to the desired location and press the Insert key again to set the pivot point.

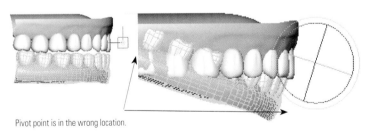

Pivot point is in the wrong location.

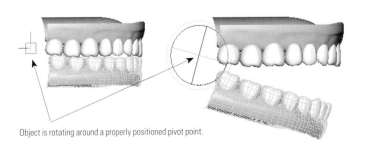

Object is rotating around a properly positioned pivot point.

Move/Rotate/Scale Tool

This tool incorporates the Move, Rotate, and Scale manipulators into one tool. Select Modify > Transformation Tools > Move/Rotate/Scale tool to use this tool.

Transformation Tools

To work quickly and efficiently in Maya, the QWERTY hotkeys offer a fast way to access the transformation tools. These tools are located at the top left corner of the Maya workspace. Select, Move, Rotate, Scale, and the Show Manipulators Tool, plus an extra space for the last tool you used, are all a part of the QWERTY toolset.

Use the QWERTY shortcut keys on your keyboard to select and transform the objects in your scene.

Reset Transformations

Once you have manipulated an object, you may not be satisfied with its new transformation. To reset your object to its original position, select **Modify > Reset Transformations**.

Freeze Transformations

Select **Modify > Freeze Transformations** to keep your current position as the default position. This means that your modified position will have values of 0 for Move and Rotate in the X, Y, and Z axes and a value of 1 for Scale.

Scaling Options

The Scale Manipulator allows you to change the size of an object both proportionally and non-proportionally. The default coordinate system for scaling is local.

Move Options

Double-clicking on the Move Tool icon brings up the following four coordinate systems: Object, Local, World, and Normal.

Each object has its own X, Y, Z coordinates. To view an object's coordinates, select **Object** in the Options window. Changing an object's coordinates to **Local** aligns the object's axes to its parent's axes, ignoring any transformations made to itself.

World is the default coordinate system for the Move Tool. When World coordinates are selected, the object moves in World coordinate space where the Y-axis always points up.

Normal coordinates work at a component level displaying NUV and is useful for CV manipulation. N represents the Normal direction of the surface. At this level, you can move across the surface in both N, U, and V directions.

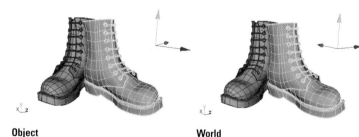

Local   **Normal**

Object   **World**

2D Transformations

When transforming an object using the Move Tool in the top, front and side views, you are constrained to move only in two dimensions. When using the Rotate and Scale Tools in an Orthographic view, you can transform an object in both two and three dimensions.

Rotate Options

The Rotate Tool menu offers three rotate modes to pick from - Local, Global and Gimbal.

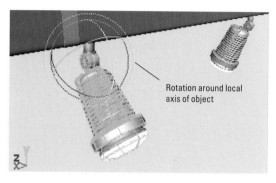

Rotation around local axis of object

Local

Local is the default setting. Local allows you to rotate an object in object space with the axis rotating along with it.

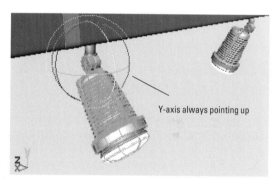

Y-axis always pointing up

Global

Selecting Global coordinates means the object will rotate within world space with the Y-axis always pointing up. In this mode, the rings never change position.

Virtual Sphere that allow you to move in all directions disappears

Gimbal

When Gimbal Lock is on, you can rotate your object only one axis at a time.

Duplication

The Duplicate Options window allows you to create copies of the objects in your scene. This saves you from having to rebuild identical versions of objects that have been already created.

There are many options to choose from when making a duplicate. You can Translate, Rotate, and Scale the object you duplicate and specify the number of copies you need. Maya also lets you choose whether or not you want to make a geometry copy or a geometry instance of the selected object.

To duplicate the surface curves of an object, select an isoparm and choose Edit Curves > Duplicate Surface Curves.

Translate, Rotate, Scale
You can enter offset values for the Translation, Rotation, and Scale of duplicated objects in these fields.

Number of Copies
Specify the number of copies to make a selected object. The range is between 1 and 1000.

Smart Transform
This applies transformations to subsequent duplicates of an object.

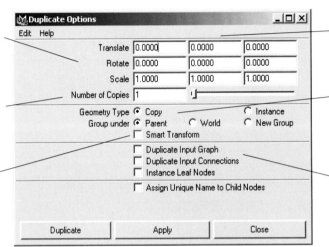

X, Y, Z Axes
The three columns beside Translate, Rotate, and Scale represent the X, Y, and Z axes in order from left to right.

Geometry Type
There are two ways to duplicate an object. You can make a copy or an instance of the geometry.

Duplicate Input Graph and Input Connections
You can copy a selected node and all of the connections feeding into it.

Duplicate with Smart Transform

When duplicating an object using Smart Transform, Maya takes into account the transformation made from the last duplication and applies the same transformation to the new duplicate. For example, if you want to create a staircase, you can select the first step and duplicate it using Smart Transform. Move and rotate the duplicate step until you are happy with its position. Duplicate the second step using Smart Transform. This time, the third step will already be in the right position.

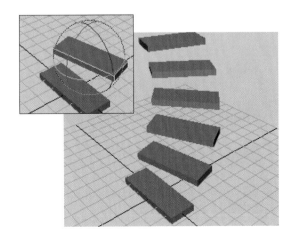

Instancing

Maya does not create new geometry for an instance. An instance is essentially the same object displayed twice, taking up less system memory.

An instance of an object is given its own Transform node. You can make transformations such as Rotate and Scale on each instance as well as apply different textures and shaders without affecting other instances.

Although they do not share Transform nodes, instance copies share the same Shape node. If you change the shape of one instance, all other instances will take on the same shape.

Instances of an object share the same Shape node. Changing the shape of one object will change the shape of all Instances.

Radial Duplication

To create a radial duplication around the pivot point of a selected object, select the Duplicate Options window and enter both a Rotate value and the number of copies you need. For example, to create the palette below, the pivot point of a single piece was snapped to the end vertex around which the duplication was made.

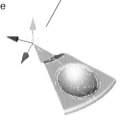

Pivot Point

The above palette piece was duplicated around the Y-axis at a rotate value of 36 and number of copies set to 9 to complete the palette.

Mirror Duplication

To create a mirror image of a selected object, open the **Duplicate Options** window. Depending on the axis you want to duplicate along, type in -1 in the appropriate axis field next to the scale option.

Mirrored Shoe

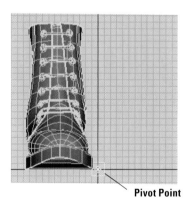

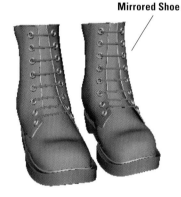

Pivot Point

Duplicate Along a Path

Animated Snapshot allows you to duplicate objects along a path. This is a very useful modeling technique that uses the Time Range as well as the start and end time, and By Time value set in the options window as the determining factor for the number of duplications created. To use Animated Snapshot, select both the object and path you want to snap to on frame 1. Select **Animate > Paths > Attach to Path**. This will snap your object to the path. Pick your object and select **Modify > Animated Snapshot**. Maya will duplicate your object from the start to end points on your path.

Duplicate Input Connections

Objects that are duplicated using Duplicate Input Connections share the same Construction History. This means if you were to edit the input attributes of one object, all downstream connections inherit the same values.

Shared Construction History   **Duplicated Node**

In the above example, the sections of the selected object have been increased, thereby changing the sections of the duplicate.

Duplicate Upstream Graph

By duplicating upstream graph connections, you can make a copy of the selected node and all connections feeding into it. The duplicates do not share Construction History.

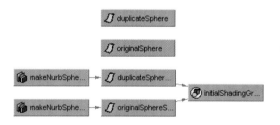

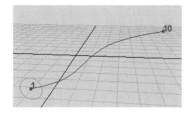
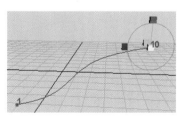
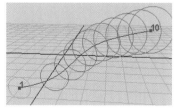

Animated Snapshot can be used to create duplicates of an object along a path that can then be used as a modeling guide.

Snapping

The snapping tools let you snap to grids, curves, points, and view planes. These tools used in conjunction with the transformation tools allow you to control the position of both an objects pivot point and components as you work.

Snapping plays a key role in many workflows used in Maya. In any operation where objects must be joined, the snapping tools can be used for precise placement. Making an object live is also a method of snapping, where the objects can be snapped onto the live surface.

Press X – Snap to grids

Press C – Snap to curves

Press V – Snap to points

Snapping Icons
Snapping icons are located in the Status Line of the Maya UI. You can toggle these on and off or use the keyboard shortcuts while you work.

Constrained Snapping

Constrained snapping can be used to make all CVs on a curve snap to a straight line along one axis.

Click+dragging on the Move Tool handle and pressing the X key on the keyboard will snap all selected CVs on a curve to the nearest grid line.

To get this snapping technique to work, you must set the **Move** Tool options to **World** and uncheck Preserve Component Space.

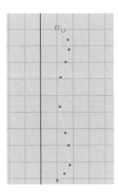 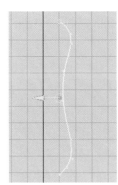 

Original Curve Shape   **Select Curve CVs**   **Constrain CVs to A Grid Line**

Displaying Points

To snap to NURBS or polygonal vertices, display the points you want to snap to. You can display the vertices of objects in a scene by choosing **Display > Nurbs Components** or **Display > Polygon Components** and select the Component type you want to display.

Grid Snapping

The grid is a plane that can be viewed in the Orthographic and Perspective views. To snap an object to the grid, either toggle on the Snap to Grids button or press the X key on the keyboard. To modify the size of the grid and the grid subdivision, select **Grid > Display** and change options in the options window.

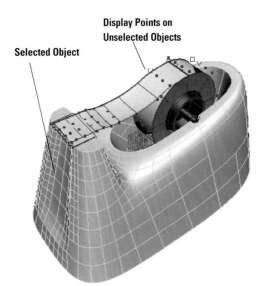

Display Points on Unselected Objects

Selected Object

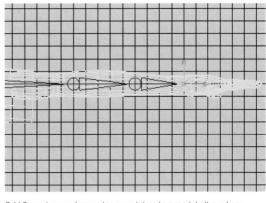

Grid Snapping can be used to snap joints in a straight line when building a skeleton.

Point Snapping

Toggling on Point Snapping allows you to snap vertices or pivot points to another point.

To use Point Snapping, select the object or component you wish to snap and select the Move Tool. Press the V key on the keyboard and middle mouse click on the vertex you wish to snap to.

In the example to the right, the pivot point of the scooter has been snapped to an edit point on a path.

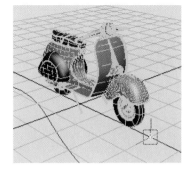 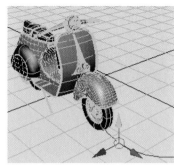

Snap to Curves

Snap to curves can be used to snap along any isoparm, curve or poly edge. This technique is very useful when used to snap pivot points to specific areas on a curve. Since pivot point location is the determining factor for most transformations done in Maya, the ability to precisely snap your pivot point to a curve is very useful.

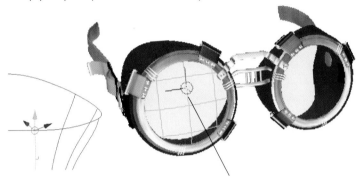

Using the Snap to curves tool allows you to snap to any point along a curve. This tool is useful to complete a Birail operation since all curves must be connected.

While pressing the C key on the keyboard, hold down the middle mouse button to click+drag on an isoparm. This will allow you to snap pivot points along existing surface lines.

Snap Align Objects

To snap one object to another, Maya offers you several tools that you can use. The Align Tool displays a manipulator that allows you to choose how to snap objects based on their bounding boxes, while the Snap Together Tool allows you to snap two objects based on their surface orientation.

You can also snap objects together based on their components. To do so, select a control point (CV, vertex, or surface point) on the first object and Shift-select a point on the other. Choose **Modify > Snap Align Objects > Point to Point**. The first point selected will snap to the second point taking the whole object with it.

Live Objects and Construction Planes

Making an object live allows you to snap a curve along the UV space of its surface as you draw. Edit points are drawn directly on the surface of a live object. Objects that are live are green and are not shaded. Once a curve has been drawn, it can be moved around and will remain constrained to the topology of the object because it is a Curve on Surface. Construction planes can also be assigned as live objects. They cannot be rendered, but can be transformed and rotated to a desired angle and used as a guide when drawing a curve. The construction plane behaves like the ground plane which is infinite in size. However, making an object live limits you to snap to the size and shape of the object.

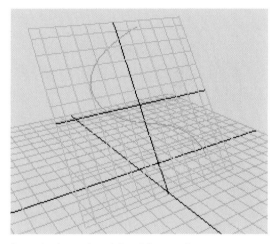

Construction planes can be made live and allow you to draw a curve that is constrained to the plane surface.

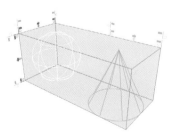

The Align Tool displays an easy to use manipulator.

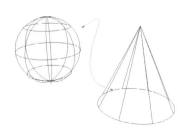

The Snap Together Tool lets you pick the surfaces to snap.

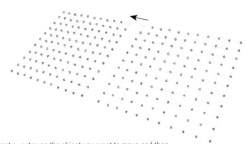

Select a vertex on the object you want to move and then shift and select the vertex you want to snap to.

Artisan

Painting with Artisan is an intuitive way to make selections, sculpt surfaces, and paint values on selected surfaces, as well as over multiple surfaces at a time.

Artisan Brushes

Using an Artisan brush is much like using a real paint brush, with the ability to paint different shapes and opacities. The advantage of using an Artisan brush is that you can select and modify the values of selected surfaces quickly, receiving visual feedback while you paint. Using a stylus pen in conjunction with the Artisan brush allows you to apply pressure-sensitive brush strokes while you work.

Stylus
Using a stylus pen with the Artisan brush allows you to increase and decrease the pressure while you paint, much like using a real paint brush.

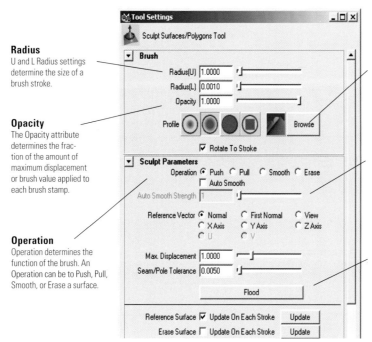

Radius
U and L Radius settings determine the size of a brush stroke.

Opacity
The Opacity attribute determines the fraction of the amount of maximum displacement or brush value applied to each brush stamp.

Operation
Operation determines the function of the brush. An Operation can be to Push, Pull, Smooth, or Erase a surface.

Profile
There are several brush profiles to choose from when changing the shape of your brush stamp.

Sculpt Variables
Sculpt Variables allow you to change the direction in which an operation will occur.

Flood
Clicking the Flood button will apply your settings to the entire surface of all selected objects.

Sculpting

Both NURBS and polygonal surfaces can be sculpted using Artisan. Adjusting attributes such as the Radius, Opacity, and Operation allow you to control the degree of influence of each brush stroke.

Sculpting with Artisan is a very useful technique when building organic models. Using the Sculpt Surfaces Tool is much like building a statue in clay where you have the ability to intuitively mold your surface.

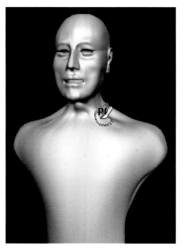
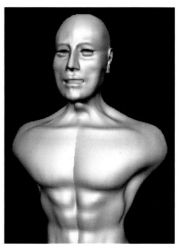

Artisan Sculpt Surfaces Tool allows you to intuitively mold organic models. The above example shows a torso before and after it was sculpted in Artisan.

Selecting

The Paint Selection Tool allows you to select and deselect CVs, polygonal vertices, edges, and faces using an Artisan brush. There are several selection types to choose from when using this tool. You can Select, Unselect, and Toggle selections. There are also global selection options that let you Select All, Select None, and Toggle all selections. You can determine the shape of your selection by choosing different brush shapes.

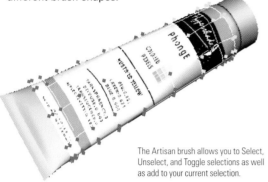

The Artisan brush allows you to Select, Unselect, and Toggle selections as well as add to your current selection.

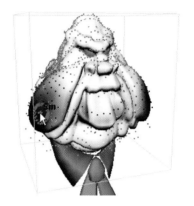

Selection Type:
- ⊙ Select
- ○ Unselect
- ○ Toggle
- ☐ Add to Current Selection

Texture Paint

The Maya Paint Texture Tool allows you to paint directly onto a 3D surface. In the settings window, you can set the color value for your brush stroke as well as the brush depth. You can also create other texture types such as bump maps and transparencies.

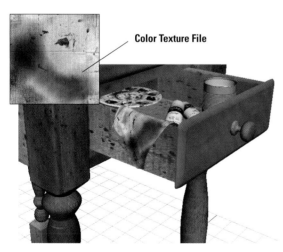

Color Texture File

Assign File Textures

The above image shows a color file texture that has been created by painting directly onto a cloth with the Paint Texture Tool. In the options window, you can set the size and image format for your texture file.

Painting Values

Changing values, such as cluster weights or soft body goal weights, allows you to create organic quality animations. With an Artisan brush, you can directly influence the way a surface moves over time by painting values to different areas of a surface.

Values applied using Artisan range between 0 and 1. These values are represented by a gradation from black to white that acts as a visual guide when you paint.

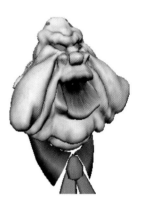

Painting Goal Weights

In the above example, an Artisan brush was used to paint goal weights on a soft body character. Both cheeks have been weighted so that when the head moves from side to side, the cheeks move more slowly than the rest of the face.

MEL Extensions

The Script Paint Tool allows you to paint MEL script effects directly onto a surface with an Artisan brush. These effects can be objects, procedures, and values.

To load a script into an Artisan brush, put your script into the Scripts directory. Select **Modify > Script Paint Tool** and click the **Setup tab**. Type the name of your script in the Tool Setup Command field and press the **Enter** key. Depending on your script, you may be prompted to enter more paint setting instructions. Once you have done this, you are ready to apply the effects of your MEL script using an Artisan Brush.

Painting Cloth Properties

Artisan can be used to create cloth properties such as density, thickness, and clothDamping with the Attribute Paint Tool. To paint cloth properties, select **Simulation > Properties > Paint Property Tool** found under the Cloth menu set. You can apply properties to selected portions of a cloth panel without affecting the entire panel. Paint attributes such as bendAngle can be used to apply creases in specified areas of a garment. You can also paint properties across more than one garment at a time.

Painting Wrinkles

Using the bendAngle attribute, you can paint wrinkles on garments. This attribute is found in the Cloth Paint Property tool window.

MEL Scripts

MEL (Maya embedded language) is the Maya scripting language. MEL is used to execute almost all functions found within Maya. Like most programming languages, MEL has its own command language which can be used to make the most of Maya.

Where Is MEL Used?

Using MEL allows you to extend the existing UI functionality in Maya. MEL can be used to customize and speed up the process of your production workflow. Also, with MEL you can write expressions for complex character animations, create macros to quickly perform repetitive tasks, build procedures, and create your own custom UI elements.

User Interface
Most of the Maya user interface is created using MEL scripts.

Marking Menus
Marking menus (menus that pop up over the current mouse position) can be customized to add shortcuts to your MEL scripts.

Command Line
The Command Line is found at the bottom left of the Maya user interface and can be used to execute MEL scripts and commands.

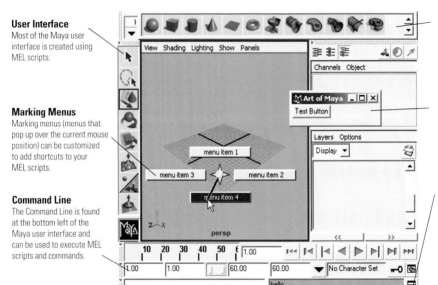

Shelf
Saving several MEL commands to the Shelf can be a timesaver when undertaking repetitive tasks.

Custom User Interface
MEL can be used to create windows with buttons and sliders that have been customized for your scene.

Script Editor
The Script Editor can be used to input and execute MEL scripts as well as offer feedback while you work.

MEL Commands

MEL commands can be typed in the Command Line and the Script Editor. More than one command can be executed at a time by inserting a semicolon (;) between commands. It is important to be consistent with uppercase and lowercase naming conventions because MEL is case sensitive.

Scripts comprising more than one MEL command can be quickly accessed by creating Shelf buttons or hotkeys, or incorporating such scripts into the marking menus accessible from the Maya Hotbox.

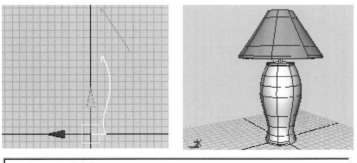

revolve -axis 0 1 0;

This simple MEL command executes the command revolve along with the Command Flag axis, giving Maya instructions to revolve the selected curves around the Y-axis.

Command Flags

Command Flags give Maya instructions on how to execute a command. Command Flags are distinguished by the dashes placed in front of them separating them as Flags.

Command Flags can determine attributes of an object such as the scale, position, and name depending on the Flags used. If you wanted to create a NURBS sphere with the **Start Sweep** starting at 0 and the **End Sweep** at 180, you would type the following in the Command Line or Script Editor: sphere -ssw 0 -esw 180;

In this case, sphere is the command and -ssw 0 -esw 180 are the Flags giving Maya instructions on how to execute the command. Visit Maya online documentation for a list of Command Flags and their descriptions.

The Script Editor

The Script Editor can be opened by clicking on the Script Editor icon to the right of the Command Line or by selecting **Window > General Editors > Script Editor**.... This window is divided into two sections: the History section and the Input field.

The History section is a feedback window that displays MEL functions that have been executed while working in Maya. With your middle mouse button, you can drag strings of code from this window into the Input field to help develop your MEL scripts. The History section can be used as a learning tool to help build upon your MEL scripting knowledge.

You can directly type and execute strings of MEL code in the Input field. In this field, you must use the Enter key on the numeric keypad to execute a command; using the Enter key on the alpha-numeric keypad takes you to the next line.

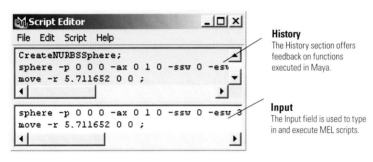

History
The History section offers feedback on functions executed in Maya.

Input
The Input field is used to type in and execute MEL scripts.

How to Use a MEL Script

A MEL script is a file that contains MEL commands, procedures, or both. MEL scripts should be saved in the scripts directory where Maya will look for them.

Before using any MEL script, it is important to read the header information describing the purpose of the script. The header states the usage of the script and whether or not there are any variables required to execute it. It is also important to be aware of any reference the script may have to other scripts, which would also have to reside in the Scripts directory to be found by Maya.

There are two ways to execute a MEL script. One way is to type the script name in the Command Line and press the Enter key. Maya will search the Scripts directory for a .mel file with the same name and execute it. You can also type the script name in the Script Editor and execute it using the Enter key on the numeric keypad. The Script Editor can be used to review or edit the script within Maya.

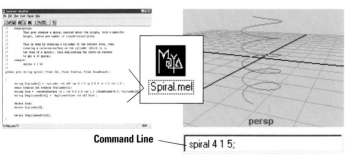

Command Line

A Text Editor can also be used to write MEL scripts that can be accessed by typing the name of the procedure in the Maya Command Line. In this example, *spiral.mel* is saved under the same name as the procedure "spiral" and is placed in the scripts directory. This script requires the user to type in the name of the procedure with a specific height, radius, and the number of turns to create a spiral that is centered about the origin.

Adding a Macro to the Shelf

A macro is a combination of several Maya commands that have been saved to the Shelf, hotkey or marking menu. Macros are timesaving features that take repetitive tasks and combine them into a single button. Macros can be created by copying pieces of MEL code from the Script Editor and creating a shortcut on the Shelf to execute several MEL commands at once.

Macro
To create a macro, highlight several commands at once and drag them to the Shelf using the middle mouse button.

Building Procedures

A procedure is code that has been written in the Script Editor or a Text Editor outside of Maya and can be stored in memory. When writing a procedure, it is important to write a description of what the procedure is meant to do. The description should be written with comment tags (//) in front of it so that once the script is executed, Maya will know to ignore these lines. The power of procedures is that they do more than simply execute commands, they are able to pass arguments from one procedure to another, store variables, and support arguments that require user input.

Building a Custom User Interface

With MEL, you can build your own custom UI with information relative to your scene. Since most user interface elements are created using MEL, you have the power to create custom windows with buttons, sliders, and other controls to modify your scene.

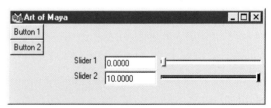

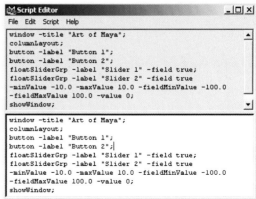

This simple MEL script creates a window with the title "Art of Maya," specifying button and slider names, and slider values.

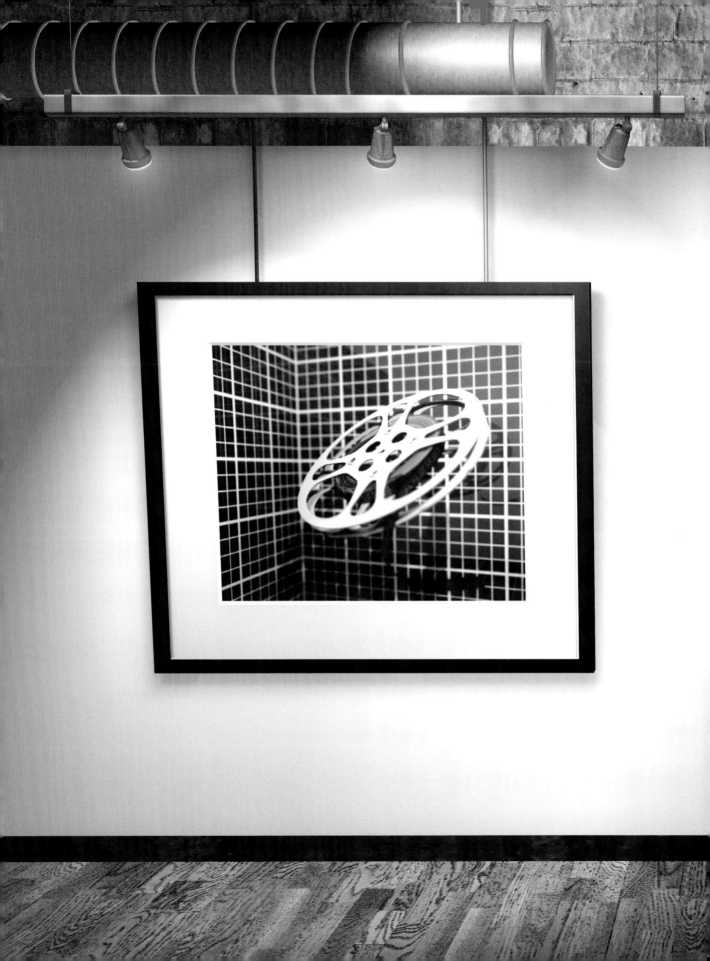

Animation

When 3D artists animate, they paint with motion instead of color. As an object
moves, rotates, or changes shape over time, it is being animated. This motion
can be at a constant speed or it can accelerate or decelerate. At times, this
motion will attempt to mimic real-world events such as an object falling off
a table, while at other times, it will take the form of an actor telling an
audience a story.

Models that are animated must be set up with mechanical properties that
define how they work. To have a door open and close or a drawer slide in
and out, 3D artists must understand the mechanics of their models so they
can animate them.

There are a number of tools for creating motion in Maya. In some cases 3D
artists will animate all the parts of an object separately. In others cases, they use
higher level controls to help streamline their workflow. Situations can even be
set up where the animation of one object controls that of another.

Animation Techniques

When you animate, you bring to life otherwise static and motionless objects. You take aspects of the object such as its position, size, shape, and color and change these over time. If these changes are set up properly, you create motion that instills character and life in the object.

In Maya, there are a number of ways to animate an object. Using a bouncing ball as a common example, it is possible to explore the different animation techniques available in Maya. In a real project, you will most often combine several of these techniques to achieve the best results.

Setting Keys

Setting keys, or keyframing, is the most fundamental technique for animating in 3D on a computer. This technique involves recording attribute values as keys for one or more objects at particular points in time. As you set multiple keys, you can play back the scene to see your object animated.

Setting keys gives you a great deal of control over timing. When you animate using keys, you generate animation curves that plot the key values against time. These curves are great tools for analyzing and editing the motion of an object. Other animation techniques are usually combined with some keyframing. Most animation you do in Maya will involve some form of setting keys.

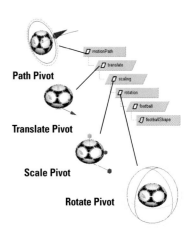

Path Pivot

Translate Pivot

Scale Pivot

Rotate Pivot

Hierarchical Animation

You set many of your keys on the Transform nodes of your object. By grouping an object to itself, you can set up different nodes with their own pivot points and orientation, then key them on their own. This added complexity isn't really required for a bouncing ball, but can be very useful for more complex objects where you want different levels of animation.

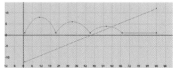

Animation Curves

By setting keys, you map the attribute's value to time. The keyframes are then connected by an animation curve that helps define the attribute inbetween the keys. The Maya Graph Editor shows you the speed of the motion and lets you reshape the curve.

Keying Attributes

By setting keys on attributes at different times, you define the motion of an object.

For example, Translate X is keyed at the beginning and end of the bounce.

Translate Y is keyed with an up and down motion that is fast near the ground and slow near the peak of the bounce.

Secondary Motion

Rotate Z defines the rolling of the ball; scaling of the ball is used to indicate its impact with the ground.

When building a hierarchy for motion path animations, it is always helpful to reserve a node for the motion path.

Path Animation

Path animation involves attaching the object to a curve where points on the path are used to determine where the object will be at particular points in time. It is easy to understand the way an object moves around in 3D space through a path, since its curve clearly depicts where the object is going.

Method 1

A curve is used to represent the path of the bouncing ball. This method lets you describe the path of the bounce by shaping the curve, but timing the bounce requires the setting of several motion path keys to lock down the motion.

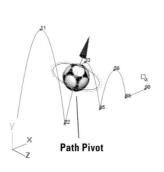

Path Pivot

Method 2

Here, a curve is used to replace the X and Z translation of the ball while the Y translation, rotation, and scaling are keyed normally. This method is ideal if you want to animate the ball bouncing along a curved path, which might suit a cartoon-style bounce.

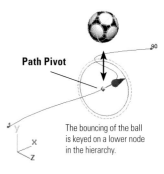

Path Pivot

The bouncing of the ball is keyed on a lower node in the hierarchy.

Animation Techniques

Set Driven Key

Set Driven Key allows you to control, or "drive," the value of one attribute with another attribute. The relationship between the two attributes is defined by an animation curve. The driving attribute can be used to drive multiple attributes. For example, the rotation of an elbow joint could drive a bulging bicep muscle and the wrinkling of a sleeve.

Custom attributes can be added to a control node, then connected to other attributes in the scene using Set Driven Key. This creates centralized controls.

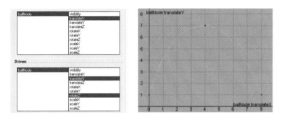

Drivers

Set Driven Key lets you use one attribute to drive other attributes. Here the Translate X of the ball drives the Translate Y and roll of the ball. As the ball moves forward, the bouncing action takes place. The resulting animation curves map the keyed attributes to Translate X instead of time.

Expressions

Another way of animating object attributes is through expressions. Expressions can be mathematical equations, conditional statements, or MEL commands that define the value of a given attribute. Expressions are evaluated on every frame. You can animate using an expression when you have a mathematical relationship that you want to achieve. In the case below, the absolute value of a sine wave creates the bounce of the ball.

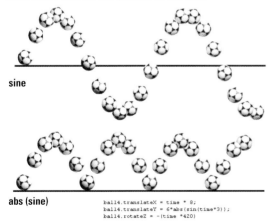

sine

abs (sine)

```
ball4.translateX = time * 8;
ball4.translateY = 6*abs(sin(time*3));
ball4.rotateZ = -(time *420)
```

Bounce Expression

A sine wave placed on time creates the bouncing motion; an absolute value function keeps the motion in positive Y and the forward motion is driven directly by time. Other multipliers are used to control the size of the bounce and the phase of the motion. Expressions are evaluated at every frame of the animation.

Non-linear Animation

Non-linear animation uses animation clips that contain keyframed motion. These clips can be cycled and blended with other clips in the Maya Trax Editor. For a bouncing ball, a single bounce clip could be cycled, then blended with a clip of the ball rolling. These clips can be moved, scaled, cycled, and blended. You can also add and subtract clips from the Trax Editor to quickly explore different animation options.

Bounce Clip

Keys are set for the up and down and forward motion of a single bounce. This one bounce can be cycled to create a number of cycles.

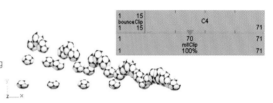

Roll Clip

Here, a clip is created for the rolling of the ball. This clip contains keys for the Rotate Z, Translate X, and Translate Y of the ball.

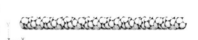

Blended Clips

The blending of the two clips has the ball bounce several times while getting closer to the ground and rolling forward.

Dynamic Simulation

To animate a ball that is bouncing off a series of objects or against a non-flat terrain, a dynamics simulation is required for the most realistic results. The ball can be turned into a rigid body that is propelled forward using dynamic attributes. Forces such as gravity or wind can then be applied to the ball to bring it to the ground.

Objects in the scene can also be turned into rigid bodies so the ball will collide with them. If they are passive, they will not be affected by the collision, and if they are Active Rigid Bodies, they will move as the ball hits them. In the end, the simulation can be baked to turn the motion into keys.

Initial Velocity

When an object is set up for dynamics, it can have attributes such as initial velocity and initial spin that give it a starting motion.

Active Rigid Bodies

An active object is affected by forces and by collisions with other Active Rigid Bodies. Active objects will animate during a simulation.

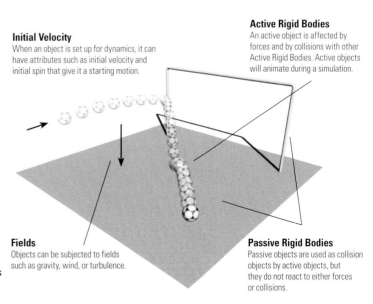

Fields

Objects can be subjected to fields such as gravity, wind, or turbulence.

Passive Rigid Bodies

Passive objects are used as collision objects by active objects, but they do not react to either forces or collisions.

Setting Keys

For an object to be animated, it must change over time. For example, a car might move forward or a light might blink on and off. To animate these changes in Maya, you need to set keys for the car's Translate X attribute or for the light's intensity. Keys are used to mark attribute values at specific times. Then, animation curves are used to determine the value in-between the keys.

As a 3D artist, setting keys is one of your most important techniques. This animation technique can be easily applied to your objects and the results can be easily edited. Once you are familiar with this technique, you will soon find that you spend less time setting keys and more time editing the motion.

Keying Attributes

When you set keys, you key values for one or more of an object's attributes at specific frames in time. These keyframes set the values, while tangents set at each key determine the interpolation inbetween the keys. This interpolation results in an animation curve that can be edited in the Graph Editor. This editing feature helps you control the quality of your motion.

Keying Attributes

In Maya, virtually every attribute is keyable. As you learn more about the different nodes available in Maya, you will begin to discover unique possibilities for animating your models. For example, if you keep an object's Construction History, you can set keys on the Input node's history. You can also set keys on attributes belonging to lights, materials, cameras, and other node types.

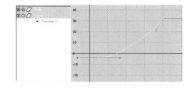

Step 1: keyframes
Keys are set for at least two points in time. You can set keys for one or more attributes at the same time. The keys are then stored as animation curves.

Step 2: Animation Curve Shape
In the Graph Editor, you can view and edit the animation curves. At each key, there are tangents set that define the shape of the curve.

Step 3: Playback
When you play back an animation, the object uses the keys and the values defined by the animation curve to create the resulting motion.

The Time Slider

Timing is one of the most important components when creating an animation. You must ensure your key poses are timed properly and that the inbetween motion achieves the desired results. The Time Slider lets you play back or "scrub" your animation to evaluate this timing. You can also edit timing of the keys.

Last Frame
Next Frame
Next Key
Play

< Backward | Forward >

Object or Character Keys
Keys show up as red lines in the Time Slider depending on which object or character you have selected.

Selecting and Modifying Keys
You can click+drag over several keys using the Shift key. This creates an editing bar. You can use this to move keys by dragging on the center arrows and scaling keys by dragging on the end arrows.

Right Mouse Button
With selected keys, you can then click on the right mouse button over the Time Slider to access a pop-up menu allowing you to cut, copy, and paste keys. You can also change tangents on the selected keys.

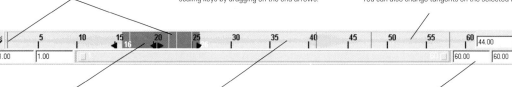

Scrubbing
Click+drag in the Time Slider to quickly preview the motion. You can drag with your middle mouse button to change time without updating object values.

Sound
You can import a sound file into Maya, then load it into the Time Slider using the right mouse button. The audio waves will be visible to help you synchronize your keys.

Time Range
The animation's Range and Playback Range can be set separately. This makes it possible to preview subsections of a larger animation by updating the Range Slider.

How To Set Keys

There are a number of ways to set keys in Maya. Each one offers a different way of recording time and value information. In some cases, you may want to set keys for a number of objects, and in others, you may want to set keys for a single attribute. The results are always the same as animation curves are created for any attribute for which you set a keyframe. The only difference lies in choosing a workflow that meets your needs.

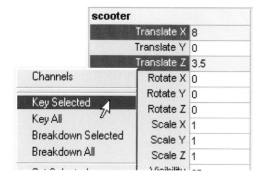

Channel Box
The Channel Box always displays the keyable attributes of a selected object. The Channel Box also lets you highlight one or more channels and then select **Channels > Key Selected** to set keys for the highlighted attributes on all the selected objects.

What is Keyed?

Generally, you set keys on attributes belonging to selected objects. You can further control which attributes are keyed using either the Set Key options, where you can work based on keyable attributes or the manipulator handles, or the pop-up Character Menu, where you only key character-specific attributes.

Keyable Attributes
By default, the Set Key command sets keys for all keyable attributes of a given object or character set. Attributes can be set as either keyable or non-keyable from **Window > General Editors > Channel control**... The keyable attributes are visible in the Channel Box and can be keyed with the **Animate > Set Key command**. Animated attributes that are non-keyable retain the keys set while keyable.

Manipulator
Keys can also be set using your manipulator as a reference. In the **Set key** options, you can choose to either use the manipulator or the manipulator handles as the keyable attribute. Therefore, keys would be set depending on which manipulator you are working with. This allows you to focus your keyframing on the attributes you are currently editing.

Character Menu
If a character has been selected from the Character menu found under the playback controls, only that node will be keyed with **Set Key**. The use of this menu assumes you have chosen a character-focused workflow when setting keys. You can set the character to None to set keys on other objects in the scene.

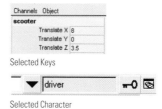

Selected Keys

Selected Character

Set Key
The Animate > Set Key tool is designed to create keys for as many keyable attributes that exist on selected objects or characters. If a character is selected from the character pop-up then it is keyed. Otherwise the selected object is keyed.

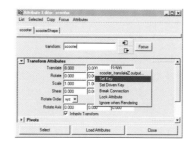

Attribute Editor
When viewing attributes in the Attribute Editor, you can click the right mouse button over individual attributes and choose **Set Key**. Since this window shows both keyable and non-keyable attributes, you can use this method if you need to key an attribute that does not appear in the Channel Box.

Hotkeys
A fast and easy method for setting keys is through hotkeys. Hitting the S key will set a keyframe for all keyable attributes on the selected object or character set. **Shift w, Shift e, Shift r**, will set keys for just the translation, rotation, or scale of an object.

Prompt
One of the **Set Key** options is to use a prompt window to let you set the keys for multiple points in time. For example, you could set a key for frames 5, 10, and 15 all at once using this window. The same attribute value would be keyed for each of these times.

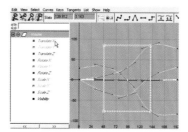

Autokey Off   AutoKey On

Auto Key
Auto Key lets you key automatically as you edit objects in your 3D views. Auto Key will set keys whenever the value of an animated attribute is changed. Make sure to turn this option off when you have finished using it.

Viewing and Editing Keys

To view and edit keys, you can focus on the animation curve's shape or its timing. Select **Window > Animation Editors > Graph Editor** to access the animation curves and define their shape and timing. Select **Window > Animation Editors > Dope Sheet** to focus on timing. In both windows, you can set the attribute value, edit tangents, and cut, copy, and paste keys.

In the Graph Editor, you can edit the weighting of the tangents. This feature allows you to create more control in between motion. This is in addition to the various in and out tangents that you can set in both windows using the menus. As you become more proficient with the Graph Editor curves, you will begin to appreciate the Dope Sheet where you can easily make more general edits.

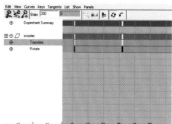

Graph Editor
This window offers a view of the animation curves themselves. This makes it possible to view the inbetween motion and edit curve tangents. You can also move keys around and edit their values.

Dope Sheet
The Dope Sheet focuses on keys. You can select keys hierarchically and edit them using this window. For example, you can use the Dopesheet Summary to edit keys for all the selected objects.

Animation Curves

When attributes are keyed, their values are mapped against time. All the keys for a single attribute are joined into an animation curve. Tangents at each key define the shape of the animation curve, or the value of the attribute in between the keys. The slope of the curve determines the attribute's speed. Thus, to control the quality of the motion, you must tweak and edit your curve.

Graph Editor

The Graph Editor is your main tool for manipulating the shape and timing of animation curves. You can edit the timing and basic tangent types in the Time Slider or the Dope Sheet, but the Graph Editor is the best place to view the animation curve's shape and use tangents to edit that shape. Once you have a better understanding of how the curve shapes work, the Time Slider and Dope Sheet will be easier to work with.

Anim Curve Nodes
Every animation curve has a dependency node that can be found by selecting Up and Downstream Connections in the Hypergraph or Hypershade window. In the Attribute Editor, you can view each key, its value, and tangents. This information is easier to visualize in the Graph Editor.

Loading Objects
By default, your selected objects are loaded into the Graph Editor. From the List menu, you can choose to load objects manually. This makes it possible to keep an object loaded in this window even if it is not selected. Active characters are always displayed in this window.

Stats
The values of each key can be viewed and edited here. The first field is time and the second field is value. If you select multiple keys, editing the stats will give all the selected keys the same time or value.

Curve Slope = Speed
The animation curve's slope shows the speed of the motion. A steep slope means fast motion, while a flat slope means static motion. An increasing slope indicates acceleration and a decreasing slope indicates deceleration.

Outliner
Loaded objects are shown in the Graph Editor's Outliner. You can then expand the different nodes to view the attributes that have been keyed. Only keyed channels are displayed.

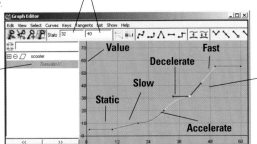

Tangents
There are several different tangent types, and each key on a curve can have its tangency set individually. Tangents can also be broken, allowing for different tangents into and out of a key. Tangents can be manipulated interactively by the user through the use of tangent handles, to refine the shape of the curve.

Transforming Curves

You can use the Move and Scale transformation tools from the QWERTY menu to edit keys. The left mouse button lets you select keys and the middle mouse button transforms. The Graph Editor also has a special Move Tool called **Move Nearest Picked Key** that lets you select a group of keys, then move them individually with a click+drag near the key.

Buffering Curves

As you edit your animation curve, you may want to refer back to the position of the curve before your edits. Buffered curves give you a ghosted version of the start curve for reference. In the Graph Editor, select **View > Show Buffer Curves** and any curves that have been edited will display a buffer curve.

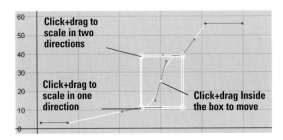

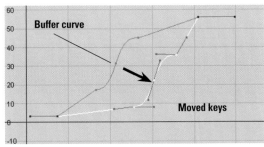

Scale Manipulator
If you select Edit > Transformation Tools > Scale Keys Tool from the Graph Editor menu, you can set up a manipulator to work with keys. You can move selected keys by click+dragging in the middle of the manipulator and you can scale by click+dragging the edges and corner points.

Display Buffer Curves
The buffer curve shows the curve's initial shape before editing. To update the curve to match a new shape, click on the **Buffer Curve Snapshot** button. To go back to the buffer curve, click on the **Swap Buffer** Curve button.

Animation Curves

Curve Tangents

While keys define the locations of points on an animation curve, curve tangents define the curve's shape and determine what the curves look like between the keys.

You can assign curve tangents to the whole animation curve or you can set them on a key-by-key basis. You can also separately set the in-to and out-of key tangents by assigning different tangent types to each.

You can assign tangent types to your keys in the Graph Editor, Dope Sheet and Time Line. The Graph Editor offers the best view of the results.

After you have used the other tangent options to set up the curve, you can use the Fixed tangent setting to ensure the tangents don't change if you move the keys around.

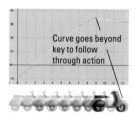

Curve goes beyond key to follow through action

Spline
With this tangent, the in and out tangents of the keys are aligned to create a smooth transition along the curve, resulting in a more organic motion.

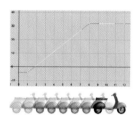

Linear
This tangent has no tangency at the keys and the motion is linear between keys. This results in a very mechanical motion.

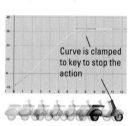

Curve is clamped to key to stop the action

Clamped
This option uses linear tangents when the values between keys are similar or the same, and spline tangents when the values between keys are different.

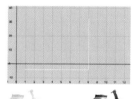

Stepped
This tangent goes flat out from the key until it hits the next key at which point it immediately changes value. This results in a jerky motion, and it is useful for on/off attributes.

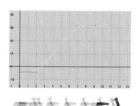

Flat
This tangent is flat at the keys, but the curve is smooth between them. It is useful for ease-in and ease-out motion where an object accelerates into motion then decelerates to a stop.

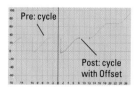

Pre: cycle

Post: cycle with Offset

Pre and Post Infinity
If you select View > Infinity in the Graph Editor, you can see how the curve is extended in time. Select options from Curves > Pre Infinity and Curves > Post Infinity to repeat your animation beyond the keys in different ways. This is particularly useful if you want to cycle your animation. This repeating animation will run no matter what the time range is set to.

Tangent Weights

Weighted tangents allow you to scale the curve tangent to create more steep slopes in an animation curve to further finesse the shape of curves. By weighting the curves, you can go beyond the Maya built-in tangents.

By default, animation curves are not weighted but new key's tangents can be made weighted tangents by setting the Animation Preferences. To use weighted keys, you must first select the animation curves, then select **Curves > Weighted Tangents**. You can then select the desired key and choose **Keys > Free Tangent Weight**. Now when you move a tangent handle, the tangent is scaled to indicate the changing weight. Then you can select **Keys > Lock Tangent** to preserve the new weight if you choose to further position the tangent handle.

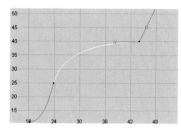 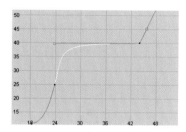

Adjusting Weights
With a weighted animation curve, you can free the tangents to allow for scaling. This adjusts the weight at that key and changes the shape of the animation curve. This option makes it possible to create the shape of animation curve you need. These curves are more complex than default curves. Therefore, you should only weight a curve if you are going to adjust the handles.

Breakdown Keys

Breakdown keys have a relationship with the two normal keys that surround them. If the timing of either of these is adjusted, the Breakdown keys are updated to suit.

You can create Breakdown keys in place of normal keys by selecting **Animate > Set Breakdown**. You can also select normal keys and convert them to Breakdowns in the Graph Editor by selecting **Key > Convert to Breakdown**. Later you can convert them back to keys.

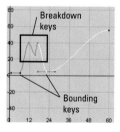

Breakdown keys

Bounding keys

Timing of Breakdown keys is updated

Bounding key is moved

Editing Surrounding Keys
When you edit one of the bounding keys, the timing of your Breakdown keys is edited. This allows you to maintain timing relationships between the participating keys. You can still edit the Breakdown keys without affecting the surrounding keys.

Motion trails and ghosts are ways to display the animation of your objects over time in 3D in the view ports.

Motion trails are curves that get updated with the keyframing of your objects. They can display frame numbers and different styles of curves, such as points or locators. To create a motion trail, select an animated object, then **click** on **Animate > Create Motion Trail**.

Ghosts do the same thing as the motion trails, except that you can see the actual geometry before and after the current frame. Create a ghost by selecting **Animate > Ghost Selected**.

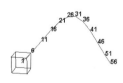

Hierarchical Animation

When you create models in Maya, they are often built of many pieces, each represented by its own Transform node in the scene hierarchy. To help you organize these parts and for others to understand your models, you can build up hierarchies using grouped Transform nodes.

These hierarchies also play an important part in how you animate. For example, if you were to group together all the parts of a door (handle, hinges, wood), you could set the pivot point of the Root node of the hierarchy at the location of the door's hinges. Then, you could animate the door opening and closing by rotating around this pivot point. If this door is grouped or parented to an airplane node, then as the plane flies in the sky, the door will move without losing its ability to open and close.

Building a Hierarchy

To build up a hierarchy, you need parent and child relationships between different Transform nodes. You can accomplish this by either parenting or grouping nodes.

Parenting
Parenting makes one object the "child" of another. The child inherits the motion of the parent transform. You can parent nodes using either **Edit > Parent** or by dragging one Transform node onto the other in the Hypergraph window.

The Workings of an Object Hierarchy

The role of a hierarchy in animating objects is to define the mechanics of the object. Object groups are used to define the moveable parts of your object, while pivot points and local axes define rotational axes. Therefore, as you build models in Maya, it is important to decide which parts of the model will actually move and also decide how they will move. This will make it possible to build hierarchies that support the animation process.

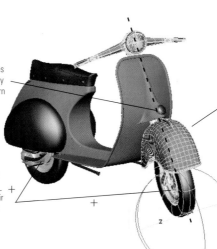

Local Axes
The local axes of the steering_assembly node are angled to match the required axes of rotation of this part. Now you can simply rotate around the X-axis of this node to turn the wheel.

Local Pivot Points
Because the wheels need to rotate around their centers, the pivot points for the front_ tire and back_tire nodes are located at their centers. These pivot positions are required for the wheels to animate correctly.

Local Axis and Pivot Point
Each Transform node in a hierarchy has its own pivot point and its own local axis. The pivot point defines the center of rotating and scaling animation, while the local axis defines the orientation. By setting up different nodes in your hierarchy with different pivot points and local axes, you can establish very sophisticated mechanics for the objects you animate.

Grouping
If you group two objects, you make them children of a third node that has its own pivot point. Transforming this node affects both children. You can group nodes using either **Edit > Group** or by selecting **Edit > Create Empty Group**, then click-dragging the children onto the empty Transform node in the Hypergraph window or simply parent them.

Hypergraph View
To animate the scooter, it had to be grouped into parts that would either move or rotate during an animation. These moveable parts include the main body, the handlebar, the kick stand, and the two wheels.

Children Move with Parent
As you rotate the steering_assembly node, the nodes below it (like the front_tire node) are also rotated. If you move the Root node, all the parts move. This is a noted benefit of working with hierarchies.

Selection Handles
If you are in Object Selection Mode but still want to select specific nodes in a hierarchy, such as the Root node, click on **Display > Component Display > Selection Handles** for the parts you want to easily select.

Order of Operations

Within a single Transform node, transformations are calculated in the following order: scale, rotation, and then translation. In many cases, this is the exact order you want. In some cases, you may want to achieve a specific effect not allowed by this order. You can, therefore, group the Transform node to itself a couple of times, then use a different node for each kind of transformation. The order of these is now under your control. Shown below is a simple example of why it makes a difference which kind of transformation comes first.

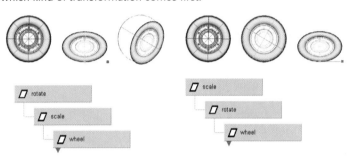

Scale/Rotate
In this example, the scale of the object is calculated first and then the scaled object is rotated. As you can see, there is distortion in the shape of the object because the center of the Rotate node is no longer at the center of the wheel.

Rotate/Scale
By having the Rotate node below the Scale node, the rotation is calculated first. No distortion occurs this time because the rotate pivot point is always at the center of the wheel and the scale pivot point works properly at the base.

Control Nodes

As you group together the parts of your model, you may want to set keys on attributes from many different levels of the hierarchy. Rather than digging through the Transform nodes to set keys, you can create a high-level control using either custom attributes or Character sets. You can build a Control node by manually adding attributes to one node of your hierarchy, such as the Root node, then using these attributes to drive other parts of the model. Character sets let you collect different attributes from different nodes into one place. Building of higher level controls is well worth the effort because these controls make animating hierarchies easier. The less selecting animators have to do, the faster they can go.

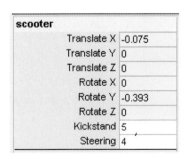

Custom Attributes
Select Modify > Add Attribute to create a custom attribute on any node in your hierarchy. These attributes can drive attributes on many different nodes using reactive animation techniques such as Set Driven Key, expressions, or direct connections. These attributes can also have built-in limits to define a range of motion for the attribute.

Character Sets
Select Character > Create to build a Character set. You can add and subtract attributes using the Relationship Editor or Character menu. These attributes have direct one-to-one connections with the original nodes. If you key either the Character set or the original node, they both share the resulting animation curves.

Avoiding Gimbal Lock

When rotating an object, it is possible to place one rotational axis right on top of another. This is known as Gimbal Lock. From then on, two of the axes lead to the same result when animated. To avoid this result, add extra nodes and use one node for each rotational axis. Now the rotation of one axis does not limit your ability to rotate around the other axis.

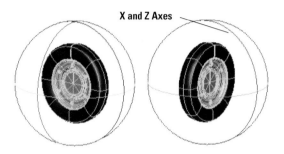

Gimbal Lock
In the Rotate Tool options, you can view a Gimbal manipulator that shows you what Gimbal Lock is. If you rotate 90 degrees around the Y-axis, you can see that the X and Z axes are now on top of each other. With a grouped hierarchy of three nodes, you can avoid Gimbal Lock by using each node for a different rotational axis.

Skeleton Joints

Skeleton joints can be used to create hierarchy. When you draw joints, a hierarchy is built where each new joint is a child of the previous joint. The pivot point of each joint is shown in 3D space and a bone icon is drawn between the pivots. This gives you a visual representation of the hierarchy that you can select and manipulate. While skeletons are generally designed for use with characters, you could use them to help control any type of object.

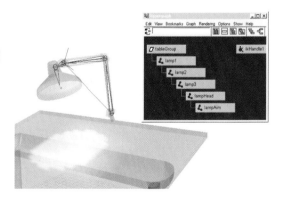

Joint Chains
A joint chain is a hierarchy of nodes. This hierarchy uses joint and bone icons to make the hierarchy visible in the view panels. This hierarchy also works with tools such as inverse kinematics that offer another method of controlling and animating the hierarchy.

Path Animation

When you animate with keyframes, you are focused on setting up poses for your objects at different points in time. With path animation, you use a curve to control the motion of your object. Using the curve's shape as your guide, you can plan the path of your object. Your object can then be animated along the curve using motion path features such as Follow and Bank to control the object's rotation.

A Typical Motion Path

To set up a path animation, start by drawing a curve. Next, select the object's root node, then the curve, and then choose **Animate > Paths > Attach to Path**. This places the selected node on the curve and uses position markers to indicate where the start and end of the motion will be.

When you attach to a path, a motionPath node is created that has attributes you can work with for added control. By default, your object will simply move along the path. There are a number of options available for motion paths that let you control rotation and timing along the curve.

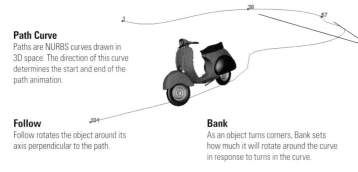

Path Curve
Paths are NURBS curves drawn in 3D space. The direction of this curve determines the start and end of the path animation.

Follow
Follow rotates the object around its axis perpendicular to the path.

Bank
As an object turns corners, Bank sets how much it will rotate around the curve in response to turns in the curve.

Adding Motion Path Markers

It is possible to create more position markers by setting keys on the motionPath node's **U Value**. This lets you control timing along the curve. A position marker is created each time the **U Value** is keyed. To help you position and set keys, you can use the motionPath node's manipulators. These can be accessed using the **Show Manipulator Tool** or Set Path Key.

Local Axes and Pivot Point

Local Axes and Pivot Point

The local axes and pivot point of an object play an important part in path animation. The pivot point determines which point is placed directly on the path and the local axes are used to determine the object's orientation relative to the path. Select **Display > Component Display > Local Rotation Axes** to view the local axes. You can then either move the pivot point or rotate the axes to suit your needs. You could also group the object to itself to create a new node with its pivot point at the origin and its axis aligned to world space.

Position Markers

The object is animated along the U direction of the curve. Position markers are used to indicate where the object will be along U at a particular time. You can select the markers by clicking on the time indicator then the **Move Tool** can be used to edit the point's position on the curve.

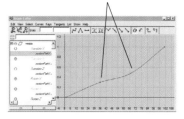

Graph Editor

The position markers actually represent keys that have been set on the motionPath node's U Value attribute. You can edit the value and timing of these in the Graph Editor.

INPUTS	
motionPath1	
U Value	0.894
Front Twist	0
Up Twist	0
Side Twist	0

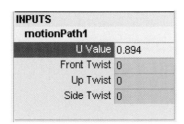

Manipulator

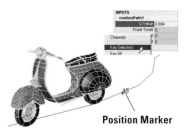

Position Marker

Step 1: Highlight Input Node
Select the node that was attached to the path. In the Channel Box, you will find a motionPath Input node. Highlight this node to view the attributes that can be used to control the object on the path. This node must be highlighted for the next step.

Step 2: Show Manipulator
With the motionPath Input node highlighted, select the **Show Manipulator Tool**. This brings up a manipulator that lets you move the object along the path. You can click+drag on the yellow dot (not the arrow) to drag the object along the path.

Step 3: Key Selected
Update the current time. Move the object along the path using the manipulator. Highlight the motionPath node's U Value attribute in the Channel Box, then select **Channels > Key Selected**. This places a new position marker along the path.

Curve Parameterization

When you draw an animation curve, its parameterization values are set depending on the type of curve you create. In some cases, the U parameter values are not evenly spread along the curve and are concentrated in certain areas. By default, this parameterization is ignored and the object is animated evenly along the complete length of the curve, but you can choose to animate using the actual U values on the curve.

Default
The object ignores the actual parameterization of the curve and animates evenly along its whole length. This gives you an even speed along the curve. To speed up and slow down, you would have to add position markers.

Parametric Length
The object follows the U parameter directly, which means that it speeds up in areas with fewer edit points and slows down in areas with more edit points. The timing along the path is affected by the curve's parameterization.

Follow and Bank

In addition to controlling the position of an object along the path, you can use Follow and Bank to control the rotation. With Follow, you determine which axis is pointing down the curve and which is pointing up. The object then rotates around the Up Axis based on the Front Axis points along the curve's Normal. Bank adds some rotation around the third axis based on how much incline you want the object to have as it turns corners. The more the object turns into corners, the greater the Bank value.

Banking

Follow
For Follow, you choose a Front Axis and Up Axis for your object. This is where the object's local axis becomes important. The Front and Up axes you choose will depend on which direction your local axis is pointing.

Bank
The Bank limit sets how much the object rotates as it leans into a turn. Bank Scale sets how much of the banking is used. A Scale value between 0 and 1 can be used to soften the banking. Set Bank Scale to -1 to lean out during a turn.

Keying Twist

If you want more control over the rotation of your object along the path than the **Follow** or **Banking** options provide, you can set keys on the **Twist** attributes using the same method as keying the **U Value**. This adds orientation markers similar to the position markers. You can select these markers and later rotate them to edit the results. You would key a **Twist** attribute if you wanted your object to spin as it moves along the path.

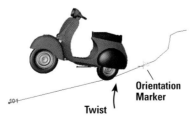

Orientation Marker

Twist

Orientation Markers
When you set keys on the motionPath node's Twist attributes, you get orientation markers that show the frame and the rotation axis. Like position markers, these markers are represented in the Graph Editor as keys.

World Up

If a path curve is drawn in 3D space instead of flat on the ground, some flipping may occur where the path twists. This is because the default World Up is pointing in one direction. You can set **World Up** to **Object Up** and your object will point toward another object. The new object's name needs to be entered in the motionPath node's **World Up Object** field.

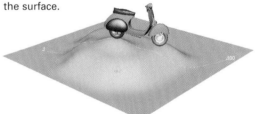

Flipping

World Up Object

How to Avoid Flipping
The flipping that occurs with the default path is alleviated when World Up is set to Object Up and a locator assigned to a second motion path is used as the Up vector guide.

Curve-on-Surface Paths

It is possible to attach an object to a curve on surface path. This ensures that your object moves along the surface. You can also set the object's **World Up** attribute to always be **Normal** to the surface.

Animating Along a Surface
You can use a curve-on-surface in a path animation to ensure your object moves along the surface. If you later update the shape of the surface, the path curve will remain in the surface's UV space.

Flow

To make your object's surfaces bend with the path, select the object after it has been attached to the path and click on **Animate > Paths > Flow Path Object**. This applies a lattice to the object that will deform the surfaces.

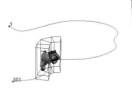

Lattice Options
When applying Flow to an object, you can choose to place a lattice on either the object or the whole curve. Your object must be made of deformable geometry. This means that objects like trimmed NURBS surfaces would need to be converted to polygons.

Non-linear Animation

Non-linear animation allows you to put a large number of keyframes into a single editable clip that offers high-level control over the animation of your objects. After setting up your attributes as a Character Set, keyframes can be set and then stored in poses and clips that you edit and mix together to quickly create animations.

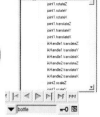

The Trax Editor

The Trax Editor is where you bring together and blend the different clips, poses, and motion capture data. These sequences are created by capturing keyframes from Character Sets as either clips or poses. The Trax Editor is used to edit and mix a layered sequence by moving, scaling, cycling, and blending the clips on any number of characters. These clips are stored in the Visor view and are not part of the main Time Line until they are layered in the Trax Editor.

Character Sets

A Character Set can be built from any attribute you want to animate. Only Character Sets can use the non-linear animation work-flow. Character Sets are a custom collection of attributes derived from other nodes. Subcharacter sets can also be created to let you focus on specific areas of a character. You can learn more about these sets in the Character Animation chapter.

Clips
Clips contain keys for Character or Subcharacter node attributes. Clips can be offset, trimmed, and scaled in the Trax Editor tracks.

Cycling Clips
Anim clips with repeating motion, such as walking, can be cycled. Press Shift and drag on the bottom corner of a clip to cycle it, or set the Cycle value in the Channel Box.

Holding Clips
Press the Shift key and drag on the top corner of a clip to hold its final position, or set the Hold value in the Channel Box.

Clips and Poses Library
The different clips and poses used by your characters are kept within your scene and can be displayed in the Visor under the Character Clips and Character Poses tabs. Any unused clips and poses are displayed under the Unused Clips and Unused Poses tabs.

Poses
Poses are a special type of clip that only contain keys for a single frame.

Tracks
Clips and poses can be layered using multiple tracks. Select **Modify > Add Track** to add a track to a highlighted character. Tracks can locked or changed to solo or mute.

Visor
You can click+drag with your middle mouse button a source clip or pose to insert it into the Trax Editor. You can also access them directly from the Library menu in the Trax Editor.

Moving and Scaling Clips
Click+drag on the center of a clip to move it within a Trax Editor track. This will change the clip's Start Frame. You can also move clips to another track. Click+drag on the edge of a clip to scale the clip to speed it up or slow it down. Using the Shift key allows you to select multiple clips at the same time.

Blends
Clips can be blended to create transitions between animated sequences. Each Blend has an associated curve that can be used to edit the shape of the transition.

Motion Warping
Extra keys can be set directly on the character on top of the clips. These keys are non-destructive and do not alter the actual clips and poses.

Weigthing
When you animate the weight of a clip, a visual representation of the Weight curve appears on the clip.

Creating Clips

A library of clips and poses is necessary to offer you enough material for mixing in the Trax Editor. The clips are collections of keyframes that can then be manipulated as one object. These clips are stored in the Visor and manipulated in the Trax Editor. Each clip also has animation curves that you can edit in the Graph Editor.

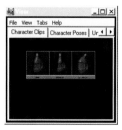

Set Keys on Character Set
Select the current Character Set from the main Character menu, or the Time Line pop-up menu. Press the s hotkey to set a key for the entire Character Set.

Create Source Clip
Select **Animate > Create Clip** to turn the keys into a clip. You can choose to leave the keys in the Time Line to make other clips or remove them.

View in Visor
The clip now appears in the Visor. To create Clip swatches, select **View > Grab Swatch to Hypershade/Visor** in the Render view panel.

Adding Clips and Poses

Once you have created a clip, it goes into the Visor as a **Source Clip**. This clip is associated with your character and can then be dragged into the Trax Editor, where it becomes an **Anim Clip**. The anim clips are connected to the source, but they can be edited independently.

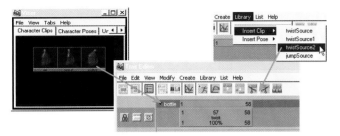
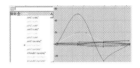

Drag Clip from Visor
Open the Visor where the clips and poses are listed. Click on a clip or pose with your middle mouse button and drag it to one of the character's tracks in the Trax Editor. You can then edit its attributes.

Select Clip from Library
Another quick way to access the clips in your scene is from the Library menu. Simply select a clip or a pose to add it to the current character track.

Source Clip

When you create a Source clip, all the keys on your character are captured even if they are outside the chosen time range. The **Source Start** and **Source End** attributes set how much of the animation will be used by the clip. This sets the in and out points of the clip, which can be very useful when working with motion-captured animation.

Source clips with their Pose attribute turned on are stored in the Poses tabs of the Visor.

Start and Duration
In this example, you can see that the anim curves for the source clip cover over 100 frames. The highlighted area shows the parts of the curves used by the clip as defined by the **Source Start** and **Source End** attributes.

Source Start

Source End

Pose
A pose is a clip with its Source End set to 1. These values are set for you when you select Animate > **Create** Pose.

Anim Clip

Anim clip attributes define the position, scale, cycle, hold and weight of a clip. These values are updated when you interactively edit the clip in the Trax Editor. To access these values, double-click on the clip in the Trax Editor.

Start Frame
This is the clip's Start Frame in the Trax Editor.

Pre and Post Cycle
These settings determines how many times the clip will be repeated before and after the clip itself.

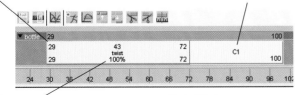

Scale
The scale lets you speed up or slow down the clip's timing. All the anim curves in the clip are affected by the scale, which offers a time warp.

Cycle Offset
An **Absolute** offset returns the values to their start position after each cycle, while a **Relative** offset adds the values from one cycle to the next.

Blending

When you have two clips that either overlap or are separated by a few frames, you may want to create a Blend to establish a smooth transition between the clips. To Blend, simply select the two clips, then click on **Create > Blend** in the Trax Editor. This Blend remains connected as you move the clips around.

Without Blend
Without Blend, the animation plays through the first clip, then jumps to the second clip and so on. This creates a break in the motion.

With Blend
With blend, there is a more gradual transition from the first clip to the second in the area where they overlap.

Graphing Clips and Blends

While clips do offer a high level of control, you may still want to go back to the level of individual keys to make changes. You can make edits to the anim curves associated with both clips and blends. This feature allows you to refine your motion at any time in the process.

Graphing Keys
To see the clip's animation curves, select a clip, then click on **View** > **Graph Anim Curves**. These curves are shared by the Source and Anim clips.

Graphing Blends
To reshape the weight curve to control the Blend, open the Graph Editor, then select the Blend icon in the Trax Editor.

Splitting and Merging Clips

As you begin mixing clips, you may find that you want to break up a clip to add to the middle of its animation or stretch out a middle section to adjust its timing. You might also want to take several blended clips and create a new combined clip that is easier to manage in the Trax Editor. Splitting and Merging allow you this kind of control.

Splitting Clips
To Split a clip, select it, move the current time to where you want the split to occur, then click on **Edit > Split** in the Trax Editor.

Merging Clips
To Merge clips, select them, then click on **Edit > Merge** in the Trax editor. One key per frame will be created for the blended area of the clips.

Character Redirection

Select **Character > Redirect** to add a translation and/or rotation redirection control to the current character. The controls appear at the origin of the character.

When a character is redirectable, you can change the translation and orientation of its already established animation.

Reactive Animation

The term Reactive animation is not one that you will find in the Maya UI. It is used to describe a number of different tools that all serve the same basic purpose. These tools all set up situations where one or more objects react to the animation of other objects.

This idea of cause and effect can be seen every day. When you open up a refrigerator, its light turns on, when the wheels of a car rotate the car moves forward, or when you raise your arm, your clavicle bone rotates. By applying reactive animation techniques in Maya, you can create these kinds of relationships.

Direct Connections

The Maya Dependency Graph displays the connections between node attributes. In most cases, Maya generates these connections for you, but you may want to build your own in the Connection Editor to support a specific animation. One limitation of this approach is that the values are linked absolutely and only these simple relationships can exist.

Connection Editor
This window allows you to make a direct connection between two attributes. Simply highlight an output node attribute, then click on the desired input node attribute to connect them. The connection can only be made between two attributes of the same data type. For example, a Float to Float, or Integer to Integer.

Translate X > Translate Z
In this example, the Translate X of the boot is linked to the Translate Z of the ball. As the boot approaches the ball, the ball moves out of the way. If the boot moves back, the ball moves back.

Translate X

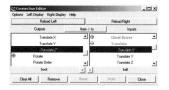

Translate Z

Dependency Graph
If you select two nodes and click on the Up and Downstream Connections button in the Hypergraph window, you can see whether the two nodes are connected. To find out which attributes are connected, move your cursor over the line between them.

Set Driven Key

Set Driven Key is another reactive animation tool. It allows you to choose one object attribute to drive the value of another. The driver attribute and the driven attributes are mapped to an animation curve that can be shaped and refined in the Graph Editor. These curves limit the motion and define the quality of the motion.

Set Driven Key lets you build high-level control attributes. You can add new attributes to the Root node of an object, then use these to drive one or more attributes lower down in the object's hierarchy or even on other objects altogether. In the end, setting keys on the driver will result in a change on the driven objects.

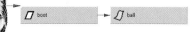

Step 1: Set the Driver and Driven
Select Animate > Set Driven Key >Set, load one object as the Driver and at least one object as the Driven. Highlight one driver attribute and as many driven attributes as you want from the list.

hand_control.indexCurl = 0

hand_control.indexCurl = 10

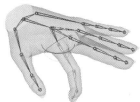

Step 2: Set a Key
Click the Key button. Now the Driver attribute and the Driven attributes are mapped to each other. Think of the Driver as replacing time in the animation curve.

Step 3: Set More Keys
Update the Driver's value first and then the Driven attribute values. Set another key. Repeat this for as many Driver values as you need to define your motion.

Step 4: Refine the Curve
You can now reshape the animation curves that connect the attributes. This will refine the motion. Later, you can set keys on the Driver, which in turn animates the Driven.

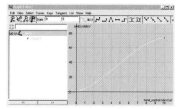

Reactive Animation

animation

Constraints

Constraints offer a way of controlling transform attributes on objects. There are a number of constraint types and each offers a different method of controlling an object.

The key advantage of this technique over a direct connection, is that you can constrain an object to more than one target object. The weighting of these targets can then be adjusted or animated to shift the constraint from one target to another. This is a very powerful tool for controlling objects and characters.

To constrain one object to another, first select the target or constraint object, then Shift-select the object to be constrained. Then, from the **Constrain** menu, select the constraint type that you want to use.

Constrained Object
This is the object that you want to control. Since some constraint types affect an object's orientation, be sure to check the local axes to help you set aiming, or up axes, in the constraint options.

Target Objects
It is possible to select one or more targets for your object. You can choose to add all the targets at once or you can add them later. Once a target is set up, you can use its transformations to control the constrained object.

Rest Position
With Set Rest Position, you can set where in world space your constrained object is positioned when its target weight is 0.

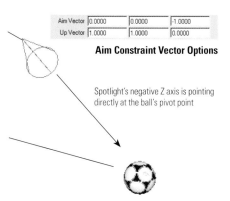

| Aim Vector | 0.0000 | 0.0000 | -1.0000 |
| Up Vector | 1.0000 | 1.0000 | 0.0000 |

Aim Constraint Vector Options

Spotlight's negative Z axis is pointing directly at the ball's pivot point

Aim Constraint
Once the aim constraint is applied, the constrained object is oriented to point at the targets based on a defined aim axis. If there is more than one target, then the object will attempt to aim at all of them based on their weighting.

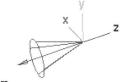

Vectors
For some constraints, you must set vectors for the up or aiming of your object. These should be defined based on the object's local axes. To aim this spotlight you would need to use its negative Z-axis.

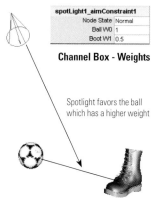

spotLight1_aimConstraint1	
Node State	Normal
Ball W0	1
Boot W1	0.5

Channel Box - Weights

Spotlight favors the ball which has a higher weight

Weighted Constraints
The constraint creates a node for each of the targets. You can adjust or animate the target weights to create different results. Be sure not to set a target's Weight to 0 unless another target is available.

Constraint Types

Point Constraint
Constrains an object's position to match the target objects.

Aim Constraint
Constrains an object's axis to point at the target objects.

Orient Constraint
Constrains an object's axis to match those of the target objects.

Scale Constraint
Constrains an object's scale to match those of the target objects.

Parent Constraint
Constrains an object's transformations to follow those of the target objects.

Geometry Constraint
Constrains an object's position to lie on a surface.

Normal Constraint
Aligns the object's axis to the normals of a surface.

Tangent Constraint
Aligns the object's axis to the tangent of a curve.

Pole Vector Constraint
Controls the orientation of a Rotate Plane IK chain.

Expressions

In cases where the connection you need between attributes must follow a more complex relationship, an expression will often solve the problem. Using either mathematical equations or embedded MEL scripts, expressions let you define the value of an attribute, or how two or more attributes work together.

You can add an expression to an attribute by right-clicking on the attribute name and selecting **Expressions**. This opens the Expression Editor where you can create the script. This technique is more technical than the other reactive animation techniques and is most effectively used once you become comfortable with the Maya embedded language (MEL).

Expression Editor
Expressions are written in the Expression Editor or in a Text Editor. The expression is linked to an attribute and is stored with its own name. You can recall an expression later by using the By Expression name filter in the Expression Editor.

Rotating Wheel
Here, the rotation of the wheel is driven by an expression that uses the forward motion of the scooter and divides it by the circumference of the wheel. The equation can be built from the fact that the circumference is 2 x π x radius.

Utility Nodes

In the Hypershade window, you can select **Create > Utilities** and choose from a number of special nodes designed to help build shading groups. Some examples include a **Multiply Divide** node, a **Condition** node, a **Clamp** node, **Reverse** node, and a **Plus Minus Average** node. By dragging other nodes into the Hypershade window, from the Outliner, you can then Shift+drag nodes onto each other to connect attributes using the Connection Editor. These nodes are most commonly used when building shading networks but can be used for a variety of things.

Plus Minus Average
A Plus Minus Average node is used to position the Root node of this character, which has its pivot point on the ground, between the two feet. The translate attributes of the two feet are connected to the node's two inputs and then the averaged output is connected to the Root node. A Utility Node can be a viable alternative to writing an expression.

Rigid Body Dynamics

In Maya, you can recreate the effects of real-world forces using dynamic simulations. These simulations are used to calculate an object's transformations based on fields such as gravity and turbulence. This approach can offer a more natural-looking motion than setting keys, and can yield a few surprises that wouldn't happen if you were controlling every aspect of an animation.

Another situation in which a dynamics simulation is useful is when you have too many objects to animate individually with conventional keyframing, especially when these objects collide.

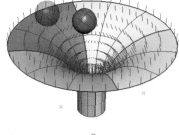

Animating Rigid Bodies

To use dynamic simulations on your objects, your objects must first become either Active or Passive Rigid Bodies. This designation tells Maya to include the object in a simulation. The motion of a rigid body is defined by the various forces that are applied to it. Collisions can also play a key role in the resulting simulation.

Normals
Always make sure your surface Normals are pointing outward to tell the Dynamics solver which part of a surface should be used for collisions.

Dynamic Constraint
A dynamic constraint creates limits for your active objects. For example, you could use a hinge so that the object can only rotate around a single axis at the hinge pivot.

Active Rigid Bodies
An Active Rigid Body is affected by forces and reacts to collisions with other rigid bodies. These are the objects you want to animate using the simulation.

Fields
A field is a force that influences the motion of your Active Rigid Bodies, such as gravity or turbulence. A field must be assigned to an Active Rigid Body for it to have any effect.

Keyframed Objects
You can set keys on Passive Rigid Bodies and this motion will be used as part of the simulation. Active Rigid Bodies cannot be keyframed and must instead be affected by either forces or dynamic constraints. A rigid body state can be keyed from active to passive and vice versa.

Passive Rigid Bodies
A Passive Rigid Body is not affected by forces and will not react to collisions. Instead, Active Rigid Bodies can collide with it.

Rigid Body Attributes

Just like a bowling ball bouncing on a slick alley would react differently than a basketball on rough pavement, you must set up how your objects will be influenced by forces.

Several Rigid Body Attributes can be used to affect the motion of the object and its collisions. These attributes are found on the object's rigidBody shape node. You can use these to control the quality of the simulation.

For added control, you can set keys on these attributes. For example, a spaceship's impulse setting could be keyed from 0 to -10 to slow it down.

Mass
The Mass alters how it is affected by forces. A lighter object is affected more while a heavier object is affected less.

Bounciness
Bounciness determines how much energy a rigid body gets when a collision occurs. A low value means a collision will slow an object down, while a value above 1 will actually propel the object. Just like friction, the resulting bounce is a product of the two colliding objects even if one of them is passive.

Initial Velocity
You can set an Initial Velocity and an Initial Spin to give an object a little push at the beginning of a simulation. This velocity is only added at the beginning of the simulation.

Friction
Friction determines how much the collision of an Active Rigid Body affects its motion. When setting friction, you must consider the friction on both the colliding objects. The resulting friction is a product of both values.

Impulse
An Impulse, or Spin Impulse, is an instantaneous force applied to a rigid body on each frame.

Center of Mass
The position of an object's Center of Mass has a strong influence on how it reacts to forces. A Center of Mass that is low on an object can help stabilize it, while a higher Center of Mass would make it more likely to fall over.

Damping
Damping is like air resistance. Higher values mean more resistance.

Running a Simulation

To simulate a ball bouncing off of the ground, you need Active and Passive Rigid Bodies as well as a gravity field. Using the four steps outlined here, you can run the simulation, then bake the motion into keys that you can manipulate in the Graph Editor. The challenge when setting up any simulation is to make sure your rigid body and field attributes support the kind of motion you want.

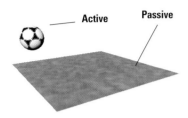
Active Passive

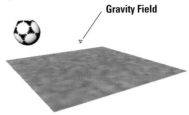
Gravity Field

Step 1: Create Rigid Bodies
Select objects you want as active objects, then click on **Soft/Rigid Bodies > Create Active Rigid Bodies**. Select objects you want as passive objects, then click on **Soft/Rigid Bodies > Create Passive Rigid Bodies**. The active objects will be able to be affected by forces and collisions.

Step 2: Add Fields
Select your active objects, then choose a field from the **Fields** menu. In most cases, you will use gravity along with some other field, such as turbulence, which can add some variation to the motion. You can also choose to add forces to some of the Active Rigid Bodies and not to others.

Note: Adding fields to a non-rigid body object will automatically turn that object into a rigid body.

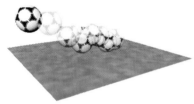

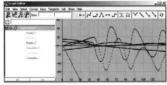

Step 3: Run Simulation
Use the playback controls to play the simulation. Make sure that your Playback speed is set to Free in your Animation preferences. If you don't like the results, play with the rigid body attributes on your active and passive bodies and re-run the simulation.

Step 4: Bake Results
To convert the simulated motion into keys, select the Active Rigid Bodies, then click on **Edit > Keys > Bake Simulation**. A key is created for every frame. Select **Edit > Delete by Type > Rigid Bodies** if you want to delete the rigid body or set **Ignore** to **On** and **Collisions** to **Off** on the rigidBody shape.

Dynamic Constraints

To help control the motion of the Active Rigid Bodies, you can apply one of five dynamic constraints. To add a constraint to an object, select **Soft/Rigid Bodies > Create Constraint**. This will assign the constraint and if the object is not yet a rigid body, it is converted.

The applied constraint has its own node that can sometimes be parented to other objects. The position of this node can be set using the constraint icon. Be sure to position the icon correctly before running your simulation because it does influence the results.

Hinge
Hinge constrains the Active Rigid Body so that it rotates around a line in space. You can see that the hinge icon has been moved to create the swing effect shown here. It was rotated by editing the rigid hingeConstraint Transform node attributes.

Nail
Nail constrains an Active Rigid Body to a point in space. This point can be parented to other objects that can be animated using keys.

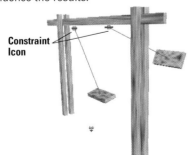
Constraint Icon

Dynamic Relationships

When you apply a field directly to an active object, you form a relationship between the objects. You can also use the **Fields > Affect Selected Object(s)** command or the Relationship Editor to link fields and active rigid bodies that were created separately.

Dynamic Relationship Editor
To build relationships between existing fields and your Active Rigid Bodies, select the **Window > Relationship Editors > Dynamic Relationships**.

Solvers

Dynamic animations in Maya are driven by sets of mathematical rules known as solvers. Solvers allow Maya to imitate physics. In complex scenes it may be more efficient to have more than one solver. Organizing the dynamics of your scene into groups of objects that interact with each but not with other groups of objects, simplifies the work that each solver does.

Collision Layers

If you have too many objects colliding during a simulation, you may want to put some of the objects on different collision layers so you can control which objects will hit each other. You can set an object's collision layer in the rigidBody node's Performance Attributes section or in the Channel Box.

Performance Tips

If your simulation is running slowly, simplify the solution by using one of the default stand-in objects in the rigidBody node's Performance Attributes section, or bake the simulation on a simpler object, then copy the animation to a higher quality model.

Interactive Playback

The solver Interactive Playback mode lets you interact with dynamic objects as you playback. For example, you can shake an object with jiggle applied to it to view the effect immediately.

Pin
Pin constrains two rigid bodies together. If one of them is passive, it can be animated using keys.

Spring
Spring constrains an Active Rigid Body to either another rigid body or a point in space with elastic-like qualities.

Barrier
Barrier constrains an Active Rigid Body such that it cannot pass by a plane defined by the constraint icon.

Modeling

Modeling is the process of creating shape and form on screen. Models in Maya can be hard objects with sharp edges or organic objects with a softer look. Using one of several geometry types, 3D artists can build surfaces, then push and pull points to change their shape.

Modeling on the computer can be a challenge at first because the goal is to mimic 3D objects on a 2D screen. In this chapter, 3D artists will learn how to use manipulators and different view panels to navigate this virtual world so they can focus on sculpting and building their models.

While building good looking models is important, 3D artists must also be aware of how the model will be used down the line. Models might need to bend or twist or simply move around your scene. Also, how surfaces are texture mapped will depend on how they were built. Therefore, 3D artists must make important choices at the outset about what kind of geometry they need and how it will support their animation pipeline.

Geometry

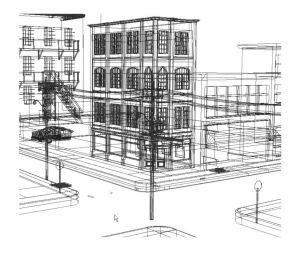

The mathematics of geometry is used by the computer to determine what you see on the screen. The Maya user interface gives you tools to edit geometry without having to understand the math behind it.

In order to build complex scenes, you need to understand how to manipulate geometry and how the geometry will be animated and texture-mapped down the line. A good-looking model is only complete when it satisfies the needs of all aspects of the animation process.

Points, Curves, and Surfaces

Points, curves, and surfaces are the basic geometric elements that you will use to create and manipulate 3D objects on the computer.

The creation of surfaces from points and curves is the essence of modeling in Maya. Sometimes, you start with an existing surface and manipulate its points to define shape and form. Other times you start with carefully constructed lines or curves that are then used to build a surface. Either way, you will work to give a physical presence to these basic geometric elements.

Building a Scene
Above is a wireframe view of a street scene. Complex scenes can be redrawn more quickly when viewed without hardware shading or texturing.

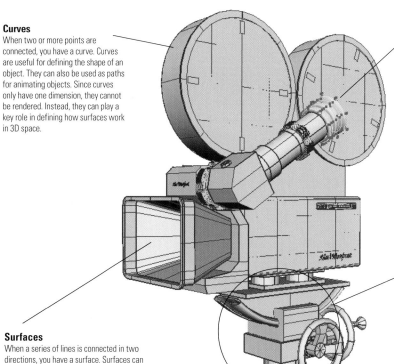

Curves
When two or more points are connected, you have a curve. Curves are useful for defining the shape of an object. They can also be used as paths for animating objects. Since curves only have one dimension, they cannot be rendered. Instead, they can play a key role in defining how surfaces work in 3D space.

Points
Points are defined in three dimensions using X,Y,Z coordinates. In Maya, control points are used to help define the shape of object types such as curves (CVs), surfaces (vertices, edit points), and lattice deformers (lattice points). Points are also very useful as references for snapping.

Objects
One surface is often not enough to fully define an object in 3D. When a series of surfaces is positioned in relation to each other, you begin to get more complex models. These models require grouping to bring together the parts into a selectable hierarchy that can work as a single object, while not denying you access to the individual parts.

Surfaces
When a series of lines is connected in two directions, you have a surface. Surfaces can be textured and rendered to create 3D images. When you shine light onto a surface, you can see the shape of the surface as gradations of tone and highlight.

Geometry

modeling

63

Geometry Types

One of the first decisions you have to make when you start a project is how you are going to build your models. There are four types of geometry– polygons, NURBS, Subdivision, and Bezier surfaces.

You can use any geometry type to create either simple or complex models. You can use one geometry type as a starting point for another or you can build models that combine geometry types. In general, if you are building organic shapes, you will probably use NURBS or Subdivision Surfaces. They will give you smooth surfaces and have the fewest control points, making edits to the surface easier. Since NURBS are limited to a four-sided patch, there are limitations to the types of organic shapes you can make from a single surface. This is where it is beneficial to use Subdivision Surfaces because they can represent many more types of shapes with a single surface. If you are building non-organic shapes, such as a desk or wall, it is easier to use polygons because they easily make shapes like corners or edges. If you are building a surface that combines hard edges with an organic shape, Subdivision Surfaces work well. In this chapter, you will learn more about your options so you can decide on the geometry that best suits the way you want to work.

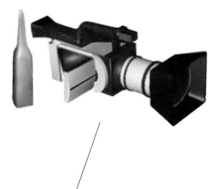

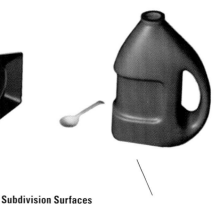

NURBS

NURBS geometry is spline-based. The geometry is derived from curves and surfaces approximated from the surface's control vertices (points) locations. NURBS allow you to start with curves that are then used to generate surfaces. This workflow offers precise results that can be easily controlled. All NURBS surfaces are four-sided patches, although this shape can be altered using the Trim Tool.

Polygons

Polygons are shapes defined by vertices that create three, four or n-sided shapes. Polygonal objects are made up of many polygons. Polygons can appear flat when rendered, or the Normals across adjacent faces can be interpolated to appear smooth.

Subdivision Surfaces

To create objects with Subdivision Surfaces, you need some understanding of both NURBS and polygonal modeling. Subdivision Surfaces are mostly built using a polygon mesh as a base and then refined. The advantage of using this geometry type is that detail is added only where needed, and it creates smooth surfaces like NURBS but does not have the limitations of being four-sided patches.

Scene Hierarchy View

Within the Hypergraph window, you can view the objects in the scene and any parent sibling relationships between them. An object will have a Transform and a Shape node. The Transform node contains information such as translation, rotation, and scale. The Shape node contains information such as History, Tessellation, Render Stats, and Object Display. When you select an object, the Channel Box will display information for both the Transform and Shape nodes. If you are using the Attribute Editor, the Transform and Shape nodes will be represented by different tabs.

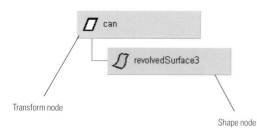

Transform node

Shape node

Tessellation

The Maya renderer requires polygonal objects in order to be able to execute rendering calculations. Therefore, NURBS and Subdivision Surfaces are broken down into triangles, or tessellated, during the rendering process. The advantage of letting the renderer tessellate a spline based model is that you can set the quality of your tessellation to match the size and scale of your object in a scene.

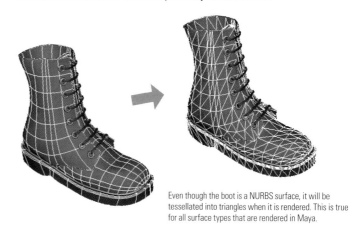

Even though the boot is a NURBS surface, it will be tessellated into triangles when it is rendered. This is true for all surface types that are rendered in Maya.

Modeling Techniques

Choosing the geometry type that best suits your model will depend on several factors, such as how the model is going to be used, how complex the model has to be, whether the model will be animated and deformed, and what kind of texture maps will be used. If you are unsure of what type of geometry to work with, it is possible to begin with NURBS because it can be converted to polygons or Subdivision Surfaces later. Polygons, however, cannot be converted to NURBS, but can be converted to Subdivision Surfaces.

Starting with Primitives

One of the most common ways to create a model is to begin with a primitive shape. This simple shape is then molded or expanded to add more detail. This technique using polygons is frequently used for developing environments and characters for interactive games. NURBS primitives, such as spheres and cylinders, are commonly used to begin organic modeling of objects such as body parts. A polygon cube is a good place to start a Subdivision model by simply converting it to a Subdivision Surface and then beginning to extrude.

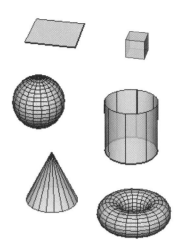

Primitives
Primitives can be made of NURBS or polygons. All primitives have the option of having different spans and sections.

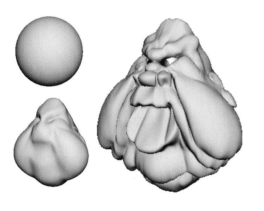

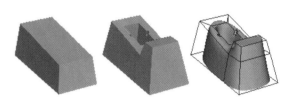

The model on the left was created from a NURBS primitive sphere that had several spans and sections in both directions to have sufficient detail. The Artisan Sculpt Surfaces Tool was used to create the main shape, which was then tweaked with CV manipulation. The model above began as a polygon cube. It was then scaled, had faces extruded, and was finally converted to a Subdivision Surface.

Network of Curves

For more precise surfaces, a network of curves can be used to control the shape and parameterization of the surface. Surfaces can be created from curves, trim edges or isoparms. For industrial type of modeling, creating a network of curves is essential for smooth and precise surfaces. There are several tools within Maya to create a network, such as Snap to curves and Point Snapping, intersecting and projecting curves, Animated Snapshots, curve rebuilding, and surface curve duplication.

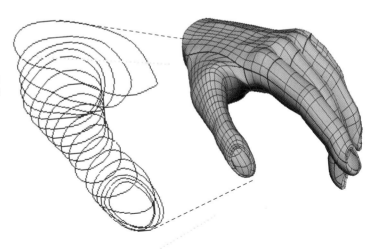

The thumb was created using a profile curve for the base of the thumb attached to a motion path. The curve was scaled and deformed at the end of the path to the shape of a thumbnail. Finally, an Animated Snapshot was performed to create the curves to use for a Loft.

Symmetry

Most objects in life, whether they are organic or industrial, have symmetry. Modeling only half the object and mirroring it offers an efficient method for completing the entire object. This technique is widely used for industrial design, but can also be used for organic shapes such as heads and bodies. A helpful tip for viewing a mirrored copy update interactively while you work on one half, is to use an Instance duplication with a negative scaling instead of a regular copy.

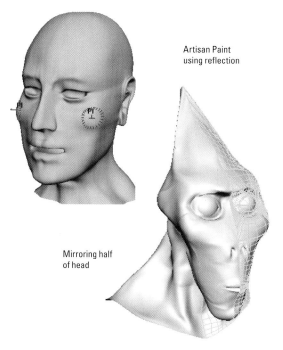

Artisan Paint using reflection

Mirroring half of head

The human head is one surface and not mirrored. Instead, it was created using the Artisan Paint Tool with the Reflection feature that sculpts on both halves at the same time. The alien head was modeled as one half and mirrored as a -1 scale in the X-axis.

Organic Modeling

When the surfacing tools are not sufficient to create the shape you are looking for, direct control point manipulation sometimes is the only solution. Artisan is an excellent tool for creating broad shapes but it can be difficult to use in tight areas where you may need to manipulate only a few CVs or vertices at a time. Manipulating on such a fine level is an art in itself that demands patience and skill.

Selecting the points for manipulation can be the first challenge because it is easy to accidentally select points on the back of the model. Artisan paint Selection Tool can be handy for selecting or deselecting points since it works on the surface under the brush and does not affect points on the back surface. Also, being able to hide unselected CVs lets you focus on the surface without the clutter, making it easier to change your selection. On NURBS models, when hulls are on, they also offer good visual clues as to where the CVs are in space. After the selected CVs have been modified, use the keyboard arrows to pick-walk to the next row.

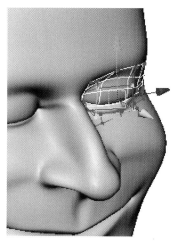 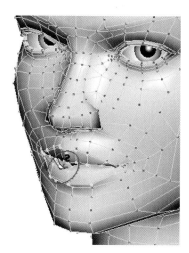

The left model displays only those CVs that are being modified. By pressing F, the view is focused to center on whatever is selected, making tumbling the camera easier for evaluation of the affected surfaces. The model on the right uses the Paint Selection Tool to select front surface vertices, avoiding wrong selections on the opposite side of the model.

Patch Surface Modeling

This method of modeling requires more planning than the others. This method creates a surface out of many smaller NURBS surfaces that have surface continuity and, typically, the same number and positioning of isoparms.

The planning stage of patch modeling involves deciding where the cutlines are to be positioned and what the parameterization of the surfaces will be. The Stitch and Rebuild Surface Tools are used extensively to create surfaces with this method.

Rotoscoping

If the model needs to have exact proportions or is being developed from a sketch, you can import reference images as backdrops and rotoscope (or trace) them. Maya Image Planes are objects in the scene that can display images or textures. Each Image Plane is attached to a specific camera, and provides a background or environment for scenes seen through that camera.

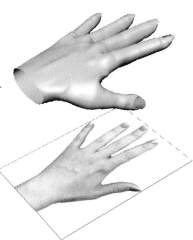

An Image Plane is used as a guide to model a hand. Image Planes can use single image files, a numbered sequence of image files, or a movie.

Working with Curves

The basis for most NURBS surface is the creation of NURBS curves. In most cases, the curve is created by placing control points in space. The decision to use the CV curve tool or the Edit Point Curve Tool depends on the precision of the placements of the control points. If the positioning is approximate and will be refined, the CV Tool is appropriate. If the points need to be in specific positions, the Edit Point Tool will place the curve where you click and the CVs for the curve will be created based on the positions of the edit point.

Drawing Curves

To create curves, Maya has several tools that use different techniques to generate a line. In all cases, the resulting lines are simply curves with edit points, CVs, and spans. By choosing the right tool, you can get to the desired shape more easily. In some cases, the tool creates a curve that has a History node, which gives you extra attributes to tweak while editing the shape. You can set the curve degree and the parameterization before drawing the curve, or you may draw a curve, and then edit the degree and parameterization later.

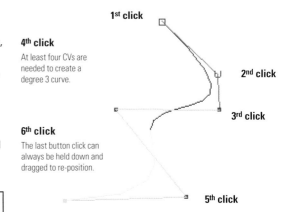

1st click

4th click
At least four CVs are needed to create a degree 3 curve.

2nd click

3rd click

6th click
The last button click can always be held down and dragged to re-position.

5th click

TIP
While drawing a CV or an edit point curve, you can press the Insert key to go into an edit mode where you can interactively move the last point drawn. Click the Up and Down arrows to move and edit other control points on the curve. Press Insert again to continue drawing.

Editing curves

A NURBS curve can be modified to create any shape. This process may require the addition or removal of control points, or manipulating the position of points to change the tangency of the curve.

To modify a curve, you can select and move the CVs or edit points, or you can use the Curve Editing Tool to reshape the curve directly.

Curve Editing Tool
This tool lets you edit the curve from any point along the curve and the associated CVs will move accordingly. This technique does not require you to select any CVs or edit points.

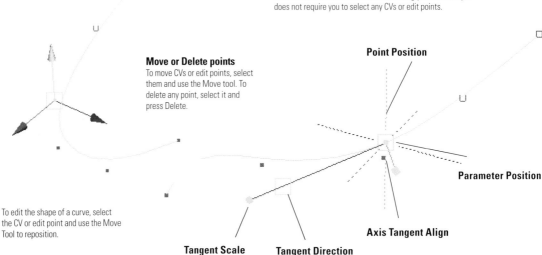

Move or Delete points
To move CVs or edit points, select them and use the Move tool. To delete any point, select it and press Delete.

To edit the shape of a curve, select the CV or edit point and use the Move Tool to reposition.

Point Position

Parameter Position

Axis Tangent Align

Tangent Scale

Tangent Direction

Curve Points

A curve point is an arbitrary point on the curve. It can have the same position as an edit point, but it's a different type of curve component. You might select a curve point, for example, to insert a knot, cut a curve into two parts, or attach a Point-on-Curve deformer.

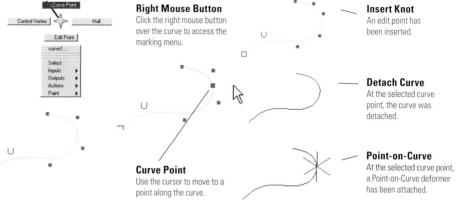

Right Mouse Button
Click the right mouse button over the curve to access the marking menu.

Curve Point
Use the cursor to move to a point along the curve.

Insert Knot
An edit point has been inserted.

Detach Curve
At the selected curve point, the curve was detached.

Point-on-Curve
At the selected curve point, a Point-on-Curve deformer has been attached.

Duplicate Surface Curves

You can create new curves from an isoparm, Curve-on-Surface, or boundary (edge) curve. There are many reasons to duplicate surface curves. For example, lofted surfaces are typically made from repositioned duplicates of several isoparms.

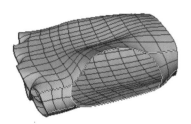

Isoparms are selected from 4 surfaces.

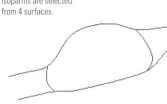

Curves are created from the selected Isoparms.

The curves are intersected, cut and attached.

The advantage to using curves created from surfaces is that they will retain the same parameterization as the surface. This is also the case if the curves are duplicated to create a network for lofting.

Starting with Simple Curves

When creating curves, it is recommended that simple curves be used at the start. More detail can be added as needed. The EP Curve Tool offers the ability to create a curve with only two points which is handy for creating a straight curve in 3D space.

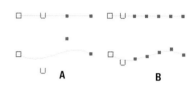

These two curves have the same shape, except the second curve has far more CVs than the first. For curve A to have a wave shape, only the movement of two CVs is required, whereas curve B requires the tweaking of five CVs. The greater the number of CVs, the more difficult it is to maintain smoothness.

Rebuilding Curves

Rebuilding curves is essential for building clean surfaces. This process can reduce geometry and reparameterize the curve.

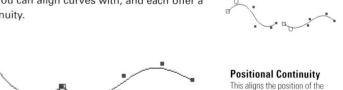

Curve B has the same shape as A after it has been rebuilt using the Rebuild Curve Tool.

Aligning Curves

Curves can be aligned and/or attached to other curves. There are three main methods you can align curves with, and each offer a different type of continuity.

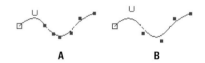

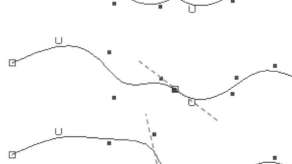

Positional Continuity
This aligns the position of the curves at the first CV.

Tangent Continuity
This aligns the curves by using the second CVs.

Curvature Continuity
This aligns the curves by matching the curvature to the third CV.

NURBS Surfaces

The foundation of a NURBS surface is the NURBS curve. To create NURBS surfaces efficiently, you must be proficient in creating good curves. The same principles behind NURBS curves are applied to NURBS surfaces since the two are related. There is an obvious difference: a NURBS curve has only one direction, while the NURBS surface has two directions. The two directions on a NURBS surface have an origin and together they define the Normals of the surface which determine the front and back of the surface. Being aware of these surface properties will help when using certain modeling and rendering operations, such as attaching surfaces or texture placement.

Anatomy of a NURBS Surface

The components of the NURBS surface are very similar to those of the NURBS curve, except the edit points are not moveable. NURBS surfaces have CVs, hulls, and spans which define the shape of a four-sided surface. NURBS models, whether they are organic or industrial in nature, generally are made up of several adjoining four sided patches. As with the NURBS curve, it is desirable to define surfaces with the fewest evenly spaced isoparms or CVs. As earlier stated, the quality and type of curve will affect the characteristics of the surface. However, the surface parameterization can be modified after creation by duplicating the surface curves at the desired locations and re-lofting.

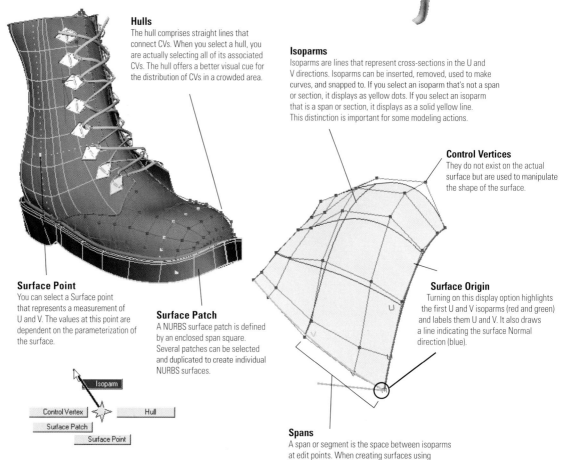

Hulls
The hull comprises straight lines that connect CVs. When you select a hull, you are actually selecting all of its associated CVs. The hull offers a better visual cue for the distribution of CVs in a crowded area.

Isoparms
Isoparms are lines that represent cross-sections in the U and V directions. Isoparms can be inserted, removed, used to make curves, and snapped to. If you select an isoparm that's not a span or section, it displays as yellow dots. If you select an isoparm that is a span or section, it displays as a solid yellow line. This distinction is important for some modeling actions.

Control Vertices
They do not exist on the actual surface but are used to manipulate the shape of the surface.

Surface Point
You can select a Surface point that represents a measurement of U and V. The values at this point are dependent on the parameterization of the surface.

Surface Patch
A NURBS surface patch is defined by an enclosed span square. Several patches can be selected and duplicated to create individual NURBS surfaces.

Surface Origin
Turning on this display option highlights the first U and V isoparms (red and green) and labels them U and V. It also draws a line indicating the surface Normal direction (blue).

Spans
A span or segment is the space between isoparms at edit points. When creating surfaces using Revolve, Primitives, and Loft, or rebuilding them, you can specify the amount of segments or spans.

NURBS Marking Menu

Building Surfaces

The majority of the surfacing tools begin with creating curves defining the surface. In some cases the curves are used to create simple surface that are then rebuilt and modified by CV manipulation. Other times, the curves are used to create much more complex surfaces that would be difficult to attain otherwise. To help you understand the operation of the tools, view the Help Line as you scroll through the menus.

Loft: Select curve(s), isoparm(s) or trim edge(s)

Birail Surface

The Birail Tool creates a surface by using two or more profile curves that sweep along two rails. The profile curves must intersect the rail curves to create a surface. Profile and rail curves can be isoparms, Curves-on-Surface, trim boundaries, or boundary curves of an existing surface. The advantage of this tool over the Loft is greater control with the addition of rails.

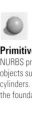

Primitives

NURBS primitives are common geometric objects such as spheres, cubes, and cylinders. Primitives are often used as the foundation for other shapes.

Deformed Half Sphere

Trim Surface

To create a trimmed surface, a closed Curve-on-Surface is required. There are various ways of creating these curves which will be discussed later in this chapter.

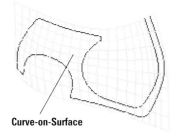

Curve-on-Surface

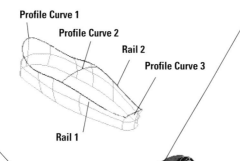

Profile Curve 1
Profile Curve 2
Rail 2
Profile Curve 3
Rail 1

Extrude Surface

The Extrude Tool creates a surface by sweeping a cross-sectional profile curve along a path curve. The profile curve can be an open or closed curve, a curve isoparm, a Curve-on-Surface, or a trim boundary. The extruded surface on this model creates a lip for the scooter surfaces and gives the illusion of depth.

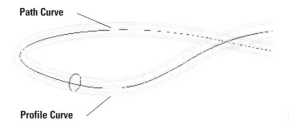

Path Curve
Profile Curve

Fillet Blend Surface

The Fillet Tool creates a seamless blend between two surfaces. The three types are: Circular Fillet, Freeform Fillet, and Fillet Blend. These terms are discussed later in this chapter.

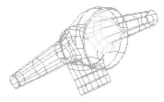

Freeform Fillet

Loft Surface

A Loft surface is created when a surface is applied to a series of profile curves that define a frame. There must be at least two curves or surface isoparms, and ideally the same parameterization for each curve, to achieve a clean surface. If the curves have the same curve degree and parameterization, the Loft surface will have the same number of spans in the U direction.

Curve 1 **Curve 2**

Revolve surface

The Revolve Tool creates a surface defined by a profile curve that revolves around a defined axis. The use of construction history is very useful to tweak the shape after the revolve operation. The front fender began as a revolved surface that was then scaled, deformed, and finally trimmed. The tire and rims are simple revolves.

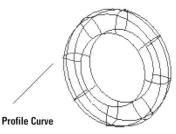

Profile Curve

Trims and Booleans

When modeling with NURBS in Maya, some shapes are not easy to model using a basic four-sided patch. The Trim Tool lets you define one or more areas on a surface that can be trimmed away. When these tools are used, the trimmed area is not visible and does not render, even though its CVs still exist. This gives you the ability to untrim the surface if needed. The NURBS Booleans tool automates a trim operation by setting up and defining the trim areas, then performing the trim itself. In general, trims and booleans are used for non-deforming surfaces, although fillet blends will let you connect two trimmed surfaces that are deforming.

Using the Trim Tool

The Trim Tool uses Curves-on-Surface that are either closed or meet the edge of the surface to perform a trim. The following example has a Curve-on-Surface created by projecting a NURBS curve in the front view. The curve gets projected onto anything in its path in the front view.

Curve-On-Surface

Trims are created using Curve-on-Surface as the trim edge. These curves can be placed onto the UV space of a surface in the following ways:

Draw on Live Surface
Make the surface Live, then draw a CV or edit point curve onto the surface's UV space.

Project Curves
Draw a curve in 3D space, then project it from any view panel onto the surface.

Intersect Surfaces
By intersecting two surfaces, the line of intersection becomes a Curve-on-Surface on one or both surfaces.

Circular Fillet
A new fillet surface is created which creates a Curve-on-Surface at points of contact on both surfaces.

Step 1
Draw a curve representing the profile of the area to be trimmed on the surface. The curve needs to be closed or drawn such that it overlaps any edges of the surface to be trimmed in the Orthographic view. This curve is then projected using the Project Curve on Surface function. By default, this tool will project using the active view. In this example, it was the front view.

NURBS curve used for projection

An enclosed Curve-on-Surface is created from the projection on both surfaces

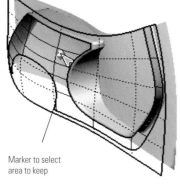

Marker to select area to keep

Direction of projection

Step 2
When the Trim Tool is active, it will prompt you to select a surface with a curve on it. The surface will then turn into a dotted wireframe mode prompting you to then select the area that will be kept (default setting). You can click on any other areas if there is more than one surface to keep.

Step 3
Press Enter to complete the operation. Repeat these steps to any other surfaces with curves on them. Remember that any surface that is trimmed can be untrimmed at any time using the Untrim Surfaces function.

THE ART OF MAYA

Intersecting Two Surfaces

A paint palette is a good example to show how you can create a Curve-on-Surface on both surfaces in order to use the Trim tool. Here, a sphere is used to intersect with a revolved surface.

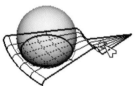

Step 1
Set up a partial revolve for the base. Give it a 36-degree angle with two segments and center it on the X-axis. Create a NURBS sphere and position it to intersect the palette base.

Step 2
Select the surface and the sphere and then select **Edit Surfaces > Intersect Surfaces**. Make sure Create Curve On is set to Both surfaces. Now you have curves on both surfaces.

Step 3
Select the **Edit Surfaces > Trim** tool and indicate what area of the palette and sphere you will keep.

Step 4
Trim the sphere using the Shrink Surface option so that the geometry is cut back after the trim.

Fixing Trim Gaps

After a trim operation is performed, you may notice that there are gaps between the surfaces in the software rendering. This can be rectified by increasing and adjusting the Tessellation attributes on the surface such as Curvature Tolerance or Smooth Edge. See the Rendering chapter for more information.

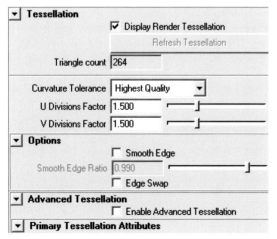

Shrink Surface

This option causes the underlying surface to shrink to just cover the retained regions. This permanently changes the surface geometry and cannot be restored by untrimming, unless you Undo the operation.

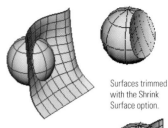

Surfaces trimmed with the Shrink Surface option.

When untrimmed, the intersecting surface shrinks. You cannot return to the original surface after this operation.

NURBS Booleans

NURBS Booleans offer a faster workflow for creating trimmed surfaces. Using a selection of surfaces as a starting shell and a second selection of surfaces as a boolean shell, you can union, subtract, and intersect to create new trimmed surfaces.

Union Boolean   **Intersect Boolean**   **Subtract Boolean**

Tools That Create Trims

There are a number of tools in Maya that result in trimmed surfaces. You should recognize which tools create trims because these surfaces may require extra attention when setting tessellation. If you want to deform your surface during animation then you should avoid the use of these tools. The following tools create a trimmed surface:

Set Planar
The isoparm or curve must be planar to create this surface.

Fillets
A new fillet surface is created which creates a Curve-on-Surface at points of contact on both surfaces.

Text Tool
The curves are used to create planar surfaces.

NURBS Booleans
Booleans automate an intersect surface with Curve-on-Surface and then trims.

Round Tool
It rounds off any corner where two surfaces meet.

Joining Surfaces

When modeling NURBS surfaces, there are instances where one surface is not sufficient for completing the object and more than one surface may need to be joined together. Modeling organic shapes where one surface must blend seamlessly into another requires an understanding of how the surface was created and how it will be deformed. The four main options for joining surfaces are: attaching, aligning, stitching, and surface fillets.

For best results with any of these options, you should have the same number of aligning isoparms and the same surface direction on both surfaces. The Surface Editing tools can prepare the surfaces for direction and rebuild them to match parameterization before joining them.

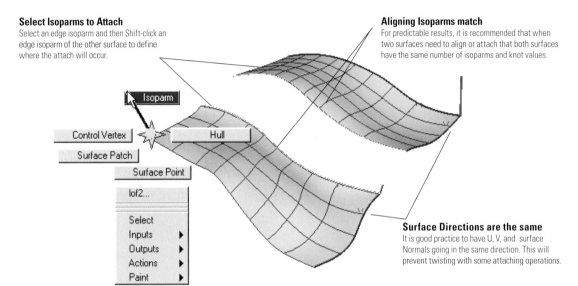

Select Isoparms to Attach
Select an edge isoparm and then Shift-click an edge isoparm of the other surface to define where the attach will occur.

Aligning Isoparms match
For predictable results, it is recommended that when two surfaces need to align or attach that both surfaces have the same number of isoparms and knot values.

Surface Directions are the same
It is good practice to have U, V, and surface Normals going in the same direction. This will prevent twisting with some attaching operations.

Attach Surfaces

The Attach Tool creates a single surface after the attach. The two main options are Blend and Connect. Blend Attach modifies both surfaces slightly because it tries to maintain continuity. Connect Attach simply moves the isoparm of the second selected surface to the first. The result of the Connect does not have surface continuity and introduces a multiknot when using the default settings.

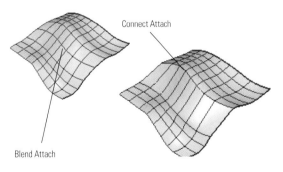

Connect Attach

Blend Attach

Notice how Blend Attach moved both edges to the center while Connect Attach only moved the bottom surface edge to the others without tangency.

Align Surfaces

The Align Tool aligns two surfaces with the selected type of continuity. This tool also has an Attach option which is executed after the align. There are more controls in this method than the Attach like Continuity Type, Modify Position, or Modify Boundary (which are the same as Align operation for curves). With the Attach tools it is important which surface is selected first. However, with the Align, you are able decide which surface(s) need to be adjusted to align.

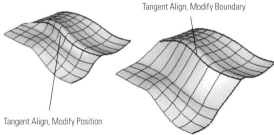

Tangent Align, Modify Boundary

Tangent Align, Modify Position

Both of these alignments have tangential continuity, but the first has positional modification on the bottom surface. The effects of Modify Boundary are similar to those of Connect Attach, except the alignment has tangency.

Surface Fillets

When a surface fillet is used between two surfaces, it creates a new surface between them. The three types are: Circular Fillet, Freeform Fillet, and Fillet Blend. Generally, Circular Fillets are used primarily for industrial models, and the other two for more organic shapes. Fillet Blends lend themselves well to character models where surfaces, such as fingers, need transitions to trimmed holes on other surfaces. The construction history allows the surfaces to be animated while it retains continuity. Also, the History node can adjust whether the fillet is created along the entire edge of both surfaces or only a portion of them.

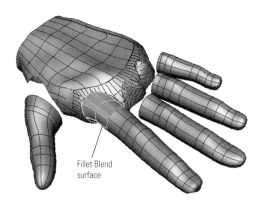

Fillet Blend surface

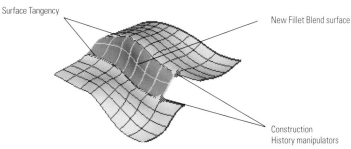

Surface Tangency

New Fillet Blend surface

Construction History manipulators

Stitch Surfaces

The Stitch Tool is used on NURBS surfaces to sew points or edges together. This tool is primarily used to keep surface edges together while they are being deformed, but is also used as part of the modeling process. The technique of patch modeling, where there are several NURBS surfaces that must have surface continuity, is where Stitch can help pull those surfaces together smoothly.

The Stitch Tool can work three ways: stitching points like NURBS surface points or CVs; stitching two edges at a time; or by Global stitch which stitches multiple edges within a specified separation gap.

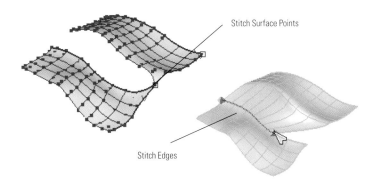

Stitch Surface Points

Stitch Edges

The left diagram shows two CVs on a NURBS surface being stitched together. The adjacent diagram shows the History node being adjusted after two edges have been stitched together.

There are several key steps involved with creating surfaces that can be stitched. The following sample shows how a cylinder and a plane would be stitched together to create seamless deformations.

You should take particular notice of the rebuilding steps and the close proximity to continuity that make the surfaces more compatible. Also, it is very important to delete history before you actually stitch the surface.

To attach the fingers to the palm, holes need to be created. Curve-on-Surfaces were created by intersecting cylinders to the front of the palm. The palm was then trimmed. Finally, the Fillet Blend Tool was used to create a smooth blend from the fingers to the palm. For animation, the Fillet Blends would not be bound into the skeleton and, instead, the construction history would be used to maintain continuity. A more desirable technique is patch modeling, which is covered later in this chapter.

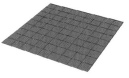
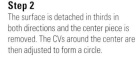

Step 1
A NURBS plane with 12 spans in both directions.

Step 2
The surface is detached in thirds in both directions and the center piece is removed. The CVs around the center are then adjusted to form a circle.

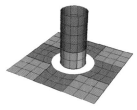
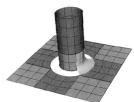

Step 3
A NURBS Primitive Cylinder with 12 sections and 6 spans is rotated 15 degrees to align with patches and then detached at the 2nd last isoparm. Then the bottom cylinder piece is detached equally in quarters.

Step 4
The to-be stitched surfaces are rebuilt using the # of Spans parameterization option. The cylinder piece can either be stitched or aligned to plane. This is repeated for all the pieces.

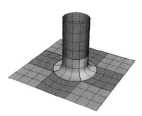
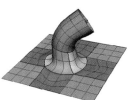

Step 5
All the construction history is deleted from all the surfaces. Set the Global Stitch options for Closest Knot and Equal Params.

Step 6
Select all the surfaces and apply a Global Stitch. The various surfaces will maintain tangency as the parts are animated and deformed.

Patch Surfaces

Patch surface modeling refers to creating a model made of several NURBS surfaces that make up a continuous mesh-like surface. The advantages of modeling this way are even parameterization that helps with texturing, and the model is generally lighter in geometry. However, this technique requires much planning and practice to achieve decent results. It is not uncommon to rebuild the model several times before finding the right density and areas where the surfaces will meet. With this technique the surfaces are continuous without trims, and isoparms match on both surfaces. Tools such as Detach, Attach, Rebuild, and Stitch are used extensively. You will find yourself using the Global Stitch function as a tool for positioning the surfaces, and then deleting the construction history.

Modeling a head is a good example to demonstrate the main issues with patch modeling. The following example explores a general workflow to incorporate several modeling techniques covered in this chapter.

Patch Surface

A patch is a NURBS surface with a certain number of span in U and V. A patch can be stitched with another patch, as long as they both have the same amount of spans or with a multiplier of 2.

High Density

In tight spots, the density of patches can create unwanted wrinkles. Thus, you need to add resolution only where needed. If your model is to be converted in polygons, these places will have a lot of faces.

Stitches

Stiching two patches together means to establish a relation between the surface Normal in order to give a smooth feeling. It is recommended to stitch on flat spots and not in creases. If you delete the history on stitched geometry, you will lose the relationship between the patches.

Circular Patches

There are three kinds of patches: Open, Close, and Periodic. An opened surface is usually shaped like a rectangle. A closed surface has its two opposite edges overlapping. Finally, a periodic surface is like a closed surface, except that there is no border edge (like a cylinder).

Symmetrical Geometry

You can save a lot of time by modeling only one half of your symmetrical or almost symmetrical geometry. You can then mirror the model and modify it to suit your needs.

Muscular Structure

Before you start modeling an organic model, take some time to think about the musculature under the skin and how the geometry should react when it is stretched and compressed.

In this case, try looking at yourself in the mirror or look at different body pictures like the ones on this page. Understand that the deformation concept is an art in itself and you might need several tries before getting the expected results.

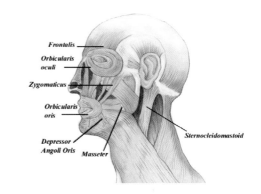

Rotoscoping

When a model needs to have exact proportions, or is being developed based on drawings or pictures, you can import images as references and rotoscope them when modeling. Maya Image Planes are the perfect tool to display images or textures. Each image plane is attached to a specific camera and provides a background or environment for scenes seen through that camera. You can then keep them in your scene for all the modeling stage.

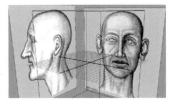

Planning Ahead
Once the design of the character has been established, you can speed up your modeling by having a front and side view that can be brought into Maya.

Image Planes
To create image planes in Maya, select the desired Orthographic camera, and open its Attribute Editor. Under the section Environment, click on the Image Plane Create button. You can then select an image file to be displayed in the viewport.

Creating the patches

This section is the most tedious workflow in patch modeling, but the result is really worth the shot. Every set of four curves must be used to create a patch. Each patch must then be rebuilt to get a good surface parameterization, and then stitched together. The history plays a big role at this stage, since adjusting the surface could potentially split seams apart.

When you stitch surfaces together, a good workflow is to use a Blinn shader on your model. The Blinn shader gives you good specular feedback on how your patches meet and how seamless they look once attached.

The Global Stitch is the tool you will use to hold all these patches together.

Surface Parameterization
A good parameterization is to have the U and V range from 0 to N number of spans. That can be done with Edit NURBS > Rebuild Surfaces.

NURBS Surface History		
Min Max Range U	0.000	4.000
Min Max Range V	0.000	8.000
Spans UV	4	8
Degree UV	3	3
Form U	Open	
Form V	Periodic	

Adding Details

By now, you should have a good knowledge of rebuilding and stitching surfaces. It is now time to add details and enhance the look of our model.

Since the continuity of all surfaces will be maintained when manipulating control points, refining and adding details to your geometry will be easier.

Curves

One technique is to start a patch model by drawing and connecting a curve network over the image planes. If your model is to be symmetrical, only bother doing half of the model and eventually mirror the geometry.

Each curves is a junction between two patch surfaces. Patch surfaces are made up of four sides (except for periodic surfaces), and should follow the muscle underneath the skin. Carefully placing your curves is the key to a good model.

It is not an obligation to draw all your curves in one stretch, but it is a good way to learn and get used to the procedure. Experienced modelers will be able to create the patches as they go, but it is because they already know exactly how and where to distribute the patches.

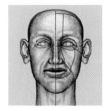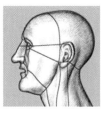

Head Structure
The placement of the curve shown here is the generic start for a head model. It is a good start to learn patch modeling, since most heads will be using a similar layout.

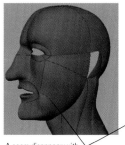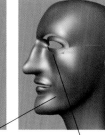

A seam disappear with the Stitch Tool.

A Blinn shader shows uneven seems.

Workflow Choices

Now that you have the cleanest geometry possible, you need to decide whether you want to continue using the patch model for animation and deformation, or if your workflow requires that you convert the geometry into polygons.

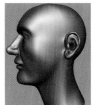

Convertion
When converting your model, you can keep the history and tweak the patch's control points instead of numerous polygonal vertices. Doing so will greatly accelerate blendShapes creation.

Polygon Modeling

Polygons can be defined as a number of connected points that create a shape or face. Points are connected by edges that surround the resulting face. A face can exist as triangles, quadrangles (quads), or n-gons. Joined together, they create a polygon mesh. A polygon mesh can either consist of the Primitives that come with Maya, can be a complex shape that results from using the Maya polygon editing operations, or can be a polygonal mesh resulting from a conversion from NURBS, Subdivision Surfaces, Paint FX, Displacement, or Fluids.

Polygon Components

Each polygon mesh consists of components that are modifiable to help create and edit the mesh. These main components are vertices, edges, faces, and UVs. There are polygon editing operations in Maya that allow you to edit these components. While you will need to select the individual components you wish to modify, by setting Convert Selection to On in the **Polygons > Tool Options menu**, Maya will automatically switch to the right component type for a given edit operation and perform the operation as instructed.

Polygon Creation

To create a polygon shape, select **Polygons > Create Polygon Tool**. After placing a point, use the middle mouse button to alter its position.

After the 3rd click, the polygon can be completed by pressing Enter. The dashed line represents the final edge.

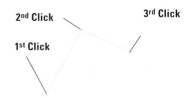

You can continue to place points until the desired shape is achieved. Press Enter to finish.

Vertices
A vertex is a point in 3D space. Three or more connected vertices make a face. Press F9 for Vertex Selection mode.

Selected Vertices

Edges
Edges connect vertices by drawing a straight line between them. A single edge can be moved, scaled, or rotated. Press F10 for Edge Selection mode.

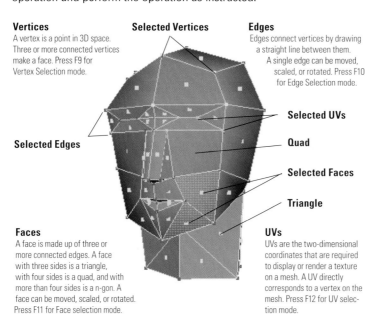

Selected UVs

Quad

Selected Edges

Selected Faces

Triangle

Faces
A face is made up of three or more connected edges. A face with three sides is a triangle, with four sides is a quad, and with more than four sides is a n-gon. A face can be moved, scaled, or rotated. Press F11 for Face selection mode.

UVs
UVs are the two-dimensional coordinates that are required to display or render a texture on a mesh. A UV directly corresponds to a vertex on the mesh. Press F12 for UV selection mode.

Non-planar Polygons

When working with quads and n-gons, you should be aware that any vertex that lies off the same plane as the other vertices creates a non-planar face. To avoid this when creating or appending polygons, you can set **Polygons > Tool Options > Keep New Faces Planar to On**. If this situation occurs as a result of a modeling operation, then either triangulate the non-planar faces or use the cleanup operation to tessellate faces with four or more sides. While non-planar faces can be rendered in Maya, they may cause problems if you are creating a polygon mesh for export to a game engine.

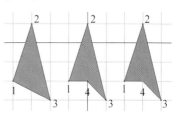

The first shape has only three sides and by nature is planar. The second and third shapes have four sides each, but appear to be planar.

The third shape has the fourth vertex on a different plane than the other vertices of its face. The third face is considered non-planar.

Use the right mouse button over the model to access a marking menu that will allow you to change selection modes interactively. This method allows you to select multiple component types.

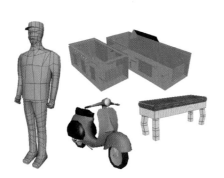

Polygon Objects

All of these objects were created from polygons. Some models (like the scooter and the gallery) were created with a specific polygon count target in mind. This means that these models do not exceed a certain number of polygon faces. While these restrictions apply to game content, models created for software-rendered output often do not fall under these restrictions.

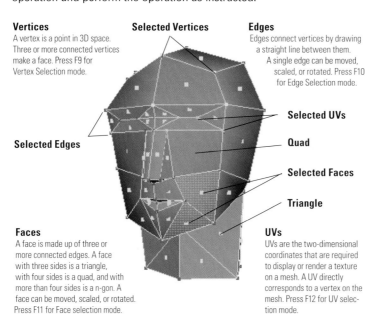

Polygon Primitives

Maya includes a number of polygon primitives that can give you a starting point for your model. These primitives, with the exception of the plane, are closed shapes and all primitives are created with a default set of UV information. These primitives have construction history and their subdivisions can be modified before or after creation.

Sphere   Cube   Cylinder   Cone   Plane   Torus

Modeling a Head

Using some of the more common polygon modeling tools, the steps for creating a polygonal head are illustrated below.

A default cube was created and then smoothed by selecting **Polygons > Smooth**. The two rear bottom faces were then extruded to create the neck and the front lower edges were moved down to create the chin.

The lower faces of the front were split for the nose and the middle edges were moved up to create the eyebrow area. The nose and eyes were created by splitting faces in the appropriate areas and then moving vertices to get the desired shape.

The mouth was created by splitting the faces in the mouth area and then moving vertices.

The eyes and neck were further refined and then the edges of the model were smoothed in the proper areas.

Extruding Faces

You can further refine your shape by extruding the face of a polygon. This extrusion operation inserts faces at the edges of the face to be extruded and allows the selected face or faces to be moved, scaled, or rotated from their original position. If you are extruding multiple faces and want them to maintain a cohesive shape, set **Polygons > Tool Options > Keep Faces Together to On**. This only inserts faces at the edges on the border of the selected faces. Otherwise, faces will be inserted at every edge. This tool can be found under **Edit Polygons > Extrude Face**.

Splitting Polygons

The Split Polygon Tool allows you to divide a polygonal face. You can also use the tool to insert vertices on an edge. To assist you, the tool has options that allow you to set how many Snapping Magnets you want and the Snapping Tolerance for the magnets. By setting Snapping Magnets to 3, the edge being split will have three equally spaced division points. Increasing the Snapping Tolerance increases the influence of the magnets. With a Snapping Tolerance of 0, the vertex can be added anywhere on the edge. A tolerance of 100 will force the vertex to snap directly to the division points.

Joining Objects

Sometimes you will create the individual parts of a model and then want to join them together. For objects to be joined, they must match certain criteria. The objects must be combined to create a single object and must have their Normals pointing in the same direction. Combining objects will create a single object with construction history relating back to the original objects. The separate pieces of the new object are called shells. Shells are pieces of an object that are not connected to the rest of the object by shared edges. Objects that are combined with opposing Normals will give an unexpected result when their edges are merged. This is because their edges run in different directions. This is true for appending polygons between shells as well.

Face four is selected. This is the face that will be extruded.

After the extrude is complete, new faces were added at the edges of the extruded face.

A common use of the Split Polygon Tool is to divide a face in half. This is done with a tolerance of 100.

However, the face can be split any way you want as long as the last vertex ends up on an edge.

The torso and arms are selected and ready to be combined. **Use Polygons > Combine** to do this.

The three objects have been combined into one object. However, there are three separate shells.

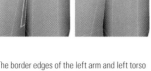

The border edges of the left arm and left torso opening are selected and the **Edit Polygons > Merge Multiple Edges** operation is applied. The arm and torso now share common edges and the holes in the left side of the torso and left arm are closed.

The same steps as before are applied. But, the result is different because the edge direction of the two shells are opposite each other. Maya was able to merge the front edge of the right arm and the rear edge of the torso, but could not continue and stopped merging edges.

Here you can see the problem. The left arm and torso have their Normals pointing out, while the right arm's Normals are pointing in. You could solve this by selecting a face on the right arm, select **Edit Polygons > Normals > Reverse > Options**. Set the Mode to Reverse and Propagate, and press Reverse Normals. The right arm Normals now follow the rest of the object and the edges can be merged properly.

Poly Smooth Proxy Modeling

Poly Smooth Proxy is a powerful tool enhancing high resolution polygonal modeling, based on low-resolution envelopes called a proxy. Basically, a smooth proxy is a duplicate of a given mesh, for which a smooth was applied and connected to the lower resolution mesh. The original polygon is the proxy mesh and the new, smooth polygon is the smooth mesh.

Any polygonal tool works on the Smooth Proxy mesh, thus subdividing, reshaping, and animating a rough model (with fewer components to worry about), allowing you to see what the smoothed mesh will look like. Once done modeling, you can then keep any or both of the low or high geometry for animation or rendering purposes.

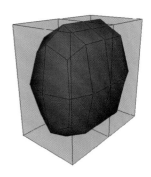

Low Resolution
At any stage while modeling with polygons, you can select **Polygons > Smooth Proxy** to create a connected and smoothed representation of your mesh.

If you are working with other types of geometry, simply convert your models to polygons using the **Modify > Convert** menu.

Smooth Proxy
Several options can be set in the Smooth Proxy option box, but most of them can be changed in the Channel Box when the construction history is still available.

Perhaps the most valuable attributes are the Exponential Level and Linear Level, which controls the smoothness of the high resolution model.

Refined Proxy
Once you have added minimal resolution to the desired location, you can be sure to get the lowest geometry for the best smoothed result.

You can keep the low resolution model and apply deformers or textures to it. The results will be automatically transferred once you apply a polygon smooth on the model.

Smoothed Object
You can boost up the subdivision level before renders, keeping any other steps light and easy to manage since you kept the minimal amount of vertex and faces while manipulating the geometry.

Mirror
The Mirror option creates a symmetrical smooth proxy about the +X, -X, +Y, -Y, +Z, or -Z axis (mirror direction). When Mirror is on, adjustments that you make to one-half of the smooth proxy are automatically mirrored onto the other half.

Share Transform Node
You can specify if you would like to share the transform node between the proxy and smooth mesh. This allows you to control whether the smooth mesh is transformed when you transform the proxy mesh.

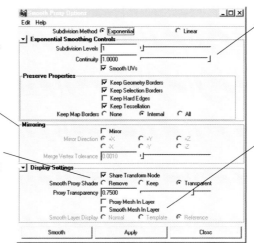

Smooth Proxy Shader
Smooth Proxy Shader controls the appearance of the proxy mesh's material. Transparency assigns a new Lambert material with partial transparency to the proxy mesh. Remove eliminates the material connection from the proxy mesh. Keep maintains the original connection between the proxy mesh and its material.

Layers
When Proxy Mesh In Layer is turned on, a new layer is created so you can control the visibility of the proxy mesh. The same applies when the Smooth Mesh In Layer is turned on, but for the smooth mesh.

Mirroring

If the Mirror option is turned on when creating a Smooth Proxy, Maya automatically duplicates your geometry on the desired axis and merges the overlapping vertex. Modifying one-half of the smooth proxy automatically updates the mesh on the opposite half of the smooth proxy. This whole process is making symmetrical modeling much more easier.

Symmetry

Sometimes when creating geometry, an artist will model only one half and then create a symmetric model to view the completed model. Mirror is a quick way to see how the model is taking shape as you go. All the polygonal tools (in this case Extrude), are compatible with this technique.

History

You would usually use mirror for modeling an object, not animating it. Otherwise, the object's animation would be symmetrical. Once you are done modeling, delete the history to get rid of the mirroring.

Subdivision Method

The Exponential and Linear smoothing algorithms both smooth equally, but they offer different controls for the resulting topology.

For example, Exponential has an option to maintain soft and hard edges, while Linear has options to better control the number of resulting faces.

You can switch between the two methods by changing the Method attribute on the polySmoothProxy node. Most of these options can be found on the **Polygon > Smooth Tool**.

```
OUTPUTS
  polySmoothProxy1
              Method  Exponential
    Exponential Level  1
         Continuity  1
        Smooth UVs  on
       Keep Border  on
     Keep Hard Edge  off
   Keep Map Borders  Internal
       Linear Level  1
    Divisions Per Edge  1
       Push Strength  0.1
         Roundness  1
```

Linear Smoothing Controls

The following options are available when you choose Linear under Subdivision Method:

Linear Level

This controls the number of times Maya performs smoothing. The higher the value, the smoother the object and the more faces are generated.

Exponential Smoothing Controls

The following options are available when you choose Exponential as the Subdivision Method.

Divisions Per Edge

Using this option, you can more easily achieve a balance between smoothness and a low polygon count.

The face count increases as a result of dividing each face. Maya divides each face by splitting the existing edges. The value you set is the number of splits Maya makes. A value of 1 means Maya splits each edge once, a value of 2 means Maya splits each edge twice, and so on.

Exponential Level

Type a number in the Exponential Level attribute to increase or decrease the number of times Maya performs the smoothing operation. This also increases or decreases the object's smoothness. The divisions range from 1 to 4. The higher the value, the smoother the object.

Continuity

The value you enter here determines the degree of smoothness that must be applied on the subdivided faces.

Push Strength

Controls the overall volume of the resulting smooth surface. Use higher values to scale outward or lower values to scale back.

Smooth UV

Specify the Smooth UV value if you want to smooth the UV mapping along with the geometry. This option gives you more control over smoothed and textured models.

Roundness

Creates a bulge in the surface by scaling vertices around the center of the original faces. Use higher values to scale these vertices outward or lower values to scale them back. For Roundness to have an effect, Push Strength must be greater than zero.

Keep Borders

When turned on, this option preserves the properties of the border edges of the geometry. That means if you have a hole in your geometry, the smoothing algorithm will keep the hole as is. If this option is turned off, the border will be smoothed.

Keep Hard Edges

If you have changed the hardness or softness of edges (for example Edit Polygons > Normals > Soften/Harden), turn this option on to transfer those settings onto the higher resolution mesh.

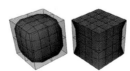

Keep Map Border

This attribute is used by both Exponential and Linear subdivision methods. If a map edge is shared by only one map polygon, then it is a map border edge. A connected series of such edges is a map border. Turn this option on to preserve the UV border.

Subdivision Surfaces

Subdivision Surfaces in Maya are surfaces created using a combination of polygon and NURBS modeling techniques. There are several advantages to using Subdivision Surfaces: the surfaces are continuous, meaning there's no need for stitching; Subdivision Surfaces can have arbitrary topology (they are not limited to four-sided patches as NURBS are); and they are extremely easy and quick to use.

Anatomy of a Subdivision Surface

Subdivision Surfaces allow you to add detail only where needed. This is accomplished by having several hierarchical levels of detail on the surface. There is a base mesh, or "level 0" mesh, that offers general control, and each finer level (up to 12) allows more control points for precise modeling. The different levels are referred to as "finer" and "coarser" levels.

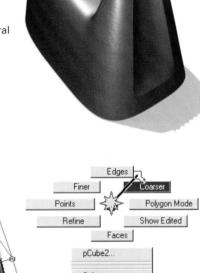

Subdiv Mesh Edge
A Mesh Edge can be moved, moved in Normal, scaled, and rotated.

Partial Crease
You can select one or more edges at a time to modify. This edge has been set with a Partial Crease to achieve a rounded edge.

Subdiv Mesh Point
The "0" represents the hierarchy mode at "level 0" or "Base Mesh."

Full Crease
You can select one or more edges at a time to modify. These edges have been set with a Full Crease to achieve a sharp edge. You are also able to Uncrease if creased.

Subdiv Marking Menu
Clicking the right mouse button over a Subdivision Surface will bring up a menu that gives quick access to common tasks.

Creating Subdivision Surfaces from Polygons

The most efficient method of creating a Subdivision Surface is with a simple polygonal mesh.

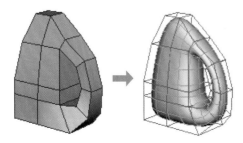

Creating Subdivision Surfaces from NURBS

To convert a NURBS surface to a Subdivision Surface, you can simply convert it using the Create Subdiv command. This will create a Subdivision Surface for every NURBS patch selected. Therefore, to have a continuous Subdivision mesh, you must attach the surfaces. A similar method is to convert the NURBS surfaces to a polygon first. The surfaces are then combined and the edges merged before converting to a Subdivision Surface.

Proxy and Hierarchy mode

There are two modes used to edit a Subdivision Surface, Polygon Proxy mode and Hierarchy mode. Both can be easily accessed from the marking menu.

Polygon Proxy Mode

Polygon Proxy Mode allows the user access to polygon tools that can operate on the Subdivision base mesh. In this mode, a polygon that matches the base mesh (level 0) of the Subdivision Surface is displayed in wireframe. Because everything is connected through construction history, in Polygon Proxy Mode, you can use polygon tools and functions to indirectly modify the base mesh of the Subdivision surface.

Hierarchy Mode

You can switch to this mode and back to Polygon Proxy mode at any stage of modeling. Hierarchy mode allows you to use a simple polygon as a starting point and add detail only where needed.

In Hierarchy mode, you can view the points, edges, or faces at any level of the hierarchy, manipulate them (rotate, scale or translate), keyframe them, etc. Also, you can increase the level of detail in areas of the hierarchy and you can crease edges and vertices. To create points at finer levels, select existing points and then use the Refine option.

Mirroring Subdivision Surfaces

To mirror a Subdivision Surface, use the Mirror command found in the menu **Subdiv Surfaces > Mirror**. This is a different command than duplicating with a negative scale.

Attaching Subdivision Surfaces

The Attach function allows you to attach two selected Subdivision Surfaces and create a new single Subdivision Surface. For the attach to work, the selected surfaces must have the same number of polygonal edges at the base mesh level. The Threshold settings are defined in the polygon Merge Multiple Edges Tool.

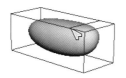

In Polygon Proxy Mode, many of the polygon tools are available to modify Subdivision Surfaces. The above image demonstrates how the Split Polygon Tool can be used to create an extra face that is then extruded, and how a face can be deleted on the bottle to create an opening.

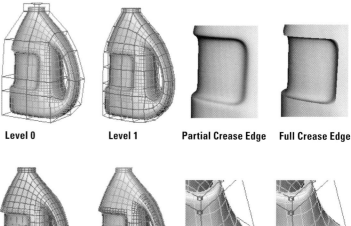

Level 0 **Level 1** **Partial Crease Edge** **Full Crease Edge**

Level 2 **Level 3** **Partial Crease Vertex** **Full Crease Vertex**

Depending on the complexity of the base mesh, there may already be a few hierarchy levels from when the Subdivision Surface was created. This example of the bottle had only level 0 and level 1 after the conversion to a Subdivision Surface from a polygonal surface. However, at level 0, after the top face was removed for an opening and Partial Creases were applied at level 1, level 2 and 3 were created. You can also create a denser mesh at any given component using the Refine command. The remaining images illustrate the differences between Full Creases and Partial Creases on edges and vertices.

Texturing Subdivision Surfaces

As with a polygonal surface, to apply a texture to a Subdivision Surface, the surface must have UVs. Subdivision Surfaces inherit UVs from the polygonal or NURBS surfaces you created them from. To create UVs, switch to Polygon Proxy Mode and use the polygon mapping tools.

Shaders need to be applied in the Hierarchy mode to the whole surface or by selecting faces at level 0 or 1. If more detail is needed at the base level, you can add faces manually or increase the detail on the base mesh using **Subdivision Surfaces > Collapse Hierarchy**.

Tessellating Subdivision Surfaces

Tessellating a Subdivision surface produces a polygon with a surface that corresponds with the Subdivision Surface.

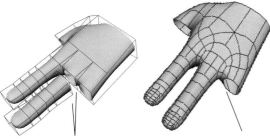

Same number of edges **Single Subdivision**
at base level **surface after Attach**

Construction History

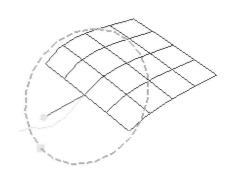

When you create a surface or use deformers or certain modeling tools, Maya keeps a construction history on the object. A construction history is a record of the options, geometry, modeling, and deformation actions that you used to create the object. You can use the construction history to modify an object by making simple changes to the original elements of the history.

This is an incredible resource for animation and modeling. As with almost everything else in Maya, the construction history can also be animated.

Accessing Construction History

There are several ways to access the Input nodes of an object. The simplest way is to use the Show Manipulator Tool. The object and the Input node need to be selected to use the tool. The Channel Box offers an easy way to select any Input nodes. This example demonstrates how the History node for a revolve operation can be modified.

History List Inputs/Outputs
This selects the History Input or Output of the selected object.

Construction History On/Off
By default, this button is on. If it is turned off, there will be no Input node for any new objects/commands.

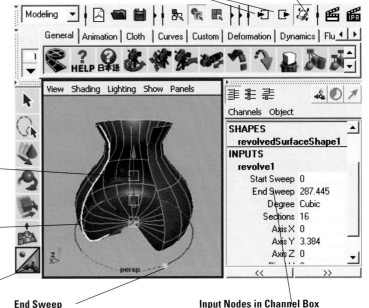

Axis and Pivot Manipulators
You can modify the axis angle that the curve was rotated around and the location of the center pivot point.

Profile Curve
Any manipulation to the profile curve will directly affect the shape of the revolved surface.

Show Manipulator Tool
This tool lets you access the Input node of an object with history.

End Sweep
This lets you interactively adjust the completeness of the revolve in degrees.

Input Nodes in Channel Box
When an object is selected, any Input nodes would be listed here. You would then need to highlight it to access the attributes.

Selecting the History Node

These are alternatives to the Channel Box and the Hypergraph window when you want to access the History nodes. In all cases, the object must be active or the cursor must be over the object when accessing the marking menu. Once selected, the node will appear in the Channel Box or Attribute Editor.

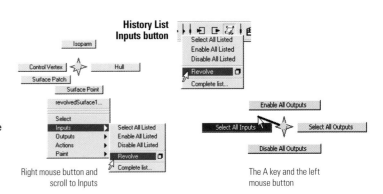

Right mouse button and scroll to Inputs

The A key and the left mouse button

Working with Construction History

As you create and modify a surface using the tools, Maya keeps a record of it. There can be several Input nodes for any given object that can be selected individually or all at once using the methods on the previous page. Some tools such as Loft, Revolve, and Extrude have a Partial Curve option that creates sub-curves that allow you to select a minimum and maximum position value for the curve(s) used to create the surface.

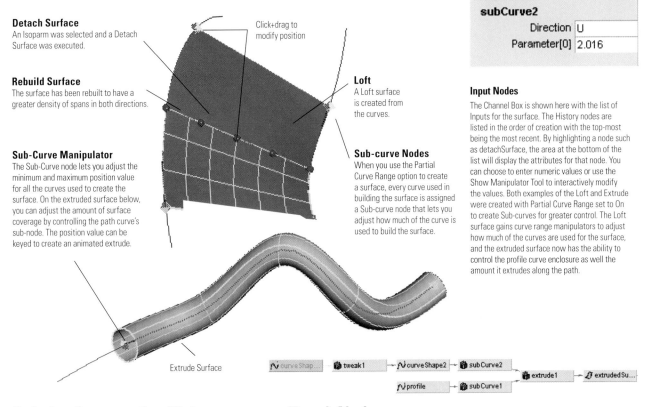

Detach Surface
An Isoparm was selected and a Detach Surface was executed.

Click+drag to modify position

Rebuild Surface
The surface has been rebuilt to have a greater density of spans in both directions.

Loft
A Loft surface is created from the curves.

Sub-Curve Manipulator
The Sub-Curve node lets you adjust the minimum and maximum position value for all the curves used to create the surface. On the extruded surface below, you can adjust the amount of surface coverage by controlling the path curve's sub-node. The position value can be keyed to create an animated extrude.

Sub-curve Nodes
When you use the Partial Curve Range option to create a surface, every curve used in building the surface is assigned a Sub-curve node that lets you adjust how much of the curve is used to build the surface.

Extrude Surface

SHAPES
loftedSurfaceShape1
INPUTS
detachSurface1
rebuildSurface1
loft1
subCurve1
subCurve2

Direction	U
Parameter[0]	2.016

Input Nodes
The Channel Box is shown here with the list of Inputs for the surface. The History nodes are listed in the order of creation with the top-most being the most recent. By highlighting a node such as detachSurface, the area at the bottom of the list will display the attributes for that node. You can choose to enter numeric values or use the Show Manipulator Tool to interactively modify the values. Both examples of the Loft and Extrude were created with Partial Curve Range set to On to create Sub-curves for greater control. The Loft surface gains curve range manipulators to adjust how much of the curves are used for the surface, and the extruded surface now has the ability to control the profile curve enclosure as well the amount it extrudes along the path.

Deleting Construction History

You can see how the construction history list can grow very long. Depending on the complexity of the scene, or if you are going to bind a surface to a skeleton, it is good practice to delete the construction history of the object for optimization. You can choose to delete on an object basis or a scene-level basis using the menu item **Edit > Delete by Type > History**, or **Edit > Delete all by Type > History**. Although it is possible to delete the last History node in the chain, this may lead to unpredictable results.

Throughout the modeling process of a typical workflow, History is deleted when you have what you need. A good example of this process is using a lattice deformer to sculpt a surface. If you were to simply delete the lattice after sculpting, the lattice would disappear and the surface would snap back to its original shape. Instead, you would need to select the surface and delete the history. The surface would then keep the new shape without the lattice.

Tweak Node

A Tweak node essentially contains any translation information that would be normally applied to a CV. For example, if a deformation is applied to an object and then the CVs of the object are modified, the translation information relative to the original position of the CVs are stored on this node.

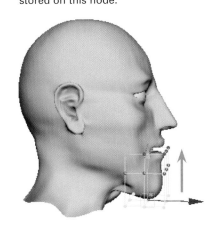

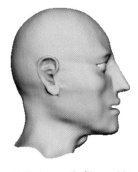

A lattice is created for CVs around the chin that were deformed to create a smaller chin. The surface was selected and the construction history was deleted. Only the new surface remains with the modifications.

Modeling for Animation

To create an animation in today's software, 3D artists must understand the pipeline from concept to rendering at a much deeper level then ever before. Animators need to foresee all the different stages from modeling to animation to rendering before ever starting a scene. Planning is the key to a successful production.

After carefully creating a storyboard, you begin the modeling process, keeping in mind how the model will ultimately be animated and textured. You must decide up front whether the model will be built from NURBS, polygons or a Subdivision Surface. The answer lies in the questions: Will the object be deformed? Will it be seen from afar or up close? Also, if you plan to use construction history to animate, you must plan to retain the history and not delete it after completing the model.

Animating logos is a good example to highlight these issues; how to decide the best route for modeling and creating hierarchies for the animation stage and, finally, how to get good results when rendering.

Camera Animation

Animating the camera in your scene is one of the easiest ways to create an animation. Since there are no deformations on the object, the only issue you need to deal with is the level of detail of the model. Generally, the closer you get to a model, the higher the tessellation.

Object Animation

Text or logo creation and animation can, at times, be a challenge to achieve. Transforming logos can appear easy enough, but it still requires planning. If you import vector artwork from a software package like Adobe® Illustrator® into Maya, it will be made of NURBS curves. Maya also has its own Text Tool that uses fonts installed on your system. If the animation will present the logo in front view only and the artwork only has move, scale, and rotate transformations, you may only need to create planar surfaces from the curves and then animate. Or, you may want the logo to have some depth or components of the logo may need to be animated independently from each other. If the latter is the case, some hierarchical setup is needed. For example, each letter of a word can have its own Transform node. Planar surfaces for the faces of the type would need to be created on a letter-by-letter basis. Otherwise, each letter face would be grouped as a single planar surface.

To give 3D logos a more weighty appearance and a polished feel, a beveled edge can be applied. The Maya Bevel tools offer several options for controlling the Depth, Extrude Depth, Corner Type, and Bevel Shape Type. The direction of the curves on imported vector artwork has an impact on how the Bevel tool creates the surface.

The bevel on the left has surfaces going in the wrong direction because of the direction of the curves. The object on the right was created after the curve direction was reversed.

The surfaces of each letter were created individually, allowing each letter to be rotated around its own axis.

This could not be achieved if all the surfaces were created at once because the geometry would be one object for the entire word.

Hardware Shaded   **Final Software Rendering**

Deforming Object Animation

Over the years, logos have become more elaborate and so have their animations. They have a personality all their own and deforming them as you would characters is standard practice. Creating a model that can withstand extreme deformations while maintaining its pristine edges without ripping at the seams is the biggest challenge of this type of work. It is for this reason that trimmed NURBS surfaces are not ideal for deformations. An ideal surface is a continuous one, such as a polygon mesh or a subdivision surface.

Polygonal logos can be achieved through different means. Rather than building objects with the polygon tools from scratch, it is always easier to use existing curves. Imported vector-based artwork is still a better starting point. NURBS surface tools can be used to create extruded and beveled logos and can then be converted to polygons using the NURBS to Polygons operation.

Display Tessellation vs. Render Tessellation

There are two types of tessellation: one for displaying in shaded mode and the other for displaying it as rendered. On the left, the first image shows how the logo appears in the Maya workspace in shaded mode. As you can see, there are many gaps in the trimmed surface. However, it will not render like this in the final software rendering. The Display Resolution can be adjusted from Display > NURBS Smoothness > Custom. The Render tessellation is adjusted from the Attribute Editor of the Surface Shape node.

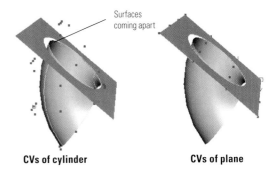

CVs of cylinder   **CVs of plane**

Deforming Trim Surfaces

These two surfaces have have been trimmed and then deformed by a Non-linear Bend deformer. It is clear that the two surfaces do not retain their position to each other and gaps appear. This is because the CVs in the cylinder are in very different positions than those in the plane, making it very difficult for surfaces to stay in position.

Bevel Plus

The best and easiest way to create logos is to use the **Surface > Bevel Plus tool**. You can achieve excellent geometry results using curves from Maya or vector-based artwork. The tool will create History nodes that lets you adjust the resulting geometry at any time.

The output surfaces can either be nurbs or polygons for which you can set the geometry sampling. Each pieces of the resulting logo will be separate, giving you more control for animation and deformation. If the geometry is a polygon mesh, you can combine the different pieces, so you will only have to deal with one mesh.

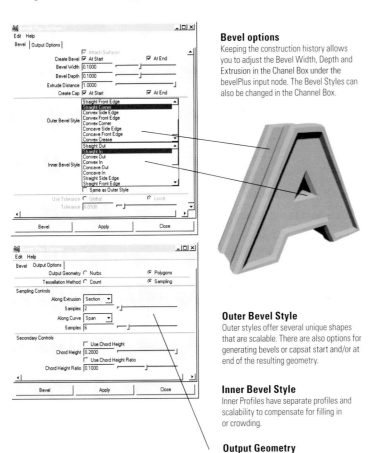

Bevel options

Keeping the construction history allows you to adjust the Bevel Width, Depth and Extrusion in the Chanel Box under the bevelPlus input node. The Bevel Styles can also be changed in the Channel Box.

Outer Bevel Style

Outer styles offer several unique shapes that are scalable. There are also options for generating bevels or capsat start and/or at end of the resulting geometry.

Inner Bevel Style

Inner Profiles have separate profiles and scalability to compensate for filling in or crowding.

Output Geometry

On the Output Options tab, you can specify how you want the resulting geometry to be created.

The above example was created using the Text Tool to create the curves, then the Bevel Plus Tool was used to create the deformable object. The result geometry was attached to a motion path and finally, was turned into a Flow Path Object to deform along the path.

Deformations

In the real world, some objects are hard and some are soft. The surfaces on the soft objects can be bent and folded into different shapes. This kind of surface deformation can be set up and animated in Maya.

Pushing and pulling the control points on a surface deforms its shape. Yet, to sculpt every surface point-by-point can be time-consuming. Maya offers deformation tools that give 3D artists a higher level of control. A deformer applied to one or more objects can be used to achieve bending and twisting by editing a few control points or attributes.

Deformers can also be used as modeling tools because they are great for reshaping a surface. In the end, by deleting the construction history on the surfaces, the deformer disappears, leaving the new twisted surface.

The deformer attributes or control points can be animated to reshape an object over time. Deformers can also be bound to skeletons to help animate characters. Simulated deformations can then be used to create realistic draping and cloth effects.

Deforming Objects

Many objects in our 3D world are able to change their shape – a soft chair gives as someone sits in it, a rubber ball squashes and stretches as it hits the ground, human skin bends as the elbow rotates. To achieve these kinds of effects in Maya, surfaces have to be able to have their shape animated. This means animating the positions of control points instead of simply translating and rotating the whole object.

A face with no deformations.

Types of Deformation

In Maya, there are a number of ways to change or deform the shape of an object. These deformers can be used to help you model surfaces or animate organic forms. While there are a set of tools in Maya called deformers, there are other tools that change the shape of objects. By becoming familiar with all of these techniques, you can best decide which one can be used in your work.

The same face after using surface deformation to reshape the nose, add a smile, round out the cheeks, widen the chin, and make folds for eyelids.

Deformers

Maya has a category of tools called deformers that either perform a specific type of surface deformation such as twist or bend, or make the process of deforming a surface easier in some way. For example, a lattice is a cage-like manipulator made of a small number of lattice points. Each lattice point controls several control points in a specified region of the surface. Moving one lattice point can affect many control points on the surface that would be difficult to select and move individually.

CV and Vertex Edits

The most rudimentary method of deforming a curve or geometry is to select component level control points and translate, rotate, or scale them. This is useful when you need to move a surface point to a specific location.

Simulated Deformations

Maya has features for simulating properties of clothing and soft dynamic moving materials like curtains, flames, and flags. A soft body is a geometry object whose control points are controlled by particles and dynamic fields such as turbulence and gravity.

Skeleton Chains

A skeleton chain consists of joint nodes that are connected visually by bone icons. Skeleton chains are a continuous hierarchy of joint nodes that are parented to each other. You can group or bind geometry (skin) to these joint hierarchies. You can then animate the joints (usually by rotating them) and the geometry will be animated. Binding geometry to a skeleton causes the geometry to be deformed as the skeleton is animated. For example, you could rotate a neck joint and the geometry around the neck joint would rotate as well.

Deforming Objects

deformations

Deformer Sets

When a deformer is created, certain control points of the surface will be affected by it. The control points that are affected by a given deformer are said to be part of that deformer's membership. Maya keeps track of which control points are members of which deformers by using sets. It is possible to add or remove control points from a deformer's set membership by selecting **Deform > Edit Membership Tool**.

A non-deformed sphere with its CVs displayed.

The same sphere with a lattice deformer applied. The top rows of lattice points have been moved up to deform the sphere.

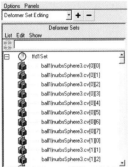

Alternatively, an explicit list of the CVs belonging to this set membership can be viewed and edited by selecting Window > Relationship Editors > Deformer Sets...

To select the lattice, click on Deform > Edit Membership Tool. This highlights the CVs on the sphere that are affected by the lattice. The yellow CVs are part of the lattice's membership.

A row of CVs is removed from the lattice's membership with the Edit Membership Tool. Now the deformer has no effect on those CVs.

Deformer Order

One of the many powerful and flexible features of deformers is the ability to layer multiple deformers together. For example, you could apply Bend, Lattice, BlendShape, Skeleton, and Cluster deformers on the same object and all will interact to produce the final deformation. However, the order in which Maya evaluates these deformers does affect the final shape. Fortunately, you have control over the order in which the deformers are evaluated.

Click+drag to reorder

Here, a Squash deformer is added first, then a Bend deformer second. Notice that the deformation looks a little strange.

The order of deformation is reversed here so that the Bend deformer is evaluated before the Squash deformer. The result is a more even deformation of the surface.

To access the List of History Operations window, place the cursor over the object and use the right mouse button and select Inputs > Complete list... This window displays a list of Input nodes connected to the text object. Click+drag the middle mouse button on the list of items to the left to change the order Maya evaluates these Input nodes.

Artisan Sculpt Surfaces Tool

Maya Artisan™ provides you with a set of brushes to sculpt detailed organic models, for both simple NURBS surfaces and polygon meshes. You can push, pull, smooth, or erase deformations on your model and even add a texture map to further displace it.

Select Edit Surfaces > Sculpt Surfaces to use the Artisan Sculpt Surfaces Tool. This is an easy way to paint deformation onto a surface interactively.

The model after the Sculpt Surfaces Tool has been applied. This second image uses a higher detailed surface, allowing subtle definition and wrinkles to be added.

Non-linear Deformers

Non-linear deformers control the deformation of the surface using simple deformation "handles". These handles have easy-to-use attributes that can be changed to affect the characteristics of the deformation for each different non-linear deformer. These deformers are great for modeling objects into otherwise hard to form shapes and can also be used to animate the shape of the object to give it character. These deformers can be applied to polygons, NURBS, and Subdivision Surfaces.

There are six non-linear deformers in Maya: **Bend, Flare, Sine, Squash, Twist,** and **Wave**. These deformers can be applied to an object by selecting the geometry, then choosing a deformer from **Deform > Create Nonlinear**.

The term non-linear is used because the amount of deformation does not necessarily have to be the same across the entire surface. For example, if you have a model of a tree that you want to sway in the wind, you can make the trunk of the tree bend more at the top and less at the bottom. This ability to control deformation "dropoff" and regions of deformation is built directly into most of the non-linear deformers.

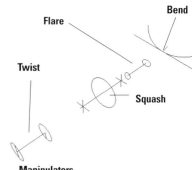

Manipulators
Every non-linear deformer has a manipulator handle that lets you deform interactively. To access a handle, select it, click on the Show Manipulator Tool, then click on the deformer in the Input section of the Channel Box.

Flare
The neck of the drill is a cylinder that is stretched and widened using a Flare deformer. This is an example where a deformer is used to model a shape.

Twist
The drill bit is modeled by applying a Twist deformer to a sphere.

Bend
The drill handle is shaped using a Bend deformer.

Squash
As the drill handle cranks, an animated Squash deformer can be used to bulge the body of the drill. This helps add character to the object.

Modeling with Non-linear Deformers

The drill bit begins as a scaled NURBS primitive sphere with high detail. The control vertices (CVs) on the top "pole" of the sphere are selected and moved to elongate the drill bit. The shape is then flattened by scaling. Detail is added at the tip by manually adjusting CVs.

A **Twist** deformer is added to the overall shape. The geometry becomes pink when selected, indicating that the surface is connected to the deformer. The effect of the twisting is localized to influence only a specific region of the geometry by adjusting the deformer handle. As a result, the twist coils become more compressed and the finished shape is produced.

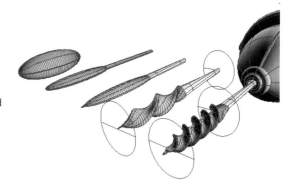

Non-linear Deformers

deformations

91

Positioning the Handle

A deformer handle can be selected and transformed around the scene just like any object. The position of the deformer handle, with respect to the object that it is deforming, affects how the surface is deformed. For example, you could animate the position of a Wave deformer through a plane so that the ripples originate from a different location on the surface.

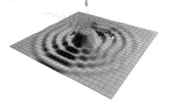
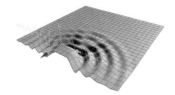

The Wave deformer handle is positioned in the center of an object. The waves radiate outward from the center or the handle.

The handle is translated to the edge of the geometry and the shape of the deformation follows along. The position, orientation, and scale of the handle can all be controlled. If desired, the geometry can also be moved.

Animating Non-linear Deformers

Non-linear deformers can be animated and combined with other features in Maya to add character to your animation. For example, a relationship can be established between the rotation of the drill crank and the amount of squash/stretch on the body of the drill. This could be done manually or by using the Maya Set Driven Key feature. As the handle rotates between 0 and -360 degrees in Z-axis, the Expand attribute on the Squash deformer changes between 0 and 5.

Step 1
At Frame 1, set Rotation of crank to 0, and Expand to 0.

Step 2
At Frame 19, set Rotation of crank to -130, and Expand to 4.

Step 3
At Frame 28, set Rotation of crank to -240, and Expand to 3.7.

Step 4
At Frame 1, set Rotation of crank to -300, and Expand to 1.2.

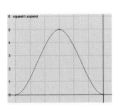

A Graph Editor curve showing the Expand attribute changing values between 0 and 5 as the rotation of the handle changes.

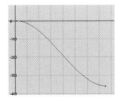

A Graph Editor curve showing handle rotation changing values between 0 and -360 every 45 frames.

INPUTS	
squash	
squash1	
Envelope	1
Factor	-0.1
Expand	5
Max Expand Pos	0.498
Start Smoothness	0
End Smoothness	0
Low Bound	-0.796
High Bound	0.648

This is the Channel Box for the Squash deformer. The Expand attribute is colored, indicating that in this case it is controlled by the rotation of the crank.

Deformer Nodes

The attributes for non-linear deformers can be edited in the Channel Box or with special manipulators. Selecting the deformer handle loads it into the Channel Box. The top section displays the deformer handle with its position and orientation; the Inputs section contains the actual deformer.

For example, clicking on the **twist1** node in the Inputs section displays the attributes specific to the twist deformer. With **twist1** highlighted in the Channel Box, pressing T will display a custom manipulator that is specific to the selected deformer. Controls on the resulting manipulator correspond to attributes listed in the Inputs section of the Channel Box.

> **Tip**
> Group the deformer handle and the object together so they can be scaled, rotated, or translated together.
>
>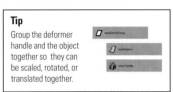

High and Low Bounds

It is possible to influence the extent to which a deformer affects a surface. The High and Low Bounds let you define the deformed region of the surface. There are manipulators to help with this task.

Click+drag on the center of the circle to change the **High Bound**. This defines the end of the surface region that the deformer will influence.

Click+drag on the center of the circle to change the **Low Bound**. This defines the beginning of the surface region that the deformer will influence.

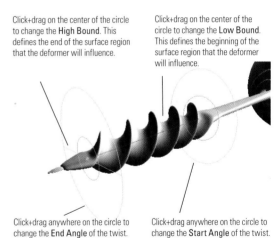

Click+drag anywhere on the circle to change the **End Angle** of the twist.

Click+drag anywhere on the circle to change the **Start Angle** of the twist.

Deforming Particles

Not only can you deform geometry, but you can also deform particles. You can also combine particle deformation with forces. Particles can be affected by any deformers except skinning and blendShapes.

Here, particles were assigned a Sine non-linear deformer.

Deformers

Lattices, clusters, wires, sculpts, and wraps are deformers that can manipulate a large number of points using simpler objects and, therefore, offer a mechanism to animate points in a more controlled and predictable manner. lattice, cluster, wire, sculpt and wrap deformers are used in both the modeling and animation process, with the focus being more heavily on animation. These deformers are located under the Deform menu and each offers a unique solution for deforming surfaces.

When any deformer is used as a modeling tool, you can use a Delete History operation to bake in the deformations. If you are not satisfied by the resulting deformation, you can simply delete the deformer and the surface will snap back to its original shape.

Lattice Deformer

A lattice deformer surrounds a deformable object with a cage-like box that you can manipulate to change the object's shape. Operations such as translation, rotation, or scaling can be applied to the lattice object or to the components to deform the underlying surface. The lattice can encompass the entire object or any number of control points. Even a lattice can be deformed since it is also a deformable object.

When a lattice is created, there are actually two lattices created: an influence lattice and a base lattice, the latter of which is invisible by default. When the influence lattice is edited, the resulting deformed surface is generated by calculating differences between the lattice points of the influence lattice and the base lattice.

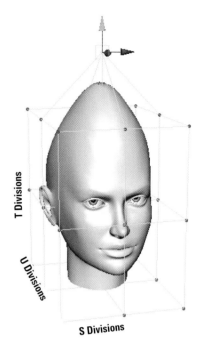

T Divisions
U Divisions
S Divisions

 ffd3Lattice ffd3Base

Lattice Deformer
You can specify the lattice's structure in terms of S, T, and U divisions. The greater the number of divisions, the greater the lattice point resolution.

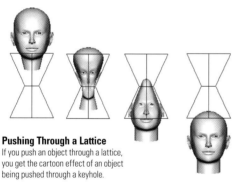

Pushing Through a Lattice
If you push an object through a lattice, you get the cartoon effect of an object being pushed through a keyhole.

Wire Deformer

Wire deformers are like the armatures used by sculptors to shape objects. With a wire deformer, you use one or more NURBS curves to change the shape of objects.

In character setup, wire deformers can be useful for setting up lip and eyebrow deformations. Wire deformers can also be useful for shaping objects during modeling. To create further wrinkling effects, you can also use the Wrinkle deformer.

Soft Modification Tool

The Soft Modification Tool lets you push and pull geometry as a sculptor would pull and push on a sculpture. The amount of deformation is greatest at the center of the push/pull, and gradually falls off further away from the center.

The Soft Modification Tool is located in the Toolbox. The corresponding action is **Deform > Soft Modification**.

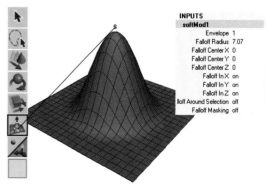

INPUTS
softMod1
Envelope 1
Falloff Radius 7.07
Falloff Center X 0
Falloff Center Y 0
Falloff Center Z 0
Falloff In X on
Falloff In Y on
Falloff In Z on
lloff Around Selection off
Falloff Masking off

History
Every time you use the Soft Modification Tool, a Deformer node is created, allowing you to go back to previous nodes and make changes. These nodes can also be animated just like any other deformers.

Flexors

Flexors are special deformers designed for use with rigid skinning. They provide various types of deformation effects that improve and enhance the effects provided by rigid skinning. There are three types of flexors that can be attached to a skeleton: lattice, sculpt, and joint flexors. Once they are applied, the joint is usually rotated to see the effect of the flexor and further adjustments can be made. Set Driven Key is an ideal tool to set up a relationship between the flexor and its affecting joint.

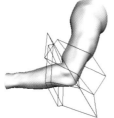

jointFlexor12	
Creasing	1.3
Rounding	1.4
Length In	-4.2
Length Out	1.4
Width Left	0
Width Right	0

Wrap Deformer

The function of a Wrap deformer is similar to that of a lattice deformer with some slight differences. The most obvious being that a Wrap deformer can be made from a NURBS or polygon mesh and be any shape. Just like the lattice, the wrap also creates a base shape and any difference in position, orientation, or shape between the base shape and the wrap influence object results in a deformation of the surface. This technique uses an influence object with fewer points than the object you are deforming. The primary visibility is turned off for the wrap deformer so it does not render.

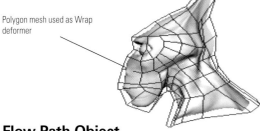

Polygon mesh used as Wrap deformer

Flow Path Object

The Flow Path Object function creates a lattice around the object that has been animated on a motion path. This technique allows the object to deform to the shape of the curve. There are two options: around the object or around the path curve. They both achieve the same look unless you decide to add deformations to the lattice.

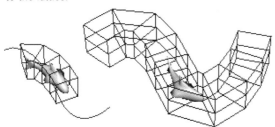

Clusters

Using clusters solves some fundamental problems for keyframing control points. These points can only have their position in space animated because they don't have a Transform node. Clusters are deformers that create a set out of any number of control points from one or more multiple surfaces and provide them with a Transform node. Once a cluster has been created, you have the ability to keyframe their scale, and rotation based on the clusters' Transform nodes pivot point. You can also group clusters into a skeleton hierarchy.

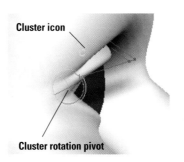

Cluster icon

Cluster rotation pivot

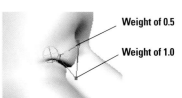

Weight of 0.5

Weight of 1.0

Six CVs around the top eyelid are clustered and weighted. The pivot point for the cluster is then placed at the center of the eye so the surface deforms around the eyeball. Without a cluster and pivot point, the eyelid would move straight through the eyeball.

After creating a cluster, you can assign a percentage to the CVs that controls the amount the points will move via the **Deform > Paint Cluster Weights Tool**. For example, if a control point is weighted 1.0, it will move 100 percent of the transformation. A value of 0.5 will only transform 50 percent. The top row of CVs for the eyelid are weighted 0.5 and the bottom 1.0. This allows for nicer tucking when the eye is open. Otherwise, the top of the eyelid would recess too far into the head with a value of 1.0.

The above left image shows how a cluster was created with the weighting at the default value of 1.0. The adjacent image shows the same cluster, but with the CVs weighted in a tapering effect. The selected CVs are shown in the Component Editor with their assigned weight.

Weighted Deformers	Joir ◄ ►
	cluster1
nurbsPlaneShap	
cv[8][14]	0.224
cv[9][14]	0.325
cv[10][14]	0.391
cv[11][14]	0.442
cv[12][14]	0.447
cv[13][14]	0.451
cv[14][14]	0.252
0.0000	0.00 1.00
.oad Component	Close

Sculpt Deformer

Sculpt deformers are useful for creating any kind of rounded deformation effect. For example, in setting a character for animation, you could use sculpt deformers to control a character's cheeks or to bulge a bicep. When you create a Sculpt deformer, select components to only affect that region of the model.

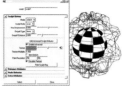

The Sculpt Tool can be very useful for simple bulging effects, but it also allows for much more complex deformations. For example, you can use a NURBS surface that itself deforms to create a more organic feel, or you could use a texture map where you can paint the deformer influence.

Simulated Deformations

Maya has tools that are used to simulate dynamic motion, such as the subtle motion of a flame or the detailed wrinkles of a character's shirt. These effects can be quite complex and are difficult to obtain using manual adjustment of control points, curves, and/or surfaces. Fortunately, Maya uses Dynamics solvers to calculate the various control point positions for you so the resulting object behaves dynamically without excessive manual adjustment and keyframing. To achieve the desired effect, Maya has controls that influence this dynamic behavior.

Soft Bodies in Maya

An object's control points can be dynamically controlled in Maya using soft bodies. When a soft body is created, a particle is placed at each control point on the object. These particles can then be moved or influenced using fields (gravity, turbulence, etc.), goals, and expressions. You might use soft bodies for creating a waving flag, candle flame, or jiggling surface. The flagpole attached to the rear of the scooter uses a soft body curve to wave back and forth.

Step 1
The curve on the right will become dynamically controlled and will take the shape of the destination or "goal" curve on the left. Both curves have the same number of CVs. The goal curve was bent into shape using a nonlinear Bend deformer. The amount of bend (curvature) on the goal curve was animated so the goal bends back and forth repeatedly.

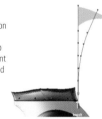

Step 2
The curve on the right has been made into a soft body using **Soft/Rigid Bodies > Create Soft Body** in the Dynamics menu set. The red dots shown in the image represent particles. When a soft body is created, one particle is created for each CV of the selected object. Collectively, all of these particles are stored in a particle object whose attributes can be edited.

Step 3
The curve on the left was explicitly defined as a goal for the curve on the right using **Particles > Goal**. Each particle becomes "attracted" to the CVs of the goal object. The characteristics of this attraction are controlled by adjusting the Goal Weight and Goal Smoothness attributes on the particle object.

Step 4
Since there are goal weights less than 1, the flag overshoots the goal and will begin to snap back. The lower the goal weight and goal smoothness, the more the soft body will overshoot its target.

Step 5
A skeleton chain is created containing one joint for each CV in the soft body curve. The soft body curve is then used as the spline curve for an Spline IK solver setup. The Spline IK solver uses the motion of a curve to control joint rotations. Thus, the motion of the soft body curve controls the rotations of the skeleton joints within the skeleton chain.

Skeleton chain

IK handle showing Spline IK solver controlling joint rotation

Step 6
Finally, a thin cylinder is used as the flagpole. Smooth skinning is used to bind the geometry to the joints. In turn, the geometry deforms to follow the joint rotations.

THE ART OF MAYA

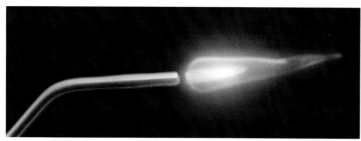

Acetylene torch flame animated using soft body goals

Soft Body Surfaces

Soft bodies are not limited to curves. NURBS and polygonal geometry, lattices, Wrap deformers, motion paths, wires, and other objects can take advantage of the dynamic behavior of soft bodies.

Step 1
Two goal surfaces are created by lofting a series of scaled circles. The inner red wireframe represents the goal shape of the inner flame and the outer blue wireframe is the goal shape of the outer flame.

Step 2
The goal surfaces are duplicated and made into soft bodies by selecting Soft/Rigid Bodies > Create Soft Body. The soft body geometry contains a particle for each CV for each surface. The goal surfaces are hidden.

Step 3
A volume turbulence field is created and centered around the particles to randomize their motion. The moving particles cause the CVs to move and, thus, produce a flowing deformation of the surface.

Step 4
The tip of the flame has a tendency to wrinkle in on itself causing creasing in the surface. This is common when applying randomized motion directly to surface control points.

Step 5
Select Soft/Rigid Bodies > Create Springs to create springs that are added between the particles at the tip of the flame to help maintain shape and volume in the geometry. Springs provide individual control over stiffness and springiness so this interaction can be optimally tuned. Alternatively, a Lattice deformer could be added to the surface geometry and subsequently made into a soft body instead of directly making the geometry a soft body. Since a lattice averages the deformation of control points across affected regions of the geometry, it is less likely to result in creasing in the final surface.

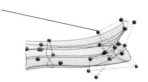

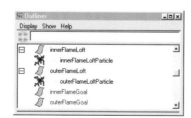

The goal attributes are adjusted to control the behavior of the particle attraction to the goals. The inner and outer particle objects each have their own goal controls.

The Outliner shows the two soft body surfaces and their corresponding particle objects. The goal objects are listed but dimmed since they are hidden.

Jiggle Deformers

Jiggle deformers let you cause points on a surface or curve to shake as they move, speed up, or slow down. You can apply jiggle to specific points or to an entire object. In the context of jiggle deformers, the term points means CVs, lattice points, or the vertices of polygonal or Subdivision Surfaces.

A useful technique is to apply jiggle to an influence object that underlies and alters the skin.

Be aware that you can create two or more jiggle deformers on different points of a single object. You can get the same effect more simply by applying a single jiggle deformer to the points and adjusting the jiggle weights.

Before rendering a scene using jiggle deformers, you must create a jiggle cache. A jiggle cache is a file located in your current project that contains the jiggle state at every frame in the scene. A jiggle cache also allows you to playback your scene without slowing it down for simulation calculations.

Step 1
Object components are selected so that only the selected points gets affected by the newly created jiggle deformer.

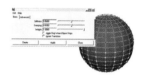

Step 2
Adjust the jiggle node's attributes for better results to suit the context in which it is going to be used.

Step 3
You can paint the weight of the jiggle's affected region using the Artisan Tool under Deform > Paint Jiggle Weights Tool.

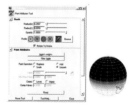

Step 4
View the jiggle reaction with animation. If needed, tweak the jiggle node's attributes for optimum results.

Step 5
Create a jiggle cache to speed up your playback or just before rendering. You absolutely need to create a cache before rendering or else, unpredicted results will be rendered.

Character Animation

One of the most challenging and rewarding forms of computer graphics is character animation. Here, 3D artists combine the transformation of a digital skeleton with the deformation of a skinned surface, to set up a character that walks, talks, and moves around in 3D space.

Of course, a character doesn't have to be a human or an animal. Any object that is animated with expression and tries to speak to the audience through its actions is considered a character. In fact, the same techniques used to animate a dog might be used to animate a dancing bottle, a tiger or a tree.

Maya allows you to combine all the controls found on different parts of a character into one or more character sets. This makes it easier to pose characters and work with them in the Maya non-linear Trax animation system. These techniques help 3D artists set up characters that can be animated throughout a production with consistent and easy-to-use controls.

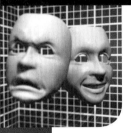

3D Characters

A 3D character is a digital actor. Whether your character is a tin can that bounces with personality, or a photorealistic human being, the animator will need to control it easily, and interactively. The specific requirements of the character's motion will dictate the complexity of the character's controls. Maya offers many tools for the creation of these digital performers.

A Typical Character

The character's mechanics must be convincing to an audience and the skin and clothing must also move and bend properly. Maya includes a number of tools that help you manage the parts that make up a typical character. This process of preparing character controls is called rigging and is used to let the animator focus on the process of animating. A fully rigged character can be quite complex as it brings together skeleton joints, surfaces, deformers, expressions, Set Driven Key, constraints, IK, BlendShapes, etc.

Skeleton Joints
Joints are used to create a framework for a character's hierarchy. The rotation of the skeleton joints defines the motion of the character; you can use inverse kinematics for even more control.

Character Controls
Using animation techniques such as Set Driven Key and expressions, you can set up attributes for controlling different parts of a character. For example, a hand joint could have attributes used to control the different finger joints.

Constraints
It is possible to constrain the kinematic controls of a skeleton to objects in your scene or even simple locators. You can then animate the constraint weights to make a character pick something up or grab hold of a fixed object.

Selection Handles
Selection handles give you quick access to parts of a character's hierarchy that are to be animated. This makes it easier to work with a character after it has been rigged up for animation.

Facial Animation
To animate facial features, you can use deformers such as BlendShape to create facial poses that can be used for talking and for showing emotion.

Kinematics
To control your skeleton joints, you can choose from forward or inverse kinematics. Forward kinematics allows you to set the joint rotations directly. IK allows you to position IK handles, which rotates the joints.

Bound Surfaces
Surfaces of a character's skin and clothing can be either parented or bound to the skeleton joints to make them move together. Binding places points from a surface into clusters that are then associated with particular joints.

Deformers
To help the surfaces bend realistically at joints, deformers such as flexors and influence objects can be used.

Character Resolution

A fully rigged 3D character includes many bound surfaces and deformers that can slow down the interactive manipulation and playback of the scene. Therefore, a low resolution character that has surfaces parented to the skeleton makes it possible to work interactively while animating, then switch to the fully rigged character for rendering. A low resolution version of a character also makes it possible to begin animating before the entire character is fully developed.

As you animate, you can use low resolution surfaces parented to your skeleton to achieve more interactivity while animating.

A Typical Character Animation Workflow

The development and animation of a 3D character involves a number of steps. Once you have a design, you must begin to build the character's model, lay down skeleton joints, and rig the skeleton so that it is capable of an appropriate range of motion. Character controls can also be set up to assist the animation process.

While it is possible to work in a linear fashion, starting with modeling and ending with rendering, most productions require some form of concurrent work to be done. An animator might need to begin laying down motion while the model is still being finished. At the same time, character deformations and texture maps may each be assigned to different parts of a team. For this reason, you may use your low resolution character to begin animating and blocking out scenes while the higher resolution character is refined and set up for deformations and rendering.

Motion Capture

As an alternative to setting keys, you can use motion capture to simulate real-life motion on a character. Generally, motion capture involves recording joint positions and rotations from an actor that are then applied to a skeleton. Motion capture works well with non-linear animation where motion capture clips can be blended together.

Motion capture offers realistic motion performances that can be imported as animation curves and applied to digital characters.

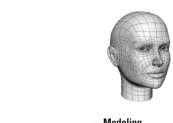

Binding Skeleton
The surfaces are bound to the skeleton and joint rotation tested. Deformers are use enhance the final look.

Modeling
Using the sketches, a detailed model is built with an awareness of how it will be bound to the skeleton later.

Character Design
In support of the story, the character is designed using sketches, storyboards, and in some cases, clay models. These visual aids give the 3D artist a clear understanding of the character and the character's range of motion and emotion.

Rendering
The final character is rendered in its final setting. You might also render the character on its own, then use a compositing package to integrate it with the background.

Integration
The animation from the low resolution character is applied to a fully rigged skeleton with bound surfaces and deformers.

Skeleton Rigging
Using sketches or the model as a guide, joints are drawn and kinematics and character controls are set up.

Animation
A fully rigged model that uses low resolution surfaces parented to the skeleton can be used for initial animation studies.

Character Sets

On a typical character, you will have many attributes on many different nodes that need to be keyed. A character set allows you to collect those attributes in one place and build up a character definition. When this character is highlighted in the pop-up Character menu, that character set is active whether or not it is selected. This feature makes it possible to easily set and edit keys for that character since it is always active. Character sets are also necessary to animate using non-linear animation through the Trax Editor since Trax clips can only be created for a character set.

Select **Character > Create** to start a character, then select **Character > Set Current Character > Character Sets** to add and subtract attributes from the set. The Character menu found near the Time Slider can also be used to highlight a character.

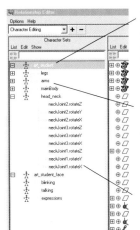

Character Sets
This set is the root of a character setup. You can have attributes assigned to the character or you can assign sub-characters to it. If you select this set and set keys, you also key the sub-characters.

Sub-Character Sets
These sets help break down a character into smaller parts in case you want to focus on one area. These sets can be set up to control specific body parts such as arms, legs, and facial features.

Keyable Attributes
For each character and sub-character set, you can choose which keyable attributes need to be brought together to effectively animate the different parts of the character.

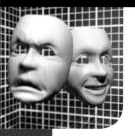

Skeletons

To give your characters a framework, skeleton joints can be drawn in 3D space to represent the bones of your character. These bones help you define and animate characters and are capable of a wide range of motion when combined with kinematic tools.

Skeleton Chains

Skeleton chains are hierarchies of nodes where the pivot point of each node is represented by a joint. The joint acts as a parent node for the hierarchy below. The joints are then connected using bones that help you visualize the hierarchical relationships in the 3D views. The resulting skeleton lets you build up a framework that can mimic the skeletal systems found in real humans and animals.

    The most important thing to remember about skeleton joints is that they are part of a hierarchy and contain many of the properties of a typical Transform node. Therefore, you can move their pivot points, re-orient their local axes, and assign selection handles for easier control.

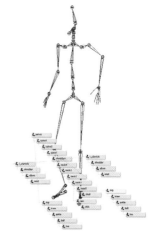

A skeleton is made up of joints. The joints are the Transform nodes of a typical character hierarchy.

Grouped Objects
When computers were first used to represent crude characters, each segment of a limb was built separately, then parented to the next limb in a hierarchical relationship. The pivot point of each limb object represented its joint. The rotation of the limbs defined the motion.

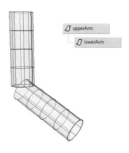

Joints
To help animators organize body parts, skeletons are used to define the limb hierarchy. Joints represent the rotational pivot points and bones represent how joints are connected. Rotating the joints defines the motion, but joints and bones don't render.

Parented Objects
For renderable limbs, you can parent surfaces into the skeleton hierarchy. The skeleton gives you control. This technique is fast and is good for non-deforming surfaces such as armor or the limbs of a robot. This method is also used for low resolution characters where speed is paramount.

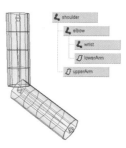

Deforming Objects
Realistic characters have joints that bend. To create a surface that deforms with the skeleton, you can skin or bind a single surface or a patch network to the skeleton. This results in CV sets that can be weighted for smooth bending of the joints.

Drawing Skeletons

The Joint Tool is used to draw skeletons. Each click adds a new joint to the scene. Bones are drawn between each joint to help you visualize the hierarchy.

    As you draw, you can click on the up arrow to go to a joint higher up in the hierarchy. As you continue drawing, the new joints branch off from this joint.

    When a joint branches off, it appears as if you can work with the two bones independently. When you select the bones connected to the branching joint, you select a single joint which controls all the connected bones.

Joints
The joints are drawn as small circles that represent the axes of the joint.

Pick-Walking
As you draw joints, you can press the up, down, left or right arrow keys on your keyboard to move around your hierarchy. The next joint you draw will branch off from the selected node.

Bones
Between each joint is a bone which is drawn like a cone. This cone always points down the skeleton chain to the next joint in the hierarchy.

Insert Key
As you draw joints, press the Insert key to edit the joint position. Press Insert again to continue drawing. You can also use the middle mouse button to reposition joints while drawing.

Editing Joints

In most cases, you will animate skeletons by rotating the joints directly or by using inverse kinematic techniques to rotate the joints for you. As you set up your skeleton, you may want to transform your joints and bones to shape the chain to match your character.

In most cases, transforming a joint also transforms all the lower, or children, joints. By editing the joint's pivot point, you can move each joint independently without affecting lower joints. Note that this edit alters the joint orientation which would then need to be corrected if the joint was going to be animated by an expression or Set Driven Key.

Rotate Joints
All the joints below the rotated joint are affected by the edit. This kind of joint edit is used the most for animating joints. This creates motion similar to real skeletons.

Scale Joints
Again, the joints below the scaled joint are affected. This edit lengthens the bone just below the joint. Scaling a joint can be used to add squash and stretch motion to a character.

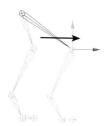

Translate Joints
All the joints below the translated joint are also moved. The bone above is lengthened or shortened.

Move Joint Pivot Point
If you press the Insert key while in a Transform tool, you can move a joint's pivot point. This moves the joint independently of the other nodes in the hierarchy.

Joint Orientation

The orientation of a joint is important for the animation of the skeleton. When you first draw a skeleton, by default, the joints are oriented to point at the next joint in the chain and align with the bone. You can also choose to align with the world space grid. As you edit joints, the orientation may be altered from your original settings.

To view joint orientations, select the joints and click on **Display > Component Display > Local Rotation Axes**. You can also go into Component Selection mode and click on the "**?**" button so selected joints display their local axes. In Component selection mode you can also rotate the local axes.

Connecting Joints

If you build parts of a skeleton separately, you can select **Skeleton > Connect** Joint to add the new limb to the overall skeleton. An example would be connecting arm or leg joints to a spine.

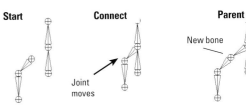

Start   **Connect**   **Parent**

New bone

Joint moves

Connect
With the Connect option, the first joint's chain moves to the second and the two joint nodes become one.

Parent
With the Parent option, the root of the first joint chain is added as a child to the second and a bone is drawn between them.

Mirroring Joints

Since many characters are symmetrical with two arms and two legs, you can build one side, then select **Skeleton > Mirror Joint** to mirror joints and their IK handles across an axis.

Before
First, you select the joint to be mirrored, then you set up the mirror plane as either XY, YZ, or XZ in the tool options.

After
The joint, its children joints, and kinematic controls are mirrored and connected back to the parent.

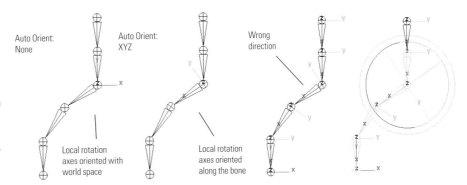

Auto Orient: None

Auto Orient: XYZ

Local rotation axes oriented with world space

Local rotation axes oriented along the bone

Wrong direction

Auto Orient
When you draw a skeleton, you can use the Auto Orient option to make sure that the joint is pointing to the next joint along the bone. This works well for forward kinematics because it makes joint rotation predictable. For situations where you may be constraining joints, you may want this option turned off. If your joint orientation is not aligned with the bone, you can either display the axes and rotate them or select the joints then select the Skeleton > Orient Joint. This will re-orient your joints, based on the settings specified in the option box.

Rotating the Local Axes
If your local axes are not aligned the way you want them, you can interactively rotate them. While in Component Mode, select the joint and display its local rotation axis, invoke the Rotate Tool, and adjust the manipulator.

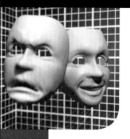

Kinematics

To make your characters move, you need to create body mechanics that are accurate to real life and have simple controls. In a typical human body, it is the rotation of joints that best describes the motion of limbs. In Maya, you can use joint rotation, but this doesn't always offer the best control as you animate. For example, you may want to move a hand while keeping a shoulder in place or move a shoulder while keeping a hand in place. This requires control which is difficult to achieve with joint rotations. In the human body, muscles offer this kind of control, while in Maya, Inverse Kinematics are used.

The two main methods of creating skeletal motion are forward kinematics (FK) and inverse kinematics (IK). These methods refer to how a skeleton chain can be animated using either joint rotations for forward kinematics or special handles for inverse kinematics. These techniques can be further controlled using character sets, Set Driven Key, and constraints. In some cases, you may even rig up a skeleton to switch between these two methods, depending on what kind of motion you need.

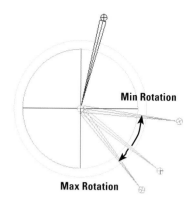

Min Rotation

Max Rotation

Joint Limits
When you view a Joint node in the Attribute Editor, you can go to the **Limit Information** section and select **Min** and **Max** values. This controls how far the joint will rotate. Most joints in the human body offer some type of limit.

Forward Kinematics

The use of joint rotations to pose a character is called forward kinematics. When a joint is rotated, all the joints lower in the hierarchy follow. This demonstrates a typical hierarchical relationship that reflects the nature of joint skeletons.

Rotating joints one at a time can involve a great deal of selection and animation. It is a good idea in a situation, such as the bending of a finger, to use a control attribute on a higher level node to control the rotation of all the joints using techniques such as **Set Driven Key**.

Joint Rotation
Rotating the joints is the main method for controlling forward kinematics. This involves rotating each joint one at a time to get the desired angle. This method offers the most control when setting up a pose.

Moving Start Joint
With forward kinematics, moving the root joint moves the whole hierarchy. This makes it impossible to place or plant the end joint to a fixed position. When using FK on a character, you will usually only move the root joint.

Moving End Joint
With forward kinematics, moving the end joint would only stretch the bone. If you want to position the end of the chain, you must use joint rotations. Inverse kinematics makes it easier to position the end joint.

Inverse Kinematics

With inverse kinematics, you can control the joint rotations for a number of joints using an IK handle. The positioning of this handle is used by the IK solver to calculate the rotational values on the joints.

There are IK solvers available that offer different levels of control. When using Single Chain, or Rotation Plane IK, moving either the IK handle or the start joint creates motion, while with the Spline IK solver, you control the joint rotations by editing the shape of a control curve.

IK Handle
An IK handle runs from a start joint to the end effector. The rotation of all the joints inbetween is affected by the movement of the IK handle. This is the fastest method for positioning the end joint.

Moving Start Joint
If you move the start joint and the IK handle has been either keyed, constrained, or has sticky turned on, the end of the chain will remain fixed. This is useful when you want to grab something or plant the feet while walking.

Moving IK Handle
If you move the IK handle, all the joints along the chain will be rotated. This makes it possible to position the end joint directly instead of as a result of joint rotations. This method is fast and precise.

Single Chain Solver

The Single Chain IK solver provides the simplest solution. By moving the IK handle the chain will update so that the joints lie along a fixed plane.

This solver is useful in situations where you want basic motion. If you were animating a leg, you could aim the knee by rotating the IK handle. This method does not offer as much control as the Rotate Plane method and does not offer a solution for joint flipping.

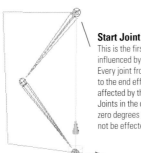

Start Joint
This is the first joint that is influenced by the IK handle. Every joint from this one to the end effector will be affected by the IK solver. Joints in the chain that have zero degrees of freedom will not be effected.

IK Handle/End Effector
The end effector is the end of the joint chain that is defined by the IK handle position. By moving the IK handle, you affect the rotation of all the joints in the chain.

Rotate Plane Solver

The rotate plane solver includes a plane that is defined using the IK handle vector as one axis and the pole vector as another. The pole vector axis can be defined by a handle that offers control over the orientation of the plane.

The ability to control the orientation of the plane is helpful for IK handles that will have a wide range of motion. Normally, as the handle hits a certain point, the solution crosses the Pole Vector axis and the joints flip. To avoid flipping, you can simply update the plane's orientation using the pole vector.

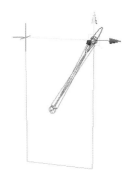

Flipping
When the IK handle axis crosses the pole vector, the IK solution is flipped. You can correct this by adjusting the pole vector to move the plane and avoid flipping.

Pole Vector Axis
This is the line between the start joint and the pole vector. This axis defines the orientation of the rotate plane in relation to the handle axis.

Pole Vector
This point is used to define the pole vector axis and rotate plane orientation. You can control the rotate plane by moving this point.

Handle Vector Axis
This is the line that runs from the start joint to the IK handle. This defines the first axis of the rotate plane. This is the axis that the plane will rotate around when the pole vector or Twist controls are used.

IK Handle/End Effector
This, by default, defines the end of the solver's influence but can be changed. By moving the IK handle, you affect the rotation of all the joints. The IK handle is a separate node that contains the pole vector and Twist controls.

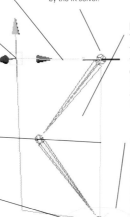

Start Joint
This is the first joint that is influenced by the IK handle. Every joint from this one to the end effector will be affected by the IK solver.

Rotate Plane
This is the plane on which the IK solver will evaluate the joint rotations. In most cases, all the joints will lie on this plane and move along it as the IK handle is moved.

Twist
This attribute lets you rotate the plane around the handle axis without moving the pole vector. It offers some secondary control over the plane's orientation.

Preferred Angle

In order for an IK handle to solve correctly, it must have a default setting for the rotations of its joints. This setting is called the Preferred Angle and can be set by selecting the start joint and then clicking on **Skeleton > Set Preferred Angle**. When an IK solver calculates joint rotations, it is in reference to these values. The preferred angles are the easiest for the solver to achieve.

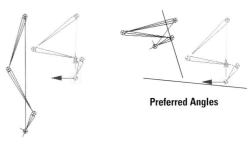

Preferred Angles

In the two examples shown above, the Preferred Angle is set differently. The first uses small joint rotations and the second uses extreme joint rotations. If you compare the motion of these two, you will see that the second rotates more at the ankle as the IK handle is moved up.

Spline IK Solver

The Spline IK solver uses a curve to control the joint rotations. This solution lets you move the CVs on the curve to reshape the skeleton. It is useful for situations where you need the joints to swing back and forth (like a tail) or where you want more local control (like a character's spine).

Clusters
To avoid going into Component Selection mode, you can apply clusters to the curve's CVs. You can then edit the cluster positions to reshape the curve.

IK Handle/End Effector
The IK handle controls the Offset, Roll, and Twist parameters for the solver.

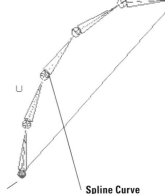

Start Joint
This is the first joint that is influenced by the IK handle. Every joint from this one to the end effector will be affected by the IK solver.

Spline Curve
You can either use an existing curve or let the Spline IK tool create one for you. Reshaping this curve generates a solution for the joint rotations.

Skinning Characters

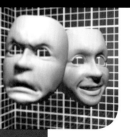

While joint skeletons with forward or inverse kinematics define an animatable framework for your character, it is the character's surfaces that are rendered. These surfaces need to be bound to the skeleton where they can bend and twist as the kinematic controls are animated. The skinning can involve not only the bending of these surfaces at joints, but also muscle bulges.

Binding Techniques

To bind geometry to a skeleton is to associate points from the geometry with joints on the skeleton. This results in skin clusters that are made up of control points. You can add and subtract points from these sets and you can set their weight to affect how they will deform. You can also add secondary deformers to handle bending and bulging.

When you first bind a surface, the skeleton's **Bind Pose** is recorded. To continue binding after the skeleton joints have been rotated or moved, your skeleton must be returned to the Bind Pose. **Select Skin > Go to Bind Pose** to go back to the Bind Pose.

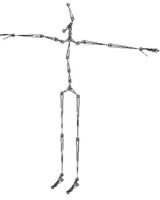

Bind Pose
IK controls and constraints can prevent you from returning to the Bind Pose. Therefore, select Modify > Disable Nodes > All to free up the joints, then select Skin > Go to Bind Pose. Afterwards, be sure to Enable all the nodes.

Parenting
If you have an element, like a fingernail, where a surface does not need to deform and its motion can be controlled by a single joint, be sure to parent it to the joint. This offers a much faster evaluation than bound surfaces.

Smooth Bind
A Smooth Bind creates clusters that overlap. The overlapping points are then weighted, depending on which joints exert the most influence. This option offers better bending of the surface, and the results can be adjusted by editing the weights. Influence Objects can then be used for secondary deformations.

Rigid Bind
A Rigid Bind breaks down the points on a surface into clusters and associates each cluster with a given joint. Therefore, the parts of a surface bend with the joints, although the points at the joints will bend harshly. Secondary deformers are used to smooth out the bending.

Indirect Binding
In some cases, you may want to apply a Lattice or Wrap deformer to your object, then bind the deformer to the skeleton. This lets you work with fewer control points and you can add or subtract surfaces from the lattice to work with updated models.

Rigid Binding

Rigid binding involves the creation of joint clusters that are made up of control points. Each cluster is associated with only one joint on the skeleton. You can apply the Rigid Bind option to a surface by selecting the surface and skeleton then choosing **Skin > Bind Skin > Rigid Bind**.

If you want to move control points from one cluster to another, you can use the **Relationship Editor**. You can also pick a joint, then select **Deform > Edit Membership Tool**. This will display the points associated with the joint and will let you add and subtract them from the set.

 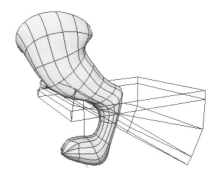

Joint Clusters
The colored CVs and joints show you the associations created during the binding process. This colored display is one of the options of the Rigid Bind tool and can be used to help determine membership.

Flexors
Secondary deformations for bends and bulges can be achieved by combining rigid binding and flexors. A flexor can be a lattice, cluster, or sculpt object that is linked to the joint's rotation.

Smooth Binding

Smooth binding involves the creation of overlapping skin clusters where the shared points are weighted automatically based on their distance or hierarchy from the participating joints. This softens the bending at joints and creates a smoothly distributed motion in the surface as it deforms. You can apply a smooth bind to a surface by selecting the surface and skeleton, then clicking on **Skin > Bind Skin > Smooth Bind.**

This method of skinning creates good results right away without requiring flexors or other deformers for good bending at the joints. Secondary deformations can be added later for bulging and other muscle-like motions using influence objects.

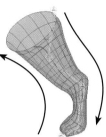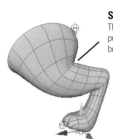

Softer Bend
The weighting of shared points creates a softer bend at the joint.

Overlapping Clusters
By overlapping the skin clusters, points near the skeleton joints become shared. When the joints rotate, these points are only partially affected because of their weighting and the softer surface's blend.

Smooth Bind Influence

In a Smooth Bind, all the points are influenced by a number of joints as set in the Smooth Bind options. No matter how many joints are influencing a point, the total weight for the point should add up to 1. This ensures that the point moves properly with the skeleton. You can visualize the weighting by selecting the joints in the **Paint Skin Weights Tool** option window or by viewing the weights in the Component Editor.

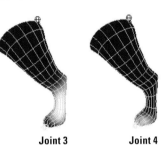

Four Joints
On this joint chain, an influence of 4 means that each point can be influenced by four joints. The images on the right show the distribution.

| Joint 1 | Joint 2 | Joint 3 | Joint 4 |

Indirect Binding

Another method used to bind geometry to a skeleton is indirect binding. In this method, a lattice deformer is applied to the geometry, then the lattice is bound to the skeleton. This lets you work with fewer skin points for setup and weighting. Indirect binding also offers more generalized deformations on the different parts of your character.

With indirect binding, you can add and subtract objects from the deformer using the **Set Membership** tool to update models without losing the work put into binding the lattice. This can be helpful if you want to begin animating before the final model is ready.

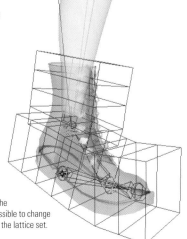

Binding Lattices
In the example shown above, you can see the lattices bound to the foot. This makes it possible to change footwear by adding and subtracting it from the lattice set.

Editing Weights

The quality of a smooth bound deformation is controlled by the weighting of its points. This weighting usually adds up to 1 and can be edited using either an Artisan brush or the Component Editor where exact values can be entered and updated.

Painting Weights
Selecting Skin > Edit Smooth Skin > Paint Skin Weights Tool lets you view a map of the weighting for each joint, then paint new weight values. These values are for the selected joint only and the overall weights of the points can be automatically adjusted to add up to 1.

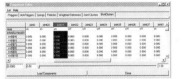

Component Editor
You can also edit the actual weight values in the Component Editor. The points can be selected in the modeling views, then their weights updated in this window. You can also hold some of the values so that you can focus your edits on the weights associated with other joints.

Influence Objects

The skin clusters of a Smooth Bind can also be affected by NURBS or polygonal geometry that is set up as Influence Objects. These can be set up using Set Driven Key to create muscle bulges.

Muscle Bulge
The mesh sitting just below the surface of the leg is set up to change shape as the knee rotates. This creates muscle deformations in the leg. You can bulge and stretch the leg surface using Set Driven Key or expressions to control this Smooth Bind deformer.

IK/FK Blending

You can pose and animate the joints of a joint chain using both FK and IK. This is called animation blending. This blending between FK and IK animation is possible because of the IK handle's IK Blend attribute. IK Blend lets you switch between posing and animating with pure FK or pure IK, as well as control the blend between the two kinds of animation.

In addition to blending IK and FK animation over multiple frames, a blend can occur over a single frame. If you want to animate an instantaneous switch between IK and FK, such as a planted, stationary hand quickly rising into the air, you should blend IK and FK over a single frame. Or, if you want to animate a motion that eases in or out of IK or FK, such as a character jumping up to grab a horizontal bar, you should blend IK and FK over several frames.

Viewing IK and FK Chains
In order to view the difference between the IK and FK skeleton chains, you must set keyframes on the joints. Doing so tells Maya that you want to use the IK/FK blending feature.

IK/FK Keys

The menu items under **Animate > IK/FK Keys** are all intended to simplify the **IK/FK keying**. Knowing these commands will help you control you skeleton chain. They become especially handy when switching between IK and FK, thus preventing unwanted results.

Set IK/FK Key
This command sets keys on all the current IK handle's keyable attributes and all the joints in its IK chain. Also, when you use Set IK/FK Key, Maya performs additional operations to ensure a smooth transition between IK and FK. You can use this menu item instead of **Animate > Set Key** when you want to key IK and FK animation on the same joint chain.

Enable IK Solver
This command turns the current IK handle's Solver Enable attribute on or off. The status of the Solver Enable attribute determines whether an IK handle's solver is active or inactive. When Solver Enable is on, you can only pose your joint chain using the IK handle. When Solver Enable is off, you can only pose your joint chain by directly manipulating its individual joints (FK).

Viewing IK/FK

Posing and animating a joint chain with both FK and IK changes the way the joints and bones are displayed in your scene view. A joint chain with FK and IK is drawn using three default or user defined colors. The blue joint chain represents the skeleton with pure FK **animation**, the brown joint chain represents the skeleton with pure I**K animation**, and the magenta joint chain represents the resulting animation blend.

Also, you can customize the colors of the **IK/FK** joint chains and the size of the **IK/FK** joints.

Connect to IK/FK
This command links the selected object to the current IK handle by adding the read-only attribute IK Blend to the object. Once the object is connected, you can select the object and use Set IK/FK Key to set keys on the IK handle and all the joints in its joint chain. You can also constrain or parent the IK handle to the object to manipulate the IK handle.

Move IK to FK
This command moves the current IK handle to the last joint in its joint chain. In a typical FK/IK rig, the IK handle does not move with the skeleton during FK manipulation and thus appears out of sync. This can cause confusion when there are many IK handles. The Move IK to FK synchronizes the IK handle's position with the end effector's position.

Joint Size
The joint and IK/FK joint size can be changed via the Display menu. You can also specify the IK/FK colors by selecting **Window > Settings/Preferences > Colors**.

IK Blend State
You might need a quick way to display whether a selected IK handle's IK Blend attribute is on or off. To do so, turn on Display > Heads Up Display > Animation Details.

Retargeting Animation

You can retarget animation data from the joints of one skeleton (source) to the joints of another skeleton (target). The source skeleton is the skeleton from which you want to retarget its animation data, and the target skeleton is the skeleton to which you want to retarget the source's animation.

Retargeting is useful when you want to transfer animation between skeletons that have the same or different proportions. Animation retargetting can save you lots of time when creating similar animations for different characters.

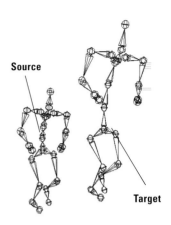

Source

Target

Joint Labels

In order to be able to retarget an animation onto another skeleton, you must use joint labels. Labels are used by Maya to transfer the animation correctly to the appropriate joints from a source to a target. As you label your joints, each label appears beside their respective joints in the scene view.

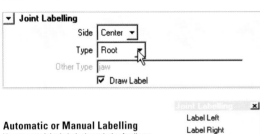

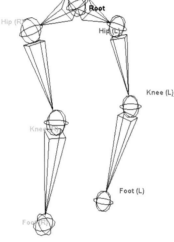

Automatic or Manual Labelling

You can set Joint Labels through the Attribute Editor or via the **Skeleton > Retargeting** menu.

You can also set the joints labels based on the names of the joints and vice-versa.

If the labels are not showing up beside your joints, make sure the Draw Label option is turned on or to select Show All Labels from the Retargeting menu.

Retargeting Solver

The Retarget Options window lets you set the retargeting solver's options.

The retargeting solver is what looks at the animation on the source skeleton's joints and retargets them to the corresponding, labelled joints of the target skeleton.

Neutral Pose

Specifies whether a defined neutral pose will be used to relate the source and target skeletons during the retarget or whether it will be a pose at a specified frame.

Lower Body

Lets you choose how the lower body animation of the source skeleton is retargeted to the lower part of the target skeleton.

Upper Body

Lets you choose how the upper body animation of the source skeleton is retargeted to the upper part of the target skeleton.

Time

Lets you specify if you want to retarget only a section or all the source animation.

Neutral Pose

In order to correctly transfer an animation, the source and target skeletons must have a neutral pose set. With these poses, Maya will be able to determine how to copy the animation, taking all the offsets in account.

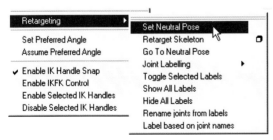

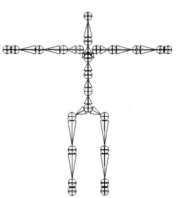

Set Neutral Pose

One of the most common neutral poses is the **T-Stance**. Once you determine a good **T-Stance**, simply make sure you use the same position for all your characters. This will simplify a lot the retargeting process. When your character's neutral pose is set, the neutralPose tab appears on the root joint's node in the Attribute Editor.

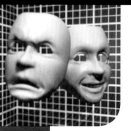

Animating Characters

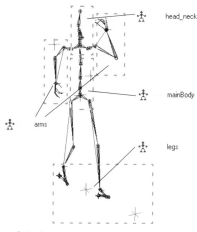

To animate a character, you must deal with a large number of attributes that are scattered around many joints, IK handles, and Transform nodes that make up the character. A number of tools can help you consolidate these attributes and make it easier to set keys on your character.

Character Sets

Character Sets offer you high-level control over your character. These sets let you collect attributes from different parts of a Character and edit and set keys on them in a single place. Keys set on Character Sets are transferred to the associated attributes.

Character Sets are given special treatment when they are highlighted on the Character menu. A highlighted character is keyed by the Set Key Tool (S key) even if its parts are not selected in the workspace. Highlighted characters also show up in the Graph Editor without having to be selected.

Sub-characters
Sub-characters can be created for different parts of a character to give you more control. These breakdowns should mimic areas that you want to animate as a group.

Character Set
This is essentially the root set of a character. It may not contain any attributes if you are using it with Sub-character sets. Select **Character > Create Character** to create one of these sets.

Sub-Character Set
A Sub-character set is a typical character set that has been assigned to a character. Select **Character > Create Sub-character** to create one of these sets. It will be assigned to the highlighted character.

Attributes
Some attributes will be part of a character or sub-character when they are created. To add more attributes, you can highlight them in the Channel Box, then select **Character > Add to Character**. You can also use the Relationship Editor to add attributes to characters.

Character Pop-up Menu
This pop-up menu found next to the timeline in the lower right of the workspace lets you quickly select and edit characters and sub-characters. The character set highlighted here is the active character.

Relationship Editor
If you select **Character > Set Current Character > Character sets...** or **Character sets...** from the pop-up **Character** menu, you open the Relationship Editor. Highlight a Character Set on the left, then click on attributes on the right to add them to the Character Sets.

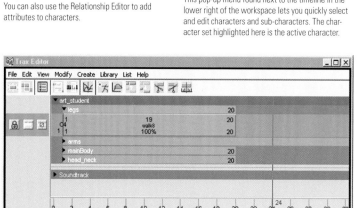

Non-linear Animation
To animate using non-linear animation, you must have character sets set up. Only character and sub-character sets will be recognized when you create clips and poses and place them into the Trax Editor.

Character Mapper
Use the Character Mapper to establish a relationship between a source and target character's nodes or attributes so that you can import and export or copy and paste animation clips between the mapped characters in the Trax Editor.

Animating Characters

character animation

109

Constraints

Constraints allow you to control a character using other objects (such as locators). Constraints let you control parts of a character like the position of IK handles with a point constraint or the rotation of joints with an orient constraint.

The advantage of constraints is that they are flexible. If an arm or leg cannot reach its constraint, it pulls away from the constraint gently rather than being abruptly stopped. When you see this pulling, you can quickly adjust other constraints to minimize the pulling of the first constraint.

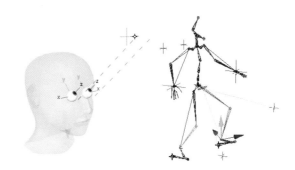

Arm
A character's hands can be constrained using point and orient constraints. You may want to parent these to the shoulders so they move with the body. If you have any finger attributes, you may want to use the locator as a Control node.

Eyes
Aim constraints can be used to control a character's eyes. These would be parented to the head but could still be moved on their own to offset the gaze. It is a good idea to use a different locator for each eye to avoid having a cross-eyed look.

Elbows and Knees
A pole vector constraint can be used to control the positioning of elbows and knees. These locators help orient the IK handles pole vector, which helps prevent the IK solution from flipping. pole vector constraints can also be parented to parts of the body.

Animated Constraint Weights

It is possible to add more than one constraint to an object. Each of these constraints is given a weight and the object will be constrained based on the average of the constraints' weights. Therefore, you can animate an object that switches from one constraint to another by keying the weights from 0 to 1. If you are animating the weights, make sure you don't set all the weights to 0. This would create a confusing situation for your object when working interactively.

Control Nodes

In some cases, you will not want to add every attribute to a character. Instead, you will want specific Control nodes that have custom attributes that are linked using reactive animation techniques (such as Set Driven Key or direct connections), to other attributes in the scene. This creates an intermediate level of control that lets you focus on fewer attributes that have control over many attributes in a central location.

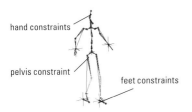

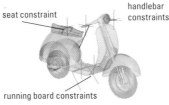

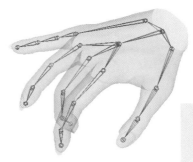

Rotate Y	0
Rotate Z	0
Finger Spread	0.4
Index Curl	3.8
Middle Curl	5.1
Ring Curl	2.8
Pinky Curl	0
Thumb Curl	0

Step 1: Character Constraints
The character's pelvis, arms, and legs are constrained to locators. The arm locators are parented to the shoulder so they move with the body, while the leg and pelvis locators are in world space. This lets you move the character freely without it being locked down.

Step 2: Scooter Constraints
The arm locators are parented to the handle-bars so they rotate with the steering mechanism. The leg locators are parented to the running board and the pelvis locator to the seat. When the scooter moves, the character constraints will also move.

l_IKhandle_pointConstraint	
Node State	Normal
L Hand W0	1
L Handlebar W1	0

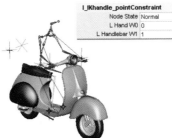

l_IKhandle_pointConstraint	
Node State	Normal
L Hand W0	0
L Handlebar W1	1

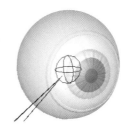

Rotate Z	0
Scale X	1
Scale Y	1
Scale Z	1
Visibility	on
Pupil	0.2

Step 3: Key Initial Weighting
While the character walks freely, the character constraints are keyed at 1 and the scooter constraints are keyed at 0. This puts the character constraints in control until the character sits down. You will want to add the Constraint node's weight attributes to a Character node to make sure they are keyed with the character.

Step 4: Key Final Weighting
As the character sits on the scooter, the character's constraint weights are keyed at 0 and and the scooter constraint weights are keyed at 1. Now you can animate the scooter and the character will follow. You might want to animate the scooter constraint weight for the pelvis up and down as the scooter goes over bumps.

Control Nodes and Manipulators
Dynamic or custom attributes can be added to specific nodes to let you animate several other joints or attributes using one control. Some custom attributes could roll a finger while others could control an eye's pupil dilation. These attributes would later be included in a character set for automatic keyframing.

110

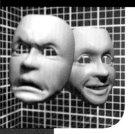

Walk Cycles

Walk cycles offer a great example of the steps you must take when animating characters. First, you need to set up a skeleton that is capable of staying planted to the ground. You must then add higher level controls that will help you animate the body. Extra hierarchy nodes can also be set up to give you added control. When you set up a character's walk cycle, you can combine the appropriate rigging with animation techniques such as constraints, hierarchies, and non-linear animation.

Rigging Up a Leg

When a character walks, one foot remains planted on the ground as the other moves up and down where it becomes planted so that the first foot can move (step forward). The foot first touches the ground with its heel, then the foot rolls to the ball and then pushes off using the toe. This heel-to-toe motion is important to a walk cycle and can be set up using a reverse foot setup. This foot is a joint hierarchy that is set up in the opposite direction as the leg joints. The leg's IK handle and some of the foot joints are constrained to the reverse foot setup, which is then used as the control for animating the foot.

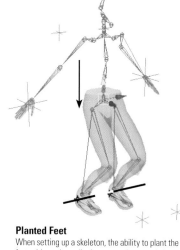

Planted Feet
When setting up a skeleton, the ability to plant the feet without them slipping or rotating out of place is crucial. The reverse foot helps makes sure the feet are planted.

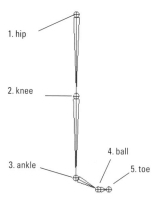

1. hip
2. knee
3. ankle
4. ball
5. toe

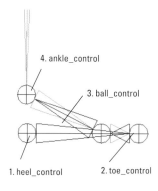

4. ankle_control
3. ball_control
1. heel_control
2. toe_control

Step 1: Draw the Joints
With Auto Joint Orient set to None, draw five joints to represent the hip, knee, ankle, ball, and toe. Draw the first three joints in the straight line and the last two as shown. Don't worry about the heel. It will be added later.

Step 2: Draw Reverse Foot
Draw a second skeleton with four joints that start at the heel, then match the positions of the toe, ball and ankle. This skeleton will be used to control the leg. Name these joints heel_control, toe_control, ball_control, and ankle_control.

Step 3: Add IK Handle
Rotate the knee joint back a few degrees, then select the hip and click on **Skeleton > Set Preferred Angle**. Now add an IK handle that runs from the hip to the ankle joints.

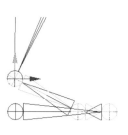

Step 4: Constrain the Foot
Point constrain the IK handle to the ankle_control joint on the reverse foot. Orient constrain the ball joint to the toe_control joint and the ankle joint to the ball_control joint. Now you can control the leg by moving the reverse foot.

Step 5: Add Pole Vector Constraint
Add a locator in front of the foot. Parent it to the reverse foot hierarchy. Pole Vector constrain the IK handle to this locator. This will help control flipping and will make sure the knee rotates when the foot rotates.

Step 6: Connect to Spine
Draw a joint chain to represent the spine of the character. Select the hip joint of the leg and the pelvis joint at the base of the spine, then choose **Skeleton > Connect** using the **Parent Joint** option. Repeat these steps for the other leg.

Adding Controls

To add high-level controls, you can set up nodes and attributes that give you automatic motion. This automation makes a character easier to animate, but may limit your range of motion down the line.

Controlling the Pelvis

Constrain the pelvis joint to a locator. Group the locator to itself so that its new pivot is between the feet. Use an Average utility node or expressions to keep the group positioned and oriented in the middle of the feet. This centers the pelvis between the feet and lets you turn corners while the original locator can be used to offset the pelvis.

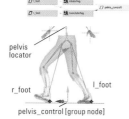

pelvis locator

r_foot   l_foot

pelvis_control [group node]

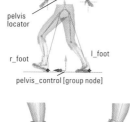

roll = 10   roll = 5   roll = 0   roll = -5

Controlling the Foot

You can control the roll of the foot by rotating the joints on the reverse foot. You can use Set Driven Key to set up a roll attribute that rotates the different reverse foot joints at key roll values. If this appears too controlled, you can choose to set keys on the various joints using a sub-character set.

A Typical Walk Cycle

Designing a walk cycle for use with non-linear animation involves two walking steps where the first and last pose of the cycle are the same. The key poses in the cycle are when both feet are planted, and when one foot is above the other. If you were to animate a run, both feet would be raised in the air rather than planted on the ground. The walk would eventually be turned into a clip and cycled in the Trax Editor.

Action Path

The movement of the feet and the pelvis can be drawn as templated curves in an orthographic window to act as guides for the motion as you set keys.

Setting Keys

The start [1], middle [3] and end [5] of the cycle are keyed first. This creates a sliding motion. The raising of the feet is then added.

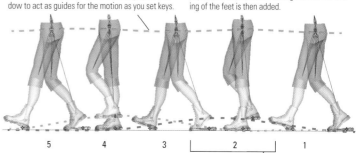

5   4   3   2   1

Start and End Positions

To make a walk cycle, the start and end poses must match in order to create motion that can be cycled. In the Trax Editor, the end frame of one cycle and the start frame of the next cycle will be merged.

Planted Feet

Throughout a walk cycle, one foot must stay planted on the ground and the pelvis must move up and down with the motion. The expression on an extra group node can keep the pelvis centered while the original pelvis joint lets you offset the pelvis as needed.

Non-linear Animation

The mixing of different walk cycles is a task well suited for non-linear animation. The Trax Editor allows you to cycle, scale, and position walk and run cycles, then blend between them.

When an IK-based cycle is placed in the Trax Editor, be sure to set its clip's **Offset** to **Relative**. This adds each step to the last. If you are using forward kinematics or motion-capture data, then **Offset** can remain set at **Absolute** since the rotates are not cumulative.

By setting up your own clips, you end up with a library of motion that can be used in other scenes. You can even use character maps to create a description of your current character that can then be used to set up a MEL connection with another character. This makes it possible to share clips between the mapped characters.

Characters

A character can be created using sub-characters to break the action down into different parts of the body. Keying an active character will key the attributes that belong to the sub-characters.

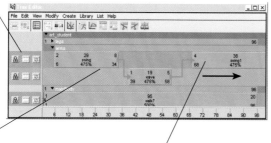

Clips

When you create clips, you can focus on the sub-characters and create motion for them alone. If you make the character active, you can choose to create clips for all the sub-characters at the same time. When the clips are laid out in the Trax Editor, you must work at a sub-character level. Poses can only be saved for active sub-characters sets.

Overlapping Action

Using your different sub-characters, you can create overlapping action. For example, you can offset the swinging of a character's arms in order to ensure that they do not coincide exactly with the character's feet. This creates more interesting motion and can be easily set up by moving clips around in the Trax Editor.

Refining the Motion

To add complexity to your walk cycles and give them more character, you can animate body parts other than the feet. The swing of the arms, the rotation of the pelvis, and the shifting of weight to the planted foot all contribute to a more dynamic walk.

If you are animating with non-linear animation, create sub-character sets for the feet and arms. This makes it easier to create overlapping action as the arms move with their own purpose.

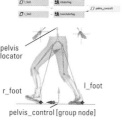

Shift weight

Hip Movement

As a character walks its hips shift over the planted foot, and its pelvis rotates. This produces a more realistic, less robotic motion than is achieved by keeping the pelvis perfectly centered between the feet. It is critical that the centering of the pelvis is controlled by a group node, while the original pelvis node is left free to create this secondary motion.

Facial Animation

O ne of the most important parts of a character is the face. Facial animation lets a character literally talk to the audience and express a wide range of emotions. In Maya, facial animation can be set up using many deformers that control all the muscle motion or you can use BlendShapes, which offer a great solution for building up and blending facial poses.

Head Models

Before animating a head, you must choose a technique for modeling it. Shown here are several head topologies using different geometry types. The most important aspect of each model is its ability to mimic the muscle movements used to create facial expressions. After that, you must consider how you will texture the model and how fast it will be to work with.

Facial Muscles
Here is a simple diagram of the facial muscles that help define the mechanics of the face. Understanding this structure will help you create facial poses.

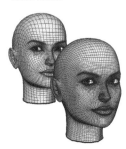 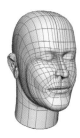 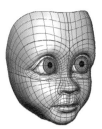 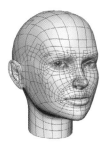

Polygonal
These two models have a structure consistent with facial muscles. The second model is a smoothed version of the first. You could animate the first model using blendShape, then smooth it later. The smooth would be slow, but it would only be needed at rendering time.

NURBS Single Surface
This model is basically a cylinder with one opening at the neck and the other at the mouth. This model works well around the mouth, but uses a lot of isoparm spans around the eye. This model is harder to texture map because 2D textures may stretch where there is more detail.

NURBS Patches
This model offers even patches that will texture map without stretching and a facial structure that matches muscle patterns. This model would require proper weighting and possibly Global Stitching to keep the patches working together seamlessly.

Subdivision Surfaces
This model shows the underlying polygonal mesh and the more detailed Subdivision head. You can animate the facial poses at the lowest level and the whole model will follow. Subdivision surfaces offer a single topology without seams.

BlendShape Setup

The BlendShape deformer lets you use several target shapes to help reshape a neutral face model. Once BlendShape has been applied, you get a series of sliders for each of the targets. Setting keys on those sliders animate the face.

To make this approach work, you can use duplicated versions of the neutral face to sculpt the targets. This will help ensure the hierarchies match and the surface topology is the same .

Once the BlendShape has been applied, you can either delete the targets or keep history and tweak the targets to refine the blends. It is a good idea to delete the targets before putting the head on your character to improve the performance.

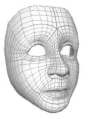

Step 1: Create a Neutral Face
Set up the neutral head. Make sure this model is grouped so that duplicates will have the same hierarchy.

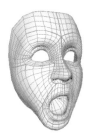

Step 2: Create Target Faces
Duplicate the head and reshape the new one to create a new facial target by adjusting the object's components.

Step 3: Apply the BlendShape
Select all the targets and then the neutral face. Select Deform > Create BlendShape.

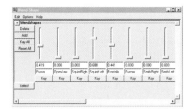

Step 4: The BlendShape Editor
Select Window > Animation Editors > BlendShape. This window gives you sliders for animating the BlendShape.

BlendShape Targets

To create convincing facial poses, your BlendShape targets must represent the mechanics of the face. The following series of faces show the kind of targets that can be used.

These targets are designed to closely resemble the muscle movements used in creating facial expressions. Later, these BlendShape attributes can be animated in the BlendShape window or combined to create more specific facial poses using the Trax Editor animation clips.

To help you model the different poses, you can set up deformers on one face that will make it possible to manipulate the surface using good generalized deformations. As you create each pose, duplicate the surfaces to produce a new face that doesn't have any deformers attached, but retains the deformed shape.

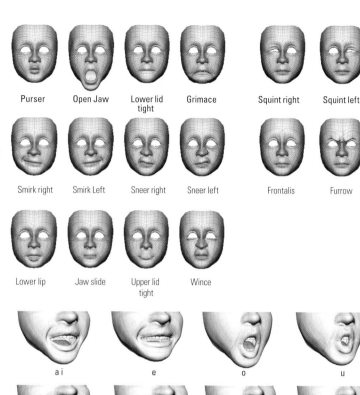

Purser　　Open Jaw　　Lower lid tight　　Grimace　　Squint right　　Squint left

Smirk right　　Smirk Left　　Sneer right　　Sneer left　　Frontalis　　Furrow

Lower lip　　Jaw slide　　Upper lid tight　　Wince

Phonemes

Another set of targets you can create are phonemes. These represent facial poses at certain points in speech. If you use the muscle targets shown to the right, you can create phonemes by blending several shapes together. These could be recorded as poses if you are using non-linear animation. Otherwise, you could choose to sculpt the phonemes yourself and make them targets.

a i　　e　　o　　u

c d g k n r s th y z　　el d th　　m b p　　f v

Non-linear Facial Animation

Facial animation is a task well suited for non-linear animation because the facial workflow is primarily pose based. Once created, these poses can be laid out in the Trax Editor and blended. Edits can be made easily to the animation by either moving the poses around or mixing in new poses.

The BlendShape attributes would be included in a Sub-character set. The poses can be created by using the BlendShape attributes to set up a facial pose and then saving a pose for the sub-character. In some cases, you may want to set some keys to create a clip that describes a more complex motion, such as a blink or phoneme.

Once you have poses for your character, they can be re-used multiple times in multiple scenes. You might even save out animation clips of common expressions typical of your character. These could then be ready for use at any time in your production.

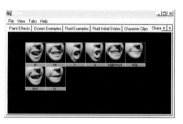

Step 1: Create Poses and Clips
Set up a facial pose using the blendShape sliders. When you are happy, select the head sub-character set, then click on **Animate > Create Pose** or **Create Clip**. Clip swatch images can be created using **View > Grab Swatch to Hypershade/Visor** in the Render view panel.

Step 2: Add the Poses to the Trax Editor
Quickly drag clips from the Visor to the Trax Editor. This allows you to block out the facial motion, although at this point, the animation will jump from pose to pose.

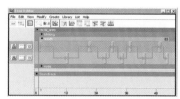

Step 3: Blend the Poses
To smooth the poses, select two of them in the Trax Editor, then click on **Create > Blend**. This creates a blend curve that can be edited in the Graph Editor.

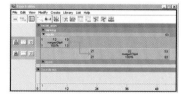

Step 4: Edit the results
Now you can move the poses around, scale and cycle the clips, and tweak the blends. If desired, you could merge some poses to form clips of complete words.

Materials and Textures

While geometry describes the shape of an object, its material describes
how its surface will appear when rendered. In the real world, when light
hits a surface it reacts to the surface qualities. Some of the light is absorbed
and some is reflected. A shiny object reflects light directly while a matte
object diffuses the light. While reflected light does not actually illuminate
other surfaces in Maya, materials and textures can be set up to simulate
the real-world reaction of surfaces to light.

To create realistic images, material qualities such as color, specularity,
reflectivity, transparency, and surface detail must all be set. Maya uses
special connected nodes called Shading Networks to set up the material
qualities of your surfaces.

Textures let 3D artists create more complex looks for their surfaces.
A texture can be a set of procedures set up in Maya or a bitmap image
created outside Maya. In either case, realistic surfaces are created by
combining geometry with well-designed textures.

Shading Your Models

While geometry defines the shape of a model, shading defines how the model's surfaces react to light and details such as color, transparency, and texture.

Maya uses Shading group nodes to tell the renderer which materials, textures, and lights will affect the final look of a surface. Shading networks are made up of nodes that define the final look of a rendered surface. Learning the proper role of each of these nodes will ensure that you build shading networks that render successfully.

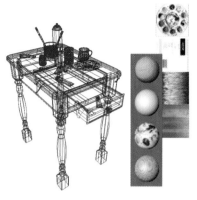

Material Qualities

Before actually looking at a more complex shading network, it is useful to consider the various material qualities that you will be trying to achieve. A basic understanding of how an object is shaded can be translated into attributes on shading network nodes in Maya.

The geometry shown as a wireframe becomes more realistic with the addition of shading networks that add color and texture.

Basic Shading
Shading shows you how the surface appears when illuminated. As light hits a surface, it defines a gradation from light to dark that makes the surface's 3D qualities apparent.

Highlights and Reflections
As a surface becomes shinier, it begins to show highlights and reflections. Specular highlights show the hotspots where the light sources are reflected, while reflections simulate light bounced from surrounding objects.

Specular highlights

Reflections

Surface Relief
Surface relief, such as bumps and scratches, helps add a realistic look to a surface. This effect can be achieved with special textures called **bump** and **Displacement Maps**.

Transparency
It is possible to see through transparent areas such as the glass on this jar, while opaque areas such as the label, cap, and paint remain solid. Transparent surfaces such as glass can also bend light. This is called refraction and can be achieved in Maya using Raytracing.

Evaluating Shading Networks

To preview shading networks and texture maps, set up a camera, then illuminate your objects with lights and render. Hardware rendering can be used to quickly preview textures and some lights while software rendering is required to explore all shading situations. More in-depth discussion of rendering types is found in the Rendering chapter. Lighting and camera information is found in the Digital Cinematography chapter.

Hardware Rendering
It offers a preview of the color of textures and up to eight lights.

Software Rendering
It is capable of rendering all shading effects such as bump, specular, shadows, and all lights.

The Anatomy of a Shading Network

Shading networks are built as nodes that control specific aspects of the shading effect. These networks define how various color and texture nodes work with associated lights and surfaces. The placement of textures on surfaces is also controlled by nodes within the network.

There are several ways to view shading networks in Maya. The Hypershade window lets you easily connect nodes and view the connected attributes. You can also double-click on any node to open the Attribute Editor. Along the way, you can zoom in and out in the Hypershade to get the complete picture. You can also view shading networks in the Hypergraph window but this view does not give you swatch images.

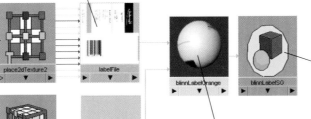

2D Texture Placement Node

A texture is mapped in 2D space when it is mapped to the UV space of the geometry. This node is used to define the texture's positioning and orientation within the UV space.

File Texture Node

File textures are bitmap images imported into Maya that can be used for texture mapping attributes such as color, bump, or transparency.

Shading Group

This node is the root of the shading network. It sends information about materials and textures, lighting, and geometry to the renderer. In most cases, you will not have to work directly with the Shading group node because the Material node is where you will make most of your texture connections.

3D Texture Placement Node

This node lets you define a position in 3D space for your texture and makes it easier to texture multiple surfaces as if they were one. The icon in the modeling views can be used to interactively establish the texture's position in world space.

Material Node

Material nodes define how the surfaces will react to light. The term **shader** is often used to describe the role played by the Material node. In general, this node will be the focus of your work as you build up all of your shading networks.

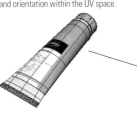

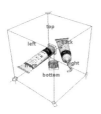

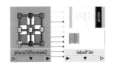

Environment Texture Node

An environment texture is used to simulate reflections on the surface. This node might be shared among several shaders and have an affect on many surfaces.

Shading Network Connections

Shading network nodes have input and output attributes. Texture mapping involves making connections between these Input and Output attributes. One way to connect them is to drag one node onto another in the Hypershade window. You are then offered a list of input attributes to map to. In this case, the Output attribute is a default attribute such as outColor. For more complex mapping, the Connection Editor allows you to select input and output attributes directly.

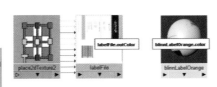

When a texture node is dragged onto a Material node, you are given a pop-up menu of possible input attributes. This makes it easy to connect two nodes together. You can also drag nodes directly onto attribute names in the Attribute Editor to connect them.

Placing the cursor over the line that connects two nodes gives you information about the connected input and output attributes. You can use this information for future reference. You can select this line and delete it to break the connection.

The Connection Editor can be used when the desired attribute is not available in the pop-up menu or when you want to make a special connection such as the Out Color R of the one node to the Diffuse of another.

Surface Materials

Materials in the real world react to light by absorbing or reflecting it. Polished surfaces are shiny because they reflect light with strong highlights, while rough surfaces have a softer look because they disperse light. A Material node is a mathematical shading model that simulates a natural reaction to light.

The Material node contains a number of attributes that let you control how surfaces are shaded. Maya includes several material types, such as Phong, Blinn, and Lambert, that each define a different shading model. The Material node acts as a focal point for shading and texturing information. It is then fed into the Shading group node where it is combined with information about lights and the geometry to be rendered.

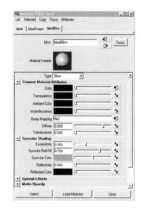

The Material nodes have attributes in two main sections. Common Material Attributes are found on most Material nodes while the Specular Shading Attributes change, depending on the chosen material type.

Material Qualities

The behavior of light when it strikes a surface in real life is quite complex. Surface imperfections can distort the angle at which light rays are reflected causing them to scatter and can also cause some light to become trapped, or absorbed. This type of scattered reflected light appears soft and even and is known as diffuse light. Very smooth surfaces have little or no surface imperfections so light is not absorbed and reflected light is more coherent or focused. When this light reaches our eyes, we see bright specular highlights. These real world behaviors are simulated in Maya with the Diffuse and Specular attributes.

Ambient Color
This attribute creates the effect of even illumination, without requiring a light source. In this image, the Ambient color has RGB values of 0.25, 0.25, 0.25 on all objects.

Diffuse
Diffuse determines how much light is absorbed and how much is scattered in all directions by surface imperfections. Rougher surfaces tend to have higher Diffuse values while smooth or mirror-like surfaces have Diffuse values that approach 0.

Color
Color is made up of red, green, and blue attributes. The color of light and reflections will influence this base color.

Transparency
White is transparent, black is opaque and other values are semi-transparent. You can also use a texture map to create the appearance of holes in a surface.

Incandescence
This attribute can be used to make a surface appear to emit light. The Incandescence attribute is not actually emitting light and has no effect on other surfaces.

Glow
This attribute, found in the Special Effects section of the Material node, can be used to add the appearance of atmospheric noise to a surface.

Specular Highlights
Specular shading attributes determine the amount of light that is reflected at a consistent angle resulting in an intense bright region called a specular highlight. Perfectly smooth surfaces will have very bright tiny highlights because there are no surface imperfections to distort the reflection angle. Rougher surfaces like brushed metals will have a softer highlight.

Combined Effect
In real life, the proportions of the specular and diffuse components of the total reflected light will vary depending on the characteristics of the surface.

Bump
This attribute lets you add surface relief by using a texture map to alter the direction of the surface Normals.

Reflectivity
This attribute controls the amount a surface reflects its environment. This environment could be a 3D texture map connected to the material's Reflected Color or actual Raytraced reflections of objects in the scene.

Reflected Color
This attribute can be texture mapped to define a reflected environment without relying on Raytraced reflections. These texture maps are positioned in world space and can be assigned to various materials to make sure the scene's reflections are consistent.

Material and Shader types

Several different material and shader types offer you distinct shading characteristics. The main difference between materials is how they handle specular highlights when rendered. Shaders are specialized materials that renders differently and specificaly for some objects.

Below are six of the most commonly used material types and five specialized shaders. Various attributes such as color, bump, and specularity can be mapped with textures and will affect the appearance of the final render.

Materials and shaders can be dragged from the Create section of the Hypershade where you can assign them and make texture connections.

After creating a Material node, you can change the material type quickly using the pop-up menu in the Attribute Editor. This will change the types of attributes available for shading.

Lambert Material

This material type is the most basic and does not include any attributes for specularity. This makes it perfect for matte surfaces that do not reflect the surrounding environment. The Lambert material type can be transparent and will refract in a Raytrace rendering, but without any specularity, it won't reflect.

Blinn Material

Many artists use this material type exclusively because it offers high-quality specular highlights using attributes such as **Eccentricity** and **Specular Roll Off**. This material type can be edited to look like a Phong material, which has sharper highlights, in cases where you need better anti-aliasing of highlights during an animation. This material is good for glass and metals.

Ramp Shader

That shader uses extra control over the way color changes with light and the view angle. You can simulate a variety of exotic materials and tweak traditional shading in subtle ways. All the color-related attributes in the Ramp Shader are controlled by ramps.

Phong Material

This material adds a sharp specular highlight to the Lambert material. The size and intensity of the highlights are controlled by the **Cosine Power** attribute. This material can also have reflections from either an environment map or Raytraced reflections. The Phong material is good for plastics.

Anisotropic Material

This material type simulates surfaces which have micro-facet grooves and the specular highlight tends to be perpendicular to the direction of the grooves. Materials such as hair, satin, and CDs all have anisotropic highlights.

Ocean Shader

The Ocean shader is a specialised shader with attributes defining realistic waves on large bodies of water. It is usually used through the **Fluid Effects > Ocean > Create Ocean command**, which automatically creates nodes required to render an ocean.

PhongE Material

This material type adds a different kind of specular highlight to the Lambert. The PhongE material includes attributes such as **Roughness** that controls the softness of the highlight, **Whiteness** that controls its intensity, and **Highlight Size**.

Shading Map Material

This material type allows you to create custom shading on surfaces. A ramp texture controls the positioning and color of the shading and highlights on the surface. If you want to emphasize the dark areas, simply darken the lower end of the ramp.

  Ramp texture

Hair Tube Shader

Hair tube shader simulates a thin tube, where the width of the tube is small enough that local shading effects can be ignored. All shading derives from the view and the tube direction. Because the highlights are spread across the entire tube width, rendering fine hairs do not require as high antialiasing levels.

Layered Shader

A Layered shader allows you to combine two or more Material nodes that each have their own qualities. Each material can be designed separately, then connected to the Layered shader. The top layer's transparency can be adjusted or mapped to reveal parts of the layer below.

Layered shaders render slower than other materials. Instead of using a Layered shader, it may be better to set up a regular Material node that uses a Layered Texture node mapped to Color. Specular and Diffuse maps can create the appearance of variations in the material qualities of the surface.

Tin material
(top layer)

Rust material
(bottom layer)

Transparency map
(top layer)

Layered shader

White areas of the map are completely transparent, while black areas are opaque. Shown above are the two materials and a map that would result in the layered shader.

Use Background Shader

The Use Background material is primarily meant for combining CG and live action components. The material is assigned to stand-in geometry that represents surfaces and objects in the live-action plate. The material then catches shadows and reflections from objects in the scene. Many of the diagrams in this book have been rendered with a white background and a Use Background material assigned to a plane to catch shadows.

Reflection catchers   Shadow catchers

To create convincing results, you must set up your lighting and position your camera to match the background image to your model. While compositing, you would remove the image plane and render with a black background. The Use Background shadows are available in the rendered mask channel.

Texture Maps

To add extra detail such as bumps, scratches, and patterns to your models, you can use texture maps. By applying textures, surface relief can be created using images instead of having to actually build a complex model, and graphic elements such as logos and illustrations can be mapped as labels.

The top and bottom plates of this movie reel are modeled with simple NURBS planes. All the detail is achieved using texture maps.

Mapping Attributes

Most attributes on materials, textures, utility nodes, and lights can be texture mapped. However, an output such as **outColor**, is made up of three channels (RGB). To connect this three-channel output to an input on another node, the input attribute must be a three-channel input such as **Color**, **Transparency**, or **Incandescence**. It is easy to see this in the Connection Editor because once you have selected an output, the inputs that you cannot connect to are grayed out.

Color Map
Mapping color allows you to create detail on your surfaces. Color maps can be used for labels as well as natural materials such as wood or brick.

Transparency Map
When mapping the material's transparency, the white areas have a value of 1, which means full transparency. This differs from other 2D and 3D programs that use 1 to mean fully opaque.

Bump Map
A bump map is used to alter the direction of surface Normals when the surface is rendered. This creates the illusion of surface detail.

Displacement Map
A displacement map is similar to a bump map, except that it is applied to the geometry rather than the shading. This creates sharper detail, especially at the edges.

Specular Map
Mapping Specular Color allows you to vary the highlights on the surface. Adding a stretched noise-like texture can produce the effect of a scratched surface.

Reflectivity Map
Mapping Reflectivity lets you specify which areas of a surface are reflective. This is different from Reflected Color, which simulates a reflected environment.

File Textures and Procedural Textures

When you texture an attribute, you can choose either File Textures or Procedural Textures. File textures are bitmaps scanned from photographs or painted in a 2D or 3D paint package. Procedural Textures are 2D or 3D plots of mathematical functions where you adjust the attributes to create different looks.

Procedural texture nodes include attributes for customizing its look.

File Textures
A file texture is a bitmap image. These textures can be very realistic if scanned from a photo. File textures can be created as tileable images where the opposing edges of the texture match up. This disguises the fact that it is a repeating texture. In the case of this brick surface, a single texture is used for the whole wall.

Procedural Textures
Procedural Texture nodes let you set attributes for different aspects of the texture. With a **Grid** texture node, you can set attributes for the size and color of the bricks. A separate **Crater** texture gives the surface some detail. The texture is then also mapped to the material node as a bump map. The luminance of the texture is used as the bump values.

Texture Maps

materials and textures

Creating Textures

To texture map an attribute, you have a number of options. You can click on one of the **Map** buttons in the Attribute Editor or you can click and drag textures within the Hypershade. It is recommended that you start by using the Map button because it opens the Create Render Node window. This window presents the texture nodes in categories that help explain how they will affect your objects.

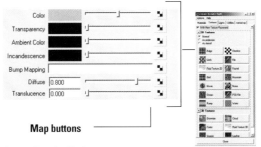

Map buttons

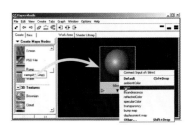

Create Render Node

To open the Create Render Node window, click on one of the Map buttons associated with a particular attribute. This opens a window with four different texture categories: 2D textures, 3D textures, Environment textures, and Other. The window's categories define the placement of the texture on the surface. Learning which textures fall into which categories will help you later if you want to use the Visor for texture creation.

Hypershade and Visor

In the Hypershade panel, you can drag a texture icon from the Visor's Create folder onto a node. A pop-up menu lets you choose an attribute for mapping to. This can be faster than the Create Render Node window, but does not categorize the nodes based on their texture placement.

2D Textures

In the Create Render Node window, the 2D textures section includes the File Texture and several Procedural Textures. These 2D textures can be mapped in one of three ways: **Normal**, **Projection**, or **Stencil**. The mapping technique determines the relationship between the texture and the surface. It also determines which placement nodes are created for you to work with in the Hypershade window.

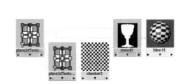

Normal Mapping

With Normal maps, the texture is mapped to the UV space of the surface. Therefore, the texture will be sized and oriented differently depending on the UV parameterization of each surface. The shading network for a Normal 2D texture map is made up of the texture node that defines the look of the texture, and a place2DTexture node that defines its placement.

Projection Mapping

This method projects a 2D texture through 3D space like a slide projector. This lets you create a consistent look on multiple surfaces. The shading network for a projection includes a Projection node that lets you choose the projection type and a place3dTexture node that defines the texture's placement.

Stencil Mapping

Stencil maps let you use either a mask file or a color key to remove part of the texture. This mapping technique is often used for labels. The shading network includes a stencil node which lets you define the masking and two place2dTexture nodes – one for placing the texture and one for the stencil.

3D Textures

With a 3D texture, objects appear to be "carved" from a solid block of granite, marble, wood or other chosen texture.

The positioning of the texture is accomplished using a 3D icon in the model view. The shading network includes the texture node and a place3dTexture node that defines where the texture is in 3D space. It can be moved, scaled, and rotated.

Environment Textures

These textures are used as either reflection maps or as backgrounds mapped to image planes. The environment maps use a 3D placement icon that sits in 3D space. The renderer then refers to this environment when calculating reflections.

A shading network that uses an environment node includes a place3dTexture node. The shape of the icon created by this node depends on the environment map you choose.

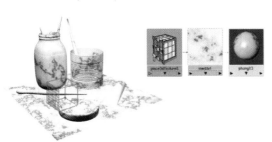

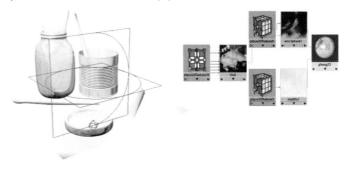

2D Texture Placement

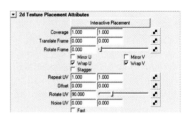

In a shading network, 2D placement is defined by the place2dTexture nodes. This 2D placement can either take place directly based on a surface's UV space, or indirectly through a Projection node. The attributes for the 2D placement let you adjust how the texture is repeated, positioned, and rotated.

Positioning the Texture

When a texture is placed on a surface, it is placed in a texture frame. This frame can be sized, positioned, and rotated, and the texture within the frame can be sized, positioned, and rotated. This positioning takes place in the surface's UV coordinate space.

The place2dTexture node contains all the information for 2D placement. You can use interactive placement to call up a manipulator for placing the texture on a surface. If a texture doesn't have a placement node default values will be applied.

Coverage
These values determine how much of the surface area will be covered by the texture frame. The texture is scaled in UV space as these values change.

Translate Frame
The position of the frame in relation to the surface's UV origin is determined by this value. The texture is also moved by this translation.

Offset
Offset is the position of the texture within the frame. This lets you move the texture independently of the frame.

Repeat UV
These values determine how many times the texture is tiled along U and V. The texture is repeated within the texture frame.

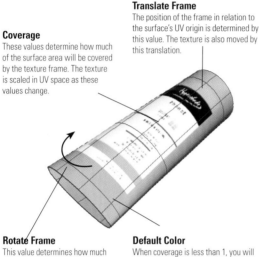

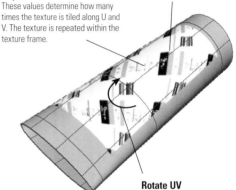

Rotate Frame
This value determines how much the whole frame is rotated. The texture rotates with the frame.

Default Color
When coverage is less than 1, you will see a gray border around the texture. You can edit this color using the **Default Color** attribute found in the Color Balance section of the texture's Attribute Editor.

Rotate UV
This value determines how much the texture is rotated independently of the frame.

Wrap, and Stagger

To give you further control over the placement of textures, you can choose to use Wrap for textures that are positioned off the surface and Stagger for working with repeated textures.

Wrap On

Wrap Off

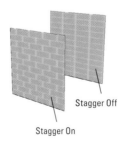

Stagger Off

Stagger On

Wrap
If the texture frame is positioned off one of the surface's edges, you can choose to **Wrap** the texture to the opposing edge or turn **Wrap off**.

Stagger
Stagger offsets every second row of a repeated texture. A grid pattern that is repeated more times in U than V can be turned into bricks using the **Stagger** attribute.

Sharing Texture Nodes

When you create a texture positioned with a place2dTexture node, in many cases, you will want to use similar placement for several different textures. You can drag the placement node onto another texture in the Hypershade window to share the placement.

The place2dTexture nodes can be shared with many textures by dragging them onto the other texture nodes in the Hypershade. Then, edits made to the placement node will affect all the connected textures. It is a good idea to share textures with color, bump, specularity, and other maps that need aligned placement.

2D Textures on NURBS Geometry

A 2D texture is positioned directly onto a NURBS surface's UV space. Ideally, the surface has been perfectly modeled and it texture maps correctly by default. However, the surface's UVs may be warped, surface Normals might point the wrong way, and the UV origin might not be where you expect it. In some cases, you may have to rebuild your surface if the parameterization is extremely stretched or compressed.

U ... **V**

Texture
Here is the file texture mapped onto the surfaces shown below. You can see that by default, the bottom left of the texture is mapped to the surface's origin, with U and V mapped along the sides.

Typical NURBS
A clean NURBS surface has its UV origin at the bottom left and its Normals pointing out. Its UV parameterization is even along its length and width and the texture maps properly. While this surface would be ideal, you are more likely to have a surface which does not map properly at first. In some cases you may even have to rebuild the surface to get a cleaner surface that resembles this surface shown here.

1.00
0.75
0.50
0.25
0.00

Even parameterization

Surface Direction
Depending on how the model was built, the surface direction might be incorrect. In such a case, you can either edit the 2D texture placement attributes to rotate and flip the texture or you can select **Edit Surfaces > Reverse Surface Direction** and either swap the U and V axes or flip either of them or both. This is also the tool used to ensure that your Normals are pointing out of the surface properly.

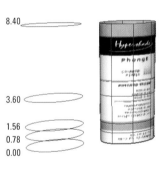

Parameterization
In case where a surface has warped parameterization, the UV values are not even and the texture appears distorted when rendered. In these cases, you can use the **Fix Texture Warp** attribute found on the surface's Shape node or a projected texture. Be aware that both these options may not look correct if the surface is deforming when animated. If this is the case, you should rebuild the surface as shown to the right.

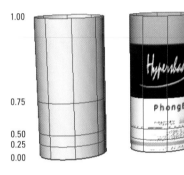

1.00
0.75
0.50
0.25
0.00

Stretched parameterization

Rebuilding Surfaces
If your parameterization is not working, you need to rebuild your surface. The **Edit Surfaces > Rebuild** tool does not fix this kind of warping. Select **Edit Curves > Duplicate Surface Curves** options and choose the direction you want. This will extract the curves you need. You can loft them again using the Chord Length option. This will give you a surface where the parameterization more closely matches the shape of the surface and the texture maps more evenly.

8.40
3.60
1.56
0.78
0.00

Chord Length parameterization

Stencil Mapping

A stencil map lets you apply a texture as a label. This is only required if your label is not square. If it is square, simply map it as a normal texture and edit the coverage and translation of the texture frame. If your label has any other shape, you can use the Stencil texture to knock out the label using either a mask file or by color keying the texture itself. Don't forget to use the texture's **Color Balance > Default Color** to set or map the color behind the label.

The green is used as the color key.

Color texture

Color texture   Mask texture

Using a Color Key
This technique uses a color from the label that will be knocked out. This color would be the label's background and should not be found in the label itself. You can sample the color using the Color Picker in the Color Chooser.

Using a Mask
You can map the **Mask** attribute with a texture where white areas would be masked and black areas would not. This functionality is also offered using the Layered Texture node where transparency can be used to mask a layer.

3D Texture Placement

When you create a 3D texture, project a texture on an object, or create an Environment texture node in Maya, an icon is placed in the scene that corresponds to the size, scale, and location of the actual texture on or around the surface. On animated and deforming objects some critical steps must be taken to ensure that your texture is consistently in the correct position on your object. You also have the option to project 2D textures on your surface using a 3D texture placement.

3D Texture Icon

Every 3D texture or environment texture you create has a connection to a 3D icon that is placed in your scene at the origin. The texture is not contained within the space of the icon if wrap is on; it extends through the entire scene. The icon represents the position, scale, and rotation of the given texture. If the 3D texture is assigned to geometry that is animated, you need to parent the 3D icon to the geometry.

Interactive Placement
When you select this option from the Attribute Editor you can manipulate handles on the icon to scale and position it.

Small Scale
Scaling the icon down compresses the texture detail shown on the geometry.

Large Scale
Scaling the icon up increases the size of the texture detail on all the parts of the model.

Rotate
When you rotate the icon, you rotate the placement of the texture on the geometry.

Fit to Group Bbox
When you select this option from the Attribute Editor, it scales the icon to envelope the entire object that the 3D texture is assigned to.

3D Textures on Deforming Surfaces

You may have a deforming object mapped with a 3D texture. When this is the case and you deform your surface, you will notice that the texture does not maintain its position on the surface as it deforms. The placement of the icon in your scene will not be enough to ensure your textures deform with your objects. In this case you have two options, either select: **Create Texture Reference Object** or **Convert to File Texture**.

A non-deforming reference object acts as a proxy for the deforming geometry.

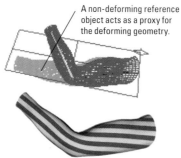

Problem
When you assign a 3D texture to a deforming object, you will encounter textures that don't stick to the deforming object.

Texture Reference Object
You can create a texture reference object in your scene that is a separate, templated piece of identical geometry with the texture assigned. The original surface references its texture information from this non-deforming copy.

Convert to File Texture
You can also convert the 3D texture to a file texture for the surface on which it is mapped. This is done by selecting the geometry and then selecting the material in the Hypershade window. In the Hypershade, select Edit > Convert to File Texture. In the options, you can set your file texture to be a specific size.

Projection Maps

A projection map projects an image onto geometry. The position, size, and rotation of the file texture is represented by the 3D icon in the scene. If you plan to animate your object, you will need to parent the icon to your object.

place2D Texture Node
This node controls the position of the file texture on the projection itself.

place3D Texture Node
This node determines the actual position of the planar projection icon in 3D space.

Projection Map Types

There are eight different types of projection that you can use for mapping a 2D texture on your surface. Each is shown here being used to map a simple checker texture to a common object for comparison. In your work, you would choose a projection type that matches the shape of your objects. The design of your texture will also be affected by this choice.

Planar
This projection type maps the texture onto objects using a single direction. It can cause stretching where surface Normals are parallel to the icon.

Spherical
This projection type maps the texture from a spherical shell. The texture pinches at the poles of the icon and will show a seam at the back unless it is tileable.

Cylindrical
This projection type maps the texture from a cylindrical shell. The texture will show a seam at the back unless it is tileable.

Ball
This projection is used for textures created by photographing a reflective ball. It maps the texture around a spherical shell. This projection has no seam but does have a single pinch point at the back of the icon.

Cubic
This projection type maps the texture from the center of a cubic shell in all six directions. The texture will appear bigger on objects further from the icon.

TriPlanar
This projection type maps the texture from three faces of a cubic shape. The projections are linear and appear to be the same size on any object they are mapped to.

Concentric
This projection type maps the texture onto objects by creating a concentric pattern from randomly selected slices of the texture.

Perspective
This projection type maps the texture from a point. You can choose a camera from the scene that will be used to define the icon's position and direction.

Environment Texture Node

There are five different types of Environment textures that can be mapped to a Material node's **Reflected Color** attribute. You can also map these types of textures to image planes to act as backgrounds for your scenes. When you create an Environment texture, a place3dTexture node is placed at the origin of the scene.

The placement, orientation, and size of the Environment icon can play a role in what the resulting reflection looks like. Different textures use this transformation information differently. In some cases, it is important to size the icon so that it surrounds the objects that are reflecting the environment, while in other cases, orientation is all that matters.

	Move	Rotate	Scale
Chrome	yes	yes	yes
Sky	yes	yes	no*
Ball	no	yes	no
Cube	yes	yes	yes
Sphere	no	yes	no

* Scale can be an issue if the Sky's Cloud attribute is mapped.

The chart explains how the reflected look of an Environment texture on a rendered object is influenced by the transformation of the placement of its icon. In some cases, the Environment placement icon will only have an effect if it is rotated.

Environment Chrome
Reflected color is mapped with the default Env Chrome texture.

Environment Sky
Reflected color is mapped with the Env Sky where the Sky Color attribute is set to a light blue.

Environment Ball
Reflected color is mapped with the default Env Ball texture using the shown file texture.

Environment Cube
Each side of the Env Cube texture was set to a varying grayscale color. The icon was scaled up to encompass the entire can.

Environment Sphere
Reflected color is mapped with the default Env Sphere texture using the shown file texture.

UV Texture Coordinates

U V coordinates are essential to assigning textures to polygons and subdivision surfaces. A UV coordinate is directly related to a vertex on the model. But the UV information is based on 2D coordinates, and therefore, must lie flat on a plane. When creating a Primitive, default UV coordinates exist. The UVs can be of an arbitrary shape compared to the model, but in order for the texture to look correct, the UVs should not overlap each other. You can see the UVs laid out in the **UV Texture Editor**. If no UVs exist on a model, any textures you assign to the model will not be visible.

Projections

To set up UV coordinates for a polygonal model, you apply projections. The projections take the UV coordinates of the model and attempt to lay them out on a plane. When applying projections, a Projection Manipulator appears allowing you to scale, rotate, or translate the manipulator. You have to decide which projection method or combination of projection methods works best for your model as you can apply a projection based on the entire object or selected faces. Projection types – Planar, Cylindrical, and Spherical – are located under **Edit Polygons > Texture**.

Planar Projection
This projection will take the UVs and lay them flat based on the X, Y, or Z- axis.

Cylindrical Projection
A projection like this is best suited to an object like a pole or a leg of a character.

Spherical Projection
This projection is best suited to an object that is round or oval in shape.

Automatic Projection

Automatic Projection is a type of projection that can apply multiple projections on a model at the same time. Based on the model, you select the number of planes that will be projected. This projection type is handy because it cuts up any overlapping UVs and lays them out accordingly.

This model, that was shown earlier in the Polygon Modeling section, was created out of a Primitive cube.

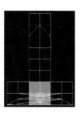

These UV coordinates are a combination of the default ones and additional UVs from the modeling operations.

These are the UVs after the Automatic Mapping operation is complete. This was done with the default settings.

Here the UVs are laid out after Automatic Mapping is completed. The UVs were selected and moved about in the 0 to 1 texture space to use up as much of the 0 to 1 area as possible. This UV information can be screen-grabbed and brought into a paint program to create texture information.

Texture Borders

When merging objects or creating multiple projections per model, texture borders are created. While this can be a desired thing, sometimes it is because of operations like reversing Normals of a face in the middle of an object. Texture borders can be sewn together to create continuous UVs.

The head above had its UVs mapped using the planar projection method. Texture borders are turned on and you can see where the individual projections were used.

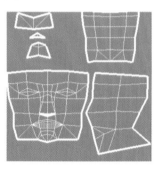

Here you can see the UVs laid out on the 0 to 1 coordinates space. If any UVs were outside this space, the texture would tile. The sides of the face were originally part of the side projection. These UVs were cut using **Edit Polygons > Texture > Cut UVs** and then sewn to the front projection using **Edit Polygons > Texture > Move and Sew UVs**.

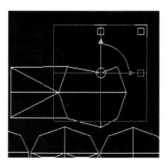

Move Component Manipulator

If you want to animate the UV coordinates of a model, select **Edit Polygons > Move Component**. This operation adds a node that can store animation data.

UV Texture Editor

You can position 2D textures on geometry by manually positioning the UVs to fit into the space of 0-1 for both U and V. This makes it possible to build textures that have many details tightly placed together to use as little memory as possible. UVs can be manipulated by using the Move, Rotate, Scale, or Move Component manipulators.

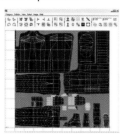

UV Editing

After the projection or projections have been applied to a model, you will probably have to do some editing of the UVs. This can require moving pieces around and sewing them to each other, or taking the UV information and maximizing it so that it makes more efficient use of the texture space. Editing UVs manually can be tedious work, especially if the model has a high polygon count. The tools in Maya allow you to perform many editing operations with one command.

Map UV Border

Edit Polygons > Texture > Map UV Border allows you to force the border of a UV mesh into the 0 to 1 texture space. This border can be made to take the shape of a square or a circle. The object that you are applying UV information to will dictate which shape is best. This operation is used in conjunction with Edit Polygons > Texture > Relax UVs.

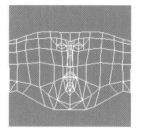

These UVs were created by using a spherical projection. This is not an ideal projection as it does not take full advantage of the texture space.

After the Map UV Border operation, UVs on the border were forced to take the shape of a square. The UV mesh may look twisted, but this is not the final result.

Relax UVs

Relax UVs takes the rest of the UV mesh and untangles it to fit within the border shape. There are options to pin the borders and pin selected UVs. The finished UV mesh gives you texture coordinates that make it easier for you to create a seamless texture map.

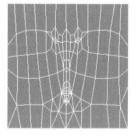
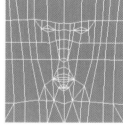

By changing the Max Iterations to 10 and applying Relax UVs twice, the resulting effect appears to be squashed. Applying Relax UVs again gives a similar result.

The face UVs were refined so it matched the model. The face UVs were then selected and Relax UVs with Pin Selected were used to layout the remaining UVs.

Layout UVs

Edit Polygons > Texture > Layout UVs is used when you have a projection with overlapping UVs. This operation will cut the UVs that overlap and lay them out in the 0 to 1 texture space.

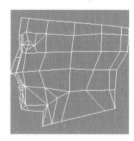
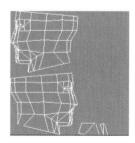

These UVs were created by using a planar projection in the X direction. Both sides of the head are overlapping, as are the back of the head and some faces for the nose.

Layout UVs were applied with the default settings. The overlapping pieces were cut from each other and laid out to fit in the 0 to 1 texture space.

This model has no UVs. You will see the steps and operations used to create the UVs.

Edges were selected so they UVs can be cut with Edit Polygons > Texture > Cut UVs. These UVs will be sewn on the face.

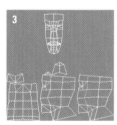

UVs were created after the Automatic Mapping operation. Some of the pieces need to be moved around and cut.

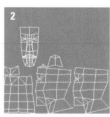

UVs were attached using Edit Polygons > Texture > Move and Sew UVs. This moved all the UVs in the texture shell.

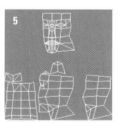

The UVs of the left side of the head were flipped so that they can be placed over the UVs of the right side.

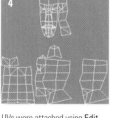

All edges are now sewn. Move the UVs close to each other as Sew UVs will average the distance between UVs.

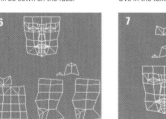

The same techniques were used for the left side of the face. UVs were moved to finish the shape.

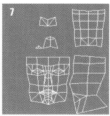

UVs were moved to overlap the UVs for the sides of the head. UVs were moved around to maximize texture space.

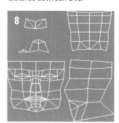

Edit Polygons > Texture > Normalize UVs was used to fit the overall UV information inside the 0 to 1 space.

Reflections

Reflections help create photorealistic images. The ability of objects to reflect their environment provides strong clues of a 3D world. As objects move or the camera pans, reflective highlights move over any reflective surface, which makes the scene look even more real. While realistic reflections are the ideal, you should remember that an audience does not usually look closely at the reflections. Therefore, simulated reflections can often be used to give the feeling of a reflected environment especially in animation.

Reflectivity = 0.1

Reflectivity = 0.5

Reflectivity = 1.0

Reflective Highlights

Reflections can be achieved using either Raytracing or reflection maps. Raytracing renders more slowly, but offers you true reflections. Reflection maps render more quickly and offer the illusion of reflectivity. In Maya, you can choose between these two types of reflections or use both at the same time for enhanced reflected detail. In the end, your decision will be based on a balance between rendering speed and final image quality.

Chrome Environment
This environment map gives a strong sense of a sky and a floor. It anchors the object to the ground with strong reflective highlights.

Reflectivity vs Reflected Color
These two attributes need to be distinguished. Reflectivity defines how much a surface will reflect while Reflected Color determines what is going to be reflected if Raytraced reflections are not used.

Environment Cube
Most of these objects and the stopwatch shown above use an Environment Cube texture that has various grayscale values assigned to the faces. This is a simple map that offers a quick way of defining a simple reflected environment. On the next page you can see how more scene-specific textures can be created.

Raytraced Reflections
The Raytraced reflections show you actual reflections of objects in the scene. Using reflections significantly adds more realism to the scene.

To Raytrace or not to Raytrace

When you set up reflections, you must decide whether you want to Raytrace them or not. At first, you would assume that Raytracing is the best way to create reflections, but in scenes with CG sets that don't fully encompass the objects, you may get nicer looking reflections from Reflection Maps. In some cases you may need to combine the two types of reflections for added photorealism.

Reflection Map Only
In this scene, you can sense a reflected environment, but you can't see objects reflected in each other. Also, the glass does not show any refraction because this scene is not raytraced.

Raytraced Only
This scene is a typical example of a problem that arises with reflecting CG sets. Since the physical environment in this scene is all white, the objects don't appear to have interesting reflections. Unless a complete CG set with four walls is built, this scene will not look as real.

Combined
This scene has both raytraced reflections and reflection maps resulting in the best of both worlds. A strong sense of a reflected environment is provided by the reflection maps and object reflections from the Raytracing.

Environment Maps

Environment maps are mapped to a Material node's **Reflected Color** attribute and offer a way of simulating a reflected environment. Maps such as **Chrome** and **Sky** use procedural information while the other maps use textures to create the simulated environment.

To create maps that represent your environment, you can use one of several techniques. Shown below are examples of the **Sphere**, **Ball,** and **Cube** techniques.

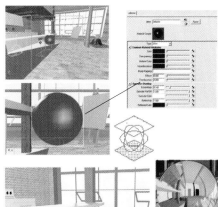

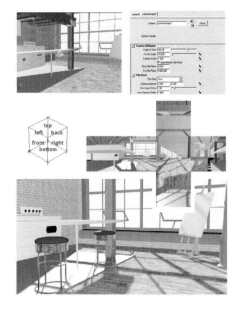

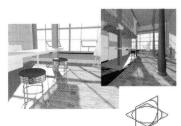

Sphere Environment Map

A rendered image taken from the back of the room is mapped to the stools using an Environment Sphere. This technique is not very accurate, but does offer an easy solution that creates results that are good enough for an animated scene.

Ball Environment Map

To create a ball texture, you need to place a sphere in the approximate location of the reflective object. Next, add a new camera and set a square resolution (ie. 512 x 512 pixels) in the Render Globals. Point the camera at the sphere so that the sphere's edges are just bounded by the resolution gate. Assign a highly reflective material with no Diffuse to the sphere, then Raytrace. The rendered sphere image can then be assigned to the stools as a Ball Environment Map. The sphere image can also be blurred to achieve a softer reflection.

Cube Environment Map

To create textures for an environment cube, you first set up a camera in the approximate location of the reflective object and hide the reflective object from the scene. Set the Aperture and the Resolution to be square, and the Angle of View to 90. This camera can then be animated over six frames to point in positive and negative X, Y, and Z directions. The scene should then be rendered. The resulting images can then be loaded into an environment cube that has its 3D placement icon located at the same position as the camera.

Raytraced Reflections

Raytraced reflections are the most accurate reflections but are slower to render than reflection maps. This render time can be optimized if you set up your scene correctly. A bit of planning will make it possible to limit the number of reflections per surface and which surfaces will reflect.

Initially, all material types, except Lambert, are created with a reflectivity setting of 0.5. This means that if you simply turn on Raytracing, the results will be slow since virtually every object will be participating. You can set the Reflection Limit too for some of your materials so that only the most important surfaces are reflective. You can then use Reflection maps for any less important surfaces.

Default Raytrace
640 x 480 - Render Time: 5:19

In this rendering, the default settings allow almost all the surfaces to reflect.

Optimized Raytrace
640 x 480 - Render Time: 3:18

In this optimized rendering, only those objects that require reflections are Raytraced.

Turn on Raytracing

To Raytrace, you must open the Render Globals window and in the Raytracing Quality section, set Raytracing to on.

Reflection Limits

The Reflection Limit determines how many reflections will be calculated. For example, if a ray hits a point on a reflective object, it bounces to a point on another surface. If the limit is 1, then the ray stops. If the limit is 2, then the ray bounces again to find another reflected surface. These extra levels of reflection are subtle and are only needed if you have a lot of highly reflective objects near each other. The Reflection Limit can be set in the Render Globals window and on the material with the lower setting taking precedence.

Can: Reflection Limit = 1

Can: Reflection Limit = 3

Optimizing Surface Materials for Raytracing

By default, every surface material type, except Lambert, has a Reflectivity of 0.5 and a Reflection Limit of 2. This means that all the surfaces will reflect if you turn Raytracing on. You can use the Attribute Spread Sheet to turn the Reflection Limit of all the materials that don't need to reflect to 0. This will allow the material to reflect environment maps but not to raytrace. You can then raise the Reflection Limit of any surfaces that need to show Raytraced reflections.

Visible in Reflections

By turning off the Visible in Reflections attribute, an object will not be considered for a reflection calculation during a Raytrace render.

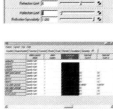

Bumps and Displacements

Bumps and displacements are used to create surface relief on an object. In most cases, it is quicker and easier to add a bump or displacement to an otherwise flat NURBS or Polygon surface to provide some detail rather than modeling the relief into the geometry.

Bump Maps and Displacement Maps

In Maya, you can choose between using a Bump map or a Displacement map or you can combine the two techniques. A Bump map renders faster and, in many cases, may be sufficient.

Bump Maps

A Bump map is used to create the illusion of surface relief. It does this by adjusting the surface normals based on the texture map's alpha values (by default). However, because the relief is only an illusion, you lose the effect along the edges of the surface and you will get no self-shadowing. It is recommended that you use square resolutions for bump maps.

Displacement Maps

A Displacement map produces results similar to those of a Bump map. However, the difference is that a Displacement map actually alters the shape of the geometry. You can use **Displacement to Polygon** to generate a polygonal model that takes on the shape of the displacement. This lets you visualize the surface detail in the interactive views.

Bump Value
You can adjust the height of the Bump by setting the Bump Depth value in the Attribute Editor.

Edges
The Bump map illusion is broken when you view the surface from the side. A Displacement map will modify the geometry.

Bump Map

File Texture or Procedural
On either a Bump or Displacement, you can map a File Texture or a Procedural Texture.

Displacement Map

Reflection and Bump Maps

Environment textures, such as Env Sky, mapped to **Reflected Color**, will not look correct when a bump map is applied. The surface will look bump mapped but the reflection map will look as though it is applied to a smooth surface. To get the proper results, connect the bump node's **Out Normal** to the Environment texture's **Normal Camera**. This tells the Environment reflection map what the bump map is doing to the surface normals.

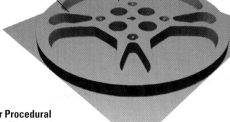

Before Connection

After Connection

Connection Editor
When you click+drag a node over another node in the Hypershade, the Connection Editor opens if the connection to be made is ambiguous.

Proper Reflections
Before you connect the bump2d node to the Environment texture node, the plane reflects as if it is flat. However, once the connection is made, the reflection takes the bumpiness of the surface into account.

Getting Good Displacement Results

The default values for Displacement maps may not produce the expected results. The following are some things you can do to improve the quality of the displacement.

Step 1: Tessellation
Adjust the tessellation on the object just high enough to capture the detail on the original surface before it is displaced. These values will work for the surface while the surface's Feature Displacement settings will set the tessellation for the displacement map itself.

Step 2: Visualize the Displacement
Map your intended displacement texture to the Color channel so it can be visualized with hardware shading in the modeling view. Turn on hardware shading and toggle on **Display Render Tessellation** to see the tessellation triangles on the surface.

Step 3: Set Displacement attributes
For each tessellation triangle, observe how much texture detail is in the triangle. If the triangle is large and the texture detail is fine, then the feature displacements **Initial Sample Rate** has to be large (from 30 to 50 or even higher). If the triangle is small and the texture details are not that fine, then Initial Sample Rate does not have to be very high (usually the default of 6 is good enough). Observe how sharp the texture details are and if there are many clean line or curved details. The sharper the features and the cleaner the lines, the higher the **Extra sample rate** needs to be. Try it at 0 and increase it only if the quality is not good enough.

Step 4: Test the Results
Use Lighting/Shading > Displacement To Polygon to bake out the displaced surface as a polygon mesh to visualize the results. If not enough detail is captured, try increasing the Initial Sample Rate. If the details are too jagged, try increasing the Extra Sample Rate. Disconnect the Displacement texture from the Color channel once you are satisfied with the results.

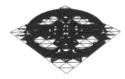

Modeling a Displacement Map

Displacement maps are great for adding detail to your models, but you might not always find the right reference material to build the maps. You can actually use Maya geometry and a projected incandescence map to build textures with accurate contour information. These maps can then be used as Displacement maps on any surface including a curved surface.

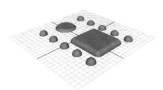

Step 1 - Create a model
Build a model that represents the surface relief that you want on your model. The detail should be placed flat on the ground.

Step 2 - Apply a ramp projection
Create a Lambert material with a grayscale ramp projection mapped to Incandescence. Project exactly to the side of the objects. The ramp defines the contours of the objects.

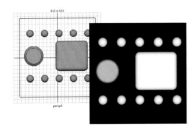

Step 3 - Render the map
Set your Render resolution to 512 x 512. Create a camera with a **Angle of View** of 1.0. A perspective camera is used in place of an orthographic camera so that you can use the camera's **Resolution Gate** to help you frame the objects. Render the scene with no lights.

Step 4 - Displace a surface
Map the resulting rendered image onto any surface as a Displacement map. Use the Alpha is Luminance option in the file node's Color Balance section. This technique can be used to create custom displacement maps.

Setting Displacement Depth

To set the depth of the Displacement, access the Attribute Editor of the texture used for the Displacement. Because the Displacement node uses the Alpha channel of the texture, you can set the depth by adjusting the **Alpha Gain** Value. A higher number produces a higher displacement. You can also reverse the displacement by using a negative number.

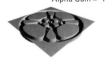

Alpha Gain = 0.35

Alpha Gain = -1.0

Sometimes after applying a displacement you will notice that the effect will make your object appear as if it has increased in volume. To fix this, adjust the **Alpha Offset** to a negative value. This creates the same amount of displacement but offsets the displacement to a point just below the surface of the geometry.

| No Displacement | Alpha Offset = 0.0 | Alpha Offset = -1.0 |

Combining Bump and Displacement Maps

In some cases, you may find it better to combine a bump and displacement in your final render. The advantage is that your object can have a greater degree of detail. Combining the maps may not be practical in an animation where the displaced object is moving or passing through the scene too quickly to warrant the extra rendering time. For a single image, the results may be worth it.

Bump Only
Using only a Bump map on an object, such as a wall, creates the appearance of surface relief.

Displacement Only
Using only a Displacement map will reshape the surface when it is tessellated and give an element of depth.

Combined
Combining the maps creates a more defined look to the brick texture by highlighting features on the brick texture as well as the spacing between the bricks themselves.

File Textures

File Textures are bitmap images that can be mapped to shading attributes. To create a File Texture, you must consider the size and shape of the surface that it is being assigned to and whether or not the texture will be repeated. This will allow you to create artwork that is properly proportioned for the surface.

There are many ways to create File textures. You can paint them yourself, or use scanned images or photos taken with a digital camera. An image editing program can then be used to manipulate the image before you save it in a Maya-friendly format such as TIFF or IFF.

Sizing Textures

When you create a texture for a surface, you must consider the shape of the surface. For example, if it is long and thin, you design the texture using those proportions. But concider resizing your textures into square images, which gives the best results when rendered.

Texture Libraries
Bitmap images are often available on CD-ROM or on the web. These collections offer high quality images that cover a wide range of surface types. A large collection of textures is available on the Alias website.

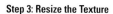

Step 1: Measure the Surface
Use the Create > Measure Tools > Distance Tool to find out the actual length (17.0664) and width (9.6) of the surface. For curved surfaces, duplicate isoparms, then use the Arc Length measure tool to determine the size.

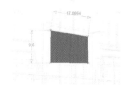

Step 2: Create the Texture
The length and width are used to create the actual artwork in a paint or illustration package. The proportions of the surface become the proportions of the texture map.

Step 3: Resize the Texture
A paint program is used to convert the image to pixels using a base-2 resolution such as 512 or 1024 for the long side. Next, create a square texture by adding pixels to extend the image's short side.

Step 4: Measure the Surface
The original proportions of the surface are used to accurately determine the 2D placement node's V Coverage (17.0664/9.6 = 1.78) and V Translate Frame ((1.78-1)/2 = 0.389) This will position the extra pixels off the surface.

3D Paint Tool

You can paint directly on any type of geometry in 3D space using either Artisan or Paint Effects brushes within the 3D Paint Tool. Texture files can be mapped to renderable attributes such as color, bump, transparency, and specular color.

The 3D Paint Tool will create blank texture files for you or it can paint on existing file textures that were created outside Maya. Alternatively, you can paint a quick scketch and then use it as a reference in another paint software.

Paint Effects Canvas

The Maya Paint Effects offers many wonderful 2D and 3D effects. It can also act as a simple paint package for creating texture maps. You can set up a canvas that is then saved and loaded as a texture.

Paint Effects offers many great paint brushes that can be used to build up texture maps. Each brush stroke is also stored in the mask channel which can be used to create transparency in your material later. You can read more about this powerful tool in the Effects chapter of this book.

Assigning Textures
Select the option box for Texturing > 3D Paint Tool. The displayed panel is based on the artisan tool. You then need to assign a File Texture to the desired attribute and set its resolution.

Painting Objects
You can paint with Artisan or Paint Effects brushes. Make sure the UVs of the painted objects are correctly layed out, if not, the results might not look like you want.

Create a Canvas
Select Window > Paint Effects to show up the panel. Select Paint > Paint Canvas. Click on Canvas > Set Size to create a square texture. Start to paint.

Paint on the Canvas
Select Canvas > Save to store the image in your sourceimages directory. Now as you paint on the canvas, the texture and the objects using it are updated. You may even want to use IPR to see the image update on the fly.

Tileable Textures

While Procedural Textures are tileable by default, File Textures have to be carefully set up if you want to use them as repeatable tiles. For a seamless look, you need to make sure that the edges match properly and that there are no definite patterns created by darker areas of the texture. Using a photograph taken of a brick wall, you can use an image editing program to create a tileable texture. You can also use Paint Effects to paint tileable textures directly.

The same brick texture is also assigned as a Bump map. This adds extra depth to the rendering of the brick.

Convert to File Texture

It is possible to convert 3D or 2D procedural textures into File texture maps. Once the convertion is done, the File textures are automatically mapped onto the surfaces.

There are some advantages and disadvantages using this technique.

Advantages:

• It is possible to touch-up or manipulate a File Texture in an Image Editor.

• It is generally much faster to render a texture than a complex procedural network.

• It is easier to fix texture problems than procedural textures.

Disadvantages:

• It is no longer possible to animate procedural texture attributes.

• The resolution of the texture is fixed.

• It can require large amount of disk space for storing and more memory during rendering.

• One File Texture is generated for each separate surface.

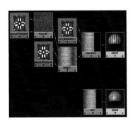

File Texture
As you can see here, the same result is achieved when a network is converted to a File Texture. It is up to you to decide weather or not to convert a network, depending on how you want to manage your project.

Step 1
A square section of the original photo was cropped out. It was also color corrected to create a lighter texture.

Step 2
The texture was tested in a repeating pattern in Maya. You can see how even though the texture appears ready for tiling, a definite pattern is visible.

Step 3
In Adobe Photoshop, the image was offset by half its value. This put the seam in the middle where you can see it.

Step 4
Using the Rubber Stamp tool, the lighter bricks were used to fix the darker areas where tiling problems were most apparent.

Step 5
A test of this texture shows a repeating pattern that works seamlessly. Only with close scrutiny can you begin to see some repeating patterns in the texture.

Convertion
The convertion consist of rendering the polygons of a surface using the same shader group.

Anti-alias
If on, sharp, jagged edges within the solid texture are blurred.

Bake Transparency
Specifies whether to compute transparency when baking lighting.

UV Range
Specifies the amount of the surface to sample in UV space.

X Resolution, Y Resolution
The horizontal and vertical resolution of the image file, measured in pixels.

File Format
Lets you choose a format in which to save the file texture.

Bake Shading Group Lighting
Bakes the lights that illuminate the selected surface into a new image file when you convert a texture or material into an image file.

Bake Shadows
Specifies whether to compute shadows when baking lighting.

Use No Lights

You can specify in a view panel to disable hardware lighting, so that no shading occurs. This is useful when you have already baked the lighting into a scene by using prelight or baking light maps and you don't want any additional hardware lighting to be added to the scene in the modeling viewports. To do so, select **Lighting > Use No Lights** in the desired view panel.

Photoshop File Textures

Adobe Photoshop files can be used anywhere in Maya, where you would normally apply textures. Maya converts a PSD file with layer sets to a Layered Texture to help visualize and work with the individual layers. You can also create a layered PSD file from within Maya in order to paint multiple channels (color, bump, specular, etc.) separately on an object in Photoshop.

You can use Maya's 3D Paint Tool to sketch out an object to act as guidelines for the areas on the Photoshop image that should be painted. At anytime, you can modify a PSD file in Photoshop, then refresh the image in Maya to see the modifications immediately.

Using PSD files

By default, Maya links a PSD file to the composite image, which is part of the PSD file. Maya can only read image and vector layers, so when the PSD node is linked to Photoshop's composite image, Maya supports anything that Photoshop supports, including layer styles, adjustment layers, text, and so on.

However, you can choose to link the PSD node to a layer set instead, in which case layer styles and adjustment layers are not supported and should be rasterized before the PSD file is read in Maya.

Using an existing PSD file in Maya

Maya artists can convert a PSD file to a Layered Texture, and see the layer sets as multiple PSD File Textures connected to a layered texture in Hypershade. If your Photoshop file is to be connected to different renderable attributes (such as color, transparency, bump, etc.), you will need to regraph the different PSD layers to plug them into the good attributes of the material.

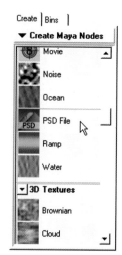

PSD File Texture Node
When mapping a texture into a renderable attribute, you can choose to create a PSD file or in the Hypershade, select Create Maya Nodes > 2D textures > PSD File.

What is a Layer Set?
In Adobe Photoshop, a Layer Set is a collection of layers that helps you better organize and manage layers. Use layer sets to easily move layers as a group, to apply attributes and masks to groups of layers, or to reduce clutter in the Layers palette.

Photoshop File Textures

materials and textures

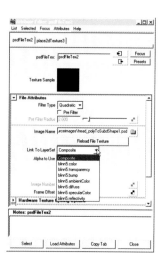

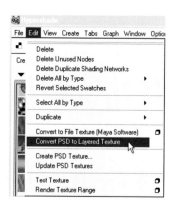

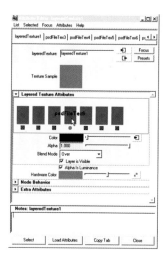

Link to Layer Set
By default, when creating a PSD texture node, Maya links the color of the node to the Composite layer. A Composite layer means the image once every layer were collapsed into one image. For your convenience, you can change this attribute to the prefered layer set found in the PSD file.

Convert PSD to Layered Texture
This command will convert a PSD file to a Layered Texture node. This action will basically split all the layer sets into their own PSD Texture node. Each one of the nodes can then be used and modified separately.

Layered Texture
If the PSD file contains alpha channels, you can specify witch alpha to use for each of the PSD Texture node. This is especially useful with the Layered Texture node, when you want to overlap textures.

135

Create a PSD file with layer sets from within Maya

When you create a PSD file from within Maya, you can select the channels to be painted in Photoshop. In order to be able to add and paint certain attriibutes, make sure the material assigned to the object supports the desired attribute. For example, if you need to paint the specular channel and a Lambert material is assigned to the object, the specular attribute will not show up in the Create PSD Texture panel.

These channels are then represented in Photoshop as layer sets, and you can add, edit, or delete any layer within a layer set. Any changes you make in Photoshop are piped back into the appropriate channels in Maya when you update the PSD node.

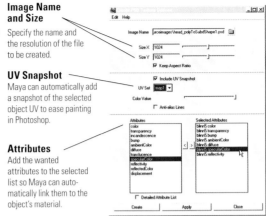

Image Name and Size
Specify the name and the resolution of the file to be created.

UV Snapshot
Maya can automatically add a snapshot of the selected object UV to ease painting in Photoshop.

Attributes
Add the wanted attributes to the selected list so Maya can automatically link them to the object's material.

Create PSD Texture Options
Select the geometry for which you want to create a Photoshop file then select Texturing > Create PSD Texture. Make sure the UVs of the selected model are within 0 to 1 space to get a good UV snapshot for painting reference.

Texture Layers
Maya will create a texture node for each channel previously selected. All the nodes are linked to the same PSD file, but to different layers within the file.

Adobe Photoshop
When the PSD texture file is openned in Photoshop, you can review the layer sets and make your changes to the image. For you convenience, a UV snapshot can be automatically generated.

Back in Maya
Once your Photoshop file is saved, you can select the modified texture node and click on **Reload File Texture** in the Attribute Editor.

Sketch out guidelines for paint application

You can use Maya's 3D Paint Tool to sketch out ("lipstick") where paint should be applied to an object. Painters can then paint more strategically in Photoshop because they can easily see where to apply the paint. This works especially well for NURBS models (that don't have UVs that you can use as a guideline), or for models with UVs that don't give you enough information to paint effectively.

Update All PSD Textures

When you modify outside Maya a PSD file that is connected to a Maya PSD node in your scene, you can update the image in Maya to show the modifications immediately. To do so, simply click on **Texturing > Update PSD textures**.

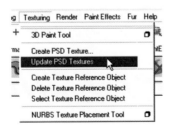

Default Attributes

	Lambert	Blinn	Phong	Phong E
Color	X	X	X	X
Transparency	X	X	X	X
Ambient Color	X	X	X	X
Incandescence	X	X	X	X
Bump Map	X	X	X	X
Displacement	X	X	X	X
Diffuse	X	X	X	X
Translucence	X	X	X	X
Specular Color		X	X	X
Reflectivity		X	X	X
Reflected Color		X	X	X
Eccentricity		X		
Specular Rolloff		X		
Roughness				X
Highlight Size				X
Whiteness				X
Cosine Power			X	

This table shows the default available channels that correspond to the layer sets that are created when you create the PSD file.

Attributes in the Selected Attributes list represent the channels to be painted. When you open the PSD file in Photoshop, each attributes listed here appears as a layer set.

Creating Texture Effects

Maya gives you the ability to create many unique and interesting texture effects. For example, the Layered Texture node allows you to layer different textures using a variety of blending techniques. Or you can take advantage of the Utility nodes in Maya. Some Utility nodes perform mathematical functions, while other utility nodes allows you to combine colors from different sources which can then be fed into one attribute. Still, others can gather certain information such as the surface normals of a geometry.

Layered Texture

The Layered Texture node lets you overlay several textures, then connect the results to a Material node. You can set or map the Alpha attribute for each layer to set its masking. You can also use Blend modes such as **Multiply, Lighten, Darken** and **Illuminate** for each layer to create effects similar to Layer modes in Adobe Photoshop. This texture node offers a lot of flexibility within a Shading network for working with textures.

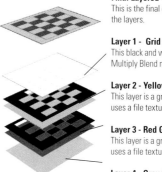

Final Layered Texture
This is the final composite of all the layers.

Layer 1 - Grid pattern
This black and white file texture uses a Multiply Blend mode.

Layer 2 - Yellow Granite
This layer is a granite texture node that uses a file texture as an Alpha mask.

Layer 3 - Red Granite
This layer is a granite texture node that uses a file texture as an Alpha mask.

Layer 4 - Grey Granite
This is the base layer. It does not need an Alpha mask.

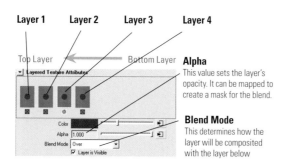

Alpha
This value sets the layer's opacity. It can be mapped to create a mask for the blend.

Blend Mode
This determines how the layer will be composited with the layer below

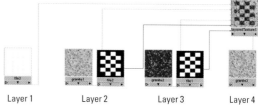

Layer 1   Layer 2   Layer 3   Layer 4

Utility Nodes

Utility nodes let you create specific effects that can be included in a Shading network. To create a Utility node, you can right-click in the Hypershade window and select **Create > Create Render Node...** then click on the **Utilities** tab. Each node can be added to the Hypershade window then connected to other nodes using the available input and output attributes. Each Utility nodes creates a particular effect and you need to understand how its capabilities relate to what you are trying to achieve.

Reverse

The Reverse node inverts the value of the input. It is useful when you have a single file texture that is mapped into Bump and Transparency. To create the proper results, you need two separate File Textures or you can use the Reverse node to invert the value that is mapped to the Transparency channel. In the example, the same File Texture is mapped to **Bump, Transparency,** and **Reflected Color**. However, the values needed for the Reflected Color are the opposite of the values needed for the other attributes. Therefore, by mapping the file texture into a Reverse node before mapping it into the Reflected Color attribute, you can use the same file texture for all three mappings.

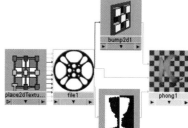

Multiply Divide

The Multiply Divide node is made up of three parts. There is an **Input 1** an **Input 2,** and an **Operator**. In this node, you can set the operator to perform either a **Multiply**, **Divide**, or **Power**. When you use the **Multiply** operation, the node multiplies the value of **Input 1** by **Input 2**. When you use the **Divide** operation, the node divides the value of **Input 1** by the value of **Input 2**. When set to **Power**, **Input 1** is raised to the power of **Input 2**.

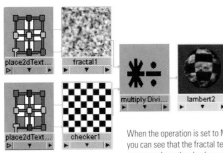

When the operation is set to Multiply, you can see that the fractal texture appears where the checker pattern is white (Value = 1). Where the pattern is black, there is no fractal, only black, as the value would equal 0.

Sampler Info

The Sampler Info node provides information about a point being shaded on a surface. With this information, you can build interesting shading networks. For example, when you connect the Facing Ratio of a Sampler Info node to the transparency channel of a **material node**, the **Sampler Info node** returns a value between 0 and 1 for points on the surface depending on their angle to the camera.

When the Normal of the surface is facing the camera, the value is 1 or transparent, and when the surface normal points 90 degrees from the camera, the value is 0 or opaque. In the example below, the **Facing Ratio** is connected to the **vCoord** of a ramp. The ramp is co nnected to the transparency of the Lambert material. Using the position of the black value on the ramp, you can control the amount of transparency on the material to get a good looking X-ray shader.

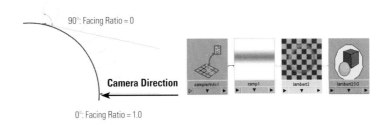

90°: Facing Ratio = 0

Camera Direction

0°: Facing Ratio = 1.0

Blend Colors

The Blend Color Utility node is made up of three main parts. First, you have two **Inputs** that each accept RGB channels. You can use these to load the color output from two textures. The purpose of this node is to Blend between these two inputs.

There is also a **Blender** attribute that controls how the first input is combined with the second input. Think of the two inputs as textures that are sitting on top of each other with the blender acting as a mask between them. If you map the blender attribute, this map will be the mask.

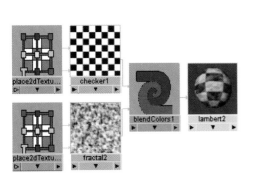

Condition

The Condition node produces a color based on a set of conditions that are specified in the attributes. This node requires at least one operation and then two color values.

You can use the Condition node to create a double-sided shader. This is done by using the Sampler Info node to provide information regarding the Normals of the surface. Using this information, the Condition node can distinguish whether the camera is looking at the inside or outside of a surface and will apply the color that is mapped to either the color 1 or color 2 channel.

By using the information of the direction of the surface Normals, Color 1 is applied to the geometry that has normals reversed to the camera, and color 2 to parts that have Normals pointing toward the camera.

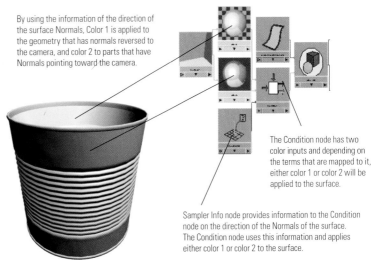

The Condition node has two color inputs and depending on the terms that are mapped to it, either color 1 or color 2 will be applied to the surface.

Sampler Info node provides information to the Condition node on the direction of the Normals of the surface. The Condition node uses this information and applies either color 1 or color 2 to the surface.

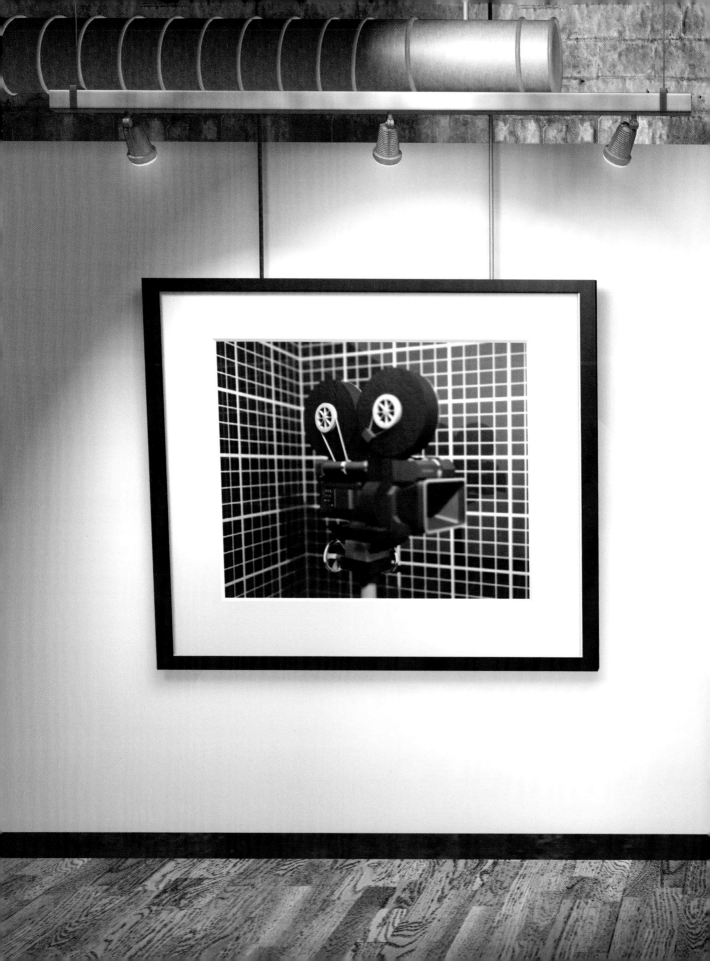

Digital Cinematography

When preparing a digital scene, lights and cameras play a very important role. Both lights and cameras make it possible to view objects, and see them in a realistic context. Artistically, they both allow 3D artists to control the look of their animation with the same creative control as a live-action cinematographer.

In some ways, the most difficult aspect of using lights and cameras in Maya is that the possibilities are endless. It is very easy to fly a camera around without a clear sense of purpose or add too many lights to a scene. The question is whether or not the creative decisions support the story being told. Therefore, it is a good idea to consider how live-action movies make use of camera moves and lighting.

Another challenge for 3D artists is to integrate CG elements and live action footage. They must take lighting and camera properties from the real world and mimic them in a scene so the audience does not have any idea the CG elements are even there.

How Lights Work

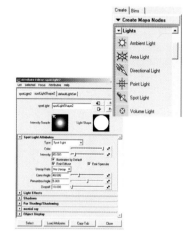

Light affects the way in which we see the world around us. Light defines the shape and form of objects and spaces, while at the same time, it works on an emotional level by setting mood and atmosphere. Learning to control light is an important 3D skill.

Cinematographers use light to illuminate the objects in the scene while supporting the scene's emotional context. The quality of light in a digital shot is equally important, although the rules are different.

Real World vs. Digital Cinematography

In the real world, light bounces. Light starts from a light source, such as the sun or a lamp, and is either bounced or absorbed by all surfaces. An object appears red because the green and blue light is absorbed while the red light is reflected. A cinematographer sets up lights, then measures the light levels, which include both direct and indirect light. This information is used to adjust the exposure settings of the camera.

In Maya, surfaces are illuminated directly by lights. There is no bounced light coming from other surfaces. This is because CG lighting doesn't bounce. Here, film isn't exposed to light and camera controls don't need to be adjusted. Light levels are, therefore, controlled using the intensity settings of the lights themselves.

Creating Lights
Lights can be created using either the Create > Lights menu or using the swatches in the Hypershade. Light attributes can be edited using the light's shape node.

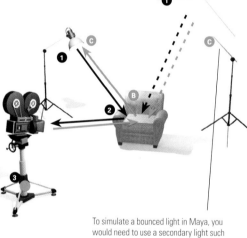

In the Real World
The film's exposure to light is controlled by the camera.

1 Light is emitted from a source with a controllable intensity. Direct light is hard, while light bounced from other surfaces is softer.

2 Light levels are measured using a light meter to determine the proper exposure settings for the camera.

3 Camera controls such as F-Stop, shutter angle, exposure time, and film speed are set to control how much light is exposed to the film.

To simulate a bounced light in Maya, you would need to use a secondary light such as an area light or an ambient light.

On the Computer
The scene's lighting is directly controlled by the lights.

A From the camera's point of view, the renderer samples a point on a surface.

B From the surface's shading group, a list of associated lights is used to determine which lights should be factored in.

C The light's attributes, such as intensity, color, and decay, are used to calculate the illumination on the surface.

Positioning Lights

Lights can be positioned using the **Show Manipulator Tool**. Each light is displayed with an eye point that defines the position of the light source and a look at point that defines where the camera is pointing. Adjusting these points sets the translation and rotation values on the light's Transform node.

The line between the eye and look at points defines the light's direction. Spot, Area, and Directional lights must have their directions set to work properly, while Ambient and point lights only require an eye point position.

You can also position a light by selecting the light, then choosing **Panels > Look Through Selected**. This lets you use the Alt key to dolly and pan the view as if it were a camera. This method often makes it more intuitive to position the light and its look at point.

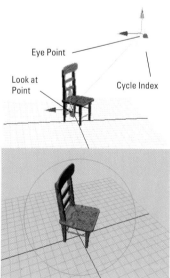

Looking through light

Light Types

Maya has several light types, each of which illuminates a scene differently. A typical scene combines a number of different light types. You can switch between light types in the Attribute Editor.

Spot

Spotlights emit light that radiates from a point within a limited cone angle. You can use this cone angle to limit the area receiving light.

Directional

Directional lights use parallel rays of light to illuminate a scene. Shading is very uniform without any hotspots. These rays are similar to the light of the sun, which hits the earth with parallel rays.

Point

Point lights emit light in all directions, radiating from a single point. This creates an effect similar to a light bulb. This light creates subtle shading effects with definite hot spots.

Area

Area lights emit light using a two-dimensional area. The area light's icon can be used to help define the light's direction and intensity. A larger area light has a stronger intensity.

Ambient

Ambient lights emit light uniformly in all directions. The **Ambient Shade** attribute adds positional behavior. Bump maps are not visible with ambient light alone.

Volume

Volume lights emit light in all direction on a finite distance, based on a light shape. The light shape can be a box, a sphere, a cylinder or a cone.

Light Nodes

When a light is created, it is built with two nodes. The Transform node holds all the information about the light's position and orientation. For most light types, scaling a light will not change its shape, or the effect of its illumination, but it will allow you to change the size of the light icon to make it more visible in the workspace. The one exception is with area lights, as their intensity is affected by scaling. The Shape node holds all the information about the light's illumination. Some of the spot light attributes can be edited using the **Show Manipulator Tool**. When using the Show Manipulator Tool to position a light, you can click on the **Cycle index** icon to access manipulators for controlling different attributes such as Cone Angle and Penumbra Angle.

Spot Light Attributes

The spotlight's Shape node contains attributes that control how the light will illuminate the scene. Since the spotlight contains the most attributes, it is used as the example here. The other light types contain a subset of the Spot Light Attributes.

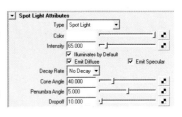

Intensity
This attribute determines how much light is emitted from the light source. As you increase the **Decay** and **Dropoff** values, you need a more intense light.

Color
You can set RGB values for the light being emitted. This will have an influence on the color of your scene.

Hotspot
The point where the light is most intense is referred to as the **hotspot**. You also know it as a specular highlight. The look of the highlight is a result of the intensity of the light and the shading qualities of the surface's Material node.

Dropoff
This attribute determines how much the light intensity diminishes as it gets to the outer edge of the light. This puts more emphasis on the light's hotspot.

Decay
This attribute determines how much the light intensity diminishes as the light gets further from its source. Therefore, if you choose to use **Decay**, you need to increase the **Intensity**.

Cone Angle
This attribute determines the width of the spotlight's cone of influence. The areas outside the cone are not illuminated.

Penumbra Angle
This attribute creates an area at the edge of the spotlight where the light fades. A larger value here creates a soft look for the light.

Light Effects

To create professional lighting effects, you have a number of tools at your disposal. You can turn on Barn doors or texture map the light's color or intensity to create Gobo effects,and you can also use Color and Intensity curves to affect these attributes over distance.

These effects offer you the kind of control a lighting technician needs to fully control the illumination of a scene. It is important to take your lights beyond the basic default settings if you want to achieve a professional look.

Light Effects Attributes
These attributes can be turned on, set, and mapped in the Attribute Editor.

Mapping Lights
It is possible to texture map the Color or Intensity of a light. These maps cover the area of the light and can be used to create Gobo or slide projector effects.

Slide Projector
If you texture map a light's Color, you get a slide projector effect. The light projects the image onto whatever surfaces lie in its path.

Barn Doors
When a lighting technician wants to prevent the light from spilling in all directions, he or she uses the light's Barn doors. Barn doors are flaps that surround the light and can be opened and closed. In Maya, you can turn on Barn doors in a spotlight's Attribute Editor. Select **Look through selected** to see the Barn doors and adjust them to block light in your scene. Using the **Show Manipulator** Tool, you can cycle to the Barn door manipulators and adjust them interactively. In the image shown here, the Barn doors are used to give a spotlight a rectangular shape that mimics a window is off the stage area.

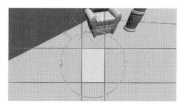

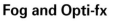

Gobos
A Gobo is a cutout that lighting technicians place in front of a light to get interesting shadow effects. To create a Gobo effect in Maya you can texture map the light's Intensity.

Negative Intensity
If you want to darken part of a scene, you can add an extra light that has a negative Intensity. This means that the light will remove light from the scene instead of illuminating it. This is a great tool for darkening the corner of a room.

Fog and Opti-fx

Fog and Opti-FX, such as glows and lens flares, let you mimic the way in which light reacts with the atmosphere, the camera's film back, and with our eyes. When a scene is rendered, glows are calculated at the end and composited onto the rendering while fog is rendered as part of the scene. Fog and glow are covered in more detail in the Effects chapter of this book.

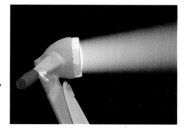

Light Fog
When you apply fog to a light, a shape is attached to the light that is mapped with a volume shader. This gives the appearance of the light beam illuminating dust and particles in the atmosphere.

Opti-FX
When you apply glow to a light, the point of the light's source can have halo and star effects. These simulate the real-life reaction of a camera's lens and film to light. The lens and retina of our eyes also react in a similar way.

Intensity Curves

Another way of controlling the decay on a spotlight is to use Intensity Curves. These curves let you specify the intensity of a light over distance in 3D space. You can use actual measurements from the scene to determine intensity.

To help measure the distance, you can constrain the light to distance locators. Select **Create > Measure Tools > Distance Tool** and place the two locators. **Point constrain** the light to the first locator and **Aim constrain** the light to the second locator. Now you can position the light using the first locator while the position of the second locator records the distance from the light to your aiming point. This distance can be used to set up the Intensity Curve.

To demonstrate how Intensity Curves work, the following diagrams show several spheres that lie on the light's illumination path. You can judge the results by comparing the curves to the illumination of the spheres. Fog has also been added to the light to further illustrate the effect of the curves.

This scene uses Intensity Curves to put less lighting on the chair while using more intense lighting on the back wall.

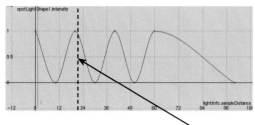

Creating the curves
Click on the Create button next to Intensity Curve in the light's Attribute Editor, then view the curve in the Graph Editor. The curve shown above is the default curve. Delete the middle points on the curve and change the distance of the second point from the default distance of 100 to a value that matches your measured distance. Later, you can add points to the curve to manipulate the illumination. The key is to remember that you are modifying intensity over distance. Therefore, you need to know the distances of objects from your light.

Simple Curve
This curve shows a linear decay from an Intensity of 5 to 1. The Distance value of the second key was taken from the Distance Tool measurement.

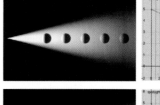

Reshaped Curve
This curve goes from an Intensity of 5 to 1 with a dip in the curve near the middle. Correspondingly, the illumination diminishes at that distance.

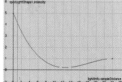

Multiple Points
The intensity jumps up and down to put the focus of the lighting on the center sphere and the background. Other objects are not affected.

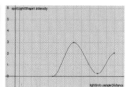

Color Curves

Similar to Intensity Curves, Color Curves let you use three curves to set the RGB values over distance. You can use these curves to create focused areas of colored light within a scene. Remember that RGB values of 1, 1, 1 create white light. You can animate the RGB values to get different colors of light. You can get the values from a color picker but you have to enter the values in the graph by hand. These curves can then be combined with Intensity Curve settings to create even more subtle effects.

Decay Regions

If you turn on **Decay Regions**, you can set up zones for a spotlight with specific start and end distances. Areas between zones have no light, while the zones themselves show the light's existing decay values. A spotlight has three regions you can work with. You can interactively edit the positioning of the Decay Regions using the Show Manipulator Tool.

White to Red to White
Three curves are used to transition the color from white to red to white over distance. This adds red to the central object while leaving the other objects uncolored.

With Intensity Curve
By combining Color and Intensity Curves, you can create more controlled lighting conditions. Here, the Intensity Curve is reshaped to create decay.

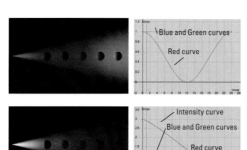

Light Manipulators
When you select a light, and then choose the Show Manipulator Tool, you can click on the cycle index to go to the Decay Region manipulators. Click+drag the rings on the ends of the regions to position them. The areas between the regions get no light at all and can be used to clip the light. This can be helpful if you want to start a light from a point other than the source itself.

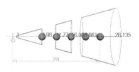
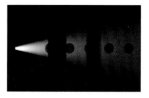

Casting Shadows

One of the most dramatic aspects of lighting is in the area of no light. Shadows add drama to your scene while helping to anchor characters and props to the ground. If your character leaps into the air, you know what is happening because the shadow and character no longer touch each other.

In Maya, there are many factors that affect the look and quality of your shadows. You can choose from Depth Map and Raytraced shadows which offer different levels of quality and speed. Sometimes light attributes, such as Cone Angle, will affect your shadows and must be taken into account. The more you know about how shadows are cast, the easier it will be to adjust the appropriate attributes.

Depth Map Shadows

Depth Map shadows are the more efficient of the two shadow types. A Depth **Map shadow** can be created by setting **Use Depth** Map Shadows to On in the light's Attribute Editor.

Depth Map shadows work by recording the Z-depth information from the light's point of view, then using this information to evaluate whether or not a point in your scene is in shadow. The diagram below shows how a spotlight evaluates Depth Map information to generate shadows. You can see that the Depth Map is generated from the light's point of view.

With and Without Shadows
Here are two shots of a scene. The first does not use shadows and the second one does. You can see how the scooter in the second image is much more grounded, and it is easier to read the scene's depth. While shadows do require extra work when you set up a scene, they are well worth the effort.

Step 1
When rendering starts, a Depth Map is created that measures how far the various objects are from the light. White is used to show surface points closest to the light, while the various shades of gray show a greater distance from the light.

Step 3
This measurement is then compared to the depth information stored in the Depth Map. If the point's distance is greater than the distance stored in the Depth Map, the point is in shadow.

Step 4
If the point is in shadow, the light's illumination does not contribute to the shading.

Note: Another light, such as an ambient light, may illuminate parts of the scene where the spotlight does not. That is why you can see the wood texture underneath the chair in this image.

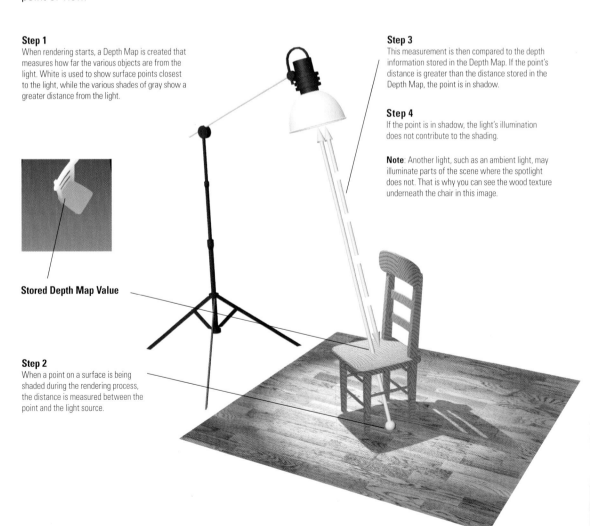

Stored Depth Map Value

Step 2
When a point on a surface is being shaded during the rendering process, the distance is measured between the point and the light source.

Raytraced Shadows

To calculate Raytraced shadows, Maya sends a ray from the camera and when this ray hits a surface, it spawns another ray toward the light. This shadow ray reports whether or not it hits any shadow-casting objects on its way to the light. If it does hit a shadow-casting object, then the original surface is in shadow.

Raytraced shadows have the disadvantage of being slower to render than Depth Map shadows. However, depending on the look you are interested in, there are several reasons why you would use Raytraced shadows in your scene. These include transparent shadows, colored transparent shadows, and shadow attenuation.

If you want Raytraced shadows, but not reflections and refractions, then set Reflections and **Refractions** to 0 in the **Render Quality** section of the **Render Globals**.

Transparent Shadows

When casting shadows from transparent objects, Depth Map shadows do not take into account the transparent qualities of a surface, while Raytraced shadows do. This may be a deciding factor when it comes to choosing which technique you will use to cast shadows.

Depth Map Shadows
When a Depth Map is generated at the start of a render, it does not take transparency into account. For this reason, the shadow generated by a Depth Map will appear solid.

Raytraced Shadows
Raytraced shadows are computed during the rendering process. Therefore, the transparency of the object is taken into account. As a result, Raytraced shadows clearly represent the details of a transparent or transparency mapped object.

Colored Transparent Shadows

Another feature of Raytraced shadows is that you can create colored transparent shadows. For example, in the real world, when light passes through a stained glass window, you see the colors transmitted by the light passing through the window onto the floor. In Maya, Raytraced shadows will automatically create colored shadows when the transparency channel on a material is colored or when it is mapped with a colored texture.

Raytraced Shadows
The color of the transparency automatically casts a colored shadow.

Depth Map Default
732 x 450 pixels
Render Time - 1x

Depth Map Soft
732 x 450 pixels
Render Time - 1.05x

Raytrace Default
732 x 450 pixels
Render Time - 1.38x

Raytrace Soft
732 x 450 pixels
Render Time - 11.87x

Default Renderings
Using the default settings built into a spotlight, the Raytrace rendering offers a sharper shadow than the Depth Map shadows. Rendering time is longer for the Raytraced scooter.

Soft Shadows
By tweaking the Depth Map shadows attributes you can see much better results. Using **Light Radius** and **Shadow Rays** to soften the Raytraced shadows, you can see how the rendering took even longer.

Shadow Attenuation

By default, Raytraced shadows look more accurate and crisp than Depth Map shadows. This can result in an undesirable computer-generated look in most cases. To avoid this, the shadows can be softened using a combination of a non-zero **Light Radius** and **Shadow Rays** greater than 1. These controls are found in the **Raytrace Shadow Attributes** section of the Attribute Editor for a light.

The biggest difference between a Raytraced soft shadow and a Depth Map shadow is that a Depth Map shadow is evenly soft around its edges. By contrast, a Raytraced shadow will dissipate or attenuate with distance from the shadow-casting object. This can be slow to render but is often used to create beautiful looking shadows in still renderings.

Depth Map Soft Shadows
The light's **Dmap Filter** value affects the softness of a Depth Map shadow.

Raytraced Soft Shadows
Light **Radius** and **Shadow Rays** define the softness of a Raytraced shadow.

Shadow Limit

When working with Raytraced shadows, you should also set the **Shadow limit** attribute. For example, if you have a shadow-casting object with several transparent surfaces behind it followed by an opaque surface, you would expect to see a shadow on the opaque surface. In order to see this shadow, set the **Ray Depth Limit** on the light to a value that is the number of transparent surfaces + 1. Be sure that the **Shadow limit** in the **Raytracing Quality** section of the **Render Globals** is not set lower than this value, or you will not see your shadow.

Depth Map Shadows

To successfully shadow your scenes using Depth Map (Dmap) shadows, you must work to get the best quality shadows with the least impact on rendering time. Various shadow attributes influence the final look of a shadow and how fast the scene will render.

To control the quality of a Depth Map shadow, there are several key attributes that affect how the Depth Map is generated and how it is used during a rendering. For example, the **Depth Map Filter Size** lets you soften the edge of the shadow, while the **Dmap Resolution** lets you generate more detailed Depth Maps. Other light attributes, such as **Cone Angle** and **Dmap Focus**, determine how much area is shadowed by the light. By learning more about these key attributes, you will be in a better position to make good shadowing decisions.

Shadow Quality
The quality of a Depth Map shadow is influenced by the shadow attributes as well as other attributes such as shading Anti-aliasing.

Dmap Resolution

This value determines the size of the Depth Map. The higher the resolution, the more accurate the details of the shadow will be. As the resolution increases, the rendering time goes up. Therefore, you should make sure that your Dmap is focused as tight as possible on the shadow-casting object before increasing the **Dmap Resolution**.

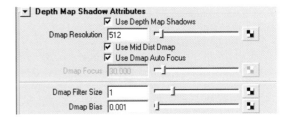

Cone Angle and Dmap Focus affect the coverage of the depth map.

Light

512 pixels

512 pixels

Depth map

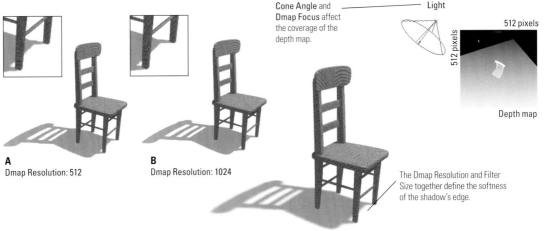

A
Dmap Resolution: 512

B
Dmap Resolution: 1024

The Dmap Resolution and Filter Size together define the softness of the shadow's edge.

Dmap Filter Size

This value blurs the Depth Map as the shadows are being rendered. This helps soften the edge of the shadows and create better anti-aliasing. The appropriate **Filter size** value depends on the resolution of your maps and how the shadow is focused on your shadowing objects. If you increase the Filter size, your render time will increase. If you increase the **Dmap Resolution**, you need to increase the filtering to get the same softness, which will also lengthen render time.

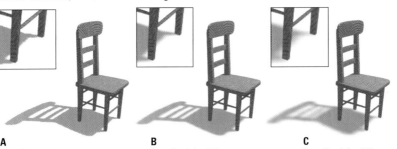

A
Dmap Resolution: 512
Dmap Filter Size: 1

B
Dmap Resolution: 512
Dmap Filter Size: 3

C
Dmap Resolution: 256
Dmap Filter Size: 3

Soft Shadows
Very soft shadows can be achieved by lowering the resolution and increasing the filter size which will render very quickly. However, with animations, lowering the resolution too much can lead to flickering shadows. You must find the right balance.

Depth Map Shadows

digital cinematography

Focusing the Depth Map on a Spotlight

As you position your lights and set your Cone Angle, you affect the area that may be included in the Depth Map calculation. If the Dmap Resolution remains the same, increasing the Cone Angle can force each pixel in the Depth Map to describe a larger area, potentially causing a pixilated shadow. It is important to learn how Maya focuses the Depth Map and how you can control it.

Shown below are several cases where the **Cone Angle**, Use **Dmap Auto Focus** and **Dmap Focus** have been set. You can see how the Depth Map relates to the actual **Cone Angle** in each case.

If not focused, a light can create a poor quality, jagged shadow. A better result may be achieved with a more tightly focused Depth Map.

Cone Angle 40 - Dmap Focus: Auto
The Cone Angle limits the size of the Dmap coverage when the light covers an area smaller than the shadow casting objects.

Cone Angle 80 - Dmap Focus: Auto
When the Cone Angle covers an area larger than the shadow casting objects, Auto Focus keeps the Dmap tightly focused on their bounding box.

Cone Angle 80 - Dmap Focus: 36
With Use Dmap Auto Focus set to Off, you can set a specific angle to focus the Depth Map on the chair.

Cone Angle 80 - Dmap Focus: 20
If you set the Dmap Focus too small, the shadow will be cut off or may not appear at all.

Reusing Depth Maps

By default, a Depth Map is generated for each light for each frame of animation. This is designed to make sure that the changing position and/or shape of animated objects is taken into account for each frame. If the lights and objects in a scene are not animated, such as camera-fly-throughs, you would only require one depth map for the entire animation.

To accomplish this, use the Disk Based Dmaps attributes found in the light's Attribute Editor to write and re-use Depth Maps. This will speed up your render time because Maya will not need to re-render the Dmap at the start of each frame.

Shown below are the three options available under Disk Based Dmaps and a description of what happens when each is used.

Directional Light Depth Maps

Since directional lights do not have a Cone Angle, **Use Dmap Auto Focus** determines the Depth Map coverage. To get accurate detailed shadows, you may need to use the manual **Dmap Focus** attribute to reduce the area covered by the Depth Map and possibly increase the **Dmap Resolution**.

Point Light Depth Maps

Point lights can each create up to 12 Depth Maps. This includes the Mid Distance Dmaps and the standard Dmaps for positive and negative X, Y, and Z axes. The light looks in all these directions, and only generates Dmaps when it encounters any shadow casting objects. You can also control exactly which axes the light can cast shadows along.

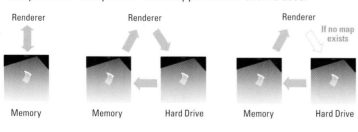

Off
A Depth Map is generated at the start of each frame. Once the Depth Map has been used to calculate shadows for that frame, it is thrown away.

Overwrite Existing Dmap(s)
The Depth Map is created and used in calculating shadows. At the same time, it is saved to your hard drive so that you can reuse it in future renderings. This new Depth Map will overwrite any existing map. You can use the Fcheck utility to view the map. Press Z in Fcheck to see the depth channel.

Reuse Existing Dmap[s]
If a Depth Map has been previously saved, it is loaded from your hard drive and reused. If there is no map then a new one is created and stored on the hard drive.

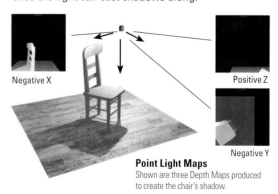

Point Light Maps
Shown are three Depth Maps produced to create the chair's shadow.

Lighting Setups

Setting up lighting involves a combination of several elements. The direction of the light, how many lights you use, and the properties of each light all contribute to the illumination of a scene. In many cases, you are attempting to create lighting that either mimics real-world lighting or studio/movie set lighting. The Importance of Light Placement

The way an object is shaded helps define its shape and form. This shading is dependent on the placement and quality of the lighting. You can, in fact, use light to sculpt an object by controlling the way its shading and shadows work together. First, you must learn how to place lights so they enhance the form of your objects.

If you set up a single light, you can see how its placement affects the look of an object. If you then add a second light, you can begin to set up more complex lighting.

Directional Light Source   Point Light Source

Shading with Light
The shading of the object is defined by its material qualities and by the angle and intensity of the light hitting it. In a simple example, you can see how the angle at which light hits the surface defines the shading.

The light is hitting the objects directly from above. The spherical shapes appear cut in half, while the rectangular shapes are only defined on one of their faces.

The light is hitting all the surfaces equally. The rectangular objects are receiving equal illumination on all faces. This makes it hard to read the shape. The object's shadow is also hidden.

The light is hitting each surface at a different angle. Now the faces are clearly defined with distinct levels of illumination. The drawer's shape is more clearly defined by this shading.

With multiple lights, each with different intensities, you get a more subtle sculpting of the form. Illumination appears less like stage lighting with the addition of ambient lighting.

Soft Lighting

When lighting a scene, you can create a softer, more diffuse look by choosing the appropriate light type and by softening the edges of the shadow and the penumbra.

Lights that emit from a single point, such as spotlights and point lights, render with hard edges and strong shading. Lights that emit from more than one point, such as an area light, give a softer look as the surface shading and shadows become less prominent. Multiple spotlights and ambient lights can also be used to create a similar look.

To further enhance the diffuse qualities of a light, you can soften the edge of a light's penumbra by adjusting attributes such as **Decay, Dropoff**, and **Penumbra Angle**. To add the same softness in the shadow edges, you can adjust the **Dmap Filter Size** and **Dmap Resolution**.

Single Light with Hard edges
This light uses default settings to create a hard look to the lighting.

Single Light with Soft Edges
Light and shadow attributes diffuse the edges of the light.

Two lights with Soft Edges
Here an ambient light is added to the scene to create less contrast. Area lights also make good secondary lights.

Multiple Lights with Soft Edges
The scene uses several key lights that are slightly offset from each other. This further softens the shadow's edge.

Basic Lighting

In animation, basic character illumination can be accomplished with two or three lights. The key light is the main light that illuminates the scene, emphasizes the character, and helps establish mood. Secondary lights are used to fill the dark areas. Sometimes, back lights are used to make sure that a character stands out from its surroundings. This basic lighting setup works well and, in most cases, you only require extra lights for background objects.

Key Lighting
The key light is the most intense light aimed at a character. In a complex scene, there may be several key lights focusing the audience on different parts of the set. This light is the hardest light in the scene and should have strong shadows.

Fill Lighting
The fill light is designed to lighten the shadow areas of a scene. This light is placed on the opposite side of the character. It is a soft light that may or may not cast shadows. Ambient and area lights work well as fill lights because they offer a more even illumination.

Scenery Lighting

If your key light does not fully illuminate your scene, you may need to add special lights. These should work with the key lights and preserve enough contrast so that the scene is not washed out.

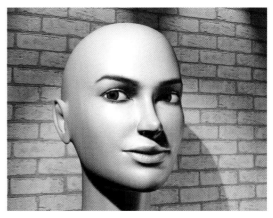

Background and Special Lighting
To illuminate a set, you often need to add lights that illuminate the background surfaces, but that do not take away from the main character. One approach is to use light linking to help you design the character lighting and set lighting separately.

Outdoor Lighting

For daytime outdoor lighting, your key light is the sun. A directional light is a good choice for this light because it has parallel rays. In a real outdoor scene, light will bounce which illuminates all the surfaces a little. Some low-intensity directional lights pointing up from the ground can help create this effect.

Shadows are sharp and clear during sunny parts of the day, while cloudy or twilight portions of the day create less pronounced shadows. On a cloudy day, you have less definition in the shading as the light is very diffuse.

Sunny Day
In this scene, a strong directional light offers the key lighting with several low intensity directional lights pointing up from the ground to mimic bounced light. Ambient light is also used to simulate bounced, diffuse light.

Light Linking

One feature available in Maya that doesn't exist in the real world is light linking. You can "tell" a surface to only be lit by specific lights or you can tell a light which surfaces it should illuminate. This lets you design lighting for different parts of your scene without affecting all of the objects. This can help speed up rendering because not all the lights in the scene will be calculated for all of the surfaces.

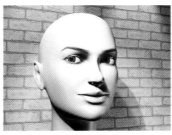

No Light Links
All the lights are being used on all surfaces. The lighting on the face is too intense.

Linked Lights
The walls have their own lights, while the face uses different lights.

light Linking Workflows
You can select Lighting/Shading > Light Linking > Light Centric or Object Centric to open up the Relationship Editor. From this editor you can set up light linking relationships by highlighting or unhighlighting items in the two lists. A faster way to link lights is to select your lights and objects, then choose Lighting/Shading > Make Light Links and Break Light Links to make the connections directly without opening the Relationship Editor. IPR is a great help when setting up light linking.

Scenery Lighting

While key lights and fill lights are built with the main purpose of illuminating your character, there is also a need to create lights that are part of the scenery. These background lights are designed to illuminate your digital set and to represent the light sources visible in the scene, such as windows or light fixtures. While there should be some logical relationship between these and the key and fill lights, the main role of scenery lighting is to make the set look realistic.

Light Fixtures

In a typical scene, there are often light fixtures that represent light sources. SinceMaya lights have no physical presence, these fixtures are created with a combination of geometry and lights. In fact, you may use more than one Maya light to help get the look of a particular fixture.

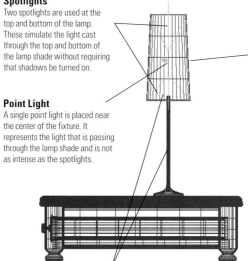

Spotlights
Two spotlights are used at the top and bottom of the lamp. These simulate the light cast through the top and bottom of the lamp shade without requiring that shadows be turned on.

Point Light
A single point light is placed near the center of the fixture. It represents the light that is passing through the lamp shade and is not as intense as the spotlights.

Incandescence Map
In the real world, the illumination of a lampshade by the light inside creates some self-illumination. You could use Translucence for this (see below), but an incandescence map offers you more control. Here, a ramp that has a gradation from gray to super white (RGB values above 1.0) is used to map the **Incandescence**.

Table Lamp
With this lamp, you would expect to be able to use a point light to do all the work. The problem is that if you use this light to cast shadows, the lampshade and maybe even the lamppost cast big, dark shadows and the lampshade appears dark on the outside. To resolve this, you need to use a few lights and some texture maps.

Casting Shadows Turned Off
On the lampshade and the lamppost you need to set **Cast shadows** to **Off** in the **Render Stats** section of their Shape nodes. This allows the point light to illuminate and shadow other objects without casting a big shadow from the lamp shade.

Translucence

In the case of the lampshade, you need to see the illumination of the light on the side of the surface that is facing away from the light. There will be other surfaces in your scene, such as blinds or screens, that may need to have light and shadows pass through them to illuminate the back side of the surface. You can accomplish this by setting the **Translucence** attribute on the object's Material node. This value will determine how much of the light will be visible on the back side of the surface.

Without Translucence
Here, you can see that the light and shadows hitting the screens have no effect on the back of the surface. To fake this with an incandescence map would be much more difficult here than on the lamp shade.

With Translucence
With Translucence set on the screen's Material node, you can see the illumination and the shadow cast by the railing. This effect works with Depth Map shadows and does not require Raytracing.

Headlights

This headlight shows a lighting situation that is not dealt with by a default light. This kind of headlight has a light bulb in its center that is then bounced off a highly reflective surface. This creates a spotlight effect where the beam of light emerges, not from a point, but from the face of the light fixture.

To achieve this effect in Maya, you can use the Decay Regions you learned about in the Light Effects section of this chapter. Put a spotlight behind the light fixture, then make sure that its first Decay Region has no length and the second starts from the face of the fixture. This will create a solid beam of light that looks great with some light fog.

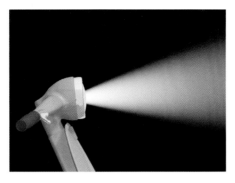

Default Light
Here you can see that a default spotlight radiates from the center of the light instead of from the fixture's front face.

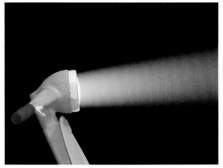

Light with Decay Regions
This image shows the use of Decay Regions to start the illumination from the face of the fixture. The light is actually behind the object.

Decay Regions
The light is positioned behind the fixture, with its cone of light aligned with the edges of the fixture's front face. The Decay Regions control the light so that there is only illumination in front of the fixture. You could also use an Intensity Curve for this, but the Decay Region manipulators make it easier to set up.

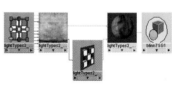

Spotlight

Decay Regions

Lighting without Lights

In some cases, you may want to have background elements that use a complex lighting setup, but you don't want to render all the extra lights. In these cases, it is possible to bake the lighting using **Convert to File Texture** found in the Hypershade window. When you select the Shading group node and the surface, then convert using the **Bake Shading Group Lighting** option, the complete shading network, including material node and lighting information, is baked into a single file texture that is connected directly into a new Shading group node and automatically assigned to the surface. At this point, lights no longer influence the shading on the surface so they can be deleted.

You could also accomplish this type of effect using hand-painted incandescence maps. If you create a grayscale image that uses white or superwhite for highlight areas and gray or black for darker areas, then this image can be mapped as an incandescence map on top of the existing textures. This gives you a lot of control but it relies on your ability to paint all the subtleties of an illuminated surface. In many cases, the baked lighting method will give you more realistic results.

Incandescence-mapped surfaces will not have shadows cast on them by your characters. You would, therefore, need a shadow pass cast from your character that can be layered onto the background during compositing.

Step 1: Original Scene
Here is a simple background set that is illuminated by a few lights. You can bake this lighting into a file texture so that the lights can be removed to optimize render time. This is a way to optimize complex scenes and is not required for the average Maya rendering.

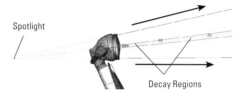

Step 2: Select the Shading Group Node
Select the Material node that is assigned to the surface you want to bake. Click on **Graph > Output Connections**. Select the **Shading Group** node and then press the Shift key and select the surface. Select **Edit > Convert to File Texture - options** and set Bake Shading Group Lighting to On.

Step 3: Converted Textures
When you **Convert to File Texture**, you are able to set a file texture size. Then Maya bakes the complete shading network into a single file texture. This file texture is mapped directly to a new shading group that has been assigned to the selected surface.

Step 4: Final Scene
With the resulting shading groups and file textures, the scene renders the same as the original but without requiring the lights. The perceived illumination is instead created by the texture maps. Now you can focus on lighting your characters.

How Cameras Work

When you first start working with Maya, the Perspective view offers you a way to tumble, track, and pan using a 3D camera. As you get closer to rendering your scene, you need to start learning more about this camera, especially in terms of how its capabilities relate to traditional cinematography.

A real-world camera uses controls, such as F-Stops, to control how much light is admitted into the camera. The Maya camera doesn't require these controls for lighting or exposure, but other controls exist to make the Maya camera act as much as possible like a real camera.

From Real World to CG Cameras

To better understand how the Maya CG camera works, it is helpful to compare it to a real-world camera. A real-world camera is designed to take bouncing light and focus it onto the camera's film. In this way, camera controls are closely linked to lighting controls. Maya deals with lighting and cameras separately. Below is a short description of why real-world cameras and CG cameras work differently.

Diameter of pinhole can cause some blurring

Pinhole Camera
The first cameras used a hole punched in a box the size of a pin to focus the light onto a back plate. This small opening would only allow a little light into the camera and the film required a long exposure to the light. The pinhole camera didn't work well in low-light situations and it could not film moving objects since the long exposure would cause the image to blur. To let in more light, the pinhole camera required a larger opening that would no longer be focused and would result in a blurred image.

Lens-based Camera
Lenses were developed to allow more light into the camera while still focusing it to a point on the film back. This made it possible to take pictures that were exposed in a fraction of a second, which, in turn, made it possible to film moving subjects. The different lenses have properties that affect the final look of a shot. The cinematographer's job is to manipulate these properties to the advantage of the film.

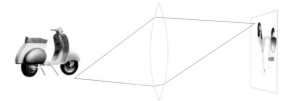

In Maya
Since CG cameras get lighting information from the surface itself, the pinhole camera model can be used without worrying about lighting levels. The CG pinhole is actually a point that has no diameter, which ensures perfect focus with no blurring in the image. Moving objects can be captured without worrying about motion blur and the camera is always in focus. While this sounds like a cinematographer's dream, in fact it means that some of these effects have to be faked in CG to make the images look real.

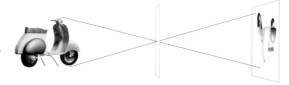

Camera Effects

In a real-world camera, the camera causes various effects including motion blur, depth of field, and lens flares. In Maya, these effects are not automatically created. You must consciously turn them on to add them to a shot.

Another real-world effect is lens distortion. This distortion is a result of the curve of the lens that causes lines at the edge of an image to bend. In the pinhole camera model, this distortion does not occur.

Motion Blur
In real life, the camera's shutter speed is often slower than a moving object and the resulting frame is blurred.

Depth of Field
This lens effect blurs objects that are in front of, or behind, the plane of focus based on a Focus Distance and an F-Stop value.

Angle of View and Film Back

In a real-world camera, the image is captured through the lens on the back of the camera, known as the film back. The film back represents the plate where the film is exposed. The distance between the front of the lens and this plate is the focal length, and different lenses are actually designated by this value. In Maya, the **Film Back** and **Focal Length** are used to calculate the **Angle of View** that defines the perspective image seen through the camera. The relationship between these two values mimics what happens in the real world so that you can use your photographic experience to help you with Maya cameras.

Film Back/Film Gate
In Maya, the Film Back is the location of the aperture plate, which is called the Film Gate. Maya includes several default Film Gates that match real-life cameras.

Aperture
The Camera Aperture settings define the length and width of the Film Gate. These measurements, along with the Focal Length, are used to calculate the Angle of View.

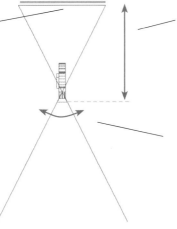

Focal Length
In Maya, Focal Length is the distance between the pinhole of the camera and the Film Back. The Focal Length describes the focal properties of a lens and is used to define the Angle of View. If you increase the Focal Length, you decrease the Angle of View.

Angle of View
This attribute offers an alternative method of changing the Focal Length. If you change either of these, the other updates automatically. In the end, the camera stores the Focal Length value and uses a built-in expression to generate the Angle of View. Artists who don't have a photographic background might find this attribute easier to work with, but when you animate, only Focal Length can be keyed.

Film Gate: 35 mm Academy

17 mm	65.68°
28 mm	42.80°
50 mm	24.76°
85 mm	14.71°
135 mm	9.29°

Focal Length Chart
Shown here are different Focal Lengths and the resulting Angle of View. Note that the Angle of View would be different depending on your Film Gate and your Film Fit.

Film Fit

The Film Gate is a metal frame that sits over the film and determines the size and shape of the exposed area of the film. In Maya, the film is actually the rendered image which has its aspect ratio defined in the **Render Resolution** section of the Render Globals window. The **Film Fit** defines the relationship between the **Film Gate** and the **Resolution Gate**. Ideally, your gates should be the same aspect ratio, but if they aren't, you can match them horizontally or vertically. To view both gates, go to the **Display Options** section of the cameraShape node.

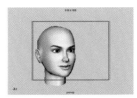

Matching Gates
In this view you can see a Film Gate of 35mm Academy and a Render Resolution of 640x480. Because the aspect ratios are similar, the gates match closely.

Horizontal Film Fit
Here the Film Gate is 70 mm Projection while the Render Resolution is 640 x 480. The Horizontal Film Fit creates a "letterbox" relationship between the two aspect ratios.

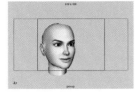

Vertical Film Fit
The Film Gate is 70 mm Projection while the Render Resolution is 640 x 480. The Vertical Film Fit creates a "Pan-and-Scan" relationship between the two aspect ratios. Film Offset can be used to pan the Film Back.

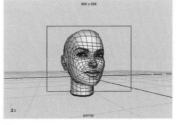

Overscan
If you select either View > Camera Settings > Film Gate or View > Camera Settings > Resolution Gate, an Overscan is set. This value shows a border area around either of the gates. If you want a smaller border, you can adjust the Overscan value in the cameraShape node.

Ignore Film Gate = Off
In this letterbox example, the Film Gate has a different aspect ratio than the Render Resolution. By default, the Film Gate will be ignored and the complete Render Resolution will be rendered. You can turn Ignore Film Gate to Off in the Render Options section of the Render Globals window if you want to achieve the letterbox look.

Clipping Planes

In Maya, the near and far clipping planes define what objects are visible in a camera's 3D view. However, by default, Auto Render Clip Plane is On, which sets the two clipping planes to include all the objects in your scene during a rendering. This can create very large distances between the clipping planes if you have objects close to the camera and far back in your scene. You can turn Auto Render Clip Plane to off if you want to limit your rendering to objects within the interactive clipping planes.

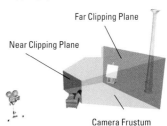

Far Clipping Plane

Near Clipping Plane

Camera Frustum

Clipped Objects
When Auto Render clip is Off, the chair that crosses the near clipping plane is partially rendered, the easel that crosses the far clipping plane is fully rendered, and the column outside the clipping planes is not rendered at all. When Auto Render clip is On, all objects are rendered.

Camera Moves

The way you position your camera and set up your lens has a big effect on the composition of a shot. Whether the camera is sitting still or being animated, you must understand the choices you can make to enhance the cinematic qualities of the shot. By going beyond the default values, you can begin working like a real-life cinematographer.

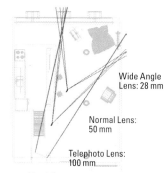

Camera Positions
To frame the scene in a similar manner for each lens, the camera is moved closer for wide angle and farther away for telephoto lenses.

Framing the Shot

When you frame a shot, you must choose how far the camera is from the scene and which angle-of-view or focal length to use. These decisions will change how the objects in the foreground, mid-ground, and background relate visually, which in turn, affects the framing. Learning to use different focal lengths is an important part of driving a CG camera to get the shot you need.

Normal Lens: 50 mm focal length
This lens is closest to the human eye. Using it as a starting point, you can explore how changes in focal length and distance create different relationships between foreground and background elements.

Wide Angle Lens: 28 mm focal length
The wide angle lens offers a stronger sense of perspective. You can get close and still see a wide area of the scene, which can be helpful in an interior space. Moving objects appear to move very fast.

Telephoto Lens: 100 mm focal length
This lens tightens the perspective. You see less of the scene and can focus on a particular area. Since the depth is flattened, distance is harder to read. Moving objects appear to move slowly.

Animating Cameras

Animating the camera is a great way to add a sense of motion to your animation. This means that you can use traditional camera moves, such as tracks and dollys, to focus on a character and enhance the 3D qualities of your scene, or your camera can fly around in a less controlled manner.

In Maya, you can animate a camera using its Transform node, which is useful, but not as intuitive as aiming the camera at a locator or creating a two-node camera which lets you control the eye point and look at point of the camera separately.

Extra Nodes

If you create a camera by selecting **Create > Camera options**, you can choose a one, two, or threenode camera from the **Animation Options**. If you create a camera with **Panels > Perspective > New**, you don't have this option.

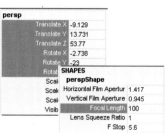

Setting Keys
You can animate a camera's position, orientation, and lens properties by first framing shots in a 3D panel. Next, choose **View > Select Camera** and set keys on attributes such as Translate, Rotate, and Focal Length.

Aiming the Camera
If you want your camera to follow an animated object, you can aim constrain the camera to the object. Be sure to set the **Aim** Vector to -1 in Z and the **Up Vector** to **1** in Y. This will point the camera correctly.

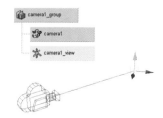

Two node Camera
With a two node camera, you can animate the eye point and look at point separately. Each has a Transform node that can be keyed, parented to another object, or sent down a motion path.

Zooming and Dollying

When you want to animate the camera getting closer or farther away from the scene, you can choose between zooming, by changing the camera's focal length, or dollying the whole camera. These two approaches yield quite different results and it is a good idea to explore each technique.

Zoom

Zoom
Changing the camera's focal length creates a zoom effect. All parts of the scene get bigger equally, which results in a static relationship between elements in the foreground, mid-ground, and background. Our eyes cannot make this kind of view change.

Initial View
The purpose of this shot is to get closer to the street front. Using both a zoom and a dolly, you can see the different ways in which the perspective reacts.

Dolly

Dolly
Changing the camera's position with a dolly gives you a stronger sense of the space. Objects pass by the frame, creating a more dramatic movement through space. This is the approach used most often with real-life cameras. This is how our eyes would get closer to an object.

Cameras on Motion Paths

In cases where you know the path you want your camera to take, a path animation can be used. You can choose to assign a one, two, or three node camera to the path and you can use multiple paths for even more control. If you want to have your camera go around a roller coaster loop, be sure to use a three-node camera and send the Up-vector node down its own path that is offset from the eye's path. This will keep the camera from flipping at the top of the loop.

Combining Zooming and Dollying

One camera move used in many horror films is the simultaneous zoom and dolly. As the camera gets closer to a character, the focal length is lowered so that the character remains about the same size in the shot. At the same time, background elements change dramatically and there is almost a sense of vertigo that can heighten a scary scene or a moment of surprise.

You can set up this camera move using **Set Driven Key** to create a relationship between the camera's Z-axis position and the cameraShape node's **focal length**. Dollying the camera along Z will create the sense of forced perspective that can create a dramatic moment for your character.

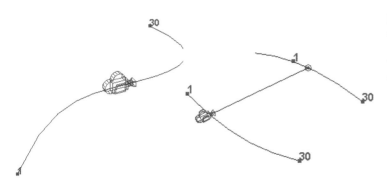

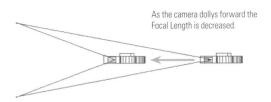

As the camera dollys forward the Focal Length is decreased.

One Node
To place a one node camera on a motion path, you must make sure the Front Axis is Z and Inverse Front is turned On. This will aim it correctly down the path.

Two Nodes
With a two node camera, you can have the eye point and look at point on different paths. You can now control the camera's tracking using these two curves.

Perspective changes
As the camera zooms and dollys, the perspective will become more pronounced and the perceived distance between your foreground and background elements change. A character at the camera's focal point would remain about the same size throughout the camera move.

Rendering

A 3D artist's ultimate goal is to create a sequence of images that can be synchronized with sound and played back as a movie. The creation of these images is the job of the renderer where surfaces, materials, lights, and motion are all taken into account and turned into bitmap images.

The art of rendering involves finding a balance between the visual complexity needed to tell a story and the rendering speed that determines how many frames can be rendered in a given time. Simple models render quickly and complex models take longer.

Therefore, the render artist brings together all the parts created throughout the animation pipeline and ensures that they render with high quality as fast as possible. This means exploring the interaction of surfaces, lights, and materials and making sure that the pixels look right in their final form.

Rendering Scenes

Rendering is where all of the work in setting up models, textures, lights, cameras, and effects comes together into a final sequence of images. In very simple terms, rendering is the creation of pixels that are given different colors in order to form a complete image. A render involves a large number of complex calculations that can keep your computer busy for quite a while. The key at this stage in the animation process is to find a way of getting the best image quality and the fastest render times so that you can meet your deadlines.

Before exploring the specific details of rendering animation sequences, it is important to realize that there are two different methods to render images: software and hardware rendering. More specifically, there are three different software renderers shipping with Maya. They are Maya software, mental ray, and vector.

The software renderers are considerably more complex than hardware rendering and requires a great deal more knowledge and understanding to get the best results. The renderer is where all of your scene data and settings are handed off to the software and render calculations are performed that result in final bitmap images. To give you some insight into what Maya actually does with your scene data during, an overview of the software render process is shown thoughout this chapter.

Hardware Rendering

Hardware shading, texturing, and lighting use the computer's graphics hardware to display objects on the screen. You can use the Hardware Render Buffer to take snapshots of each frame and save them to disk.

Because hardware is designed to perform only specific tasks, its rendering capabilities have the advantage of being very fast, but lack the sophistication of features such as some advanced shadows, reflections, and post-process effects. Hardware rendering is used primarily to render hardware-type particle effects which are later enhanced in a compositing application.

Hardware Shading
You can display hardware shading, texturing, and lighting in any view panel using the panel's Shading menu.

Hardware Render Buffer
The Hardware Render Buffer is a special window used for outputting hardware-rendered images.

Software Rendering

All three software renderers use complex algorithms to combine elements such as geometry, cameras, and textures, with the physics of light to create final bitmap images. Because some aspects of light's true behavior would be prohibitively slow to calculate, most renderers let you employ shortcuts, such as ambient lights, in place of Global Illumination to make sure that rendering times support the production cycle.

Software rendering has the advantage of being more flexible than hardware rendering. Software companies can add functionality by changing algorithms in the code without being restricted by the computer's hardware. Therefore, while software rendering is not as fast as hardware rendering, the added functionality lets you achieve more sophisticated results.

Software Rendering
You can create a software rendering in the Render view window or by using Render > (Save)BatchRender... The Batch render is always used to render animation and can be launched from a Command Line.

Software Render Process

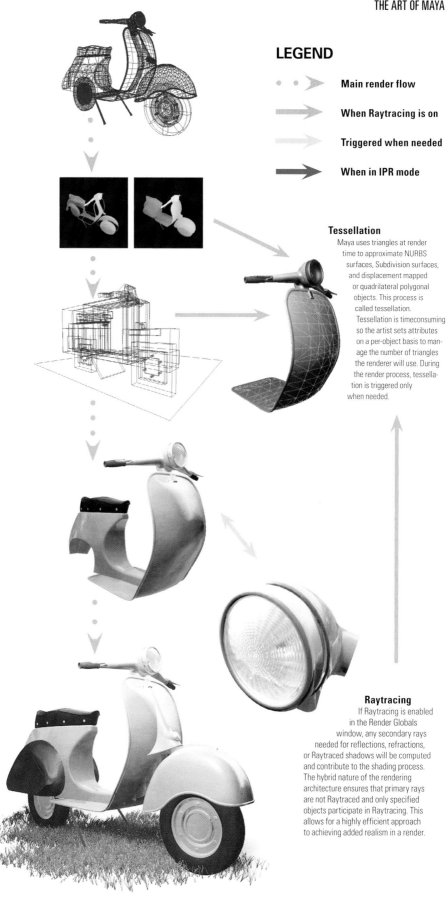

LEGEND

- ● ● ● ● → **Main render flow**
- → **When Raytracing is on**
- → **Triggered when needed**
- → **When in IPR mode**

1. Geometry Filtering
To start the rendering process, Maya determines which objects in the Maya scene file will be rendered. Any objects that are hidden, templated, or do not belong to a shading group, will not be rendered.

2. Light Depth Maps
From the point of view of each shadow-casting light, Maya renders Z-depth files called Depth Maps to be used later to compute the shadows in the scene. Two Depth Maps are created because the UseMidDistDmap is turned on by default in the light's Attribute Editor.

3. Tiling/Primary Visibility
By looking at the bounding boxes of the geometry, Maya can determine which objects are visible to the camera and approximately how much memory will be required to render them. Based on these estimates, the image is divided into rectangular regions called tiles. Each tile is a manageable amount of data for the renderer to process at one time. It is possible to explicitly set the maximum tile size (in pixels) from a Command Line.

4. Shading
Maya computes all of the texturing, lighting, shading Anti-aliasing, 3D motion blur, etc. for the visible surfaces in each tile.

Deep Raster Generation
When an IPR render is launched, a temporary file is created and written to disk in the iprImages directory. This deep raster file stores the image itself and all the data required to allow interactive tuning of shading and lighting attributes during an IPR render.

5. Post Processing
After the frame is rendered, Maya completes the final image by creating and automatically compositing any of the post process effects that you have specified. These effects include Depth of Field, 2D motion blur, Glow, Paint Effects, Fur, etc.

Tessellation
Maya uses triangles at render time to approximate NURBS surfaces, Subdivision surfaces, and displacement mapped or quadrilateral polygonal objects. This process is called tessellation. Tessellation is timeconsuming so the artist sets attributes on a per-object basis to manage the number of triangles the renderer will use. During the render process, tessellation is triggered only when needed.

Raytracing
If Raytracing is enabled in the Render Globals window, any secondary rays needed for reflections, refractions, or Raytraced shadows will be computed and contribute to the shading process. The hybrid nature of the rendering architecture ensures that primary rays are not Raytraced and only specified objects participate in Raytracing. This allows for a highly efficient approach to achieving added realism in a render.

Tessellation

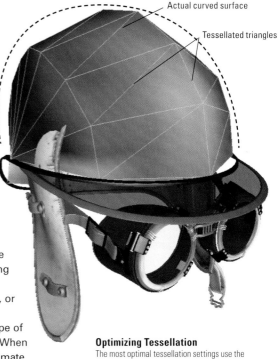

Actual curved surface

Tessellated triangles

The word tessellation comes from Latin and means the process of covering a surface in a pattern or mosaic. In Maya, tessellation is the process of converting surfaces into triangles.

Your pre-production storyboards can help guide which tessellation settings to use since they will show the position of objects during animation. Objects closer to the camera need to be more finely tessellated, while objects that remain distant from the camera can be more crudely tessellated. Careful management of tessellation settings can significantly help optimize a scene for rendering speed.

What Is Tessellation?

Maya converts NURBS surfaces into triangles during the render process because it is more efficient than rendering NURBS surfaces directly. Tessellation can also apply to Subdivision Surfaces, surfaces with displacement maps, or quadrilateral polygonal objects.

Tessellation triangles can only approximate the shape of the actual curved surface because the triangles are flat. When higher numbers of smaller triangles are used to approximate a curved surface, a more accurate and smoother shape results. However, using more triangles requires more memory and takes longer to render. For this reason, it is most optimal to carefully set the tessellation values on a per-object basis.

Optimizing Tessellation
The most optimal tessellation settings use the minimum acceptable number of triangles for a surface to look convincing. Relative to the camera, distant and less important objects should have lower tessellation settings to save on render time.

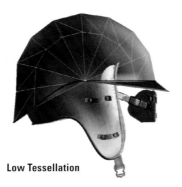

Low Tessellation

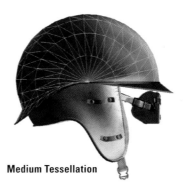

Medium Tessellation

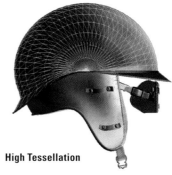

High Tessellation

Simple Tessellation Controls

The tessellation controls are found in the Attribute Editor for each object. In hardware shaded mode (as shown in the images above), **Display Render Tessellation** allows you to preview how the renderer will tessellate the surface.

Maya uses a two-pass method for tessellating geometry. The first pass, Primary Tessellation, uses a fast approach that creates a specific number of triangles in the U and V directions of the surface. The second pass, Secondary Tessellation, looks at the curvature of the surface and creates more triangles only where needed. For this reason, the second pass is sometimes referred to as Adaptive Tessellation.

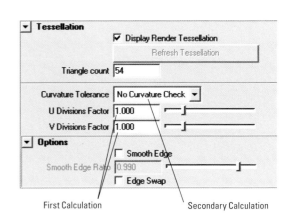

First Calculation

Secondary Calculation

Smooth Edge

Trimmed holes or edges of surfaces often require higher tessellation. In these situations, you can use the **Smooth Edge** feature to add more triangles only in the areas where they are needed, rather than increase the overall tessellation of the surface. Be careful when using this feature, as specular highlights can appear to shift where the Smooth Edge regions blend into the rest of the surface. In this scenario, you may need to turn Smooth Edge off and work with the Explicit Tessellation controls instead.

Plane with Smooth Edge On

Explicit Tessellation

The simple tessellation controls are a subset of the **Explicit Tessellation Attributes**. You should use the **Explicit Tessellation Attributes** when you are not able to achieve smooth enough results with the simple controls. These attributes offer several additional modes for the Primary and Secondary Tessellation passes.

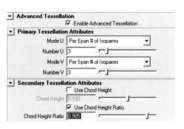

Explicit Tessellation Control

One possible way to tessellate your surfaces efficiently is to set the Primary pass to use as few triangles as possible and let the Secondary pass fill in more triangles only where needed. There are three different criteria for the Secondary Tessellation, and while it is possible to turn them all on at once, it is advisable to only use one to optimize your rendering time.

Attribute Spread Sheet

To edit tessellation of many selected objects at the same time, select **Window > General Editors > Attribute Spread Sheet**.

Using Chord Height

Chord Height is the perpendicular distance from the center of the triangle edge to the true curved surface. When Maya finds a Chord Height that exceeds the value specified in the Attribute Editor, the surface is further subdivided into more triangles. The limitations of this method are that the scale of your geometry dictates the value you need to set in the Attribute Editor and small objects can be difficult to tessellate. An alternative is to use the Chord Height Ratio.

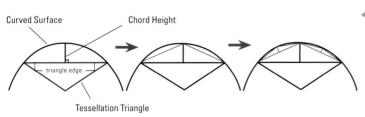

Curved Surface   Chord Height

triangle edge

Tessellation Triangle

Using Chord Height Ratio

Chord Height Ratio is also used for calculating tessellation. It is more flexible in terms of the scale of geometry because it is a function of the Chord Height as well as the triangle edge length. Chord Height Ratio = 1 – chord height/triangle edge length. As you set the Chord Height Ratio slider closer to 1, more triangles will be created.

Tessellating Deforming Objects

When rendering deforming objects, the Secondary (Adaptive) pass can cause the surface's tessellation to change from frame to frame, resulting in undesirable jittering in specular highlights or textures. To avoid this, you need to turn off all secondary criteria and rely on the Primary Tessellation pass alone.

Edge Swap

It is best to avoid tessellation triangles that are long and skinny. The Edge Swap feature can help eliminate long, skinny triangles where possible.

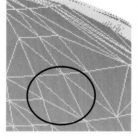   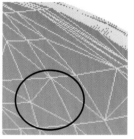

Without Edge Swap   With Edge Swap

Tessellating Trim Surfaces

You will notice that Maya automatically increases the tessellation of a surface once you trim it. This is necessary to properly represent the trim details on the surface. Smooth Edge can be used to create very smooth trim edges without having to further increase the overall tessellation.

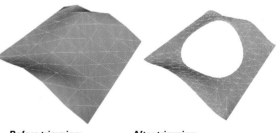

Before trimming:
No Secondary Tessellation

After trimming:
Still no Secondary Tessellation

Artifacts and Anti-aliasing

The "jaggies" or staircase-like edges associated with pixel-based images are referred to as aliasing artifacts. The term Anti-aliasing refers to software features and techniques designed to remove or reduce aliasing artifacts. This normally requires some form of increased sampling resulting in a higher level of accuracy when determining the color of pixels. This improves visual quality, but takes longer to render.

Controlling Anti-aliasing

Because aliasing artifacts can occur at various stages in a software render, the Anti-aliasing processes are controlled separately. This is an efficient approach as it allows Maya to use appropriate sampling methods at each stage.

The main Anti-aliasing controls are found in the Render Globals and the object's Attribute Editor. However, several undesirable artifacts can appear in your images that are not resolved by these settings. The most common of these artifacts and how to correct them are described on the next page.

This is a close-up of an edge of a rendered button before Anti-aliasing.

Further zooming of the button edge with Preview Quality Anti-aliasing settings.

Edge Anti-aliasing

Maya controls Edge Anti-aliasing by using an algorithm called Exact Area Sampling. You can adjust the quality from Low to Highest in the Render Globals window. The quality level tells Maya to use a specific number of visibility samples. The more visibility samples, the more accurate the information about the pixel coverage from each object. This results in better edge Anti-aliasing.

Shading Anti-aliasing

Adaptive shading allows Maya to use more shading samples only where needed in an image. You define a range of shading samples by setting a minimum and a maximum number in the Render Globals window. You then control contrast threshold values, which will determine how many samples to use within your specified range. The actual number of samples used will depend on how much a pixel's contrast with its neighbors is above the threshold values. In the case of a low contrast scene, thin specular highlights, reflections, or complex textures, you would likely need to lower the threshold values to achieve good shading Anti-aliasing. Maya provides a Contrast Sensitive Production Quality setting that does this for you. It is also possible to override the adaptive shading range on a per-object basis.

Render Globals

Multipixel Filtering

Multipixel filtering improves the appearance of thin lines and highlights to help eliminate jaggies or flickering in rendered animation. This approach renders faster than increasing the sampling. The filtering effect is controlled by adjusting the Pixel Filter Widths and the Pixel Filter Type in the Render Globals window. Reducing the Pixel Filter Widths, for example, decreases the filtering effect.

Object's Attribute Editor

Thin Geometry

You can correct the flickering of very small objects by increasing the visibility sampling (beyond the setting in Render Globals) on a per-object basis. This override is found in the object's Attribute Editor. This allows you to resolve the Edge Anti-aliasing for a small object without increasing the sample rate for all the objects in the scene.

Motion Blur

Edge Anti-aliasing becomes adaptive for motion blurred objects. It uses the same approach as the adaptive shading process where there is a range of samples and a threshold you define in the Render Globals window. In this case, the samples are visibility samples and the threshold deals with coverage instead of contrast. There is also a setting on a per-object basis to override the maximum number of visibility samples.

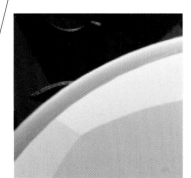

This is the same button as above, rendered with a high quality Anti-alias setting.

Shadow Artifacts

Shadows can cause artifacts that are actually the result of shortcuts deliberately used by most rendering algorithms for efficiency; they are not coding errors and they are not unique to Maya.

Raytraced Shadow Artifacts

Raytraced shadows may show dark blocky artifacts along the edge of illumination where the light falls off the surface. The computer graphics term for this is the terminator effect. It is a self-shadowing error resulting from the fact that flat triangles are used to represent curved surfaces. You can eliminate the terminator effect by increasing the tessellation.

Terminator artifact   No terminator artifact

Depth Map Shadow Artifacts

Self-shadowing errors are more common when using Depth Map shadows. These artifacts appear as dark bands or cross-hatching on surfaces facing toward the light, but can be corrected by increasing the Dmap Bias.

Use Mid Dist Dmap = OFF
Dmap Bias = 0.0

There are many self-shadowing artifacts when there is no **Dmap Bias** and the **Mid Dist Dmap is Off**.

Use Mid Dist Dmap = ON
Dmap Bias = 0.0

The Use Mid Dist Dmap feature is turned on by default which greatly reduces the likelihood of seeing any artifacts. Here, most of the self-shadowing artifacts have been eliminated.

Use Mid Dist Dmap = ON
Dmap Bias = 0.1

In some cases, you will need to adjust the Dmap Bias attribute on the light. For example, the default Dmap Bias is set to 0.001, but setting it to 0.1 corrects the remaining artifacts in this image. Increase this value in very small increments just until the artifacts disappear.

Clipping Plane Artifacts

Maya uses a near and far clipping plane to help determine the depth position of geometry relative to the camera. The closer together the clipping planes are, the more accurately Maya will be able to sort what geometry is in front of or behind other geometry in the scene. For this reason, **Auto Render Clip Plane** is turned On by default in the camera's Attribute Editor to ensure that the clipping planes will closely bind all the objects in a scene during a render.

When rendering animation, you may see artifacts that look like background surfaces showing through foreground surfaces. This occurs mainly in very large scenes with objects that are close together, such as architectural details on buildings.

Auto Render Clip Plane = Off
Near Clipping Plane = 0.001
Far Clipping Plane = 11000

To fix the problem of surfaces looking like they are inter-penetrating, turn off Auto Render Clip Plane and set the camera's clipping planes closer together. In most cases, setting the near clipping plane further out from the camera solves the problem.

Auto Render Clip Plane = Off
Near Clipping Plane = 1.0
Far Clipping Plane = 11000

Animation Flicker

When Maya renders, it filters textures, which improves the quality of the final rendered animation. If your texture appears to be flickering or crawling from frame to frame, you should set the Filter value slightly higher than 1. File textures tend to filter better than procedural textures in animation, so it is common to use the Convert to File texture tool in the Hypershade window.

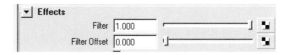

Render Output

Based on your post-production requirements, your final rendered image or sequence of images will need to suit the medium you are outputting it to. These image properties, such as size, format, and frame padding, are set from the Render Globals Window.

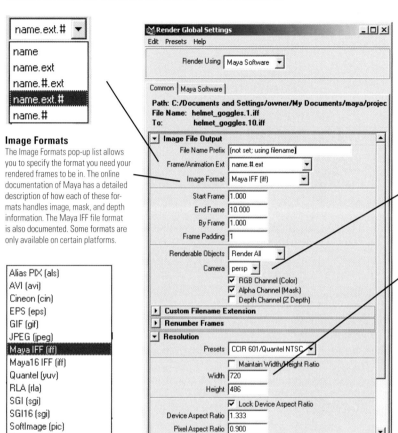

Image Formats
The Image Formats pop-up list allows you to specify the format you need your rendered frames to be in. The online documentation of Maya has a detailed description of how each of these formats handles image, mask, and depth information. The Maya IFF file format is also documented. Some formats are only available on certain platforms.

Renderable Camera
The pop-up camera list allows you to choose which camera will be used in the Batch render. It is possible to render from more than one camera in a Batch render. This Render Globals setting does not affect which camera is used while rendering in the Render View window within Maya.

Render Resolution
The Render Resolution refers to the dimensions of a rendered frame in pixels. The list of presets in Maya allows you to quickly select a resolution from a list of those commonly used in the industry.

Rendering Animation
An image file name consists of three components when rendering an animation: file name, frame number extension, and file format extension. (A combination of these three components is referred to as the file name syntax.)

The file name is the base name for all images in the animation sequence. The frame number extension represents the frame in the Time Slider in which the image is rendered. The file format extension indicates your chosen file format. You can see these combined as a preview at the top of the Render Globals window.

You need to tell Maya what frames to render when rendering an animation. After a Start Frame and an End Frame are specified, Maya renders all the frames in between by default. However, if you want to render every 10th frame for test purposes, you can set the By Frame attribute to 10. In this case, Maya only renders every 10th frame, beginning with the Start Frame number.

Channels

The color channels of a rendered image are made up of red, green, and blue (RGB). A mask channel (or alpha channel) stores information about the coverage and opacity of the objects in your scene. This channel allows you to work with your rendered images in a compositing software application like Maya Composer or Maya Fusion.

A depth channel records the distance from the camera to the objects in the scene. This is often called Z-depth and you can look at it using the Z-key in FCheck.

Maya can render an image file that contains RGB color information, a mask channel, a depth channel or any combination of the three. The flags in the Render Globals window let you choose what channels will be rendered. Some image formats do not support embedded mask or depth channels; in these cases, Maya generates a separate mask or depth file and puts it in the mask or depth sub directory of your current project.

color (RGB)

mask

depth

Rendering Fields

When an NTSC television displays images, it uses a technique called interlace, where electron beams horizontally scan all of the odd-numbered lines first and then fill in all of the even numbered lines (for PAL, even lines are scanned first). Each of these scans is called a field and they are half a frame apart in time. This means that instead of 30 frames per second, you actually see 60 fields per second (50 fields per second for PAL) when you watch television.

Rendering fields in Maya takes advantage of this interlace technique to achieve smoother motion on video. Instead of rendering whole frames, Maya renders each frame in two fields where the odd scan lines are rendered separately from the even scan lines at half-frame time intervals. The two fields are automatically put back together to form a whole image at the end of the frame render. The result is that the motion of an object in-between frames is captured in the render. In the final interlaced image, moving objects will look ghosted when viewed on your computer monitor because the monitor shows you both sets of scan lines at the same time. However, when the same image is viewed on a television screen, the objects will look correct.

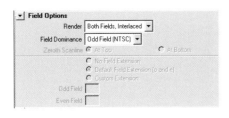

Image Formats

Maya's Render Globals lets you render your images in the specific format that you need for your production pipeline. The default image format is Maya's IFF, but you can choose from a list of many standards used in computer graphics such as TIFF, GIF, JPEG, Quantel, etc. Most of the formats are 8 bits per channel, but Maya also renders 10 bit Cineon and several 16 bit formats which are commonly used for film. Human eyes can perceive more colors than 8 bits can represent, so high-resolution formats, such as film, sometimes require better color definition to look realistic.

Maya also lets you render directly to AVI or QuickTime movies. While this may be convenient, you might also consider rendering in one of the other formats that creates separate images so that you have more flexibility. An application such as Maya Fusion allows you to create a movie from the images after any adjustments have been made.

AVI (.avi)
Microsoft Audio Video Interleaved (AVI) movie file format. Maya only renders uncompressed AVI files as these are the most common for reading into other applications.

QuickTime™ (.mov)
Apple QuickTime™ movie file format. Maya only renders out uncompressed QuickTime files as these are the most general for reading into other applications.

Animated scooter rendered as interlaced fields.

Rendering and Optimization

As you work on the shading, texturing, and lighting phases of your production, you will go through many iterations and tests before ultimately rendering the final animation. Maya's IPR, Render View, and Batch renderer allow you to move efficiently through this process. Along the way, there are several things to keep in mind to achieve optimal render times. These optimizations can take a few minutes to set up, but can save huge amounts of time in your final render. For example, consider that 10 minutes of video requires 18,000 rendered frames. Reducing your render time by 1 minute a frame will amount to saving 300 hours of render time.

Render View

The Maya Render View window allows you to launch a software render and watch the results as the file is being rendered. It can be used for everything from a quick test on a low quality render to a final production render. However, because it only renders the current frame, it is not used to render animation.

While rendering in the Render View window, Maya itself is the renderer; there is no intermediate file or separate rendering application as is the case with other renderers. Consequently, Maya does not allow you to make changes to the open scene's data as it is being rendered.

Batch Rendering

To software render your animation, you will use the Batch renderer, which can be launched inside the Maya interface or from a command line. When you start a Batch render from within an interactive session, a scene file is saved and another copy of Maya (with no user interface) is launched to do the render. This means that you can keep working on your scene in Maya while the render is in progress. For maximum speed when rendering your final animation, you should render from a command line (for example UNIX shell, DOS command prompt window) with no interactive Maya session running.

The Render Globals attributes let you specify the camera, Anti-aliasing quality, resolution, etc. for the Batch render. If rendering from a command line, there are many flags which can be set to override any Render Globals settings saved in a file. This can be very useful and efficient in cases where the scene file takes a long time to open.

Image Zoom
By default, images are automatically resized to fit into the Render View window. This means that you may be seeing your image at a zoom value other than 1.0. This scaled image will appear jagged in most cases, making it look like it has Anti-aliasing problems. Press the 1:1 button to view the image at its true size. If you still see jagged edges, adjust the Anti-aliasing settings in Render Globals.

IPR Rendering

IPR stands for Interactive Photorealistic Rendering. It is an interactive multi-threaded tool for tuning lights, shaders, textures, and 2D motion blur with immediate feedback in the Render View window. It also lets you tune Depth Map shadows without having to re-render the entire image.

IPR is designed to help you quickly accomplish 90 percent of your tuning. It is not used for final rendered images because it does not support Raytracing or production quality Anti-aliasing in order to keep the rendering interactive.

File Extension
To render out an animation, you must choose an extension with a pound (#) sign. The extension order depends on what system you are sending your images to.

Camera
You must pick the camera that you want to use for the Batch rendering.

Command Line
You can start a Batch rendering by entering a command similar to the line shown here in either a shell window or a DOS shell. This command should reference a previously saved Maya file.

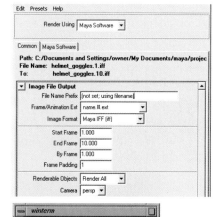

File Name
By default, the scene file name will be used for the rendered images. You can change that name here if you want it to be different.

Start and End Frame
You must set the Start and End frames. By default, this range is 1 - 10, even if your Time Range is different on your Timeline.

By Frame
You can choose a By Frame other than 1 when you want to skip frames for a test.

Lighting

If a light cannot possibly illuminate an object, you can break the link between the light and that object. Then, when Maya goes to shade the object, it does not need to evaluate the illumination contribution from that light.

To use Depth Map shadows efficiently, there are many things you can do, such as reusing the Dmaps from frame to frame for fly-through animation, or creating lights specifically to cast shadows from certain key objects to keep Dmap resolutions down.

Camera

An object's bounding box is used to determine if it intersects the camera's frustum. Keep this in mind so objects that are not visible through the camera are not unnecessarily tessellated. You can ensure this by breaking objects into smaller pieces so that the bounding boxes are smaller, or by animating the visibility of the objects.

Optimize Scene Size

The Optimize Scene Size and Delete Unused Nodes features will remove any excess clutter in the scene before rendering.

Tessellation

You should always keep tessellation to the lowest acceptable values. Over-tessellating can have a major impact on render times.

Anti-aliasing

Keep the Render Globals shading samples as low as possible. It is better to try lowering the contrast thresholds rather than increasing the shading samples. For objects that require higher numbers of shading samples, use the per-object overrides.

Memory

Maya renders an image in small rectangular sections called tiles. Normally, Maya determines the size of each of these tiles so that each one is manageable in terms of memory. However, if your render is running out of memory, you can reduce the memory usage by forcing Maya to render smaller tiles. You would do this by explicitly setting the tileHeight and tileWidth when rendering from a command line. The valid range is between 16 and 256 pixels where a tile that is 16 x 16 pixels will use the least amount of memory. The command line would look like this: Render -tw 16 -th 16 file.mb

When Batch rendering on multiple-processor machines, keep in mind that some post processes are not multi-threaded. For this reason, it is common to split up a render when dealing with effects such as glow or depth of field. For example, instead of sending 400 frames to 16 processors at once, render frames 1-100 on 4 processors, 101-200 on another 4 processors, etc. This avoids having many processors sitting idle while a single processor finishes the post process. Another important factor is that each render can only use up to 1.6 gigabytes of RAM (because Maya is currently a 32-bit application and the operating system has some memory overhead). If you have a large amount of RAM available, running multiple renders is the only way to take advantage of it.

Raytracing

Use reflection maps instead of Raytracing where possible.

An even distribution of geometry will allow for the most efficient Raytracing. Scenes with large ground planes and a dense clump of complex geometry in the center tend to cause major inefficiencies. To avoid this, turn off Visible in Reflections and Refractions for the ground plane.

If you are running out of memory in a Raytrace and have already optimized everything, try lowering the Recursion Depth to 1 in the Memory and Performance Options in the Render Globals. This will make the Raytrace slower, but will use far less memory.

Texturing

Convert to File Textures - In general, it is faster to render file textures than procedural textures. For this reason, you should consider using the Convert to File Texture tool found in the Hypershade.

Square textures - Maya performs better with square textures whose resolution is a power of 2. You should create your textures with this in mind, otherwise Maya will have to spend some time converting your textures at render time.

Texture size - The resolution of your texture should be directly related to the object it will be used on. If the object is far in the background or very small, you only need a very low resolution texture. Always keep texture resolutions to a minimum.

BOT files - If your scene has many file textures, you should work with Block Ordered Textures and the Use Cache option. These allow Maya to store all of the textures on disk in a quickly accessible tiled format. Only the portions of textures currently being used in the render will be held in a cache in RAM.

File format - Textures in formats other than IFF will need to be internally converted by Maya at render time.

Reuse nodes - It is a good idea to reuse nodes where possible, when building your shading networks.

Rendering for Compositing

Many 3D artists choose to render their productions in multiple layers and/or passes that are later combined and finished through compositing. Compositing is the process of merging multiple images into one image to create a final look.

A common misconception is that compositing is only used by large production houses where there are many 3D artists. However, smaller houses and individual artists can also benefit from the flexibility and advantages offered by compositing. While it is true that rendering scene elements separately may require more time initially, it is well worth the effort when you consider that each layer can be manipulated with color corrections, blurs, and other effects as they are brought together for compositing. You can also increase your creative possibilities by generating effects that are faster and more flexible in 2D, such as depth of field and glow, or achieve effects that are not possible with the renderer, such as blurred reflections or shadows.

Another key advantage of compositing is that if the director suddenly asks for the stone wall to be a brick wall instead, you only need to re-render the layer containing the wall. This flexibility can save significant amounts of time and allow the director more freedom to finesse the final look of the production. Compositing offers even more opportunities: you can add hardware rendered particle effects, combine 3D objects with live-action footage, and save render time by only rendering a single background frame for scenes where the camera does not move.

Rendering for Compositing Workflow

Since the basic premise of compositing is that you will be layering images to create a final product, Maya has several features to help you render objects in your scene as separate images. You can also render elements such as shadows and reflections separately, and go even one step further to render an object's color separately from the shadows that fall on it.

Using Display Layers

If you normally work with your scenes divided into Display Layers for modeling and animation purposes, these layers can be rendered separately based on their visibility. For example, if you have three layers and only two of the layers are visible, only the objects in the visible layers will be rendered. This can easily be controlled from the Command Line as well. To do this, simply make sure all your Display Layers are visible before you save your scene file. Then when you type your Render command, you will include an "-l" and the names of one or more Display Layers to render. It would look something like this:

Render -l layer1 layer3 file.mb

Using Render Layers

You can assign objects to Render Layers so that you can separate the objects in your scene specifically to meet your rendering needs. The most basic approach might be to separate objects into foreground, mid-ground, and background layers. Or, you may decide to divide the scene elements by specific objects or sets of objects such as helmet, liner, and goggles as shown in the adjacent images. In this case, you will actually increase the render time because you will render parts of the objects which will not actually be seen in the final shot. However, if you need to make changes later, you will not have to re-render the whole scene.

The Role of the Alpha Channel

The alpha channel, sometimes called a mask or matte channel, contains information about the opacity of objects in an image. The images to the right show the alpha channel for the helmet, liner, and goggles. You can see that where the helmet's visor is semi-transparent, the alpha channel is gray, and where the goggles lenses are transparent, the alpha channel is black. The opaque regions of the objects are white. These grayscale values are used by the compositing application to combine the images later.

Matte Opacity for Black Holes

The images below show what the compositing stage will look like with the images of the helmet, liner, and goggles. In the first example, the alpha channels for each image do not have any information about the other objects in the scene. For this reason, the compositing application won't know which part of which object goes in front or behind the other objects. The Maya Matte Opacity feature provides a way to resolve this.

There are three modes for Matte Opacity that allow you to manipulate the alpha channel on a per-material basis. One is the Black hole mode that allows you to resolve this compositing issue. Careful planning and use of this feature results in images with cutout regions that will composite correctly, as shown in the middle image below. Sometimes it is also possible to solve this type of problem using a Z-depth channel in compositing applications with depth-compositing capabilities.

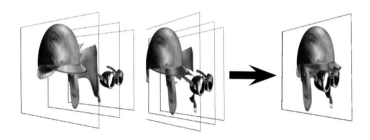

These objects were rendered as separate images without the use of Matte Opacity Black hole. They will not composite correctly.

These objects were rendered as separate images using Matte Opacity Black hole so they will composite correctly.

Render Passes

If you need to have very precise control over the color of your rendered objects and the shadows that fall on them, you can further break down your shot by rendering separate passes within any Render Layer. The term Render passes generally refers to the process of rendering various attributes of your scene separately such as color, shadows, highlights, etc. The spreadsheet in Maya Render Globals allows you to set this up. The following images show the objects rendered in two passes: color and shadow.

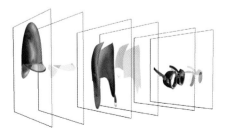

Rendering Reflections & Shadows

Maya also provides a way to create custom reflection and shadow passes. This involves the useBackground material which acts as a shadow and/or reflection catcher. To create the images below, a ground plane under the goggles has a useBackground material assigned, and the Primary Visibility is turned off for the goggles.

When the shadow pass is rendered, a black image is created with an alpha channel containing the shadow information. In the compositing phase, the alpha channel can be blurred, lightened, darkened, etc. to control the final look of the shadows.

The reflection pass shows the reflections in the RGB image and a white mask in the alpha channel. In some cases, the alpha channel would not be used in the final composite because reflections are normally added to the background image. However, if the background image is a light or white color, the alpha channel is needed.

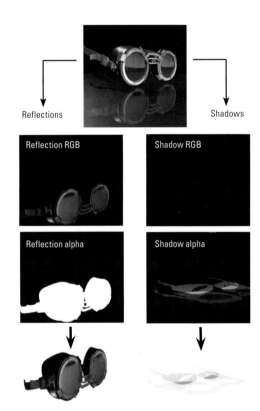

Reflections   Shadows

Reflection RGB   Shadow RGB

Reflection alpha   Shadow alpha

Edges for Composite Rendering

Turning on the Composite flag in the Render Globals will prevent the edge pixels of an object from being Anti-aliased against the background color. This is useful because it prevents an unwanted rim around the object in the final composite. The objects will intentionally appear to be very aliased before compositing, but will look perfect after compositing.

mental ray

mental ray offers all the features traditionally expected of photo-realistic rendering, and includes functionality not found in most rendering software, such as host and network parallel rendering, area light sources for soft shadows, Global Illumination, and Caustics.

mental ray for Maya supports Maya-type shaders, textures and lights, and you can import arbitrary libraries of mental ray custom shaders. Additionally, you can create your own user-written shaders, giving you the opportunity to exploit the power of metal ray to its maximum. Custom shaders can be compiled in advance, or compiled at runtime, which means that you do not need a compiler to experience the advantage of mental ray's custom shaders.

Caustics and Global Illumination

mental ray can render with Caustics, the light effects that are caused by specularly reflected or refracted light, like the shimmering light at the bottom of a pool of water.

mental ray can also render with Global Illumination, the technique used to capture indirect illumination, the natural phenomenon where light bounces off anything in its path until it is completely absorbed.

Both Caustics and Global Illumination use photon maps. A photon map is a 3D representation of the accumulated light energy at certain photon bounce points. They are conceptually similar to shadow maps, but they capture light instead.

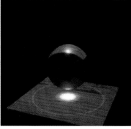

Global Illumination   Caustics

Final Gather and HDRI images

Final Gather is a fast and easy way to achieve good illumination results for architecture visualization and entertainment scenes that require credible, but not necessarily physically accurate, lighting. When Final Gather is enabled, every object effectively becomes a source of ray-emitting light, mimicking the natural world in which objects influence the color of their surroundings. When one light ray strikes an object, a series of secondary rays are diverted at random angles around it to calculate the light energy contribution from the surrounding objects. The light energy is then evaluated during the Raytracing process to add the effect of the bounced light.

Final Gather

HDRI Image

mental ray supports HDRI images as file textures. HDRI stands for High Dynamic Range Imaging. Image-based lighting uses the light and light color represented in an image you provide to illuminate the scene. An HDRI image has an extra floating point value associated with each pixel that is used to define the persistence of light at that point. A high-dynamic range image is like several images with different exposures combined to show the full range of light. HDRI images have a greater capacity to describe light accurately (by way of floating point numbers), because they store the amount of light (rather than just color) represented in a pixel. This prevents 'blown out' or extremely dark areas in an image that your eyes compensate for in the natural world. Using HDRI images with Final Gather lets you provide extremely realistic lighting.

Contour Lines

Contour lines can be placed at discontinuities of depth or surface orientation, between different materials, or where the color contrast is high, simply by using an appropriate contour shader. The contour lines are anti-aliased, and there can be several levels of contours created by reflection or seen through semitransparent

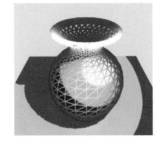

materials. The contours can be different for each material, and some materials can have no contours at all. The color and thickness of the contours can depend on geometry, position, illumination, material, frame number, and various other parameters as determined by the shader. Contour lines are especially useful for cartoon animation production.

Phenomenon

The Phenomenon concept is conceived to unify, by packaging and hiding complexity, all those seemingly disparate approaches, techniques, and tricks, most notably (but not limited to) the concept of a shader, which are characteristic for today's state of the art in high-end 3D animation and in digital special effects production. The aim is to provide a comprehensive, coherent, and consistent foundation for the reproduction of all visual phenomena by means of rendering. The Phenomenon concept provides the missing framework for the purpose of rendering in a unified manner. Phenomenon was designed to extend the concept of shaders, not replace it.

Diagnostic Modes

Since it can be hard to fine-tune all the aspects of mental ray, a number of diagnostic modes that help visualizing and optimizing the rendering process are supported. They modify the output image to include grid lines or dot patterns that indicate coordinate spaces, sampling, or photon densities. These graphs allow simple detection of insufficient or excessive sampling densities, and help to tune parameters, such as numbers of photons or sampling and contrast limits.

Grid Mode renders a grid on top of all objects in the scene, in object, camera, or world space. It's useful to get an idea of the scene scale and to enable rough estimates of distances and areas.

Photon Density Mode shows a false color rendering of photon density on all materials. This is useful when tuning the number of photons to trace in a scene, and for selecting the optimum accuracy settings for estimation of Global Illumination or Caustics.

Samples Mode shows how spatial supersamples were placed in the rendered image, by producing a grayscale image signifying sample density. This is useful when tuning the level and the contrast threshold for spatial supersampling.

BSP Mode shows the cost of creating and traversing the BSP tree used for raytracing. If the diagnostic image shows that mental ray has been operating near the limit in large parts of the image, it helps tune the BSP parameters in the options block.

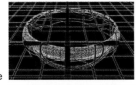

Final Gathering Mode shows Final Gathering points, as green dots for initial raster-space points and red dots for render-time points.

mental ray Shaders

There are many types of shaders in mental ray, all of which can be substituted by user-written shaders. Following is a brief description of the custom shaders available:

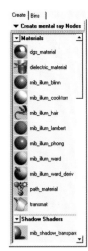

Material shaders describe the visible material of an object.

Volume shaders are used to account for **atmospheric effects** encountered by a ray. Light shaders implement the characteristics of a light source.

Shadow shaders are used instead of material shaders when a shadow ray intersects with an object.

Environment shaders are used instead of a material shader when a visible ray leaves the scene entirely without intersecting an object.

Photon shaders are used to propagate photons through the model in order to simulate Caustics and Global Illumination.

Photon volume shaders are similar to photon shaders; they compute indirect light interactions in volumes, such as volume scattering.

Photon emitter shaders are used to control the emission of photons from a light source.

Texture shaders come in three flavors: color, scalar, and vector. Their main purpose is to relieve other shaders, such as material or environment shaders, from performing color and other computations.

Displacement shaders are called during tessellation of polygonal or free-form surface geometry, a procedure that creates triangles to be rendered.

Geometry shaders are run before rendering begins. Unlike displacement shaders, which are called once per vertex, geometry shaders are responsible for creating an entire object or object hierarchy.

Contour shaders come in four different types: contour store shaders, contour contrast shaders, contour shaders, and contour output shaders.

Lens shaders are used when a primary ray is cast by the camera.

Output shaders are different from all other shaders and receive different parameters. They are used when the entire scene has been completely rendered and the output image resides in memory.

Lightmap shaders can be attached to materials to scan the surface of an object, collecting data and optionally writing a texture to disk.

Maya Vector

You can use the Maya Vector renderer to create stylized renderings for example, cartoon, tonal art, line art, hidden line, and wireframe. The vector renderer can output in various bitmap image formats, or in the major 2D vector formats such as Macromedia Flash and Adobe Illustrator.

Bitmap Format vs Vector Format

Bitmap images are mainly used to display photographs or computer generated photorealistic images. A bitmap image has two main attributes that defines its quality: the resolution and the number of bits per pixel. Both attributes together define the size of an image. The advantage of bitmaps is their ability to carry the necessary information to display photorealistic content. The biggest disadvantage is that the resolution directly affects the image quality. A potential problem is that high quality bitmaps need a lot of disk space and memory.

Vector images deal with curves and closed shapes, which can be filled with solid colors or color ramps. A vector graphic is described by two properties: outline and fill. These two properties are mathematical descriptions for shape and color. Because of this, the main advantage of a vector image is that its quality is independent of the resolution. That means you can scale a vector graphic to any size without losing detail and quality. Also, vector graphics don't take up as much disk space as bitmap images.

Fill Options
You can choose between several options of filling for your geometry:

Single Color selects the proper color based on the shader color, and can take into consideration a point light.

Two and Four Colors use two or four colors to shade each object rendered.

Full Colors shade each triangle with a solid color. It is a similar look to polygons with only hard edges.

Average Color selects the average color in a surface and uses it to fill the surface. You can influence the look of the surface by playing with the Normals of polygonal faces.

Area Gradient fills each surface with one radial gradient.

Mesh Gradient is the most expensive fill. It shades the surfaces with a close match to regular software rendering.

Edge Options
Enable this option to render your objects with an outline.

Edge Weight lets you control the thickness of the outline.

Edge Color lets you choose the overall line color.

Edge Style controls the placement of the line on either the outline of the surfaces or the entire mesh.

Edge Detail will render the sharp edges between polygons. You can specify a threshold that gives you global control about where the outlines are rendered.

Hidden Edge gives a wireframe look to your renders.

Rendering Options
These options are only available with Macromedia Flash or in bitmap rendering.

Shadows enables all objects to cast and receive shadows. Only shadow-casting point lights are rendered.

Highlights will calculate a highlight based on the material, light, and the specified number of highlight colors.

Reflections enables all objects to be traced in reflections.

Render Layer renders all layers to different files. To compose them, these files must be imported into a vector graphic software.

Usage of Vector Images

Vector graphics are mainly used for print publishing (especially diagrams), logos, and typography. Web vector formats are also very common because they have a relatively small file size and are scalable. Also, the individual elements can be easily animated and used for interaction with the user. The disadvantage is that it is hard to get realistic results with a vector graphic.

Decreasing Vector File Size

If you are using the Maya Vector renderer to create SWF or SVG files for online delivery, you may need to modify your scene and adjust the Maya Vector Render Global Settings to produce the best compromise between image quality and file size. Complex scenes and certain Maya Vector Render Global Settings can produce very large SWF or SVG files that are unsuitable for online delivery.

Here are some tips to reduce file size:
Reduce the complexity of your scene: Consider removing minor elements. Reduce the number of triangles in polygonal and Subdivision surfaces. Reduce the tessellation of NURBS surfaces.
- **Reduce the number of frames in an animation.**
- **Reduce the Frame Rate of an animation.**

Choose an appropriate Fill Style based on the objects in your scene. For certain types of objects, some fill styles produce different file sizes for results of equal quality. Avoid using Full Color or Mesh Gradient as they always create large files.
- **Turn on Combine Fills and Edges for SWF files.**
- **Increase the Curve Tolerance value.**
- **Decrease the Detail Level.**
- **Set Edge Style to Outline instead of Entire Mesh.**
- **Turn off Hidden Edges.**
- **Turn off Show Back Faces. If a surface does not render because it is facing away from the camera, manually reverse the surface's Normal.**

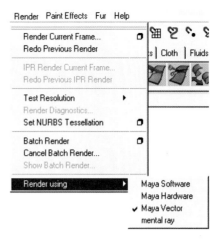

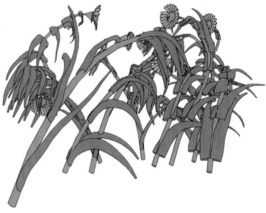

These Paint Effects flowers were rendered in vector graphic once they had been converted into polygons. The history makes it possible to keep the animation.

Notice the nice and accurate reflection on the water.

Unsupported Features in Vector Render

There are certain things in Maya that cannot be rendered in vectors. As a workaround, most objects can be converted to polygons and then rendered.

Here is a list of unsupported features:

- Bump maps
- Displacement maps
  (Use **Modify > Convert > Displacement To Polygons**)
- Fluids (Use Modify > Convert > Fluid To Polygons)
- Image planes
- Lights (only point lights are supported)
- Fur
- Paint Effects (Use Modify > Convert > Paint Effects To Polygons)
- Post Render Effects
- mental ray shaders

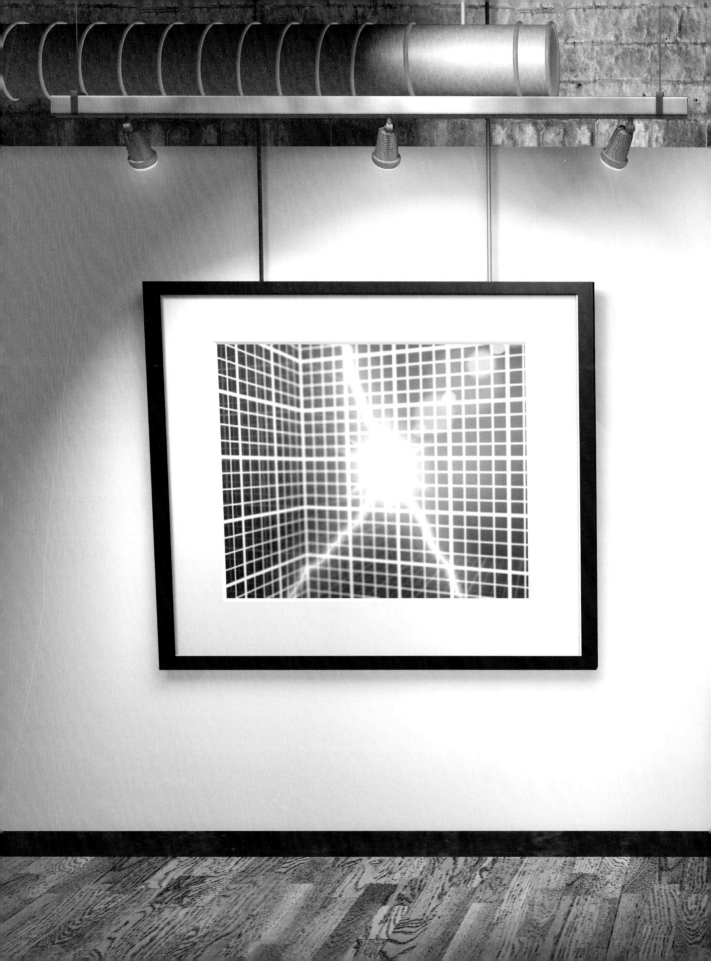

Effects

In an animation, effects are used to add visual interest to a scene. Rain, fire, smoke, and other natural effects are difficult to create using traditional surfaces and shaders. Effects tools such as Opti-FX, particles, and Paint Effects can be used to add these and other elements to a scene.

Opti-FX are basically lights that have glows and fog. They make it possible to add atmospheric effects to lights that can enhance a scene.

Particles are points in space that can be simulated using forces and dynamic expressions. The resulting motion can be quite complex and is great for creating natural effects such as smoke and steam.

Paint Effects uses a brush-based paradigm that lets 3D artists add brush strokes to their scenes that they then render using hundreds of attributes to create effects including trees, lightning, fire, and clouds.

Adding Effects

The addition of effects to a scene helps establish the final look of your animation. One of the primary uses of CG in movies and broadcast is the addition of effects to live-action shots.Effects can include explosions, fire, rain, fog, clouds, and many other natural phenomena.

Effects Tools

Maya includes many tools capable of adding effects to your scenes. In fact, you can sometimes choose between different methods of achieving the same kind of effect. Whether you use Paint Effects, Opti-FX, particles or compositing effects, the goal is always quality of the final shot. Having a vast array of effects choices helps you get the perfect look. To help you make the right choice, it is important that you understand what each tool set has to offer. Shown below is a scene that uses several different tools to create a variety of effects.

Paint Effects
In Maya, you can instantly add a variety of effects using this revolutionary brush-based technology. Creating realistic effects is as easy as selecting a preset brush and painting in already animated elements such as lightning and rain.

Opti-FX
Lights can be used to generate volumetric fog effects. Attributes such as color, intensity, spread, and fall-off can be modified to change the appearance of the fog within the cone of the light.

Particle Effects
Fire is just one of a variety of effects created through the use of a particle system in Maya. This system is made up of small points called particles. As part of a collective system, particles can be animated to create special effects using the Maya force fields, custom expressions, and/or keyframes.

Opti-FX

In Maya, lighting effects are added to existing lights so they mimic real-world situations. These optical effects (Opti-FX), include lens flare, light glow, and light fog. They can be used alone or in any combination.

Although it is possible to use these effects in any combination, it is the 3D artist's job to know when it is appropriate to use which effect. For example, a lens flare can add some realism to a computer rendered image.

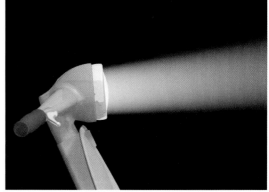

Spotlight using Opti-FX fog

Particle Effects

Particles are used to simulate complex natural phenomena. These phenomena range from rain, gases, and smoke to dust, snow, and fire. A particle system is made up of a number of particles that are usually affected by some dynamic force or combination of forces such as collisions, gravity, or turbulence.

Since particles are simply points in space, these points can be drawn onscreen in different ways. The drawing method used to display the particle is called the particle render type. Maya has software and hardware particle render types. The software particle render types (e.g., cloud, blobby, tube) lend themselves well to cloud and liquid-type effects and can be rendered with shadows, reflections, and refractions. The hardware particle render types (e.g., points, spheres, multi-points) are rendered by the graphics card and more commonly used for granular effects such as rain and sand.

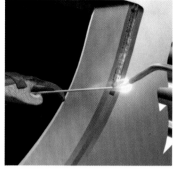

This lighting effect illustrates a lens flare in the upper right of the image and a light glow at the hottest point of the welding torch. Controls are available for tuning these effects to provide just the right balance in the image.

A welding bead is created by emitting a particle defined as the blobby render type. Where the particles overlap, they "blob" together forming a liquid-like appearance. Attributes for threshold and radius on the particles determine how large the particles are rendered and how they blob together.

Maya Paint Effects

Paint Effects allows you to use brushes to paint rendered strokes. You can paint in a 3D scene or onto a 2D canvas with editable, pressure sensitive pre-set brushes. Paint Effects includes the typical natural media brush types such as pastels, crayons, and watercolors, but it goes beyond this to create other special effects. These effects range from plant life such as trees and flowers, to hair and feathers and to particle systems such as fire, lightning, rain, snow, and clouds. Paint Effects brushes can be customized and applied to keyframe animation.

Compositing Effects

Not all effects have to be rendered directly in Maya. Using a compositing package such as Maya Fusion or Maya Composer, you can add effects in the post-production stage. Compositing software lets you color correct your renderings and add effects such as glow, blur, grain, fog, and others to turn simple shapes and forms into more natural-looking forms. If you combine a hardware rendered particle simulation with compositing effects, you can control all aspects of your work.

Rain

Lightning

Sparks

Fire

Geometry
The first layer is geometry rendered with no effects. In compositing, this layer can be color corrected to boost the image quality. The geometry could be saved out as a single image or as a series of render passes where objects can be worked on individually.

Inner Spark
These hardware rendered particles have been enhanced with several compositing effects. The sparks have been blurred, glow has been added, and color gain and brightness have been adjusted. The layer's mask will be used to knock out the image.

Outer Spark
This layer again shows some hardware rendered particles that have had some glow and grain added in compositing. These two layers show how a simple particle hardware rendering can be enhanced in post-production using compositing effects.

Final Composite
You now have the final image and can evaluate the effects in their completed form. Of course, if you don't like a part, you can rework that layer without having to re-render the whole scene.

Opti-FX

An optical effect in 3D animation is typically a re-creation of lighting qualities found in the real world. A lens flare is an example of how the virtual camera in a 3D animation can mimic the look of a real camera. A light glow effect recreates the perception of atmosphere or smoke surrounding the lighting object. A light fog effect recreates the perception of light penetrating atmosphere or a smoke-filled space. In Maya, these effects are known as Optical Effects, or Opti-FX for short.

Optical and Fog Lighting Effects

Optical effects add depth and realism to the perception of 3D lighting objects. Glows, lens flares, and halos help the light-emitting object achieve a voluminous shape. Light fog also adds depth and realism by generating and defining the perception of distance. When light fog is combined with another optical effect, the result can be a very realistic portrayal of the interaction between light and atmosphere. In Maya, the Opti-FX and shader glow effects are rendered as a post-process (added to the final rendered image after the geometry has been rendered). In a sense, the Opti-FX "pass" is composited on top of the rendered image so that the lens flare, halo, or glow appears between the virtual camera lens and the rest of the scene.

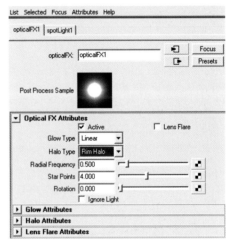

The Attribute Editor display of Opti-FX node's attributes.

Maya Opti-FX Example

The lights in Maya include the option to create optical effects associated with each light. Each light type contains a Light Effects section. This section contains entries for Light Fog and Light Glow attributes. Selecting Light Glow will create an Opti-FX node that is connected to the lightShape node and controls the optical effects associated with this light.

Spot Light Attribute showing Light Effects attributes with Fog and Opti-FX selected.

No Opti-FX applied.

Lens Flare Opti-FX applied.

Lens Flare

A Lens flare Opti-FX mimics the aberrations created by light reflecting on internal lens elements in a real camera lens. Lens flare uses camera position and the angle between the virtual lens and light source to determine the look and motion of the lens flare.

Glow Opti-FX applied.

Glow

Glows in Maya can originate from a light source or from an object's shader. The Glow attributes control the voluminous appearance around the affected region. Glows on lights can be adjusted for **Color**, **Dropoff**, and **Size**. Shader glow provides control over the intensity of the glow and the visibility of the glowing object.

Flare and Glow Opti-FX applied.

Light Fog Effects

Light Fog emanates from the light. The Light Fog attribute is located under each light's Light Effects section next to Light Glow. When Light Fog is selected, a lightFog node is created. The lightFog node has attributes to control **Spread**, **Color**, **Intensity**, and **Fall-off**.

Light Fog opti-FX applied.

Light fog Shadows

Fog lighting also obeys a light's shadow-casting ability. Where a shadow-casting object intersects a light's casted fog shape, the fog is obstructed, forming a shadow.

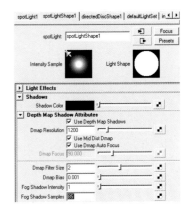

The Depth Map Shadow section of Light Effects contains additional attributes for controlling the accuracy of fog shadow intensity, sampling, and/or smoothness.

Opti-FX and shadow-casting Light Fog applied.

Decay Regions

Light fog obeys Decay Regions on spotlights. Decay Regions are zones of light intensity and fall-off. To adjust Decay Regions interactively, select the Spot Light manipulator tool. Sequence through the tool until the Decay Regions manipulator is selected, then middle mouse button (MMB) click+drag each zone or region to the desired position. The regions can also be manually designated from the Attribute Editor.

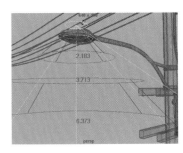

Spot light showing Decay Regions.

Particle Effects

Dynamic movement of a very large number of very small objects is accomplished using a particle system. A particle system can be used to create effects such as smoke, sparks, water and fire.

Particle Simulations

Particles are objects that have no size or volume; they are reference points that are displayed, selected, animated, and rendered differently than other objects in Maya.

When particles are animated, they are generally moved by dynamic forces. Because it would be too time-intensive to animate individual particles, their motion is derived from establishing an environment that will move the particles as the 3D artist intends. Naturally occurring and intuitive factors such as wind, gravity, or bouncing collisions can be used to animate the particles.

Particle Steam
Particles are ideal for creating steam because they can be animated using a dynamics simulation. Therefore, the particles can be affected by real-life forces.

Particles
A particle is best described as a point in 3D space. This point really has no size or shape and, therefore, its position at any point in time can be computed very quickly. This is necessary because typical particle effects can involve thousands of particles. To give particles shape and form, you can choose a Render Type that suits your simulation.

Emitter
An emitter gives birth to particles. An emitter controls attributes such as the type of emission, speed, particles per second, and direction. These attributes can be controlled using the Show Manipulator Tool for more interactive control.

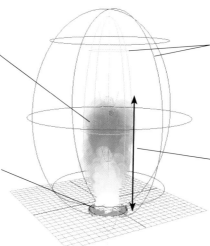

Fields
Fields create forces that affect the way particles animate. For example, you can add a gravity field to make your particles fall to the ground, or a turbulence field to disrupt their motion at a particular point. These fields can be placed in 3D and take effect when the particles pass through their volume of influence.

Lifespan
When a particle leaves the emitter, it is "born" and can be made to "die". This time period is defined as the Lifespan of the particle. Lifespan can then be used to influence other aspects of the particle such as color, opacity, and radius. Lifespan can be set for the whole particle object or for each particle individually.

Particle Attributes

Particle attributes control the behavior of particles in their environment. Some attributes control the whole particle object (Per Object) while others control each individual particle (Per Particle or Array).

Particle Fields

The motion of particles is animated by applying a force to the particles. The resulting effect is determined by the type of field chosen. Maya has three field types: stand-alone, object, and volume.

Per Object
The Add per Object attribute was used to give all the particles one color.

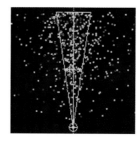

Per Particle
The Add per Particle attribute was used to give the particles different colors. During their Lifespan, particles reflect the values of the default ramp colors: red, green, and blue.

Gravity Field
A directional emitter shows the effect of a gravity field applied nearby.

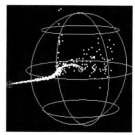

Volume Field
A directional emitter shows the effect of a turbulence field applied within a spherical volume.

Particle Emitters

When a particle is born, it is "emitted" into existence. A particle emitter is generally used to create the particles that will run in the particle system. Surface and curve objects can be emitters in addition to specific objects called emitters. Even more importantly, particles themselves can become emitters. Many popular effects are the result of a particle emitting another particle (e.g., fireworks).

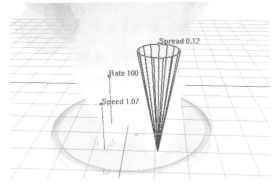

Manipulating Emitter Attributes
The Show Manipulator Tool can be used to interactively modify the emitter attributes.

Emitter Types in Maya

Emitter attributes control the initial position, direction, quantity and velocity of the emitted particles. Each type of emitter in Maya has a specific effect on the particles that are subsequently generated.

Directional
A directional emitter is much like a garden hose nozzle with control over aim and spread.

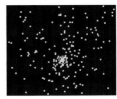

Omni
An omni directional emitter emits in all directions.

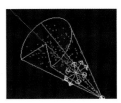

Volume
A volume emitter creates particles inside a primitive object such as a cube, sphere, or torus.

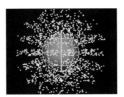

Surface
NURBS and polygon surfaces can emit particles. The surface texture color can even be transferred to the particle as it is emitted.

Curve
NURBS curves can be used as emitters.

Particle
Particles can be emitted from other particles.

Lifespan – The Birth and Death of a Particle

When a particle is born or created, it is given a set of rules (Creation Rules) that govern how the particle will react, move, and look. As it moves through its life, the particle comes under the control of other rules (Runtime Rules) that govern how the particle will react, move, and look during its life until its death. The Lifespan, which can be infinite or of a specific duration, determines when the particle dies. Most effects benefit from individual particles living for a certain time, then dying gracefully.

Many attributes that are animated on a per-particle basis get their values based on the particle's per-particle Lifespan value known as lifespanPP.

age = lifespan (death)
The top of the ramp represents the death of the particles.

Per-object Lifespan Attributes
Lifespan mode can be Constant, Live forever, Random range, or lifespanPP only.

age = 1/2 lifespan

age = 0 (birth)
The bottom of the ramp represents the creation of the particles.

Mapping Lifespan
The Lifespan of a particle system can be mapped with either a color or grayscale ramp. The ramp can be used to control the particles' attributes as they age or you can use the ramp in conjunction with other attributes such as opacity, color, and/or radius. In grayscale ramps, black equals a value of 0 while white equals a value of 1.

Opacity over Lifespan
At birth, the particle opacity is very opaque. As the age increases, the particle opacity changes in accordance with the values of the ramp. By the ramp's end, the particles are transparent (opacity zero).

Color over Lifespan
At birth, the particle color is almost white. As the age increases, the particle color changes in accordance with the values of the ramp so they become darker as the particles get older.

Radius over Lifespan
At birth, the particle radius is miniscule. As the age increases, the particle radius increases in value to 1.

Particle Instancer

Maya's particle instancing feature saves you time when you need to animate a flow of identical objects in a scene. The instances created for the particles can be animated if needed.

For example, suppose you want to create a group of flying bugs where only the placement and orientation of the bugs differ. With Maya, you can animate a single bug, then create instances of the bugs that move with the position and orientation of animated particles.

The instances are not copies. They are references to the original object. Any changes you make to the original object changes the instanced objects. You can control the motion of the individual instanced objects by animating the per particle attributes that control them.

Effects

Maya effects are built-in programs that make it easy for you to create complex animation effects such as smoke and fire. Each Maya effect offers many options and attributes for tuning the results.

Effects   ☒

Create Fire   ◻
Create Smoke   ◻
Create Fireworks   ◻
Create Lightning   ◻
Create Shatter   ◻
Create Curve Flow   ◻
Create Surface Flow   ◻

Delete Surface Flow   ◻

Smoke Effect

The Smoke effect emits smoke from a position in the workspace or from a selected particle object or geometry object. The effect uses a series of smoke images (sprites) included with the Maya software. You can alternatively use your own images. You must hardware render the resulting smoke.

The Smoke effect creates several custom attributes in the emitted particle object it creates. The custom attributes control a combination of field and emitter attributes to lessen the settings you would otherwise need to make to tune the smoke.

You'll often need to emit smoke from part of an object rather than from its entire geometry. A common technique in such cases is to emit from an invisible geometric object in that area.

Fire Effect

You can use the Fire effect to emit fire from a NURBS or polygons surface, particle object, NURBS curve, selected component of an object or even a lattice point.

The Fire effect creates several custom attributes in the emitted particle object it creates. Tweak these attributes to customize the fire to suit your needs.

It's often useful to use the Fire effect on the same geometry more than once. By setting options differently with each usage, you can create a complex look not possible with a single usage.

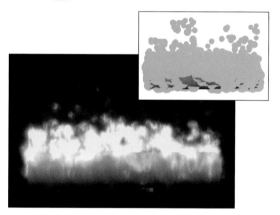

Fireworks Effect

You use the Fireworks effect to make fireworks displays quickly and easily. The effect creates a number of rockets that fly up, leave a trail as they fly, and burst. Gravity fields are also created for all particles. Initially, the effect randomly chooses colors and positions for rocket launches and bursts. You can edit these defaults later. The fireworks are rendered as streaks in software mode.

This effect will create handles on which are located several attributes controlling the fireworks' properties. Even if the default attributes give a nice, ready to render look, you can tweak it in many ways to make it do what you want.

Lightning Effect

When you create lightning, you set the Lightning Creation Controls in the Create Lightning Effect Options window to determine certain aspects. You cannot change these once the lightning is created. If you want to change them, you must delete the lightning and recreate it.

You can also set the Lightning attributes in the Options window. These attributes can be edited after you create the lightning.

To create the effect, simply select two or more objects and the lightning will be created between all of them. The order of selection determines the direction of the lightning, depending on the Creation Option you selected.

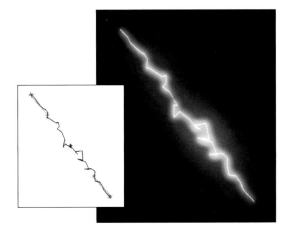

Curve Flow Effect

When you create a Curve Flow effect, select a curve and make sure that there are control points where the flow should change direction and size. Once the curve flow is created, an emitter and flow locators appear on the curve. The flow locators are visual aids that show the maximum spread of the particles during animation.

You can edit the Flow attributes of the Curve Flow effect by choosing the selection handle in the viewport. Note that the distance and size of the locators will alter the speed and spread of the particles.

There is an option to display circles for control segments and subsegments that also shows a wireframe representing the cylindrical region of flow. This gives you a more detailed view of the region of flow.

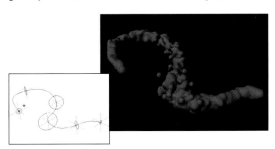

Shatter Effect

Shatter provides three methods of breaking the object: Surface Shatter, Solid Shatter, and Crack Shatter.

Once you've shattered your object, you can move the shards with the Move Tool and keyframe the motion, or you can connect the shards to a Dynamics field and let the field move the shards.

Surface shatter breaks the selected object along polygonal boundaries. You can use surface shatter to break an object into individual polygons.

Solid shatter breaks the surface of an object but keeps the interior polygons and creates solid pieces. It does not break the object along polygonal boundaries so the edges of the shattered pieces are more realistic.

Crack shatter creates cracks that radiate from selected points. You use crack shatter on an open polygonal object.

Surface Flow Effect

Surface Flow is very much like the curve flow, exept that you can create a flat surface, like a river. You get several attributes to play with when you select the flow group's selection handle.

Since the surface flows create expressions in the affiliated particle objects, you should not delete it using the Delete key or **Edit > Delete** option. There is a special menu item that ensures it gets deleted correctly.

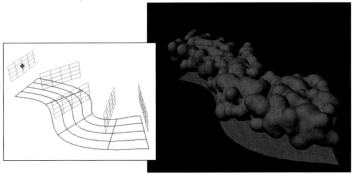

Paint Effects

Paint Effects offers a wide variety of brushes that let you add real-time effects to a scene. With this toolset, you can work on either a 2D canvas or in a typical 3D scene. This makes it possible to create either bitmap images or integrated brush strokes that can be viewed and animated in 3D. Paint Effects offers a vast library of pre-sets that make it easy to add effects to your scene with a few brush strokes. As you learn more, you can also enhance the existing brushes and even add your own to the library.

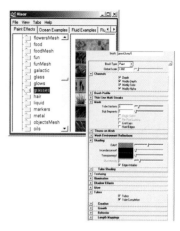

You can access all the Paint Effects pre-set brushes through the Visor. Attributes are accessed through the Template Brush window.

Paint Effects Basics

Paint Effects offers 3D artists a number of pre-set brushes ranging from a simple pen stroke to a complex brush, such as an animated tree blowing in the wind. The Attribute Editor for Paint Effects has some 274 attributes. With these attributes, you can create a number of effects brushes ranging from an oil or watercolor brush to many animated 3D brushes such as lightning, fire, hair, and plants.

Visor
From the Visor, you can access a palette of pre-set brushes. When you select a brush option, the attributes for that brush are transferred to the Template Brush.

Template Brush
The Template Brush stores the attribute settings for your next brush stroke. You can edit a pre-set brush by selecting it in the Visor and then changing the various attributes in the Template Brush window.

Paint Scene
You can use any brush to paint on any object. When you paint in a scene, your brush works in 3D space. Painting in a scene also gives you the option to have your brush animated.

Paint Canvas
In Canvas mode, you can use any brush to paint on a 2D canvas. You can then save the image out to an image file to use as a texture map.

Paint Effects Dependencies

When you select a brush and draw a Paint Effects stroke in a 3D scene, you are actually creating a curve that provides information as to where the brush will be placed in the scene. Once the curve is drawn, Paint Effects creates a stroke Shape node. This node takes shape information from the curveShape node and applies the brush properties from the Template Brush to it.

CurveShape Node
This node keeps the CV information for the curve. It defines the shape of the curve itself.

Transform Node
This node contains the actual transform information for the curve. With this node, you can modify or keyframe any animation or scale the size of your curve.

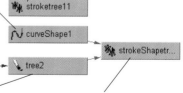

Brush Node
This node takes all of the attribute information from the current Template Brush. To change attributes of a brush once it is already painted, you change the attributes contained in this node.

StrokeShape Node
The strokeShape node contains information such as pressure mapping, sample density smoothing, and surface offset.

Painting in Canvas Mode

Paint Effects can be used to paint 2D images or textures using any of the preset brushes, or ones you have customized yourself. You can also add blurs or smears to existing paint on the canvas using preset brushes.

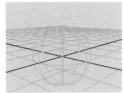

Image Size
You can specify the size of your canvas by selecting Canvas > Set Size.

Background Color
You can change the background color of the canvas while in canvas mode by selecting Canvas > Clear - ❑

Wrap Image
Turning on the wrap image feature gives you the ability to create a tileable texture.

Display Alpha
You have the option to create a mask channel with any brush stroke.

Painting in Scene Mode

When you paint in Scene mode, you paint in 3D space. In Scene mode, you can paint directly on objects, or in front or behind them. Many of the strokes that you paint in scene mode use the actual lights in the scene. Scene mode also lets you animate any brush. As in Canvas mode, you also have the option to apply a blur or smears to any brush in 3D.

Resolution
This sets how much of your brush detail will be shown in your work window. A higher setting will give you the highest display resolution of your brush stroke, but it will also take longer to refresh your screen. Rendering Paint Effects will be at full resolution regardless of this setting.

Shading
This option allows you to preview your strokes in either wireframe, shaded, or textured modes. A higher setting will take longer to refresh.

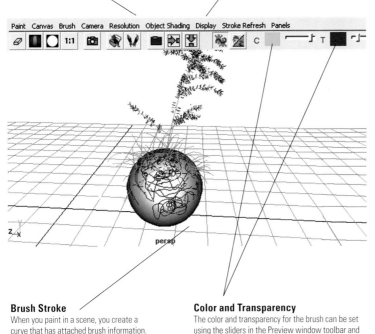

Brush Stroke
When you paint in a scene, you create a curve that has attached brush information.

Color and Transparency
The color and transparency for the brush can be set using the sliders in the Preview window toolbar and in the Template Brush Editor.

How to Paint on an Object

To paint on an object in Scene mode, you must select the object and make it paintable. You can use this application to paint objects like hair on a character or paint trees on a sculpted surface.

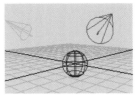

Step 1: Add Lights to Your Scene
Create and aim some lights on the object in your scene.

Step 2: Select Your Object
Select the object you want to paint on.

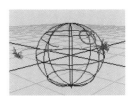

Step 3: Make Object Paintable
Select Paint Effects > Make Paintable.

Step 4: Select a Brush and Paint
Select a brush from the Visor and paint on your object.

Blending

Blending takes the shape or color attributes of a brush and combines those elements into your current brush. Selecting a brush in the Visor makes it your Template Brush. Right-click over another preset in the Visor and you are given the option to blend either shape, color, or the entire brush in varying percentages to your Template Brush.

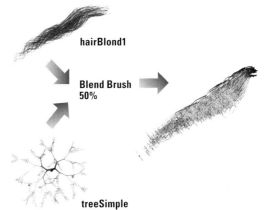

hairBlond1

Blend Brush 50%

treeSimple

Brushes

The power of painting with Paint Effects is that brushes contain a large number of attributes that make it possible to achieve almost any required effect. In a 3D scene, these attributes are stored with the brush stroke and can be edited after painting. Therefore, it is a good idea to learn the role each of the attributes plays in the look of a typical brush stroke. As you learn about the attributes, you will have more control over your own strokes.

Basic Brush Attributes

Paint Effects works by creating a series of dots along a curve. When you paint with a brush, the closer the dots are together, the smoother your brush stroke will look. Using the Attribute Editor, you can control the size, color, and spacing of these dots. This method lets you create many different effects. In the Attribute Editor, there is a setting called Global Scale. This setting scales all the attributes proportionally to your scene. If you paint a stroke that is too big, simply use a lower value for Global Scale.

Paint Effects allows you to create 2D images using a variety of pre-set brushes. You also have the option to smudge, blur, or add water to your images to create interesting effects.

Brush Profile

When you paint, you are basically creating round dots along a curve. By opening the Brush Profile attributes in the Attribute Editor, you can set how many of these dots are created and how far apart they are spaced. By setting Stamp Density, Brush Width, and Softness you can choose between a dotted line with harsh edges or a soft flowing brush stroke.

Brush Width

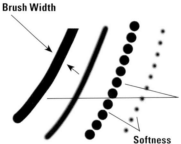

Softness

Stamp Density A low value creates a dotted line while a high value creates a smooth, continuous line.

Shading

You can shade the Color, Incandescence, and Transparency of any Paint Effects stroke. In the Paint Effects window, you will find sliders that let you change these settings quickly. For more options, you can also open the Template Brush window to make changes. If you are working in 2D canvas mode, you can only make changes to brush settings before you paint with them.

Incandescence

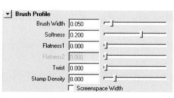

Transparency

Color

Illumination

Every brush stroke can contain lighting information. In the Template Brush window you have the option to use real lights from the scene or you can choose to have the brush be self-lit by specifying the position of the specific light. In the Illumination section of the Template Brush window, you can also adjust specular qualities such as Specular, Specular Power, and Specular Color. By doing so, you can create a 3D feel to an otherwise 2D brush stroke.

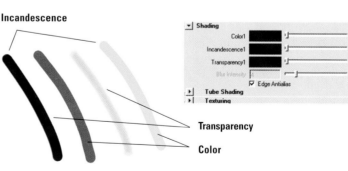

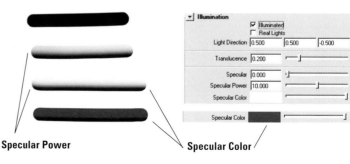

Specular Power

Specular Color

Shadow Effects

You have the option to add shadows to your paint stroke. When using Paint Effects, you can use either Fake or Real Shadows. Fake Shadows take less time to render and are usually sufficient for 2D textures or flat surfaces.

Real Shadows require you to select Cast Shadows from the Attribute Editor, and then turn on Depth Map shadows for the light you want to cast shadows. Real Shadows only work in Paint Scene mode and show up when you render.

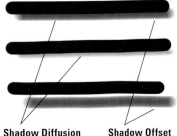
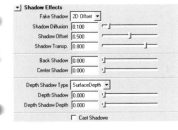

Shadow Diffusion   Shadow Offset

Texturing

You can add a texture to a Paint Effects brush using either a Checker, U or V Ramp, Fractal or File Texture. This is done by first enabling the Map Color box in the Template Brush window located in the Shading section, and then selecting what type of texture you want to map in the Texture Type box. You also have an option to choose which type of Mapping Method to use. You can map the texture to your stroke using either 2D or 3D methods.

When you enable the Map Color or Map Opacity, you will notice that as you map a texture to a stroke, there is a separate color channel for the texture and for the original shading color. The original shading color value is still used. When you map a texture to your stroke, the texture uses the colors in the texture color section. The texture then takes the original texture color and multiplies the texture color value by the color value. For example, if you have a stroke that has a Checker mapped to it, and your original color is black, you will not see the Checker effect because black equals 0. If you change the color to white (value = 1), you will see all colors in the texture section mapped to your stroke.

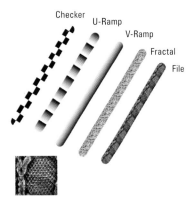
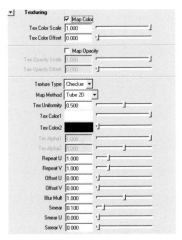

Checker
U-Ramp
V-Ramp
Fractal
File

File Texture

Mapping Methods

When you map a texture, Maya gives you the option to use different mapping methods.

Full View
Full View Mapping maps your chosen texture across the entire screen view, and reveals it where you paint.

Tube2D Mapping
Tube2D Mapping maps your texture along the part of the stroke that is visible to the camera, projected as if the stroke were flat and oriented towards the camera.

3D Mapping
The 3D Mapping method wraps the file around the actual stroke in 3D space, as if the stroke were really a tube (or in this case, a snake).

Common Values

When you explore some of the many attributes that make up Paint Effects, you will see some recurring attributes:

Values 1 and 2

Certain values have a 1 or 2 beside them. These are values that affect strokes where tubes are enabled. The value 1 stands for the base of the tube, while 2 represents the tip of the tube.

Dropout

Dropout defines the proportion of the given attribute that is randomly "pruned" to give a more natural look. For example, a Twig Dropout setting of 0 will produce exactly the same amount of twigs each time it is created, where a setting of 1 will prune all twigs.

Decay

This value defines the rate at which a factor diminishes for a given attribute. For example, setting a value of 1 for Split Size Decay creates branches the same size as the branch they are branched from. Setting a value less than one will produce them smaller than the original.

Rand

Sets the amount of randomization on a given attribute. The larger the Rand value, the higher the variation in values. For example, if Split Rand is 0, branching will occur at equal intervals along the tube. A higher value will cause the spacing to be more random.

Bias

Bias is used in conjunction with a random value for a given attribute. Setting a value for Bias will push or pull those random values towards the Bias values. For example, setting a positive value for Bias will create more wider tubes than thinner ones. A value of 0 will create just as many wide tubes as thin ones.

Tubes

A tube is an object that grows from a stroke path. To create vegetation, trees, hair, rain, and other unique 3D brush strokes, you must enable the Tubes option on a Paint Effects stroke. When you enable Tubes, a simple stroke sprouts a series of tubes. Enabling Tubes in the Attribute Editor allows you to create brushes that simulate vegetation or other organic growth. The attributes are named after the parts of a tree and are very similar in their function. However, the power of Paint Effects is that it allows you to pick which specific parts of the Tube you want to use; nothing stops you from using only some of these elements. The shape of the tube can then be shaded and lit using the same lighting as your scene.

Tube Creation

As you paint a stroke, sample points are created along the stroke. The number of sample points on a stroke depends on the settings you make to the attributes in the strokeShape node. At each sample point, a new tube can be created and any existing tubes will grow a new segment. These segments can then become branches, twigs, leaves, flowers, or buds. By setting different attribute combinations, the tubes can grow into an infinite number of shapes and sizes.

Tube Width2

Tube Width1

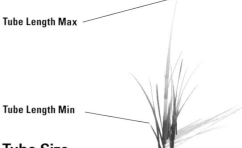

Tube Length Max

Tube Length Min

Tube Shape

At the most basic level, the shape of a tube is determined by Tube Width 1 and 2 values, which set how thick the tube will be at the base and the tip, respectively. Other attributes that affect the shape of a tube are Twist, Flatness, Noise, Wiggle, and Curl.

Tube Size

The attributes Length Min and Length Max determine the minimum and maximum length that a tube can be. A brush with a big difference in these values will create a stroke with tubes that are quite varied in height.

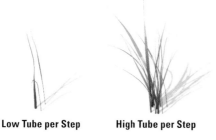

Low Tube per Step   High Tube per Step

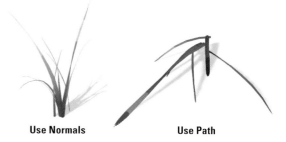

Use Normals   Use Path

Tube Density

Density is dependent on the **Tubes per Step** attribute. Increasing the value of this attribute creates more tubes at each sample point along the curve.

Tube Direction

Tube Direction specifies whether the tubes use the Normals or path direction. If you use the Normals, you can then set the Elevation and **Azimuth**, which will determine the direction the tubes point. If you use **Path Direction**, the tubes will try to follow the path of the curve you paint.

Growth

Growth is used to grow the tubes over time and have them sprout branches, twigs, leaves, flowers, and buds. Adjusting the attributes in each of these subsections allows you to simulate many natural, and some unnatural effects. Much like a shading network, it is a good idea to consider the various material qualities you want to achieve in advance. For example, if you understand how a plant looks and behaves, you will find it easier to translate these into the various Paint Effects growth attributes.

Branches
The number of branches created at each split is determined by Num Branches.

Twigs
Twigs sprout from branches or tubes.

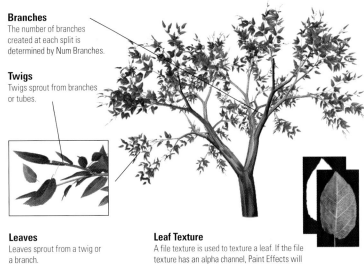

Leaves
Leaves sprout from a twig or a branch.

Leaf Texture
A file texture is used to texture a leaf. If the file texture has an alpha channel, Paint Effects will make it transparent automatically.

Flowers
Flowers grow in a radial pattern around tubes or branches.

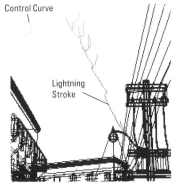

Buds
Buds sprout from the tip of a branch or twig.

Working With Paint Effects Tubes

Through the use of tubes, you can create a large number of effects such as rain, lightning, sparks, and fire. In most cases, you will pick a pre-set brush and then modify the attributes to fit into the look of your scene. When you paint a stroke into your scene, you generally paint the stroke onto your target surface.

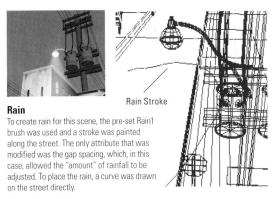

Rain Stroke

Rain
To create rain for this scene, the pre-set Rain1 brush was used and a stroke was painted along the street. The only attribute that was modified was the gap spacing, which, in this case, allowed the "amount" of rainfall to be adjusted. To place the rain, a curve was drawn on the street directly.

Lightning
To create lightning, a small stroke using the Lightning3 pre-set brush was made near the top of the transformer. A short single stroke was used to make sure that there would be only one bolt of lightning. The shading and glow attributes were set to a white and blue to create the bluish glow. Finally, a control curve was used to direct the lightning to the desired angle in the sky.

Control Curve

Lightning Stroke

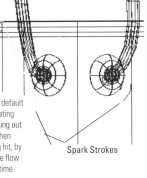
Spark Strokes

Sparks
The sparks were created by using the default pre-set sparkExplosion brush and creating two small strokes near the wires coming out of the transformer. The sparks were then set to animate only after the lightning hit, by turning on the clip time attribute in the flow animation section and by setting the time that the sparks were to occur.

Fire
Fire was created using a standard fire pre-set brush. A curve was drawn along the top of the transformer, then Global Scale was increased to create flames that matched the size of the transformer and the scene. The smoke was created using the basic risingSmoke2 brush. The animation of the flames is generated by turbulence forces that were built into the fire effects.

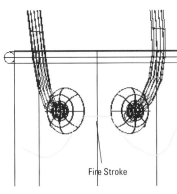
Fire Stroke

Brush Stroke

When you draw a brush stroke with a pressure-sensitive graphics tablet and pen, you modify parts of the stroke based on how hard you press as you paint. In Maya, this information is retained in the strokeShape node and offers another way of controlling how the brush information appears when rendered. In 3D scenes, you can turn curves into strokes and apply brush settings. You can also capture the brush attributes from any brush and create your own pre-set for later use.

Stroke Attributes

Strokes are the curve that the Paint Effects brush is applied to. When you paint, you will notice that painting very slowly produces a result very different from painting quickly, since there are more sample points along the stroke. In this respect, your stroke acts much like a paint brush on a real canvas. Setting attributes in the strokeShape node affects the position and number of tubes that are contained on a particular curve.

Painting Curves
The power wires in the above image were created not with geometry, but with curves that have the default template brush stroke applied.

Low Sample Density

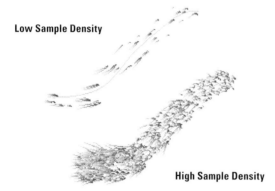

High Sample Density

Sample Density
A sample point along a stroke either starts a tube or grows a tube by one segment. If you draw a stroke slowly or with heavy pressure, there will be many more sample points in a given length as opposed to a curve that was drawn quickly or with light pressure. Increasing the sample density on the stroke that was drawn quickly can help make the brush look more similar to the one that was drawn slowly.

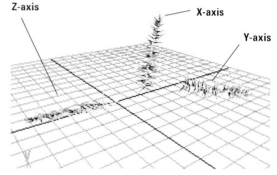

Z-axis   X-axis   Y-axis

Normal Direction
When you create a stroke on the ground plane, the Use Normal attribute is automatically turned on and set to the Up Vector. You can change this setting and have the Normals point in either X, Y, or Z directions. Any tubes contained on that stroke will grow in the selected direction. When you paint on an object, the Use Normal is turned off and the surface Normal of the geometry is applied instead.

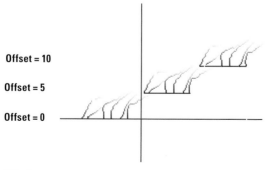

Offset = 10

Offset = 5

Offset = 0

Offset
The offset lets you set a value that will paint the brush at a distance away from the surface you are painting. For example, if you want to place some clouds in the sky, you could use a cloud brush with a high value for offset and paint on the ground plane. This will put your stroke on the surface, but your brush will actually paint the clouds away from the stroke.

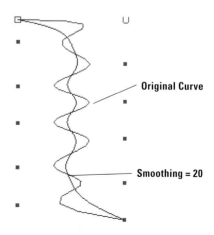

Original Curve

Smoothing = 20

Smoothing
Smoothing allows you to dampen the values between CVs on a curve to create a smoother path for your stroke. With enough smoothing, it is possible to create a straight line out of even the most drastic curve.

Pressure Mapping

The strokeShape node also contains pressure mapping information.
If you use a graphics pressure sensitive tablet, up to 3 brush-creation
attributes can be mapped to the pressure used on the tablet as a stroke
is drawn. You can access these settings by selecting **Paint Effects >
Paint Effects Tool - option**.

Combining Mappings

Pressure mapping becomes most effective when
you combine different mappings to simulate an
actual paint stroke. For example, the stroke to
the left uses scale and transparency mappings.
Pressing hard on the tablet gives you a thick dark
stroke, while pressing lightly gives you a thin,
wispy stroke.

Scale

Transparency

Softness

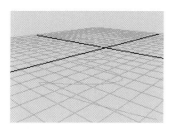

Num Leaves

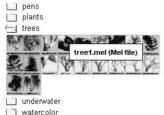

Tubes per Step

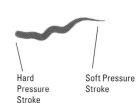

Hard
Pressure
Stroke

Soft Pressure
Stroke

How to Put a Brush on a Selected Stroke

You can apply any brush to any curve or Paint Effects stroke in your
scene. This is useful for using the same brush on multiple curves
without having to paint each stroke.

How to Create Your own Pre-set Brushes

Once you have created a brush that you are happy
with, you will want to save it so that you can use it in
the future. Maya lets you customize your workspace by
saving your brush to either the Visor or the Shelf.

pens
plants
trees

tree1.mel (Mel file)

underwater
watercolor

Step 1: Select the Stroke
In your scene, select the stroke curve.

Step 2: Load to Template Brush
Open the Visor and select the desired brush
to load it into the Template Brush.

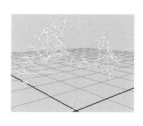

Step 1: Edit Brush Attributes
Edit the brush attributes in the Attribute
Editor or Channel Box to get a brush
you like.

Step 2: Load to Template Brush
Select **Paint Effects > Get Settings** from
Selected Stroke. This will load the brush
into the Template Brush.

Step 3: Apply the Brush
In the Paint Effects menu, select **Paint Effects >
Apply Settings to Selected Strokes**.

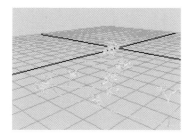

Step 4: Render Your Scene
Add lights to your scene and then render.

Step 3: Save Preset
With the brush loaded into the
Template Brush, select **Paint Effects >
Save Brush Presets**.

Step 4: Grab Icon
Switch to the Paint Effects preview
window by pressing "8" on the keyboard.
With your brush rendered, select **Grab
Icon** and click+drag an area around the
brush to create an icon.

Working with Paint Effects

Animating your brush unleashes the true power of Paint Effects. Some of the pre-set brushes already contain animation. Therefore, animating these brushes is simply a matter of pressing the Play button. An understanding of the types of animation that can be applied to a brush or stroke can take Paint Effects off the canvas and into your animated scenes.

Methods of Animating Brushes and Strokes

There are a number of methods you can use to animate a Paint Effects brush. In some cases, it is as easy as setting a start and end time for your brush. In other cases, it may involve animating an attribute on the brush itself or setting the clip range.

Animate Texture
Any texture assigned to a brush can be animated.

Animate Stroke Attributes
(clip range)
You can animate a stroke attribute, such as the Min clip and Max clip, to create an effect such as a growing vine or a burning fuse.

Control Curves
Not only can you animate the control curves, but you can also animate the attraction to those curves over time.

Attributes that Animate
You can animate the value of any attribute in the Attribute Editor for a particular brush.

Springs
Springs create an expression which causes the tubes to react to the animation of the geometry to which they are attached.

Turbulence

You can add six types of turbulence to a brush with tubes. Turbulence is created in two different ways: a Force tends to push the segments on the tube, whereas a Displacement actually moves the position of the segments on the tube. Keep in mind that the turbulence in Paint Effects is different from and has no connection with the turbulence in Maya Dynamics. Adding Turbulence to a brush will add it only to that brush and not the entire scene.

Local Force
A force is applied in the local space of the tubes.

World Force
Force is applied in world space.

Local Displacement
A displacement is applied in the local space of the tubes.

World Displacement
A displacement is applied in world space.

Grass Wind
A world space force is applied where the force applied to the tips is delayed from that applied at the roots.

Tree Wind
A world space force is used where the outermost branches have a stronger force applied than the parts closer to the root.

Springs

When you create springs, you are creating an expression which takes the force from the animated object and uses it to move the tubes as if they are springs. You can control the Stiffness, Damping and Travel of this simulated spring from the option box. You can create springs by selecting the stroke on the animated surface and applying the menu command found in **Paint Effects > Brush Animation > Make Brush Spring**.

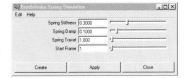

Flow Animation

The setting for Flow Animation acts as the on/off switch for many default animations that are available on a brush. Entering a value for Flow Speed other than 0 turns on the animation, and sets the rate at which these attributes will be animated. Attributes that are affected by flow speed are Texture Maps and Gap Spacing. Keep in mind that Turbulence is controlled separately from, and is not affected by, Flow Animation.

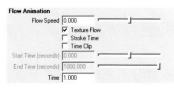

Gap Spacing

Gap spacing involves placing gaps along the length of the tube. Using gap spacing allows you to create new brushes that can mimic certain particle behaviors. The default rain brushes use gap spacing to create the effect of falling rain. Turning on Flow Animation will animate the position of the gaps along the length of the tube.

Gap Spacing

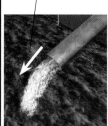

Direction of Flow

Texture Maps

Flow Animation also controls the animation of any textures that are assigned to the Paint Effects stroke. Here a Fractal texture will animate along the tube from the start to the end with a positive value for Flow Speed.

Control Curves

You can use control curves to control the shape and direction of tubes. Control Curves were used to direct the lightning in the image shown below. To control the curves, you can apply attributes that control the amount of Attract and Follow. Also, you can set the Maximum Distance that defines the distance at which the curve will stop attracting the tubes. If you use control curves, it is not a good idea to add springs because using the two together may give you unexpected results.

Animating Stroke Clipping

Min Clip and Max Clip values will allow you to set the start and end of your stroke. By animating the Max Clip value and setting the Tube completion to Off in the brush attributes, you can get the effect of a vine growing up a stop sign.

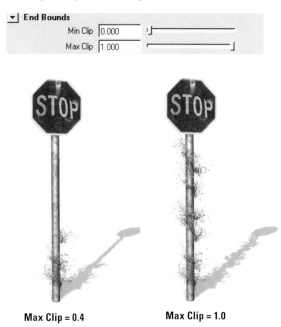

Max Clip = 0.4   **Max Clip = 1.0**

Convert Paint Effects to Polygons

You can convert Paint Effects strokes to polygonal meshes, including construction history, using **Modify > Convert > Paint Effects To Polygons**. Keeping the history might be important to you since you can keep any kind of animation on your strokes.

Converting allows you to render in any renderer, including the Maya Software Renderer, mental ray for Maya, the Maya Hardware Renderer, and the vector renderer. It allows you to have Paint Effects show up in reflections, refractions, and through transparent objects. Also, it allows you to use other polygon editing tools on them.

You can edit brush attributes and see the effect on the output mesh. Shaders that closely match the look of the Paint Effects render are automatically generated and assigned to the resulting meshes. You can optionally choose to output color per vertex and also to bake lighting onto the mesh.

Paint Effect   **Polygons**

Cloth

With Cloth, you can create realistic animated cloth within the Maya environment. Cloth gives you the ability to model garments for any animated 3D figure, apply dynamic effects, and simulate the cloth behavior.

If you are creating a simple piece of cloth like a sheet or tablecloth, you can create a polymesh or NURBS shape and make it a cloth object. Alternatively, attaching panels together for constructing a garment is similar to the way a tailor makes clothing.

Cloth Animation

Cloth simulations are driven by dynamic solvers; there are no keyframes. A number of constraint types in Maya allow you to restrict the movement of your character's clothing. Collision constraints let your character's clothing move with the character's body.

Cloth objects

A cloth object is a piece of geometry simulated as cloth. You create cloth objects from polygonal shapes or NURBS shapes. The original shape is hidden and the tessellated cloth shape is displayed. The original shape and the cloth shape are grouped under the object's transform.

With NURBS objects and certain procedurally-generated polygonal objects, you can get artificial stress lines caused by the regular tessellation. If you change the topology of the polygonal object after simulating, you have to resimulate.

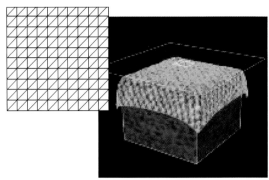

Garments

A garment is one or more panels that are seamed together to form a cloth. A panel is made up of two or more NURBS curves that are on the same plane and form a closed region.

When you create a garment from curves, Cloth creates a mesh with varying sizes of triangles that are randomly distributed. The mesh has no regularity or stress lines. This creates more natural folds.

In addition, if you change the resolution of a garment after simulating, Cloth can update the geometry without resimulating. However, you need to simulate for the cloth to move with the new resolution.

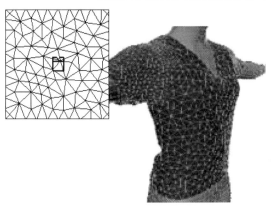

Collision Objects

In order for your cloth to drape over your model or an object, you need to make it a collision object. When you make an object a cloth collision object, Maya connects it to the cloth solver and adds three collision object attributes.

Polygonal objects, NURBS, and Subdivision Surfaces can all be used as collision objects. If your model is a NURBS object or a Subdivision Surface, Maya automatically converts it to polygons when you make it a collision object.

Dress-up Pose

It is recommended to start the cloth simulation from a dress-up pose. This will eliminate any self-collision of the garment worn by the character, and minimize wrinkling in the initial fitting of the garment.

To create a character animation, you should move your character from the dress-up pose to the position it will be in at the start of the animation. You may want to add some frames to the start of your scene to accommodate this transition, or, the cloth might not react as expected.

Draping and fitting

After you create the garment, you drape it and fit it to the character. To drape the garment on the model, you specify the model as a collision object and use the cloth solver to drape the garment over the model.

Fitting involves modifying the original garment to accommodate peculiarities of the character on which it is draped. You can influence how the cloth settles on the character using constraints and dynamic fields. For example, you can pull out wrinkles or pin portions of the garment to specific places on the character. You can assign different properties to the panels and set various attributes of the cloth to change the physical behavior of the cloth.

Once the garment has settled, you can save this initial position of the garment and begin animating.

Simulate Cloth

Once you have your cloth ready to drape over your character, you can start the simulation. The simulation is performed by the cloth solver, which assembles information on all the garments, cloth objects, bodies they interact with, and any fields or constraints applied to the cloth.

Cloth Cache

When you simulate cloth by playing through the Time Slider, Cloth creates a cache file to store all the positions of the vertices of the cloth. The cache lets you quickly preview the results of the cloth simulation without having to render to a flipbook. This offers many benefits, including scrubbing back and forth in the Time Slider and re-using a cache so you don't have to solve at render time.

Cloth Constraints

Sometimes you may want to constrain certain parts of your clothing to your character so they don't fall off. You can do this using constraints. For example, you can use constraints to make sure the pants of your character stay on, or to keep straps in a dress attached to the shoulders. In addition, you can use constraints to pin clothing together or attach items such as buttons or pockets.

Dynamic Fields

Because Cloth is fully integrated with Maya, you can use Maya's dynamic fields to affect the motion of your cloth. You create the field the same way you create a field in Maya. You connect the field to cloth using a type of constraint known as a field constraint. You can connect field constraints to cloth vertices or panel curves.

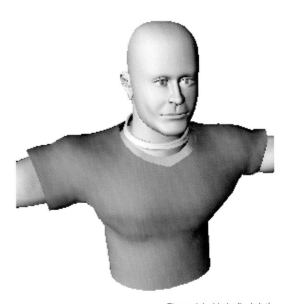

The model with the final cloth shape after the simulation.

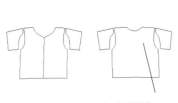

Intersecting NURBS Curves

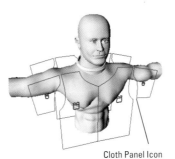

Cloth Panel Icon

Step 1
The cloth object begins as a series of intersecting NURBS curves that form the front and back shape of the shirt.

Step 2
Panels are defined for the different regions of the shirt by selecting Cloth > Create Panel.

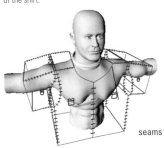

seams

Step 3
Next, one panel is defined by using Cloth > Create Garment. Seams are created where each panel overlaps. This creates a "cage" around the model and a polygonal "cloth mesh."

Step 4
The body geometry is made into a collision object by selecting Cloth > Create Collision Object. At this point, no dynamic interaction has occurred between the cloth object (shirt) and the collision object (body). Therefore, the cloth appears very loose.

Step 5
Select Simulation > Start Simulation to perform the cloth simulation. Maya applies gravity to the cloth. Based on the cloth properties set by the user, the cloth collides, interacts, and settles to take shape around the body.

Fur and Hair

Creating fur involves the simulation of realistic, self-shadowing fur and short hair. Fur characteristics are defined by a fur description, which contains the definition of all attributes for a particular type of fur like color, width, length, baldness, opacity, scraggle, curl, density, and so on. Using Maya Artisan, you can paint most fur attributes directly onto the surface and actually comb the fur and make clumps.

A hair system is a collection of hair follicles, each of which hosts a hair curve and includes various attributes for modifying the appearance and style of the hair, including a braid attribute. The hair system output can be in the form of NURBS curves, Paint Effects strokes, or both. Since Hair is a set of dynamic curves, you can also use these curves to create non-hair effects, including a suspension bridge, an octopus or other sea creature, or a lofted surface from a curve.

Creating Fur

You create fur by creating fur descriptions. Maya includes a set of fur description presets that you can use as a starting point for various fur types.

You can attach a fur description to any single or multi-surface NURBS, polygonal or Subdivision Surface model. You can then style the fur, such as shorten or lengthen the fur on some parts of the model, using attribute value maps, or by painting fur attribute values directly on the model using Maya Artisan. When you apply fur attribute value maps, or paint fur attribute values, the global fur description attributes do not change.

When you render a scene, Fur exports the description values to maps that the renderer can use.

Blending Presets
You can load Fur Preset settings into any fur description, and blend Fur Presets to get new variations.

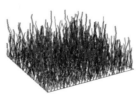

Fur Feedback
Fur feedback provides you with a representation of the fur description on your model while you work.

Bison

Dreadlocks

Gorilla

Lion Mane

Llama

Polar Bear

Porcupine

Punk

Fur and Hair

Creating Hair

The hair system is a collection of hair follicles. A hair follicle in human hair typically hosts one hair, whereas in Maya each hair follicle hosts a hair curve. The hair follicle controls the attributes and curves associated with a particular hair clump, and how the hairs attach to a NURBS or polygonal surface.

The hair system output can be in the form of NURBS curves, Paint Effects strokes, or both. If the specified output is NURBS curves, each follicle contains one NURBS curve that represents the position of the hair in that follicle. If the specified output is Paint Effects, each follicle has a hair clump (strokes) containing information about the color and shading of the hair, as well as its position. There are various attributes on the follicle for modifying the appearance and style of the hair, including a braid attribute. You can make hairs in a hair system collide with themselves and with other objects.

Hair Constraints

You can use constraints to create effects with hair curves. There are five types of constraints you can create using **Hair > Create Constraint**. When you create a constraint, the constraint is set to affect the selected hair curves. At the start frame, the hair simulation determines the nearest points on the constrained curves to the constraint node position. As the simulation runs, the constraint works only on this initial set of points, not the entire curve. The constraint type determines how the simulation deals with these points. In general you should apply constraints after modeling and determining the hair start positions and shapes. The constraint acts by applying forces to the set of points.

The Rubber Band constraint is like attaching hair with rubber bands. If the distance between a point and the constraint becomes greater than the rubber band length, a force is applied pulling it toward the constraint.

The Stick constraint is like attaching sticks in the hair, where the sticks may rotate freely about the constraint center. This is similar to the Rubber Band constraint, except that it tends to keep all the constrained points at a fixed distance from the constraint center.

The Transform constraint is like constraining the points to a block of jelly. Unlike the Stick constraint, when the constraint node is rotated or scaled it will pull along the constrained points. It can be used to simulate hair being grabbed and twisted by a hand. If you animate the constraint's scale, the hair can be pulled together or pushed apart.

The Hair to Hair constraint allows you to bind hairs together, where the hair group is free to move with respect to the constraint position.

The Hair Bunch constraint can help add body to the hair as it animates in a fashion similar to self-collision but with much less computation. The initial set of points nearest the constraint will repel each other where they overlap. There is also a slight static cling where the points stick together slightly when they touch.

Hair with Paint Effects Brush

You can assign a Paint Effects brush to the hair system. This is useful for creating effects, such as vines or ivy, for hair.

Also, to create your own hair look with polygons, you can create a mesh brush and paint a test stroke, then assign this brush to the hair system following the procedure above. Next, convert the Paint Effects to polygons. You can even texture these with hair images. The width attributes on the hair system still affect the polygons.

Hair System Anatomy

A hair system is composed of multiple hair follicles. When modifying a hairSystem attribute, it affects the entire hair system and when modifying a follicle attribute, it affects only the selected follicle.

Each follicle is composed of three curves. The Start Curves/Position is the position of the hair when it is first created. It is also the position of the hair at the start frame of the simulation. The Rest **Curves/Position** is the position of the hair when no forces are acting upon it. You can use these curves to influence the shape of the hair. The Current Position is how the hair behaves when you play the simulation, which includes dynamics.

Finally, the Paint Effects stroke is the part of the hair follicle that renders. Modifying the Paint Effect brush will change the look of the hair when rendered.

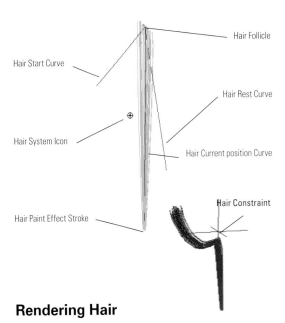

Hair Follicle
Hair Start Curve
Hair Rest Curve
Hair System Icon
Hair Current position Curve
Hair Constraint
Hair Paint Effect Stroke

Rendering Hair

Hair can be rendered using Paint Effects, so the hairs you see rendered are Paint Effects strokes. You can also convert Paint Effects to polygons and render in another renderer, such as mental ray, or output just the dynamic curves to an external renderer.

Just like any other simulation, you can create a cache file to store all the positions of the hair curves. This offers many benefits, including scrubbing back and forth in the Time Slider and re-using a cache so you don't have to solve at render time.

Fluids

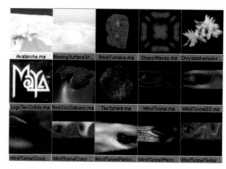

To assist you in creating your own fluid effects, a set of example fluid files is included with Maya. To access the example fluid files, initial states, and presets, select **Fluid Effects > Get Fluid Example**.

Fluid Effects is a technology for realistically simulating and rendering fluid motion. Fluid Effects lets you create a wide variety of 2D and 3D atmospheric, pyrotechnic, space, and viscous liquid effects. You can use the Fluid Effects solvers to simulate these effects, or you can use fluid animated textures for more unique, distinguishing effects. Fluid Effects also includes an ocean shader for creating realistic open water. You can float objects on the ocean surface and have those objects react to the motion of the water. Note that Fluids Effects can only simulate mixing elements that have the same density, for example, gas in gas or liquid in liquid. It does not simulate gas in liquid or vice-versa at this time.

Dynamic Fluid Effects

Dynamic fluid effects behave according to the natural laws of fluid dynamics, a branch of physics that uses mathematical equations to calculate how things flow. For dynamic fluid effects, Maya simulates fluid motion by solving the Navier-Stokes fluid dynamics equations at each step. You can texture dynamic fluids, apply forces to them, and have them collide with and move geometry, affect soft bodies, and interact with particles.

Non-dynamic Fluid Effects

3D fluids inherently require extra data to define them, which can make them very large. This extra data can slow a dynamic simulation exponentially because more calculations must be performed at every step of the simulation. For a less memory intensive effect, you can use a 2D fluid (with less data), or you can create a non-dynamic fluid.

Non-dynamic fluid effects do not use the fluid solvers to simulate fluid motion. For non-dynamic fluid effects, you create the look of a fluid using textures and you create fluid motion by animating texture attributes.

Since Maya doesn't solve the fluid dynamics equations for non-dynamic fluids, rendering this type of fluid is much faster than rendering a dynamic fluid.

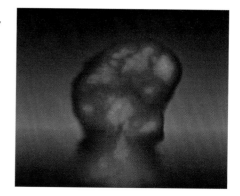

Oceans and Ponds

You can create Ocean and Pond fluids to simulate large realistic water surfaces, such as stormy oceans with foam and swimming pools. Oceans are NURBS planes with ocean shaders assigned to them. Ponds are 2D fluids that use a spring mesh solver and a height field. Also, you can add Wakes to Oceans and Ponds to create boat wakes, add additional turbulence, or generate bubbling and ripples.

Fluids

effects

Fluid Containers

A fluid container is a rectangular 2D or 3D boundary that defines the space in which the fluid exists. Fluid effects cannot exist outside a container. The fluid container is the principle component for any dynamic or non-dynamic fluid effect. Open water effects do not require containers.

Fluid containers are divided into 3D grids, and each unit of one of these grid networks is called a voxel. When you first create a fluid container, it's empty. To create a fluid effect, you need to add contents to the container and then modify the look and behavior of the fluid by modifying the container attributes.

Fluid containers can be placed within each other, but the fluids will not interact with each other. A 2D fluid container is a 3D fluid container with a depth of one voxel. The size of that voxel is determined by the Z size of the container.

3D fluids can be very large, making the solver for their dynamic fluid behavior very slow. This is due to all the extra data required to define them. In many cases, the effect you want can be achieved using simpler, less memory intensive 2D fluids.

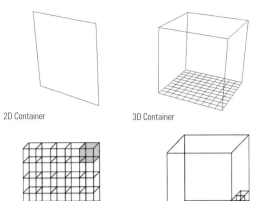

2D Container   3D Container

2D voxels   3D depth voxels

Fluid Emitter

You can add fluid properties (Density, Temperature, Fuel, and Color) to a fluid container using a fluid emitter. A fluid emitter creates fluid property values and populates the voxels of a grid with those values as a simulation plays. The fluid emitter must be within the bounds of the fluid container to emit.

Density represents the material property (the substance) of the fluid in the real world. Think of density as the geometry of the fluid. Where the Density values are highest, the Density appears more opaque.

Velocity affects the behavior of dynamic fluids by moving Density, Temperature, Fuel, and Color values inside the container. Velocity has both magnitude and direction values. Direction defines the moving fluid values' path.

Temperature affects the behavior of a dynamic fluid, causing it to rise or react.

Fuel combined with **Density** creates a fluid where a reaction can take place. Density values represent the substance being reacted, and Fuel values describe the state of the reaction.

Color applies color to Density. Color appears only where there is Density.

Density Values   Temperature Values   Fuel Values   Velocity Values   Resulting Fluid

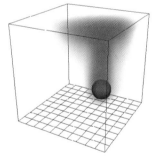

You can emit fluid from any polygon or NURBS surface that is inside a fluid container by selecting **Fluid Effects > Add/Edit Contents > Emit from Object**. The fluid emits from the surface towards the closest voxels.

Oceans and Ponds

On Ocean and Pond fluids, you can generate waves, bubbles, and ripples in the fluid surface using Wakes.

Additionally, you can float objects in your Oceans and Ponds using fluid locators. You can add these locators to objects individually, or you can use commands in the Ocean or Pond menus to quickly create a buoy, float an object, or make a boat.

There are two types of fluid locators. The ocean surface locator follows the motion of the ocean in the Y direction only. Dynamic locators follow the motion of the ocean in the Y direction, but additionally react appropriately to dynamic attributes such as bouyancy, gravity, and damping.

You can make an object float by adding a dynamic locator to it. Motor boat locators include throttle, rudder and roll attributes to realistically simulate the motion of a motor boat.

Dynamic Fluids

Dynamic fluids can enter in collision with any object. As a result, the fluid can bounce and slice on the geometry surface. It can also push an object by making the geometry an Active Rigid Body, a soft body, or a cloth.

Convert Fluids to Polygons

You can convert a fluid to a polygonal mesh, which you can then treat like any other polygon. The resulting mesh will be created based on the voxel resolution and you will need to supply a shader and texture for it.

Buoy
With a single command, you can add a NURBS sphere to your ocean and make it bob up and down in the water.

Interactive 3D

Through video games, visualization and the world wide web, 3D computer graphics have moved beyond the movie screen and into our everyday lives. Today, computer games consist of complex 3D characters and environments produced under aggressive production schedules. As such, game production has shifted away from the traditional animation pipeline, adapting new ideas such as game engines and blind data.

While many of the concepts covered in this book can be used by game developers to help them in their work, gaming environments have rules that are required to get graphics to play in the most efficient manner possible. Therefore, the kinds of models and textures that game developers can create are limited.

Recently, next-generation systems have emerged that make game platforms as powerful as the workstation used to run Maya. This means that the rules are changing and more and more of Maya toolset are becoming available for game development. This will undoubtedly open the door for very exciting interactive content in video games and on the web.

Interactive 3D

The rendering of 3D scenes into animated movies supports a narrative tradition where a story is told to an audience. The audience plays a passive role in relation to the content. In our digital world, this relationship is changing as audiences begin to demand more interaction with the content they are viewing.

The Video-game Generation

Interaction with content is most evident in video games where the main character is the viewer or "player" who makes key decisions that shape the resulting action. Players want to be immersed in new worlds where they can become the actors and the decision makers.

The ability to interact in 3D environments, similar to our own, serves to further enhance the experience. For this reason, Maya includes a number of tools designed to help game developers create these 3D environments and the actors who inhabit them.

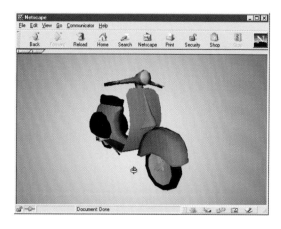

3D on the Web

While interactive 3D is most prevalent in video games, similar content is beginning to appear on the web for more mass-market consumption. E-commerce sites are beginning to use technologies such as VRML (virtual reality modeling language) to let customers preview their products in 3D.

A Different Workflow

Interactive 3D has different rules compared to film and video. Understanding these rules will help you make the best choices when deciding on such issues as geometry type, texture mapping, and the animation.

Animation   **Interactive**

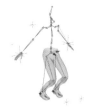 

Modeling
Models built for interactive 3D are primarily polygonal models that use controlled polygon counts to suit the gaming system. Some next-generation game systems already have support for Bezier geometry, and NURBS and Subdivision surfaces may soon follow.

Animation
When playing a game, the player drives the motion of the scene. Therefore, animation is stored in small sequences that are controlled using the joystick (the players control). For character animation, some systems support inverse kinematics (IK) and some do not.

Effects
Generally, effects are added to video games using 2D sprites that are composited on the fly. With next-generation systems, there will be support for more complex dynamics and particle effects. The limits are set by the system itself.

Rendering
Whereas an animation is rendered to a series of still frames, games use hardware rendering to present content to the player. Models and textures must be designed for real-time playback. Lighting and texturing tricks help attain faster playback.

A Short History of Gaming

Sprite-based Games

Bitmap graphics have been the driving force for video games from the beginning. These bitmaps were created as "sprites" that would be overlayed during game play in reaction to the player's moves. To preserve playability, the number of colors was limited to suit the power of the game system. To this day, games are being produced using 24 bit sprites rendered in programs such as Maya. Sprites are sometimes used in real-time games to add effects.

Real-Time 3D

Once graphics engines began supporting the display of polygons to the screen, 3D became interactive. With the creation of true 3D environments, players could now roam around a game and discover its secrets. Every year, the systems become stronger and there are fewer restrictions on the games.

1 bit B&W Pixels
~ 1980 – 1990
These games used simple bitmaps to generate the game play. Graphics could be easily created using simple pixel based paint systems.

8 bit Color Pixels
~ 1985 – 1994
Adding more colors offered richer environments, but the limited palette meant that the sprites had to be painted by hand.

24 bit Color Pixels
~ 1993 – Present
With a more complex color space, 3D programs could now be used to generate sprites. This created richer game-play environments.

Low Polygon 3D
~ 1995 – 2000
These games offer the freedom of motion within a 3D environment, but models maintained a jagged look because of low polygon counts.

Next Generation
~ 2000 – Future
The polygon counts are now becoming high enough for much smoother artwork and more stunning visual effects can now be used.

Setting the Limits

To make a game truly interactive, the game art must not interfere with the game play. Therefore, the speed at which a game can get polygons and other sprite based graphics to the screen is crucial to this interactivity.

Hardware

Games are run on both computers and game consoles. The ability of the hardware to process graphic information has a strong impact on the look of the final game. Hardware rendering is measured in Polygons Per Second (PPS) and the higher the PPS, the more complex an interactive 3D scene can be. This PPS rate is affected by textures, animations, and in-game effects, and can lower the hardwares' total PPS.

Game Engine

The game engine is the software that handles the user's input, calculates animation and dynamics, and renders the graphics to the screen. The game engine is built by the game developer to create the most sophisticated game experience possible for players. When designing a game engine, a developer must decide on a production pipeline that matches the engine with the intended hardware platform.

The Rules Are Changing

In the world of interactive 3D, the term next-generation is a bit of a moving target. Systems are becoming more powerful, game engines more open, and game developers more inventive. Also, systems are beginning to accept different geometry types and hardware rendering techniques are becoming more realistic.

As mass market uses of interactive 3D rise, these techniques will begin to be incorporated into more open standards, such as Web3D, which will help make interactive 3D a more integrated part of how we work and live.

Game Creation

To create a game environment, a game developer must put together a wide range of digital content such as 3D characters, levels, motion, behavior, textures, shaders, and lighting. This information is then given to game programmers, who build it into a real-time game. The coordination of all these parts is a complex undertaking that requires the game developer to work with concept artists, modelers, animators, texture artists, level designers, programmers, writers, and musicians, to name a few. With the ability for near photorealistic output from next-generation systems (game consoles, graphics hardware, and PCs), development teams have grown from small teams of 5 or so people, to larger teams of 30 or more.

Gaming Workflow

While a distinct workflow will vary from studio to studio, there is a basic gaming workflow. This workflow, from design document to concept art, game art, level building, and game programming, is not necessarily a linear one as all of these activities can happen at the same time. Because of the number of tasks involved, establishing a workflow at the beginning of a project can mean the difference between making a deadline and missing it.

Design and Planning
Every game starts with a design document that lays the groundwork for the player's real time experience. Characters, environments, puzzles, and music are laid out along with detailed design sketches that become the game's storyboards. The plan defines the workings of the game, while the sketches define the look and feel.

Game Art
Starting with the design sketches, 3D characters, props, and sets are built using techniques defined by the chosen game engine. Texture maps, lighting, and other game specific data are also added. Models are built for different levels of detail since props and characters in the foreground can have more detail than those in the background.

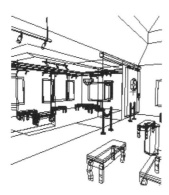

Level Building
Level building is where the various digital game art pieces are brought together to create the gaming environment. This is where many objects will be placed repetitively to make the most efficient use of game memory. The work of the level builder is designed to work intimately with the actual programming of the game.

Game Programming
This is where most 3D artists tend to be less involved. The artwork and built levels are run through a game engine designed for a specific console. Ideally, the game art is built in such a way that the programming runs very smoothly. The Maya Real Time SDK is designed to help with the transfer of 3D art to game engine.

Game Art

All the visual content created for a game, whether it be concept drawings, 3D assets or levels, can be referred to as game art. The concept drawings can be used in Maya as reference to create 3D assets. 3D assets can consist of characters models, or items for use in the game. These 3D assets can also be rendered to create sprites. Levels often use varied amounts of these 3D assets to help create a feeling of realism in the space and for items like weapons or power-ups.

Environments

Environments, or levels, comprise the world that the player sees and interacts with. These environments can be broken down into interiors and exteriors. They can be created in Maya using polygon manipulation, procedurally with height maps, or a combination of the two.

Props

Props can be items like the pictures and benches in the gallery or a key that the player must collect. Props help a game convey its realism or lack of realism. Maya toolsets allows the creation and modification of these props.

Characters

Characters help bring a game to life. A character can be the hero of the game or its evil villain. Maya character animation tools allow for the creation of animation that can breathe life into your game characters. Animation that you created can also be reused on different characters to speed up production.

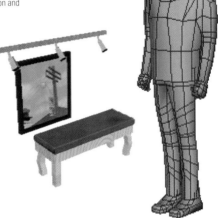

Color and Texture

The skillful use of color and texture on a model can help you imply detail. You can apply color to a model and use a grayscale texture map to suggest shading. This technique can also help you save texture memory. Maya allows you not only to paint color information on a model, but also to create textures by using Paint Effects in canvas mode.

Textures

Textures are used to add detail where no geometric detail exists. Some textures will be on what is called a decal. A decal can be a singular texture map or multiple textures laid out into a square to maximize texture space.

Color per Vertex

Color information can be stored at the vertex level and is derived from prelighting geometry, from painting the color on or setting color values at each vertex.

Lightmaps

Lighting information in a scene can be saved to a picture file that can be applied to the base texture as a light map so that lighting for a level does not have to be calculated at runtime.

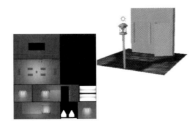

Level of Detail

One of the ways to keep frame rates consistent in a game is to use a technique called Level of Detail (LOD). With this technique, multiple versions of a model created with varying polygon counts are switched depending on their proximity to the camera.

When the model is close to the camera, the higher detailed model will be used. As the object moves farther away, the higher detail models will be replaced by lower detail models. Maya will let you take a group of models and assign them to an LOD group. This group will switch between the models based on their distance from the camera in Maya.

LOD Visualization

When setting up the LOD group, the high-detail model is selected first, with lower detail models selected in descending order. You need to have two or more objects selected to create a level of detail group. Edit > Level Of Detail > Group will assign them to the LOD node and automatically set up distances to switch models. You can select this node and change the distances that the models will switch. For example, looking at the images to the left, the top image shows a model that is closest to the camera and consists of 1422 polygons. The second image was set up to switch at 8 units from the camera; it contains 474 polygons. The third and final model of the LOD group will switch at 20 units from the camera and consists of 220 polygons. You can also use a quad with a software render of your model mapped to it as a texture map.

Blind Data

Traditionally, data such as item spawn points, environmental conditions (slipperiness, noisy floors), and condition triggers (enemy attacks, door opens, platform moves) fell into the game programmer's domain. Today, the ability to assign this information visually also allows 3D artists and level designers to control where it's placed on a model or environment.

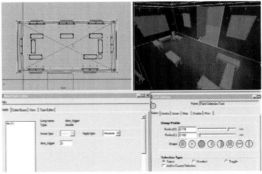

Painting Blind Data

Blind data can be painted on to components using the Artisan tool sets to help you see where the data is being applied. You can set multiple data types and assign colors to them. Here, the door trigger is being painted. You can see the color applied to the model.

Polygon Display Options

In order for a model to end up in a game engine and behave properly, certain criteria must be met. Situations like inverted Normals and non-planar faces can cause a model that looks fine in Maya to perform badly at runtime. Maya includes a number of options that not only allow you to visually see these problems, but also to correct them.

Display Options

Maya includes a wide variety of display options to help you see exactly what is going on with your polygon mesh. The ability to display the polygon count of a model or check for unnecessary texture borders can be a big help in troubleshooting your model.

Verts : 300	35	0
Edges : 620	68	0
Faces : 321	34	0
UVs : 305	62	0

Polygon Count
The polygon count Heads Up Display (HUD) provides you with valuable information about the polygon meshes in your scene. This display is broken up into three columns from left to right: total count for the scene, total count for the selected polygon mesh, and total count for the selected polygon components. This count is calculated based on whether the mesh is visible in the window.

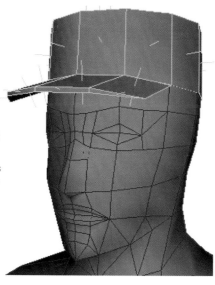

Normals

Shading and surface direction are transparently calculated by Maya. You can turn on components called Normals and modify these Normals using the tools under **Edit Polygons > Normals**. There are Normals for faces and for vertices. While face Normals can be activated in **Display > Polygon Components > Normals**, both face and vertex Normals can be turned on in **Display > Custom Polygon Display**.

Polygon Components
Maya allows you to view certain polygon components regardless of the tool or action you are using. This option can be found under Display > Polygon Components.

Vertices display can help you track down stray vertices that will cause extra polygons to be created when tessellated.

Soft/All Edges shows you which edges are hard or soft and Border Edges shows you borders that may exist in a polygon mesh.

Face Centers can help you see if faces are overlapping or intersecting each other.

UVs with UV topology turned on can help show you where texture borders exist .

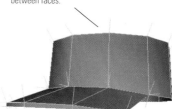

Shared Vertex Normals indicate smooth shading between faces.

Face Normals with Normals pointing in a direction away from the model.

Unshared vertex Normals indicate hard edges between faces.

Face Normals
Face Normals indicate the direction of the face. By default, Normals point in a direction away from the model. When the Normals are pointing into the model, this is referred to as inverted Normals. These inverted Normals can lead to holes in your model when transferred to a game engine because most engines only draw one side of a polygon. Any inverted polygons will not be drawn, and therefore will appear as holes in your model, even though the geometry exists.

Vertex Normals
Vertex Normals show the smoothing from one face to each adjacent face. Normals that are shared at the vertex display a smooth transition from face to face. Inversely, Normals that are not shared at the vertex display a hard edge between faces. Creative manipulation of vertex Normals can even be used to simulate shading on a surface. Maya allows you to set these Normals independent of each other and to explicitly soften or harden an edge. These Normals can be locked so that they will not be changed or updated during modeling operations.

Selection Constraints

Selection constraints can be very useful for a number of tasks. You can select faces that are unmapped, or you can select edges with a certain length for deletion. Other constraints like visibility, distance, and border selection let you further refine your selection to allow you to zero in on the geometry that you want and save you from picking the components one by one. Selection constraints can be found under **Edit Polygons > Selection > Selection Constraints...**

Faces
Here you see faces selected with the quads and inside constraints turned on. This would let you triangulate any quad faces before export to your game engine.

Vertices
The vertices were selected with inside and neighbor setting at Min 2 and Max 3. This is a good way to track down T-joints within your polygon mesh.

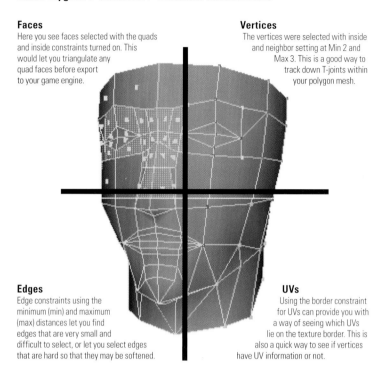

Edges
Edge constraints using the minimum (min) and maximum (max) distances let you find edges that are very small and difficult to select, or let you select edges that are hard so that they may be softened.

UVs
Using the border constraint for UVs can provide you with a way of seeing which UVs lie on the texture border. This is also a quick way to see if vertices have UV information or not.

Custom Polygon Display

Maya provides different ways for you to see the polygon components. In addition, you can see things like triangles and vertex numbers, allowing you to further examine your polygon mesh. This in-depth examination can be very important in troubleshooting your model before exporting it to a game engine. The custom display types and options can be found in **Display > Custom Polygon Display** options window.

Back Face Culling

By default, Maya shows you both sides of a model. This can get in the way when you are trying to look into an interior level or when you are trying to pick components on one side of a model. Turning Back Face Culling on can help. This option is a subsection of **Display > Custom Polygon Display > Options**.

Culling Off
As you can see from above, this level is difficult to visualize. With Back Face Culling turned off, both the faces pointing toward the camera and the faces pointing away from the camera can be seen.

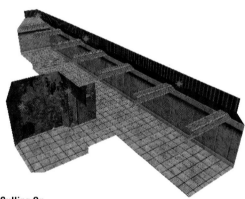

Culling On
With Back Face Culling turned on, you can see inside the level and it is easier to see texture placement. Also, you can select components on one side of the model and leave the other side untouched. The Normals of this model were purposely inverted to use this workflow tip.

Triangle Display
As mentioned earlier, triangles are the base polygonal shape. This display mode will show you how Maya decides how quads are triangulated. This triangulation is transparent to the user and only visible with this mode.

Texture Edges
This is just another way to see texture edges on your model. Texture borders show you where UVs are unshared on a polygonal model. UVs can inadvertently become unshared and this display mode can help you see them.

Non-planar Geometry
In early 3D games, non-planar faces were a big issue because the engine could not handle them. Now, most engines can. This mode helps you identify the non-planar faces as you model, and helps you minimize their occurrence.

Color per Vertex
The Color in Shaded display option allows you to see the color per vertex information applied to a model (if any). This color information can be viewed by itself or color material options like Emission can be set to see textures blended with the stored colors.

Modeling for Games

Modeling for a real-time 3D application can provide some interesting challenges. Issues like face type, face planarity, non-manifold geometry, and polygon count can force you to omit detail in one area because the geometry in another must be cleaned up. This clean up can require more polygons because certain faces must be triangulated. All of this, however, will depend on the engine you are building models for. It is always a good idea to clarify your engine requirements before you begin modeling.

Troublesome Geometry

Regardless of how careful you are when creating your models, you can sometimes create geometry that gives you problems. When you animate a character, you may see a polygon pop, or a face may even disappear. Also, geometry that may seem valid may have stray vertices or concave faces that will be a problem when the model is exported.

This edge is shared by more than two faces.

A single vertex is shared by more than two faces and no edges.

These adjacent faces have opposing Normals.

Non-manifold Geometry

Maya allows for 2 types of geometry: 2-manifold geometry and non-manifold geometry. 2-manifold geometry is geometry that can be unfolded and laid flat without any overlapping geometry. Non-manifold geometry can have more than two faces sharing an edge, two or more faces sharing a vertex but not an edge, or adjacent faces that have opposing Normals. This type of geometry can require additional clean up before it is exported.

Stray Vertices

When removing edges from a model, it is important to remember to use **Edit Polygons > Delete Edge**. If you select an edge and then press the Delete key, the edge will be removed, but the vertices at the ends of the edge will not. This will lead to stray vertices that you may be unaware of.

Edge to be deleted

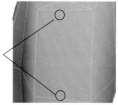

Vertices left behind by using Delete key

Delete Edge operation used. No stray vertices left behind.

Problematic Geometry

While not necessarily invalid geometry, you can create situations on a model that Maya has problems dealing with upon export. These situations, like concave faces and T-joints, can cause faces to be added where they are not wanted or sometimes cause holes to appear on your model.

Here is a single polygonal face that has a concave area in it. The problem with this is that the game engine may try to add an edge between vertices 2 and 4 to close the shape. This may cause the shape to be drawn improperly. Also, if the face overlaps another at the same place, the overlap area will flicker as the game engine tries to draw one on top of the other.

This piece of geometry has what is referred to as a t-joint. It has three triangular faces and therefore appears valid. But in this situation, all vertices are not shared. Some game engines would analyze this situation and leave a hole at the top face. Or, others would share the middle vertex to the top, splitting the top face and therefore increasing the polygon count of the model.

Other Geometry Types

As console and PC hardware evolve, their ability to display large numbers of polygons becomes less of an issue. As such, smooth surface types are quickly becoming the pressing issue. Maya toolsets allow you to create Bezier surfaces or Subdivision surfaces. You can also create a model in NURBS and convert it to one of these surface types.

Bezier Surfaces

Bezier surfaces require very little computational overhead and, therefore, are ideal for real-time applications. The use of Bezier surfaces already exists in current game engines.

Subdivision Surfaces

Subdivision Surfaces are higher order surfaces that may be adopted in the near future. The different levels of refinement they offer can be used to create adaptive levels of detail for a model.

Should I Start High or Low?

One of the decisions you may have to make before you start your modeling, is whether to start with fairly high detail and reduce the geometry for LOD or start with low detail and add more as you go along. The reduce, smooth, in-out mesh connections, and related polygon tools found in Maya can help you approach your modeling task from both ends.

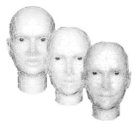

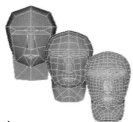

High
You can take your high-resolution model and reduce detail to get lower polygon count versions.

Low
You can start with a low-resolution model and increase detail for three LODs.

Polygon Reduction

Using polygon reduction can save you the time of taking a model and reducing its polygon count manually by removing edges and vertices. Polygon reduction in Maya is best used in small increments. Reducing the polygon count of a model by 25 percent or so at a time will give you an output that maintains the overall shape of the model (better than if you had reduced it by a larger percentage in one operation). You may have to tweak the final result. This can be found under **Polygons > Reduce**.

Original Model
Here is the original model. It is made up of quad faces.

Reduced Version 1
This version was reduced by 25 percent twice with the triangulate option set to off.

Reduced Version 2
This version was reduced by 25 percent twice with the triangulate option set to on.

Triangulation
With the triangulate option on, the reduction seemed to keep the overall shape better on this model than working with quads. This will vary from model to model. The option to turn triangulation on or off is only available in the Channel Box after the operation is complete. The method that you use for your reduction task will be dictated by the model itself.

Polygon Clean up

Invalid geometry or non-manifold geometry may cause Maya to fail on certain operations. Or, models converted from NURBS may contain geometry like small edges or faces with zero face area. **Select Polygons > Cleanup** to eliminate these situations on a model. The clean up operation can also select the problem areas and let you examine exactly what is going to be eliminated.

Original Model
Here is the hand, converted from NURBS to polygons.

N-sided Triangulated
The n-side faces of the model were selected and triangulated. For this operation, history was turned on. This operation leaves the model intact.

Faces with Zero Area
The faces were only selected and not removed. The tolerance was increased to select faces that were a minimum size based on the options. This operation actually removes faces and leaves holes in the model.

Paint Reduce Weight Tool

If you reduce a model with Keep Original turned on, you can use the Paint Reduce Weight Tool. This allows you to paint different areas on the model where darker areas will be reduced more and lighter areas will be kept as is as much as possible. As you paint on the original, the reduced version will update. To get the tool properties, select the tool's option box under **Polygons > Paint Reduce Weight Tool**.

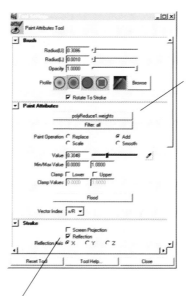

Painting
Just like any other Paint tool, you can specify how to draw and how much value to paint.

Reduction Percentage
When you specify a percentage of reduction, painting the reduce weight will keep the same amount of faces, but redistribute them to fit how you drew the weight of the reduction node on the geometry.

Reflection
You can paint symmetrically by turning on the Reflection option under the Stroke tab and specifying a reflection axis.

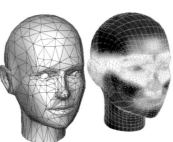

Primitive-up Modeling

With interactive games, it is important to keep your polygon count as low as possible. One technique for creating low polygon counts is called primitive-up. Using this method, you control the count by starting with a simple polygonal shape that has approximately the number of faces you want. You then reshape the Primitive, adding detail only where needed. Then you must decide what level of detail is appropriate for the model and remove polygons as needed.

When creating a low polygonal model, the balance is between smoothness and poly count. You want to add enough detail to make your model smooth, while working within a polygon count "budget."

Building a Polygonal Scooter

You have already learned how to build a scooter using NURBS modeling techniques. While that model was focused on getting realistic detail, the polygonal version of the same model would need to use much simpler geometry. Starting with polygonal primitive shapes, all of the scooter parts can be rebuilt very quickly.

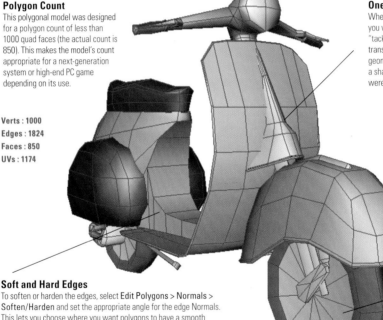

Polygon Count
This polygonal model was designed for a polygon count of less than 1000 quad faces (the actual count is 850). This makes the model's count appropriate for a next-generation system or high-end PC game depending on its use.

Verts : 1000
Edges : 1824
Faces : 850
UVs : 1174

One or Two Pieces
When adding detail to a model, you must decide if you want to integrate the detail into the model or "tack" it on. Integrating the detail leads to smoother transitions, but requires extra polygons on the base geometry to line things up. For this front detail, a sharp edge was needed, therefore, two pieces were used.

Maintaining Hierarchy
When grouping the parts of the scooter, you would follow the same principles you applied to the NURBS scooter. The hierarchy should be created to support the animation of the scooter down the line.

Soft and Hard Edges
To soften or harden the edges, select **Edit Polygons > Normals > Soften/Harden** and set the appropriate angle for the edge Normals. This lets you choose where you want polygons to have a smooth transition compared to a sharp edge.

Add Detail Later
In areas such as the wheel-well, it is important to avoid excessive detail. You can always add it later with texture maps.

Wheels

The wheels are created using Primitive Cylinders that are manipulated into the proper shape. The polygon count is controlled by how the subdivisions are set on the Cylinder upon creation. Assign different materials to the tire portion of the wheel and inner rim. By selecting the faces that represent the tire portion, you can now assign a material to those selected faces. This is referred to as per face material assignment. Do the same for the inner rim.

Step 1
Create a Polygon Cylinder. Reduce the subdivisions to 11 at the axis and 2 along the height. Increase the cap subdivisions to 2.

Step 2
Scale and Translate the vertices. You will need to work with vertices on both sides of the wheel to maintain symmetry.

Step 3
After the vertices have been positioned, soften all the edges to help give the tire a smoother appearance.

Main Body

This scooter body is created using a polygon primitive cube, vertex manipulation, and extruded faces (this is just one method — there are other methods you might want to explore such as extrude edge, for example). The goal is to add detail only where it is needed to keep the polygon count as low as possible. You will also use Harden and Soften to help shape the final form.

Step 1
Create a Polygon Cube that is subdivided along Z and Y axes but not along the X-axis. Use a templated version of the NURBS body as a reference.

Step 2
In the front view panel, manipulate the vertices to map out the shape of the body. Remove some of the faces from the wheel well area.

Front Detail

The front detail is a simple plane shaped using vertex editing. Many shapes can be easily derived by simply reshaping an existing form. The symmetrical nature of this form meant that edits had to occur on both sides of the object at the same time.

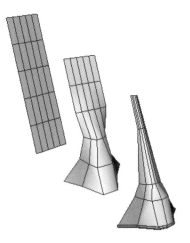

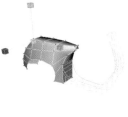

Step 3
Select and scale opposing vertices to shape the sides of the body. Scaling both vertices makes sure the edits are symmetrical.

Step 4
Select the bottom front face of the cube. Select **Edit Polygons > Extrude Face** and use the various manipulators to accurately shape the spine.

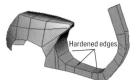

Hardened edges

Step 5
Compare the final shape to the NURBS surface. Harden the spine edges to emphasize the front face.

Running Board

A similar technique is used for the running board. A polygon primitive plane is used to start. Vertex manipulation and the Extrude tool are then used to shape the model and add detail.

Step 1
Start with a plane that has enough subdivisions to work with as it is shaped.

Step 2
Manipulate the vertices to shape the running board to suit the scooter.

Step 3
Extrude the top and bottom edges and edit the vertices to get the final shape.

Step 4
Use **Surfaces > Extrude** to create a polygonal border using curves derived from the model.

Handlebars

The handlebars use a number of smaller cubes that are manipulated into their final shapes. These separate pieces are then combined and merged to create a single object. This part of the scooter has more detail but uses the same basic techniques as the rest of the model.

Step 1
Create a polygon cube that is scaled and rotated into place. Remove the end face where it meets the stem body as a reference.

Step 2
Extrude the end face several times to create the handle. Extrude and Rotate the faces near the grip to create the base of the brake bars.

Step 3
Further extrudes and rotations are used to create the brake bar. Vertex manipulation is also used to get the extra detail in the brakes.

Step 4
Another polygon cube is created, then rotated. This will be the base of the light and has just enough subdivisions to match the needs of the light shape.

Step 5
The top faces are extruded a couple of times, then the vertices are edited to create a completed stem that is aligned with the handle.

Step 6
The front faces are extruded to create the shape for the light. A square face is built on the side of the light that matches the handle.

Step 7
The handle is merged to the light. The various edges are then hardened and smoothed as needed. Materials are assigned to the different faces.

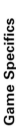

Game Specifics

There are some game specific tools in Maya that allow you to set certain attributes that are useful only to game engines. Some of these are animation based while others are color and texture based. Most of these attributes are not renderable within Maya. Maya provides ways to visualize these attributes, even if they are not renderable.

Animation Specific

Animation for games used to rely solely on the Scaling, Rotation, and Translation (SRT) of objects. Characters were segmented, which meant each movable object on a character was a separate piece. The pivot points for the object were set up at a character's joints (e.g., the shoulder and the waist). Most game engines now support animated vertices, which allow for single-skinned characters. Single-skinned characters are models that have all the parts of the character or object as a single object. Lightweight IK animation is now being implemented in some game engines that are already on the games market. Maya allows you to export this data to a variety of animation formats.

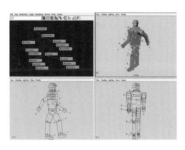

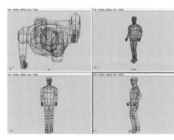

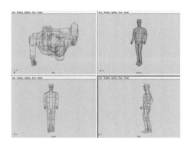

Segmented Character
Here, you see the local centers at the joints of the character. The limbs are arranged in a hierarchy so that the lower joints follow the upper joints.

Single Skin Character
This character was animated by skeletons with IK chains. The animation data was baked onto vertices at each frame.

2-Bone IK Solver
This character was animated using a skeleton with the 2-Bone IK solver. This solver is lightweight and can serve as a basis for implementing IK in your engine.

2-Bone IK Solver

This solver is lightweight and is a limited version of the Rotate Plane Solver. Therefore, it can be calculated very quickly. A 2-Bone solver is ideal for games because you generally only want to use an IK solver for the legs and arms, which only need two bones. The source code for this solver is included with Maya.

This is a good example of how the 2-Bone IK solver can be used. The solver node must be created by first loading the IK2Bsolver plugin, and then entering createNode Ik2Bsolver; in the Command Line. The solver will then be accessible as a current solver in Skeleton > IK Handle Tool > Options.

Baking Animation

Using **Edit > Keys > Bake Simulation**, you can take motion capture data and bake it onto IK handles for tweaking. Or, you can take keyframed animation and bake it down to the vertices of the model. Also, IK animation can be baked to SRT animation. Most animation data can be translated into one of the other animation types. Depending on your engine, you may require a combination of these animation types.

This baked simulation is ready for export. As you can see, the arm is deformed, but no bones or IK handles are present. When the animation is baked, the Time Line will show a keyframe for every frame. Selecting a vertex and examining it in the Component Editor while advancing frames will allow you to edit the vertex position.

Triangulation
One thing to remember when exporting your animation is that your polygon mesh may pop as it deforms. This is because Maya automatically decides how to tessellate quads and n-gons so they can be displayed and rendered properly. This tessellation can change on a frame-by-frame basis depending on how your model is deformed. It is a good idea to tessellate your model (even before you animate) to avoid having your polygons pop. To do this, use **Polygons > Cleanup > Options** and turn 4-sided faces and faces with more than four sides On.

Game Specifics

interactive 3d

213

Facial Animation

While not as precise as facial animation for feature films or television, lip-synching is making its way into real-time applications. The ability of new systems to push more polygons allows for the "luxury" of having a character's mouth move when he or she speaks. Adding a little bit more detail to the mouth area for upper and lower lips allows you to animate them when you get around to the animation task. There are a few methods for animating the lips, such as clusters, bones, Blend Shapes or simple vertex manipulation.

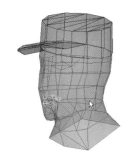

Cluster deformers have been set up around the mouth to deform the vertices around the mouth. This animation could be baked onto the model when the animation process is finished.

Skeletons and soft body skinning have been used to deform the mouth. Less precise controls have been set because the soft body skinning can influence the whole model.

Color and Texture Specific

Pre-lighting information and color can be stored at the vertex level. This data can be painted on, applied explicitly on selected vertices, or calculated from existing lighting in a scene. These techniques can help save valuable texture space and processor time.

Color per Vertex

Storing color on a model lets you enhance your textures with a base color or paint shading on a model to mimic lighting. This color information cannot be seen until you turn on the proper display. Setting Color Material Channel to None and turning **Color in Shaded Display** to on in **Display > Custom Polygon Display > Options** only allows the color per vertex (CPV) information to be seen. To see the CPV info blended with a texture, set **Color Material Channel** to **Emission**. Color per vertex information is not renderable.

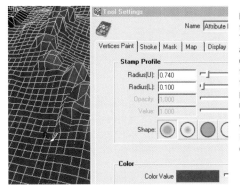

Painting colors on the model is similar to painting colors with Paint Effects. The major difference is that there are only Color value and Color Alpha options. As you can see, the ability to paint in detail is based on whether there are vertices where you want to paint the detail. If you had a denser model, you would be able to paint in more detail. Colors blend between vertices and, therefore, color information can appear in areas you do not wish it to.

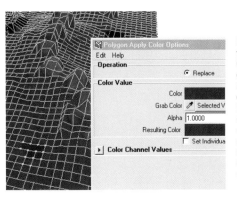

Polygon Apply Color Options allow you to select a vertex and assign a Color Value to it. These color values can also be accessed through the Component Editor. If you have applied color and want to get rid of it, it is best to use the Remove option as opposed to applying black over the color. Applying black will still leave a color value present on the model, and this redundant color information can be exported along with the rest of the model.

Pre-lighting

Pre-lighting can take lights that exist in the scene and convert the lighting and shadows into color per vertex information. This allows you to remove the lights from a scene and still have the scene look lit. This is referred to as static lighting. Static lighting can free your engine from calculating lights for a level or object at runtime. You can also sample color information from a texture while undertaking the pre-lighting operation.

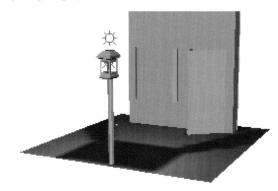

Here, you can see the lighting and shadow information applied to the floor. This was accomplished by using the Compute Shadow Maps and Ignore Mapped Channels on Surface Shaders options. Depending on the size of your scene and the number of lights in your scene, this can take a bit of time to process.

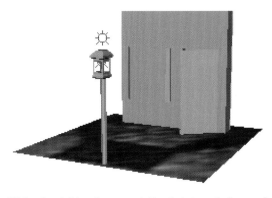

This time, the color information was sampled from the texture on the floor as well as the lighting and shadows. Where a pixel of the texture lies on a vertex, the color of that pixel is applied to the vertex underneath. A mesh with a very high polygon count could mimic the texture that was applied to it using this method.

Building Levels

The worlds that you experience in an interactive 3D application can be referred to as levels. These levels are the culmination of all the assets that have been created for the game. This can include props, characters, power-ups, and pieces of an interior or exterior environment. Often, the level itself is created out of low polygon count geometry to achieve the basic shape or feel of the space, and the props are added to help achieve a feel of realism. Using file referencing in Maya can help you add in the props and weapons that will be distributed throughout the level. To help speed up your level building, MEL scripts can be used to create a user interface for adding assets to your level.

Interior and Exterior Environments

All of the environments you might create can be broken down into interior or exterior environments. Interior environments can be inside a house, inside a ship, or any environment where your view can be blocked by a wall or door. Exteriors could be a jungle, a backyard, or any environment where you can view an infinite distance.

Interior
You will notice that the view is always blocked by walls. Therefore it is an interior level. Interior levels usually do not require any special considerations when being built.

Exterior
Here, the exterior level has a sky added in the shape of a half sphere. This sphere could be used by the game engine to create a clipping plane to minimize the distance that the camera has to calculate. Fog can also be used to establish a viewing distance.

File Referencing

File referencing allows you to reference a file and link the original source scene with the current scene. Referenced files can contain one object or multiple objects. These referenced files can be modified a bit and are re-referenced when you reload the scene. This can be of great use when building levels because it allows you to reference the assets regardless of their state of completion and continue to build the level. Once the assets are finished, then the old assets are simply replaced when the scene is reloaded.

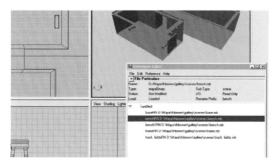

Here, the first parts of the level are being assembled. The walls, a few benches, and some lighting have been referenced in. As seen in the Reference Editor, each item has a unique name. It is in this editor that you work with the referenced files.

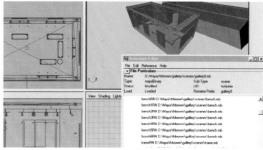

After more props are added and textured objects are swapped in, the look of the level is complete. Once the level is finished, you can import the objects from the Reference Editor to make the current scene no longer link to the source scene.

Using MEL

Using MEL in combination with file referencing allows you to create ways in which to access your assets with the click of a button or by the Hotbox. The ability to create interfaces to assets that you want added to your scene, can greatly improve your workflow. Adding MEL scripts to the shelf that incrementally scale, rotate, or translate an object can provide you with another way to improve your workflow.

Here the assets for the level have been added to the shelf through MEL scripts. This gives you one click access to your assets. You could also add a shelf button that would rotate an object 90-degrees or move an object a specified number of grid units.

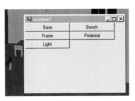

MEL was used here to create a window where all the assets for the scene can be accessed. You can create simple buttons or create an icon to help you identify the assets better.

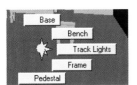

Marking menus provide another way to access your assets. All of these examples show you how easy it is to modify the UI in order to improve your workflow.

Lightmaps

The ability to take lighting and shadow information and write it to a texture file can allow you to create what are called lightmaps. Lightmaps are layered over top of the original texture to make it appear that the level is actually being lit. With the use of multiple UV sets, you can set up one set of UVs for the lightmaps and a second set of UVs for the texture maps. Multiple UVs are supported by most next-generation consoles and the blending methods in Maya will work with these systems as well as existing game systems. Setting up lightmaps is a fairly advanced workflow.

Terrain Creation

The creation of terrain in Maya can be accomplished in a number of ways. Two ways are using Heightmaps or sculpting terrain with Artisan.

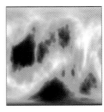

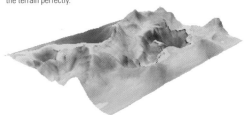

Lighting/Shading > Displacement to Polygon can be used with Heightmaps to create terrain. A Heightmap is an image file that uses white to portray the highest point on the terrain and black portrays the lowest point. A grayscale image (above left) was created based on the color image (below left). This grayscale map was applied to a NURBS plane and the displacement to polygon operation was used to create a displaced polygon mesh. The color map was then applied to the displaced polygons. This method not only provides a nice displacement with as few polygons as needed, but the color map fits the terrain perfectly.

Polygons > Sculpt Polygons Tool can be used to push and pull a polygon plane. A plane with divisions of 20 for the width and height was created and the Artisan Sculpt Tool was used to create the hills and valleys of the terrain to the right. The terrain can be refined until the desired result is achieved. Using varying brush sizes and different opacities, you can achieve even the subtlest of details. Paint Effects was used to paint the texture map for the surface of the terrain. Using this method can give you a more interactive modeling method compared to the Heightmap method. You could also combine these methods to achieve a final result.

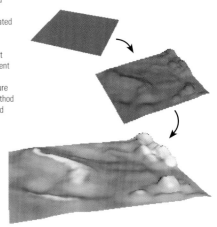

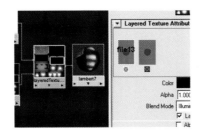

Step 1:
These are the textures used for the wall and the floor. The third texture was created using Convert To File Texture. Both lighting and shadows were turned on so that both would be saved. On the accompanying CD-ROM, you will find two MEL scripts that include the replacement UI for Convert To File Texture that has a checkbox for shadows.

Step 2:
The textures were then layered using the Layered Texture node. The lightmap was placed above the texture in the layer order. Then, the lightmap was set to illuminate the file texture. It appears the texture is being lit but in reality, no lights are being calculated in hardware. The UVs for the base texture were different for the lightmap.

Step 3:
Here is the interior of the gallery with the lightmaps applied to all the surfaces. Using lightmaps can save a game engine from having to calculate lighting at run-time. This can free the system to perform other tasks. Lightmaps are used in games often.

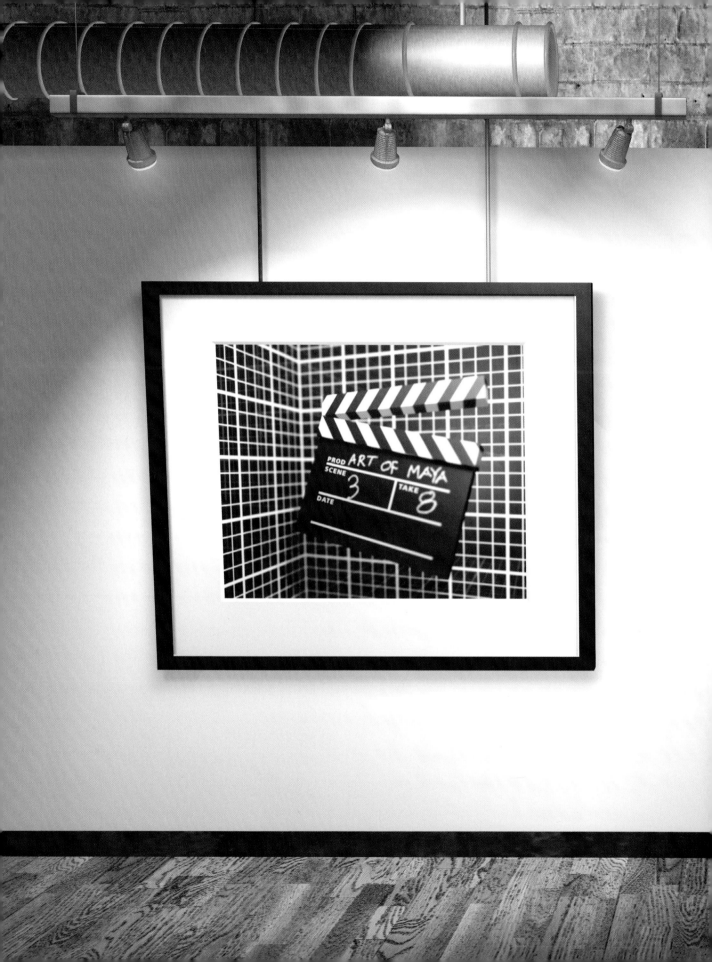

PROD ART OF MAYA
SCENE 3 TAKE 8
DATE

Production Notes

To better understand how the theories presented throughout this book are used in the real world, this chapter examines how Maya is used in production. Several companies, including Meteor Studios, Turner Studios and the Mill have all shared stories about how they used Maya to complete specific projects. These stories contain interesting insights into the various possibilities offered by Maya with many different tools and techniques.

In each case, there is a common theme of integration and productivity. Using various techniques such as character rigging, custom attributes, and MEL scripts, Maya can be set up to support technical directors, CG supervisors, and 3D artists. Efficient workflows are used to facilitate character setup as well as the integration of data from Maya in the larger production pipeline. Even smaller teams are taking a more technical approach at the outset of a project in support of more creative freedom later on.

Maya Brings Stability to the Final Frontier

Space may be the final frontier for mankind but within the world of advanced computer graphics at the Advanced Operations and Engineering Services (AOES) Medialab in the Netherlands, space is easily created and simulated with the help of Maya. Tasked with the mission of developing a short movie to scientifically showcase the upcoming Exo-Mars mission - a highly ambitious project of the European Space Agency - the AOES Medialab called on Maya to bring stability and strength to this demanding graphics project.

Making the Exo-Mars an Onscreen Reality

"The challenges on this project were numerous for our team," begins Marc Thiebaut, the senior technical director at the AOES Medialab. "They included developing the concept, design and visualization of a robotic rover mission based on scientific data from structural and mechanical engineering which is still in a development phase." Of critical importance to the project was the scientific accuracy of the visual output. As the movie was slated to be shown at space and aeronautic expositions and space-oriented scientific meetings, the details of the animation needed to be scientifically flawless. Using Maya 5 and Maya 6, both Complete and Unlimited versions, AOES Medialab dedicated two CG artists full-time for three months to complete the project. The team developed the animations and simulations using Windows®, IRIX® and Unix®.

© 2005 ESA & AOES MEDIALAB

© 2005 ESA & AOES MEDIALAB

MEL Opens the Door

When discussing the tools within Maya that made the software the perfect fit for the project Thiebaut comments, "Maya Embedded Language (MEL) opened the door for our team to develop custom tools required for the production." He continues: "we used a lot of scripted animation tools to simulate movement of the rover and this was based on the MEL expressions our team wrote. Without MEL, the job of accurately simulating the rover would have been much more time intensive."

The teams used NURBS, polygon models and the normal IK/FK tool to articulate all joints and mechanical aspects of the rover. For rendering, the team used the Maya renderer along with the mental ray renderer for specific scenes that required reflections. "We developed a tremendous number of specific shaders for the Exobiology part of the production which proved to be really stable at render time," notes Thiebaut. "We also used some of the extensive effects tools found in Maya to visualize parts of the mechanical deployment of the rover and also to simulate the rover's behavior on the rocky Mars surface."

Thiebaut concludes: "We've used Maya since version one and have never had to look at any other 3D package to meet our needs. With this high profile project, Maya proved again to be a highly valuable package to work with and the right choice for our team. We handle huge data models and it had remarkable stability during the production, which is really important for us." Best of all, Thiebaut enthuses, "the movie has been well received by our core audience - space scientists and aeronautic specialists. We couldn't be happier with the results."

MEL Empowers Oddworld Inhabitants for Stranger Results

The past 10 years have seen remarkable changes in the games industry and for Oddworld Inhabitants - the award-winning game company behind the Oddworld Universe. This universe has spawned three games and in its 10 year anniversary, Oddworld just got Stranger. In this new chapter of the Oddworld series, players step into the role of the Stranger, a mysterious bounty hunter who tracks down outlaws for cash.

With the task of creating new intellectual property along with a new game engine and new in-house team for an early 2005 launch date on the Xbox, the Oddworld game team chose Maya over other 3D game development tools to be their backbone. "Any one of these things is difficult on its own but we took the challenge to attempt all three simultaneously," comments Ryan Ellis, lead realtime artist at Oddworld.

Enter Maya

The Oddworld team began developing Stranger with two different development tools - Maya and another software package. "We realized very quickly that we had a fractured pipeline and to speed up the development process we needed to consolidate," comments Ellis. "We switched to Maya because it could handle the large data sets that our game required and it was capable of handling everything we needed; animation, level design and level and character modeling, in one package. This meant quicker turn around time for our artists and less work for our programmers."

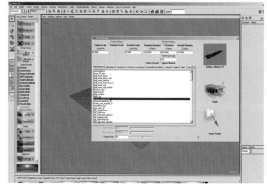

MEL Makes it Easier

Ellis admits that MEL was used for, "just about everything." When the team made the decision to use Maya as their level editor, they realized they would have to build a large suite of custom tools and pipelines and MEL became the cornerstone of that process.

They created scripts for everything from asset management to in-level artificial intelligence tools.

Ellis explains: "For example, when an in-game model is created, it needs to be exported into the correct location, preference files need to be made and hooked up, animation settings need to be applied and all of this needs to be checked into our data management system. This is a time-consuming process for our artists." He continues: "However, with MEL this is automated down to a simple click of a button. It saves us incredible amounts of time in just asset handling alone."

Another example is how the team uses an advanced decorator render for grass, plants and small trees and with Stranger, they needed control of the placement of these assets to achieve a natural sense of realism. "This meant hand-placing hundreds of thousands of small models which was impossible due to timing," explains Ellis. "So we turned to the MEL scriptable Artisan tool set. It allowed us to paint large amounts of decorators quickly and also to randomize scales and rotations for a natural feel. Our game simply would not have been achievable without such a quick and flexible system."

The API Saves Valuable Development Time

Another key tool for Oddworld was the API. The team used it to create a plug-in that could export their scenes into the formats used by their game engine. Also in that process were a number of optimizations that allowed their engine to render the geometry faster. "By creating a plugin that would convert natural Maya objects into game assets we saved a ton of time for our level artists," describes Ellis. "It meant that the artists could focus on making the art look good and not have to worry about the behind the scenes data - this is an absolute necessity for our artistic team."

"For Stranger, our goal was to make something that people had never quite seen before and that is a lofty goal to attempt," summarizes Ellis. "To achieve a goal like that you need a solid, easy to use toolset that will help to get there, not hinder you. Maya was the tool to get one step closer to achieving this."

BioDigital Systems and Maya Lead Medical Animation Advancements

The enthusiasm in their voices is unmistakable and it's contagious. The founders of BioDigital Systems, Aaron Oliker, John Qualter and Frank Sculli, are in-the-trench animators, software engineers and leaders in the emerging field of 3D medical animation. Determined to shine a light on the possibilities for 3D in the world of medicine and pharmaceuticals, BioDigital is working with such big name clients and partners as Novartis, Cornell University's Medical Center, and St. Luke's Hospital.

"The area of 3D medical software has only been around commercially for the past three to four years," begins Oliker, when describing his business and the industry. "We're still in the process of educating the pharmaceutical and medical communities about the power of 3D in their work." And BioDigital Systems is the one to do the educating. In 2002, after 18 months of intense scientific research, programming and animation, Oliker unveiled the world's most advanced, scientifically accurate 3D animated beating heart in conjunction with NYU Medical Center.

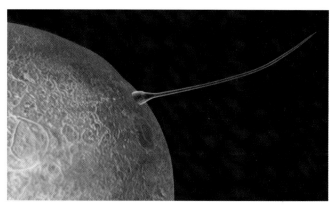

In a 2002 press release, NYU Medical Center's chief of cardiothoracic surgery, Stephen Colvin, explained: "Medical animation software is going to provide an in-depth tool for physicians to be able to take high volume, high resolution data sets, and put them into models that can be explored visually helping us understand what is going on in a particular patient."

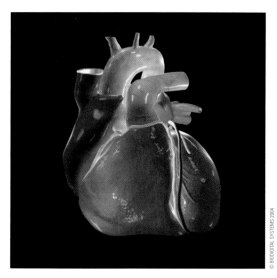

Only as Good as their Data

Using real database driven medical data, the animators can manipulate the information and feed portions of it into Maya to recreate anatomically accurate medical conditions in 3D. "For instance, the project we're currently working on with Novartis will show our virtual heart in various medical scenarios – how the heart will react in the body of a patient with high blood pressure, or how it will react if the patient has heart disease – to name a couple of examples," explains Oliker. By building their credibility and the value of 3D in the medical community, BioDigital Systems allows companies like Novartis to develop educational Web site content, rich media presentations, digital medical illustrations and CD-ROM and DVD material to educate their consumers.

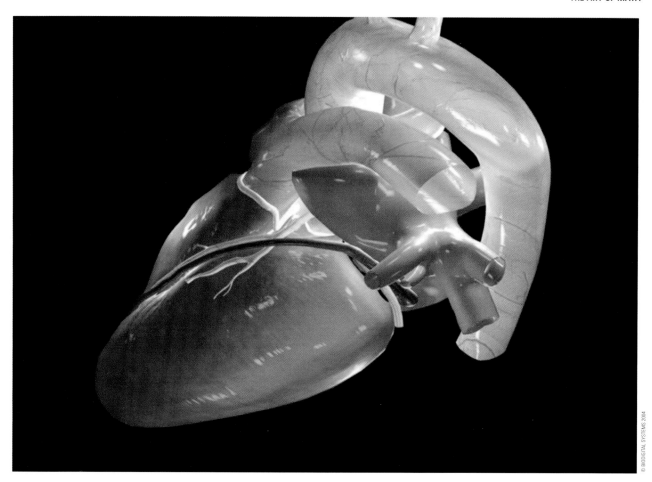

© BIODIGITAL SYSTEMS 2004

Using Maya Complete on Windows workstations for their projects, the BioDigital 3D team relies heavily on the Maya API to program and customize their unique projects. "Creating simulations is a huge part of the work we do for both our pharmaceutical clients as well as the hospitals we work with," comments Oliker. "We've been using Maya for years and chose it as our 3D tool because of the strength of its API programming abilities. There is no other 3D tool that would allow us to so easily create complex simulations."

BioDigital Systems' next goals are just as ambitious as their first 3D heart – to go beyond creating medical animations. "We believe that use of 3D in the medical community will continue to grow and we'll continue to push the boundaries – including end to end medical visualization systems used for diagnostics, training and medical education at leading teaching institutions," concludes Oliker. "The possibilities are endless and Maya is poised to be the key 3D tool for the entire medical 3D industry."

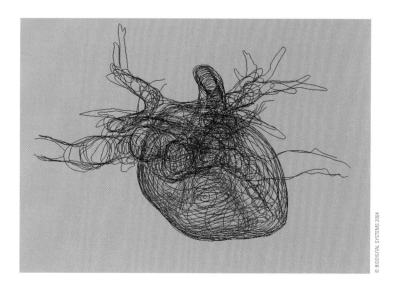

© BIODIGITAL SYSTEMS 2004

Canadian Broadcasting Corporation and Maya Support The Greatest Canadians

production notes

Canadian Broadcasting Corporation

In Fall 2004, The Greatest franchise television show began sweeping around the world and presented itself as the ultimate reality TV. Millions of people in Germany, Britain, Finland, Canada and the Netherlands, to name a few countries, voted for their country's greatest citizens. In Canada, the Canadian Broadcasting Corporation (CBC) picked up The Greatest Canadian challenge and called on their in-house creative team to design graphics supporting the stories of some of Canada's heros and icons.

The team was tasked with creating the opening stingers and interactive logos for the series along with some unique 3D and specials effects that would appear in the stories throughout the series. Of particular challenge for the graphics team was the recreation of a hydro-foil from 1918, which came from the story of Alexander Graham Bell. Described as a wing that flies through the water, the hydrofoil project needed Maya to help bring it to life.

Beyond Great Canadians

The creative team at the CBC is also responsible for generating graphics and intermingling 3D with live action and special effects for dozens of televisions shows and specials including the world-renowned, The Nature of Things and federal elections coverage. The CBC's creative team now includes eight 3D designers who have been using Alias software to create stingers, special effects and interactive logos since 1995 when the relied on the predecessor of Maya - Alias Power Animator.

"There is a whole list of features within Maya that our team here relies on including the modeling and animation tools, MEL and deformers, to name a few," comments 3D graphic designer, Frydun Mehrzad, who produced the 3D components for the Greatest Canadian opening, Nature Of Things and the recent CBC federal election package. "Maya 6 really delivers faster mental ray rendering in Maya which is so important when we're rendering out particles for broadcast quality work."

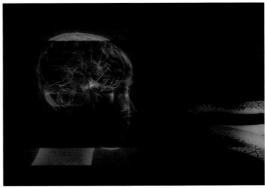

Maya Fluid Effects

Using Maya 6 on both PC and Mac OS X platforms, the re-creation took two animators approximately six weeks to complete. One strength of Maya for this project was its Fluid Effects system that was launched with Maya 4.5. Vinit Dutt Menon, one of the designers on the project explains, "We had to create a realistic body of water and make the hydrofoil interact within that environment. We developed the models using polygons and NURBS and used particles for some of the effects which we then rendered out with the hardware renderer." He continues, "We ended up creating six fantastic shots of the hydrofoil skimming across the water. Only Maya Fluid Effects could handle this kind of project the way we wanted."

Although Menon has used other professional 3D packages he prefers working with Maya in the CBC creative lab because, "with Maya creating effects is easy and its dynamics capabilities are huge. Modeling and texturing are a few more of my favorite tools – Maya essentially allows me to create any kind of effects I need."

Vinit Dutt Menon

Meteor Studios Builds Hyenas for Exorcist: The Beginning

Like a star streaking across the night sky, Meteor Studios burned its way onto the visual effects scene in 2001 and has become the largest visual effects studio in Montreal with more than 120 staff members working on both documentary and feature film projects. Now with an office in Los Angeles, the company has expanded its workforce while building up credits on high profile feature films such as *Scooby Doo 2*, *Catwoman* and *Exorcist: The Beginning*. The studio recently started work on *Fantastic 4*, scheduled to premiere in July 2005.

Attack of the Wild Hyenas

Creature animation is a key strength for the facility and they were called upon to deliver one of the most important wild animal scenes for *Exorcist: The Beginning*. The movie's visual effects supervisor, Brian Jennings, describes Meteor's role in an Animation World News article. "There's one sequence in which a character is attacked by five hyenas," says Jennings. "Harlin [Renny] had tried to get some footage with real hyenas, but they just stood there in front of the green screen. So, they shot the plates with the actor pretending to be attacked and relied on CGI for the hyenas. Meteor Studios created those shots, using hyena footage and documentaries as a reference for the animation. During plate photography, the crew had used wires to pull the actor's costume in order to simulate the presence of the hyenas biting the character. The animation of the digital hyenas was then timed with this practical effect."

With the scene containing 35-50 shots, Meteor put together close to 50 artists on the project and used Maya 5. "The real challenge for us in this scene was integrating the creature animation seamlessly with the live action shots; to make it believable as a horrific reality," says Timothy Stevenson, digital effects supervisor at Meteor. "Our skilled artists made use of every ounce of Maya's modeling, animation and dynamics strength for this job."

Blood and Dust

Meteor's team used all of different types of particles found in Maya, including blobbies to augment and extend both blood and dust effects in their scene. "The creation of the blood was a combination of Maya blobbies and a customized in-house 'blood' shader. Once implemented and approved by the client it was rendered with RenderMan to achieve the final result. This allowed us to embellish some of the practical blood effect work that the on-set FX team used in the movie and to extend the effect," describes Stevenson.

As the primary renderer they used RenderMan with MTOR. In addition, they developed their own fur solution in-house.

To create dust effects that the director was seeking, the team focused on blending live action with special effects. "There are many shots in the sequence that saw both the actors and digital hyenas shuffling and kicking up the dust in the environment," recounts Stevenson. "We had to enhance the actors footsteps and the interaction of the creatures with the ground."

Dealing with up to five hyenas per shot, the FX team designed a footprint tool based on the Maya soft body fundamentals. "This allowed us to generate dynamic footprints for the hyenas in numerous shots," explains Stevenson. "We had also designed a dust generator to handle the amount of dust interaction between the boy and all the hyenas. The use of RenderMan helped us get the desired dust look that was required for that particular environment."

Maya Embedded Language (MEL) was also an important aspect of the R&D work, helping the team in development and for providing flexibility to the tools. Stevenson explains, "MEL was a valuable component for us; allowing our artists to develop custom processes to realize the effects, and do so in a time efficient manner."

Animation Brings Hell to Life

With five hyenas wild with blood-lust in the movie, the animation and creature control had to be perfect – as if the animals were sent straight from hell.

The animation editor was of huge importance, not only for the development and keyframing of the control rig developed for the creature choreography and body animation, but also for allowing the construction of an interface for the blend shape sliders. This allowed Meteor to play with the physical structure of each hyena so that each had a unique identity. "We integrated custom rigging and simulation in the creation of the hyenas to have the skin and soft tissues react as a secondary movement, and to add a further touch to the action realized by the talented animation team," says Stevenson.

"Working on projects such as this one is an important step in the evolution of our team's capabilities," finishes Stevenson. "The challenge of producing photo-real visuals for feature film work is always an honor to accept."

To read the latest information on Meteor's projects, visit www.meteorstudios.com.

The Mill Gives Birth to Badenia Baby and Brings God to Life with Mercedes "Clouds"

Mercedes "Clouds"Released in June 2004 from The Mill, the Mercedes "Clouds" commercial posed the celestial challenge of creating gods out of clouds. The clouds had to sit perfectly in shots that already contained multiple carefully combined cloud plates with various cloud formations and movements. Once the CG clouds matched the movement of the real clouds, animation was applied. Due to the unique nature of clouds, each shot was a new challenge for the CG cloud animators and renderers.

"We work with various software packages at The Mill," comments Rob van den Bragt, t heir CG supervisor, "but the advantage in using Maya was that it had all the right pieces in one package." Using Maya Unlimited 6, the Maya team at The Mill worked on a Linux platform. He elaborates: "We had a great animation system, a powerful renderer and a strong open architecture enabling us to easily create new tools, shaders and links between animation rigs and advanced volumetric shader setups."

To create the cloud scene, a special rig was built using mainly IK and FK blending setups. Since the rig was primarily used for layout, timing and fluid emissions, it was kept fairly simple.

MERCEDES "CLOUDS COURTESY OF THE MILL

Maya Fluid Effects Do The Job

"This project was a huge Fluid Effects job," begins van den Bragt when describing the most critical tools for the project. The team tried numerous techniques and software at the beginning of the job, but nothing else came close to using true volumetric renders. "The clouds cast shadows, they had turbulence, textures were animated and varied throughout the shot. This would not have been possible with, for example, particle sprites or shader tricks," he explains.

MERCEDES "CLOUDS COURTESY OF THE MILL

MERCEDES "CLOUDS COURTESY OF THE MILL

Along with Maya Fluid Effects the team drew on the ability of MEL [Maya Embedded Language] to connect various nodes together to create desired effects and animations. "For this project we developed several MEL scripts and plug-ins," describes van den Bragt, adding, "Without them, the job would have taken much longer and would have given us many headaches."

MERCEDES "CLOUDS COURTESY OF THE MILL

The team also used MEL to automate various setups and to facilitate the artist during the CG cloud setup. Also, small GUIs were written to help with CG cloud adjustments and to give an interface to plug-ins that were made. As well, the team used particles to emit per particle fields, which helped them break up the contours of the clouds where needed.

Additionally, Maya Applied Programmer Interface [API] tools came in handy to create custom volume emitters, noise deformers, and numerous other plugins.

"The effects of this spot were really stunning and creating this type of dynamic CG cloud movement has been a first for anyone in post production," enthuses van den Bragt.

Badenia "Baby"

In Spring 2003 it was almost impossible to open up a CG magazine and not see the stunning images from another Mill project – the Badenia "Baby." The Mill's client on this project wanted to capture the realism of the baby without making it look grotesque or unappealing to the eye. They had to strive hard to achieve the balance between artistic license and reality.

"We studied a lot of baby footage to find out what made a baby a baby," explains van den Bragt. "We also spent a lot of time on proportions, as this is what sets a baby, a child and an adult apart. We had to cheat reality a little to make the baby more perfect than he would really be at that point in time. I suppose, we tried to make the baby look how a mother and father imagine the baby looks." He continues, "On the animation side, we used an advanced rig that was capable of posing the baby in every possible position, while maintaining realistic deformations and subtle skin folds. The facial expressions consisted of about 40 different subtle muscle variations for the expressions, which after combining them would give us endless expressions."

The strength of Maya for this project was its strong character rigging, animation and technical abilities. The integration of mental ray with Maya also provided to be the right solution for the job.

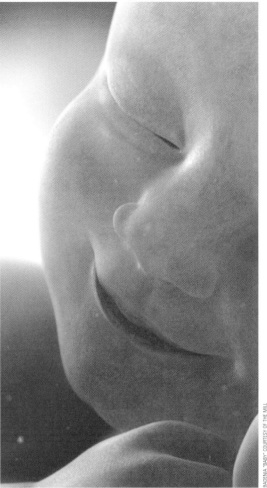

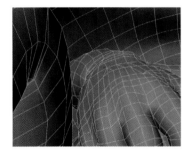

BADENIA 'BABY' COURTESY OF THE MILL

Bringing Baby to Life

The baby consisted of a detailed poly model that was subdivided using polysmooth at rendering time. The womb was made out of a NURBS surface.

For animation techniques, the team primarily used FK/IK, clusters and Blend Shapes. The rig used numerous IK handles that had the ability to be blended into forward kinematics. The clusters were used to deform the rigid binded setup. This technique, although not uncomplicated, gave them a very flexible workflow to create wrinkling and bulging. The Blend Shapes were used for the facial expressions. By splitting up the individual muscle movements of the face, the animator had more control over the facial expressions.

Rending with mental ray for Maya

Rendering proved to be a crucial element of the project due to the unique lighting requirements of the CG womb. Two factors encouraged them to stay with the renderer: its ex Rendering on the desktop was on Windows, but the renderfarm operated under Linux. Van den Bragt explains the process: "Due to the time spent with mental ray for Maya tuning the look of the skin, we needed a small number of render passes at the end. We ended up with a baby beauty, womb beauty, depth, water particle, peach fuzz and highlight pass only. Giving the compositor enough flexibility to tune the precise look we were after, the renders took only 20 minutes a frame at full PAL resolution (720x576)."

Due to the workflow The Mill applied to the job, they were able to focus on the artistic side rather than the technical side, saving them enormous time. "Maya performed beautifully," van den Bragt says. "After spending 10 weeks on the job as the lead 3D artist, I can definitely say that my father instincts had woken up! Aren't babies just the cutest ever!?!".

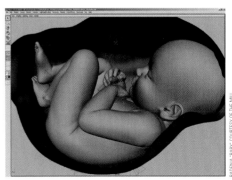

BADENIA 'BABY' COURTESY OF THE MILL

Turner Studios and Cartoon Network Create Virtual Cast of Characters for Miguzi

Based in Atlanta, Georgia, Turner Studios is a diverse, exciting, full-service broadcast production division of Turner Broadcasting System, Inc. that provides resources for all the Turner Entertainment Networks worldwide. Along with services such as live and post-produced video and audio production and on location remote film and video production they have an in-house, award-winning full service visual effects group, Turner Studios Effects. The group offers design, art direction, compositing, 3D animation and virtual set integration to the Turner networks around the world.

The team of about a dozen computer graphics artists who serve all the Turner networks are required to be very flexible and efficient. Blaine Cone, director of computer graphics, Turner Studios explains: "Our team could be working on a bold sports open one day and then an elegant spot for Turner Classic Movies the next. To meet the demands of the various networks, we're all seasoned generalists, ready to take on every aspect of a CGI project individually or as part of a team."

A Virtual Cast of Characters for Miguzi

In 2004, Turner Studios and Cartoon Networks launched Miguzi, a programming block on the Cartoon Network that airs six days a week and features cartoons that are introduced by a cast of virtual characters. Erin, the primary host, is surrounded by her intergalactic friends in a space ship that has crash-landed deep in the ocean.

Using Maya Complete and Maya Unlimited on a Windows platform, 12 animators over a three-month period used Turner Studio's primary 3D package – Maya – to animate Erin, her cast of friends, the environment for the Miguzi opening, the show promos and bumpers.

Chris Higgins, project lead for Miguzi and senior CGI animator at Turner Studios talks about the assignment: "With this project we were faced with an extremely tight timeline. We also had the challenge of learning RenderMan and MTOR (Maya to Renderman plug-in) within this constraint."

"We knew upfront that the most critical areas of importance to this project would be character rigging, animation, lighting and shading through MTOR," continues Higgins. "We also knew that Maya's strength is its overall depth, so we were confident that we could accomplish what needed to be done."

Turner Studios and Cartoon Network

production notes

The Effects team used a combination of modeling types, which depended on the model's design and intended use. They used NURBS mostly for inanimate objects and low-resolution polygons for characters, which were then rendered as MTOR Subdivisions. "In terms of animation we bound skeletal structures with both IK and FK, blend shapes for facial rigging, along with non-linear deformers for additional animation," describes Higgins. "We used RenderMan via the MTOR plug-in on the Windows platform in order to achieve a high quality render with rich colors and an overall soft look."

With rave reviews from media and their viewing audience, the Turner Effects team continues to turn out award-winning animation and special effects at a record pace.

"The Miguzi project reflects a growing trend of more and better character-driven 3D animations for broadcast television," Cone concludes. "Maya allows us to hit the ground running and turn around a quality product in a very short timeframe."

Alias' Maya Provides Core 3D Animation Software for Lord of the Rings trilogy

A great film starts with a great story. But, it also takes an outstanding director and in some cases, highly experienced and talented computer animators and digital-effects artists to help bring that idea to fruition in a visually compelling way.

So it has been with director Peter Jackson's trilogy of films based on author J.R.R. Tolkien's epic classic, *The Lord of the Rings* .

When The Fellowship of the Ring hit theaters in December 2001 ,thanks to Jackson's vision and the skilled artists and animators at Weta Digital, viewers marveled at its otherworldly 3D environments, fantastical 3D creatures, armies of CG soldiers and peasants and photorealistic digital doubles. A year later, New Line Cinema released The *Two Towers* . Once again fans gazed in awe at the big screen, where they were treated to roughly 920 phenomenal digital effects shots.

The release of the third and final episode in the trilogy, The Return of the King ,was the cinema highlight of the 2003 holiday season with 1,500 outstanding digital effects shots.

Joe Letteri , visual effects supervisor, **Randall William Cook** , animation designer and supervisor, and **Matt Aitken** , digital model supervisor, offer up their thoughts on working on The Lord of the Rings trilogy.

Q: Describe your approach to bringing the CG creatures to life in the Lord of the Rings trilogy.

Matt Aitken : We evolved a custom hero modeling pipeline for the trilogy because we wanted the creatures to work at a level we hadn't achieved before, [one] we didn't think anybody had achieved before. One of the things that made this possible early on was the ability to pull data sets of five million polygons into Maya and work with them – the ability to do this was essential to make this pipeline work. If we hadn't been able to do that, we wouldn't have embarked on this path. embarked on this path.

Joe Letteri : WETA's creature pipeline is set up so that we can model, rig, and animate in Maya. Our animation puppets are set up for fast posing and playback. We create our creatures to make it as easy as possible to achieve motion that is natural for each one. But, we also make sure that we have the ability to animate that creature when it gets into a more unnatural pose, such as when it has to collide with another creature. Then we use MEL [Maya Embedded Language] to create more intuitive controls that wrap up all these levels of detail so that animators can concentrate on performance.

Q: Tell us about Gollum's facial animation.

Letteri : Gollum's facial system is an amazing blend of the physical with the artistic. All of the shapes that Gollum makes are completely based on the muscles of the human face and how they influence not only the surface of the skin but also each other. Each of those shapes is completely sculpted by hand; there is no physical solve going on, so even the most complex interactions of muscles had to be broken down into a smaller set of controls that reconnected to everything else going on in the face. That gave the animators the ability to set a pose by thinking about its key features, and the facial system would take care of the secondary muscles. For example, if you raised the lips in a smile, the muscles of the cheeks and around the eyes would respond correctly and automatically. Then you could layer in secondary animation to create subtle or broad variations in performance.

Q: What were some of the technical challenges you were faced with?

Aitken : Creating believable digital doubles was one of the large technical challenges we faced. Cloth and hair are key components to creating doubles that are exact replicas of the original characters. Maya Cloth coming on stream was a huge benefit for us in terms of being able to move from using Dynamation-style, simple spring mesh approaches to simulating cloth, using a much more custom-oriented, tailor-made package for doing cloth of different weights and cuts.

We pushed digital doubles to a level at which they haven't really been seen before. In film two, an actor leaps onto a horse and he switches to a digital double full frame in the middle of that shot. To this day people ask me how the guy got up on top of the horse. Of course that brought us into film three where we had a scene showing Legolas on the Mumakil, which was built on the success of that one shot in film two.

The Lord of the Rings Trilogy

production notes

235

Q: How did Maya play a role in the Lord of the Rings picture?

Randall William Cook : Maya entered the picture very early on. I was shown several selections of software and had the chance to test drive them. Based upon my experience in animation, I found Maya to be the most comfortable interface for me, coming to it from a non-technical, non-coder orientation. What I like best about Maya is that whenever any of us needed a new tool, somebody could write it and plug it into Maya and make it work. And, of course, the whole series of blend shapes for the Gollum facial system was something Maya was able to absorb very neatly and handily.

Aitken : We've had a relationship with Alias for a long time. Wavefront Explorer was our key 3D technology on The Frighteners , which was the biggest show WETA had done to date: 570 visual effects shots in 1995-96. I think it's interesting that the life of the Lord of the Rings project coincides with the life of Maya. We went into early pre-production in late 1997 and got a beta copy of Maya about that time. Both The Lord of the Rings and Maya grew here at WETA. We established a 3D pipeline around Maya. As Maya evolved we were able to extend the approaches we were taking and push the envelope in terms of the way we were doing things.

Index

Index

⦿Alias® | LearningTools

Novice/New to 3D

Looking for a better understanding of 3D space and the concepts and theory behind working in Maya? Want a highly visual tour through 3D space? Try *The Art of Maya*, a full-color illustrated guide to working in 3D or get hands-on experience through one of our Maya Beginner's Guide DVDs. The Maya Beginner's Guides provide you with a step-by-step, highly visual guided learning experience to help you understand how to animate, render and create dynamic effects in Maya.

Intermediate

Transitioning to Maya from another 3D package? Looking to improve your general skills when using Maya? Choose from our Learning Maya family of books. Explore Maya through theoretical discussions, step-by-step instructions and with helpful instructor-led chapter overviews - the Learning Maya books are must-have reference materials for any Maya user. Delve deeply into *Character Rigging, Modeling, Rendering, Dynamics, MEL,* and *Maya Unlimited Features.*

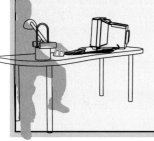

Step 1

Step 2

Step 3

Want to Learn More?
Visit
www.alias.com/store
and check out our books and
training materials.

Advanced

Are you a seasoned Maya user looking for time and money saving tips and techniques? Want to understand how your industry peers have successfully solved their production problems? Select from our extensive selection of Maya Techniques™ DVDs and learn from pros like Jason Schleifer (Weta Digital, Dreamworks/PDI); Tom Kluyskens (Weta Digital); Erick Miller (Digital Domain); Paul Thuriot (Tippett Studio) and more.

Alias | LearningTools

Maya Beginner's Guide Series

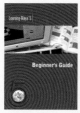

Step 1

Learning Maya Series

Step 2

Step 3

Maya Techniques Series

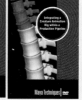

OTHER **tools** TO COMPLEMENT YOUR Maya Experience

IMAGE COURTESY OF RAIMONDO DELLA CALCE

Maya Memberships

 Bronze

Designed for anyone interested in Maya, the Bronze Membership program gives you increased access to the Maya community pages of the Alias website — at no extra charge. These pages contain valuable Maya learning resources and information about the software including: selected Maya Personal Learning Edition resources, Maya-user discussion forums, information on Maya-specific news and events — even software updates. As a Bronze program member you can also register to receive the Alias monthly corporate newsletter at www.alias.com/bronze.

Silver

The Maya Silver program is available to customers, students and Maya Personal Learning Edition users who are ready to start advancing their Maya skills from the beginner to the intermediate level — or intermediate to advanced. It gives you quick, online access to a huge range of learning resources including: downloadable Maya Learning Tools movies, tutorials; Weblogs from experienced Maya users and Alias' Principal Scientist; and the Maya Mentor interactive, learning environment plug-in (www.alias.com/community). You also gain access to a high-resolution texture database and a Maya-user discussion forum, as well as information on the latest computer graphics industry developments.

Part of the program's value, comes from the fact that all materials are authored and/or reviewed by Alias' Maya Product Specialists — so the information is accurate, up-to-date and relevant in today's 3D marketplace. And because these materials are efficiently organized on one website, you won't spend countless time searching for information.

The Silver Membership rate —19.99/ month* ($149/ year) — even includes a one-year subscription to *Game Developer* or *Animation magazine* and 30 days of personal help using the learning resources. Those who subscribe annually also get a bonus Maya Learning Tool DVD worth $69.99. www.alias.com/silver.

Platinum

The top-tier, Maya Platinum Membership program is designed to help professional Maya users maximize their investment in the software. Because the Platinum Membership service was developed based on feedback from the Alias global user base, it delivers the features that customers want. This includes priority access to all Maya updates and upgrades, extensive technical support — 18 hours per day on weekdays and 12 hours per day on weekends — greater licensing flexibility, and access to an extensive range of Maya learning resources such as tutorials, a technical solutions database, best practices documentation, all the features included in the Silver Membership (outlined above) and more. From now until June 30th, 2005 Platinum Membership also includes a one-hour, personal training call with a Maya Support Engineer. If you are looking to gain the competitive edge that comes with being among the first to have leading-edge Maya technology and world-class technical support, consider Maya Platinum. www.alias.com/platinum.

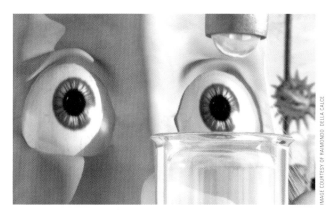

IMAGE COURTESY OF RAIMONDO DELLA CALCE

Maya MasterClasses

Ever watched an effects-laden blockbuster and wondered: how do they do that? Now you can find out through a Maya MasterClass. MasterClasses are 90-minute seminars taught by CG-industry experts and Maya Product Specialists covering a wide range of topics. Each intermediate or advanced level class is focused on techniques and workflows that will help you solve specific production challenges. To find out about Maya seminar events taking place near you visit www.alias.com/masterclasses .

*All prices in US dollars.

Maya Learning Tools

Get ready to learn Maya from the comforts of your own space. Our wide selection of Alias Learning Tool books and DVDs were developed to put you on the road to Maya proficiency — and then mastery. You'll learn from Maya Product Specialists and CG-industry experts as they share their production techniques and workflows with you. Whether you're just beginning to explore 3D or are looking to improve your speed and efficiency, Alias Learning Tools — with prices ranging from $19.99 - $129.99 are an affordable, accessible option. Find out more about Maya Learning Tools at www.alias.com/learnmaya.

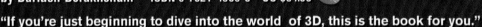